KEN TYRRELL

THE AUTHORISED BIOGRAPHY

KEN TYRRELL
THE AUTHORISED BIOGRAPHY

MAURICE HAMILTON

CollinsWillow
An Imprint of HarperCollins*Publishers*

First published in 2002 by
CollinsWillow
an imprint of HarperCollins*Publishers*
London

© Maurice Hamilton 2002

1 3 5 7 9 8 6 4 2

A CIP catalogue record for this book is
available from the British Library

ISBN 0 00 714376 1

Set in Minion with Univers Display by
Rowland Phototypesetting Ltd, Bury St Edmunds, Suffolk

Printed and bound in Great Britain by
Clays Ltd, St Ives plc

The HarperCollins website address is
www.fireandwater.com

Photographic acknowledgments
All photographs supplied courtesy of the
Tyrrell family collection with the exception of the following:
GP Library 3t, 4t, 7t, 11t, 15c; **LAT** 3c, 4c, 8t, 8b, 9b, 12b, 14t,
14c, 15t, 15b, 16t; **Phipps/Sutton Motorsport Images** 3b, 9cr, 10 (all),
11c, 11b, 12c, 13 (all), 14b; **Sutton Motorsport Images** 5b, 6b,
7c, 9cl, 12t, 16c, 16b.

*For Eoin, who introduced me to Ken
and all the good times that followed*

Contents

Acknowledgements

I would like to be able to say that this book was Ken's idea, but it wasn't. Despite numerous attempts to discuss the subject, the conversation was always brief. 'No,' he would say. 'Why should anyone want to buy a book on me?' End of story.

Despite Ken's typically self-effacing attitude, his family were of a different view. Here, indeed, was a story worth telling, and I am deeply indebted to Kenneth and Sandy Tyrrell, and Bob and Alison Tyrrell, for their support and encouragement from start to finish. My only regret is that Norah Tyrrell will not be able to read the account of a life in which she played a quiet but seriously influential part. Norah's fortitude and dignity when recalling her long and wonderful life with Ken was one of the reasons why the writing of this book became so compelling.

I would like to pay particular thanks to Sir Jackie Stewart who gave so generously of his time, not only to write the foreword with such care and compassion but also to provide memories and anecdotes without which this book would have been the poorer, if not impossible to write.

I am also most grateful to Jean Albrecht, Warwick Banks, Mark Blundell, John Blunsden, Keith Boshier, Alan Brown, Martin Brundle, Diane Cant, Phil Cant, Graham Collyer, Gerard 'Jabby' Crombac, Derek Daly, Neil Davis, Ron Dennis, Eric Dymock, Mark

Gallagher, Mike Gascoyne, Wil Griffiths, François Guiter, Alan Henry, Nick Henry, Charles Hewlett, Roger Hill, Ian Hunter, Stefan Johansson, Steve Leyshon, John Love, David McErlain, Tony Maggs, Bert Orris, Jo Ramirez, Nigel Roebuck, Jody Scheckter, Stacey Simkins, Alan Stait, Nigel Steer, Danny Sullivan, Stuart Sykes, Henry Taylor, Paul Tear, Sir Frank Williams, Colin Woods, Eoin Young and the staff at the Surrey History Centre.

And, finally, thank you to Michael Doggart and Tom Whiting of CollinsWillow for taking on the project and allowing the story of a wonderful man to reach fruition.

Bibliography

Autocar
Autocourse (Hazleton Publishing)
Autosport
The *Guardian*
The *Independent*
Motor Racing
Motor Sport
Motoring News/Motorsport News
The *Observer*
The *Surrey Advertiser*

The Chequered Year, Ted Simon (Cassell)
Cooper Cars, Doug Nye (Osprey)
Faster, Jackie Stewart and Peter Manso (William Kimber)
Formula 1 Register, Paul Sheldon and Duncan Rabagliati
   (St Leonards Press)
The Grand Prix Tyrrells, Doug Nye (Macmillan)
Grand Prix Who's Who, Steve Small (Travel Publishing Ltd)
It Beats Working, Eoin Young (PSL)
The Motor Racing Register 1964, 1965 and 1966 (Foulis and MRP)
Ken Tyrrell, Surviving Formula 1. A Mark Stewart Production

Foreword by Sir Jackie Stewart OBE

It is difficult to know where to start when writing a foreword for a book about Ken Tyrrell. He had so much to do with my life and my career as a racing driver. He contributed enormously to all three of my World championships and 25 of my 27 Grand Prix victories. Without Ken Tyrrell I could not possibly have had the career I enjoyed in motor sport.

Maurice Hamilton knew Ken extremely well. Maurice was part of a small group of people in the press corps who followed and reported on Ken's life in motor sport, and Ken had a great deal of time for him. Maurice was Ken's sort of man, someone he could trust, someone he 'liked reading', someone who could appreciate the qualities and principles of the life Ken lived. I suspect that if Ken is looking down from on high he will be more than pleased that Maurice has written this book, even though Ken's modesty was such that he didn't like talking about himself.

One of Ken's greatest assets was his practical approach. Almost all of his motor sport success as an entrant was based on his no-nonsense direct methods while going about his business. That's not to say he wasn't deeply passionate about the sport, which he loved. From the time he stepped away from the day-to-day running of his timber merchant business, his whole life was dedicated to his team and his beloved Norah. He had a first-class relationship with his two sons, Kenneth and Bob, and was besotted with his grandchildren and, in later years, great grandchildren.

Much has been written about the fact that he and I had no written contract during the halcyon days of our partnership. The reason was really quite simple: we didn't need one. I trusted Ken implicitly, and I suspect Ken felt the same about me. This is something that is most unlikely to occur in the world we live in today, and I suppose it's just one of the things that made our relationship so special.

In this book, the reader will enjoy many aspects of the remarkable life of Ken Tyrrell, and he surely did enjoy his life. If Ken had a friend, you knew that person was going to be all right. Whether it was someone he talked to about his business, or his shooting friends, they all had to pass the Tyrrell test of being genuinely nice people.

Ken Tyrrell was a decisive man. As a team principal he made the decisions; there was never any doubt about that. He looked after his employees and they gave him loyalty and dedication in return. Ken was known as not always being a placid man. When he got excited – not necessarily upset, just animated in conversation – there was the famous Tyrrell 'froth job'. This left you in no doubt that he either disagreed with you vehemently and seriously wanted to change your mind on the subject, or he was so excited and thrilled about what he was telling you that there was little chance of you not having to be towelled down afterwards. Ken's recovery rate from these outbursts was almost instantaneous. Anyone unfamiliar with his ways could easily have thought that such a tirade of clearly deep feelings was the end of any friendship that had existed. The fact was that Ken Tyrrell would state his point as strongly as he knew how, then would quickly return to 'normality' as if nothing had happened.

Since Maurice started writing this book, the love of Ken's life, Norah, has also passed away. He and the 18-year-old girl he met in Edinburgh had shared 58 years of a loving marriage. The two were inseparable, both sharing the same values and integrity that made them a shining example to those who knew them. Norah died with deep sadness and loneliness in her heart. The loss of Ken, the separation from the man she so dearly loved, was unbearable for her. She had contracted cancer, but it was when Ken died that her will to live seemed to disappear. Her need to be close to her deepest love was granted by the grace of God.

For my wife, Helen, and our two sons, Ken and Norah were a couple who were not just special, but unique. Ken was a remarkable man with remarkable values who celebrated life in its fullest form. He despised those who behaved in a manner that jeopardized or threatened the code of living about which he felt so strongly. For people whose integrity he questioned he had little time. Some of the things that have come my way in life he would have approved of, some others would no doubt have been on the receiving end of a 'froth job', but I certainly would not be the man I am today, not just as a racing driver but in so many other ways, without his influence. Ken was a man of all seasons who came through the grass roots of motor racing to reach the highest peaks with dignity, integrity and energy. I am clearly writing this foreword as a person who had enormous affection and respect for him, but Maurice's extremely well-researched book will magnify what I have said in these few words about a great British gentleman.

Ken would have loved to have seen Her Majesty the Queen's Golden Jubilee being recognized with deep affection, particularly in Great Britain. He and Norah would have been part of the celebrations, hand in hand on the Mall. He, like many others, would have had tears in his eyes and would surely have been wearing something very patriotic. I have an image in my mind of Ken Tyrrell wearing Union Jack pyjamas and standing to attention beside his bed, a 78rpm gramophone record playing 'God Save the Queen', before retiring for the night. He was a loyalist to the core, a very special man whom Great Britain and its motor sport community were blessed to have.

Sadly, Ken was never recognized by any government in the honours lists over the many years during which he contributed so much to our sport and the reputation of our country. It is one of my deep regrets that this never occurred. However, this book will help a great number of people fully to applaud and respect this amazing man. I am proud to have been asked to write its foreword.

Introduction

On 31 May 1952 the *Surrey Advertiser* carried an artist's impression of the west front of Guildford Cathedral. Building work had been interrupted by World War Two and the caption announced that, rather belatedly, construction was due to recommence.

Ken Tyrrell probably gave that edition of the weekly local newspaper nothing more than a cursory glance. His mind would have been on other things. The piece appeared on the day of the timber merchant's first motor race, and his second was taking place at the weekend, so any thoughts about the completion of the cathedral are bound to have been subjugated. Even if Tyrrell did find time to admire the drawing, he would never have thought that almost 50 years later the cathedral would be needed to accommodate those wishing to remember his remarkable life. In fact, he never could understand the fuss, right up to the moment when he succumbed to cancer on 25 August 2001.

The Service of Thanksgiving for the life of Robert Kenneth Tyrrell was held on Thursday, 15 November at 2 p.m. sharp. If you wanted a neat summary of the man you needed only to look at the list of participants: the Band of the Royal Air Force Regiment, Dame Kiri Te Kanawa, the Chris Barber Jazz and Blues Band, former world champion Sir Jackie Stewart and silversmith Paul Tear, a friend of Tyrrell and a keen shot. An eclectic mix, but one that set the tone for a motor racing reunion brought about by a man who would have enjoyed every minute of it.

With typical modesty, Tyrrell would not have believed that 500 people would wish to pay such a tribute to someone who was friend, father figure, family man, passionate believer in his sport and all-round good bloke. If the musical accompaniment was diverse, then so was the congregation. The British Racing Drivers' Club – which Tyrrell, despite failing health, helped steer through difficult times – filled the body of the church, the many grey heads reflecting an association covering almost five decades. Drivers were plentiful. From those who competed against Tyrrell's various teams to those who drove for him, the cross-section illustrated the dramatic changes motor racing underwent during the Tyrrell era. But it was the lesser-known faces at the back of the cathedral that told the most significant story about Ken's popularity. Here were the old hands from the Tyrrell Racing Organization, now retired or spread across various motor sport workshops, but still keeping in touch and happy to recall the team's 33 Grand Prix victories and three World championships.

Diversity and variation were everywhere. From Dame Kiri's powerful but haunting rendition of Strauss's 'Morgen' to the jazz band jigging slowly and joyfully to the exit while playing 'The Saints Go Marching In', the service set exactly the sort of tone which would have received Ken's full approval. Everyone wore a smile as they shuffled towards the great west door which had been portrayed in that drawing nearly 50 years before.

Guildford Cathedral stands in a commanding position on Stag Hill, overlooking the Surrey town. With perfect timing, the afternoon sun shone on the steps. The RAF band, there to commemorate Tyrrell's service as an engineer during World War Two, played on the lawn. The entire area resembled a motor racing paddock spanning the ages as acquaintances were renewed and memories invoked, Ken's great grandchildren representing the future. Time, for half an hour or so, seemed to stand still.

Jean Alesi, the former Grand Prix driver, had flown in from

France. Smartly dressed in a dark topcoat, Alesi was in constant demand as his former mechanics sought out the Frenchman to say hello. Alesi, who went on to drive for Ferrari and Benetton, maintained that his season and a half with Tyrrell was one of the happiest periods of his Formula 1 career. 'It was a dream,' he said. 'The best place for me to start. I'll never forget Ken's face when I finished fourth in my first F1 race. He was standing there, in the pit, with this big, big grin. He was so happy. That was Ken.' Jean moved off to find Ken's wife, Norah. To say they embraced with gentle, unspoken warmth, like a mother and son, is not an exaggeration. That was Ken's legacy too. His team and everything associated with it was family, and they were out in force on the steps of the Cathedral Church of the Holy Spirit on that wonderfully mellow afternoon.

Despite several attempts to persuade him, Ken refused to sanction a biography since he genuinely believed there would be no interest in his life or his achievements. The memorial service indicated otherwise, and it did not take long to set this book in motion, if only because the story is unique and revolves around a remarkable man.

Ken Tyrrell was the first person I interviewed after becoming a professional motor sport writer in 1977. Prior to that, I had watched from the other side of the fence as his cars set the standard during the previous decade. There was never any doubt that this was the man I wanted to talk to first. Typically, Ken not only agreed to see me, a complete stranger and novice, he also suggested we meet over a pre-dinner gin and tonic. The interview lasted for more than an hour. It was to be the first of many we would enjoy between then and his retirement in 1998.

During that time, he kept a fatherly eye on my progress, offering advice and admonishment in a sometimes robust manner that left me in no doubt about his sincerity and seriousness. But, as Alesi said, 'That was Ken,' and you held him in no less regard for his forthright method of communication. Indeed, it helped to build an appreciation of why his workforce considered Ken to be more than simply the boss.

Ken Tyrrell was as straight as a die. His integrity was beyond reproach, a virtue which became old-fashioned and increasingly rare as the sport's basic values were trapped between pure competition and the more unsavoury ethics of commercial expediency. Yet his passion for motor racing, and everything associated with it, never wavered. He truly loved his job, even during the difficult times that followed the halcyon days of what now seems a pioneering era.

In these days of multi-million-dollar budgets, executive jets and clean-air factories, it is hard to believe that a small group of Tyrrell's mechanics not only manufactured a Formula 1 machine in a shed in a wood yard but also raced that car to victory in the World championship. It is the equivalent of building and servicing Concorde in a wartime hangar at Biggin Hill. For Tyrrell, that was quite normal. Just as everything else had been from the moment he set off for his first motor race back in May 1952.

On 31 August 2001 the *Surrey Advertiser* carried his name on the front page; the headline read FATHER FIGURE OF GRAND PRIX RACING DIES AT 77. Inside, a tribute by Graham Collyer, the paper's editor and a staunch supporter of the Tyrrell team, encapsulated the local man made good. 'The Ken Tyrrell story is one of *Boy's Own* proportions,' wrote Collyer. 'He was the council house boy who, after flying with Bomber Command in the Second World War, became a self-made business man with enough money to fund his own Grand Prix racing team, one good enough to beat the rest of the world.'

Had he been able to read his obituary, Ken would surely have been bemused. It had always been thus. Over the years, those inside and outside the world of motor sport might have shown huge respect for his achievements, but Robert Kenneth Tyrrell never heeded the applause.

Maurice Hamilton
Cranleigh
June 2002

1

Never Too Young

A few weeks after Ken Tyrrell passed away, someone in the family idly wondered about his trophies. Where were they? And just as important after all this time, what state were they in? Given Ken's attitude to such fripperies, predictions were gloomy.

Ken had been very clear on the matter: on the day, trophies were the posh reward for a job well done, but that was it. Within five minutes the silverware had become a nuisance, an awkward piece of clutter someone had to carry home. Given half a chance, Tyrrell would have dispatched such items to the bin along with the detritus of a race weekend. The Grand Prix that had so recently consumed his every waking moment was history. So was the trophy, but not in an important sense: it meant as much to Tyrrell as his used boarding pass from the return flight. It was forever time to move on and think about the next race, the next challenge.

The cups were found mouldering in the attic of the family home. Blackened by age and neglect, some were completely unrecognizable, but all of them hinted at remarkable stories, the only tangible remains of significant victories. The inscriptions were barely legible, but the facts behind them had matured with time. These were Tyrrell milestones, casually tossed aside. The 1968 Dutch Grand Prix – the first win for Ken's Formula 1 team. The German Grand Prix from the same year – a truly epic drive by Jackie Stewart, the man who would claim most of Tyrrell's 33 Grand Prix victories and all three of his World championships. The 1971 Monaco Grand Prix – another virtuoso performance by Stewart. The 1978 Monaco Grand Prix – Tyrrell's last in the principality. And so it went on, about 20 cups in all, tarnished evidence of a unique contribution to motor racing history.

It was as if Ken could scarcely believe that such acclaim had come his way. After all, he had not been besotted by the sport as a boy. He knew nothing about it until he went on a day trip with his local football club to Silverstone. It might have been a chance encounter at the age of 27, but that race meeting would shape the rest of Tyrrell's life. It would make him an internationally recognized figure even though he felt truly at home only in his beloved rural environment on the edge of the North Downs in Surrey.

Ken Tyrrell was born on 3 May 1924 in West Horsley, a small village just off the winding road linking Guildford and Leatherhead. His father, Leonard, was a gamekeeper; his mother, Selina, a cook from Milford Haven. They had met when working in service on a local farm, and Ken first saw the light of day in the workman's cottage where they lived. His earliest memory was as a five-year-old, crying his eyes out because he missed his mother during his first day at the village school, a tearful display which earned a rebuke from his elder sister Irene, who claimed he was nothing but a mummy's boy. On reflection many years later, Ken admitted that Irene was probably right.

Irene and Ken had two stepbrothers, Arthur and Bert, and the family later moved to council cottages not far away in East Horsley. Ken recalled it as a happy home which never wanted for anything thanks to his father always being in work and his mother's deft skills as a housekeeper.

Ken and his sister left school at 14, Irene going into service as a housemaid at the nearby Rowbarns Manor while Ken started work as a delivery boy for the village chemist. It was to be the first of many jobs, Ken having failed the entrance exam for Guildford Technical

College. Disappointed but never downhearted, he transferred his natural enthusiasm to pumping petrol, acting as a sawyer's mate, and then to training as a bench mechanic repairing lighters at the Ronson factory in Leatherhead.

Not long after the outbreak of World War Two, Arthur joined the army as a dispatch rider and was one of the many to be evacuated from Dunkirk, only to survive that and lose his life in a motorcycle accident a few months later. Ken's earlier attempts to join the RAF as a boy had been unsuccessful owing to another failed entrance exam, but in 1941 circumstances dictated that the armed forces had become less choosey; as Ken put it so graphically in a later interview, 'All you had to do to get in the RAF was cough while the doctor held your balls. With a war on, that was the new entrance exam.' Even so, he did not take any chances. He gave his date of birth as 3 January 1923, so as far as the RAF knew – or cared – their latest recruit was 18. In fact, when he signed up on 10 April 1941 he was the best part of a month short of his 17th birthday. But he was in!

Ken immediately passed two important exams, achieving marks good enough for acceptance as an airframe fitter and a member of aircrew. It was his first experience of fulfilling a major personal ambition. The second such achievement, and one that would prove the most important of his life, would follow unexpectedly. And exceptionally quickly.

Norah Isabel Harvey was the youngest of seven children and an enthusiastic regular at Edinburgh's dance halls. It was while following the usual etiquette one night at the Palais de Dance, where the ladies sat on one side of the hall and the men on the other, that a tall RAF officer strode over and asked her to dance. 'I wasn't that impressed at first,' recalled Norah. 'He was a bit brash; I thought he had a bit too much to say for himself. But he ended up walking me part of the way home. I was living with one of my sisters because my parents had died when I was quite young. My father was from Addlestone in Surrey and had come north as a soldier and married my mother, who was from Melrose. I would never have believed for

3

a second that I was about to do that in reverse with this Englishman who was walking me home.' It was indeed an unlikely scenario. Ken was stationed in Scarborough, but had been called before an aircrew selection committee in Aberdeen. Edinburgh was nothing but a quick diversion on his way back to base.

As far as Norah was concerned that was the end of the matter. 'I worked in the main post office in Princes Street,' she continued. 'A week or two later, I was coming away from work, and Ken was standing outside on the pavement. He had come all the way up to Edinburgh, not knowing where I lived, only where I worked, because we had said goodbye that night and that was it. He asked me out. I didn't know it at the time, but he had sold his pride and joy – a Biro pen – in order to pay for the evening!

'He went back to Scarborough the next day, but said he was going home later to see his mother and father in Surrey, and he asked me if I'd like to come. I had only seen him a couple of times. But, for some reason, I agreed. His mother wasn't all that impressed with me; after all, I was only 18 years old. I spent a few days with them before Ken went back to Scarborough and I returned to Edinburgh. Not long after, I received a letter saying I could be conscripted. This was in May 1943; we had known each other about two months. I wrote a letter to Ken saying I had to have an interview and it looked as though I was going into the WAAF [Women's Auxiliary Air Force].'

This presented a problem for Ken. He did not see the WAAF as the right sort of place for Norah, particularly as he had other plans for his girlfriend, so he asked for compassionate leave on the grounds that he wanted to get married. When his commanding officer asked why he was in such a rush, Ken explained that his prospective wife had been called up, adding with a chortle, 'And you know what happens to girls when they join the WAAF!' The CO stood up, left the room, returned with a WAAF section officer and said to Ken, 'So, Flight Sergeant Tyrrell, you were about to tell me what happens to girls when they join the WAAF. Please proceed . . .'

4

Between them, the officers made Ken sweat. But he got his leave.

'I knew he didn't want me to go into the WAAF,' said Norah, 'but I didn't know he was working on getting time off. The next thing, he sent a telegram, asking if I would marry him. I said yes. Many times during the years that followed he would ask me why I had agreed, and to this day I don't really know! It was probably because I was on my own. It was one of those things, although there was obviously something about this guy.

'We were married in my church, St Paul's in York Place, on 15 June 1943. It wasn't a big wedding by any means because we had very little money. I remember my family was furious because I was the youngest. We spent that night at my sister's, and the next day we went off to Scarborough. We had enough money for just one day away. I recall sitting on the wall outside a boarding house while Ken went inside to try to get a room. I remember thinking that we hardly knew each other.'

Not long after their brief honeymoon, Ken had a few days' leave and it was decided a visit should be paid to his parents. Before Ken and Norah reached East Horsley, Ken's mother was killed when a timber lorry – a terrible irony in view of Ken's future occupation – mounted the pavement. She never did see Ken and Norah as a married couple.

On 6 August 1946 Flight Sergeant 1336942 Robert Kenneth Tyrrell received his release papers. The certificate, signed by one Wing Commander Hughes, said that Ken had been given a 'VG' for character, the attached note explaining that, 'VG is the highest character which can be awarded in the Royal Air Force. The character assessment reflects the airman's conduct throughout the whole of his service.' For both proficiency and ability as a member of aircrew, he was awarded 'Superior', the second of five grades ranging from 'Exceptional' through 'Satisfactory' to 'Inferior'. The RAF did not mince their words, a trait Ken fully understood and appreciated.

His logbook showed a total of 268 flying hours in daylight, 216 in darkness. His experiences in Halifax and Lancaster bombers had ranged from circuits and landings to a night raid on a synthetic oil plant in the Ruhr in November 1944. Night missions could take six hours or more, during which time Ken would in all probability have been on his feet. The flight engineer's panel faced forwards on the Halifax, which meant Ken had his back to the pilot and navigator. According to experienced hands at the game, once airborne it was better to stand up and make use of the extra headroom provided by a handily placed astrodome in the roof of what was a very cramped cockpit. And all this while the bomber was being buffeted by flak at low altitude.

The logbook also showed that Ken had flown with a variety of pilots in February 1945, an unusual situation created by his regular pilot being grounded thanks to making a spectacular landing. Ken flew as part of a crew of six officers comprising a pilot, navigator, engineer, wireless operator and two gunners. The wireless operator, Stacey Simkins, remembers the incident that almost brought an end to more than simply the man's future as a Halifax pilot.

'At that time, the RAF was taking pilots that didn't exactly have twenty-twenty vision; in other words, they wore glasses. They were issued with goggles that had corrected lenses in them. Our pilot at the time – he was a good lad, a bit airy-fairy maybe, but a decent chap – was in this category. Only we didn't know it. Neither did we know that he'd sat on his goggles and broken them. But, instead of putting in for a new pair, he wore his ordinary glasses. They say lightning never strikes twice in the same place – well, he sat on those too. Then he carried on flying without his glasses. When we found this out later on, it explained why we had the sort of experiences where we sometimes took off on the field beside the runway and occasionally finished up on the field beside the runway when we came back down again.

'On this particular night, he came in and he landed at the wrong end of the runway, more or less at the far end. What he should have done was pull his throttles right back, put his brakes on like mad, and start praying. Of course, because Ken was the engineer, he was right up front and saw what was happening. Ken told me later that the pilot panicked and, instead of pulling the throttles back, he pushed them forward!

'This was at RAF Pocklington in Yorkshire, and, as luck would have it, a previous landing had had brake trouble and the aircraft had careered off the end of the runway and gone through the wire fence between it and the road. The fence had caused the aircraft to slew and it had gone down the road for a bit. So, instead of going at full throttle into a fence, which wouldn't have done us a great deal of good, we went through the hole, straight across the road, through a hedge, across a field, through another hedge and we were just about getting to the end of that field when the undercarriage decided it had had enough. That's how we finally came to a halt.'

There was no time for an inquiry, but the pilot, a bank manager, was removed from flying duties. This was a blow for the remainder of the team because it meant they had become, in RAF parlance, 'spare bods', or reserves should another crew need a stand-in. Nonetheless, they stayed in touch and made the most of what little leisure time was available.

'We heard that our navigator, "Smudge", was at a place eight miles away and they were having a dance,' recalled Simkins. 'So Ken and I, er, "borrowed" a couple of bikes and got ourselves there. We went into the mess and played darts and had a few drinks. Then the dance started and there were more drinks. Ken and I got a bit too high, took over the stage and the microphone and gave them a rendition of songs I can't repeat here. I'm not sure if Ken sang his favourite that night, but it was, "Dan, Dan, the Waterworks Man". I'll never forget it. It went like this:

I'm Dan, Dan, the waterworks man, round to stop your water.
Every day from morn till night,
I shout out, "Missus, is your water all right?"
I ain't the bloke who brings the coke,
Ain't no railway porter;

*I'm Dan, Dan, the waterworks man, the man who brings your
water.
How's your water? All right!*

'We would do that chorus and Ken would sing the verses, many of
which were unrepeatable. Anyway, we woke the next morning to
discover they had stuck us in a room in the mess. They took us back
to our camp in a car, so Gawd knows what happened to the bikes!'

Simkins also remembered that, though Ken might have enjoyed a
good time socially, he was deadly serious when it came to his job.
'You always felt he knew exactly what he was doing. He made sure
he didn't have any slip-ups. He was always on the ball. As a bloke,
you couldn't have asked for better. He joined in with everything;
never got nasty about anything. He was a great man.'

When the war ended, Ken was transferred to Transport Command and spent six months as an air quartermaster on Avro Yorks
flying to the East. These were relentless trips, typically six hours
from Lyneham to Malta, with five more legs of a similar length
before reaching Dum-Dum airport in India. 'These exotic places
didn't impress me,' Ken remarked later. 'I made myself a promise
that I would never live outside England.' It was a promise he would
keep, although his future career would entail more global travel
than he could ever have imagined.

Of more immediate importance was finding a job and a place to
live. Wing Commander Hughes had completed Ken's release papers
with a handwritten note. It said: 'During this NCO's service with
this squadron, he has proved himself keen and conscientious in
carrying out all his duties. He has an excellent record in the RAF and
is confidently recommended for any employment.' The question
was, where?

Ken and Norah already had an extra mouth to feed following the
arrival of baby Kenneth on 18 June 1944. The family moved in with
Ken's father, Leonard, who had married for a third time. Living
in the small terraced cottage at East Horsley was to prove difficult,

particularly for Norah. 'That was purgatory,' she recalled. 'Kenneth had just turned two years old. I couldn't do anything right. They'd say, "Ken wouldn't like that," or "Ken doesn't do it that way," or "You don't light the boiler like that," or "Clean the stairs – no, not that way!" And, of course, they didn't think I could cook. I just wanted to be away from that place but there was nowhere to go. We had no money and the council wouldn't countenance a house. It was dreadful.'

Bert Tyrrell was skilled at tree felling, and he asked Ken to join him. Tyrrell Brothers started out as a small business, lopping and topping trees in local gardens. Given the shortage of coal in the immediate post-war years, demand for wood was high. The tiny yard, tucked away at the end of a muddy track known as Honeysuckle Bottom, quickly became well known. It was not uncommon to have lorries travel from all parts of the Home Counties and queue there at dawn, waiting for whatever was on offer.

Honeysuckle Bottom, on the fringe of East Horsley, adjoined a narrow road crossing a densely wooded part of the North Downs. During the war the road had been closed for the storage of ammunition and a Nissen hut placed at each end, the most northerly of the two positioned by the entrance to Honeysuckle Bottom. It occurred to Ken that the abandoned hut might make a home of sorts; rudimentary maybe, but better than the increasingly tense environment Ken and Norah were being forced to endure at Leonard Tyrrell's place.

'Ken suddenly said, "Let's go!"' recalled Norah. 'One Sunday morning, we broke into the Nissen hut and became squatters! It was full of rubble; I can't begin to tell you what it was like. The only thing we had was thick carpets which Ken had brought back from India. During the first week, Ken went off to work and I got rid of the rubble. It was a big hut. We had to light the fire to heat water for breakfast – for everything really. We weren't short of logs, of course, so we got it warm and painted the inside. The council charged us rent, we put in a toilet and so on, and it actually became quite nice.

Even though it was cold in the winter because the metal roof was so high, we put up with it. After the war, you did what you could. You didn't get two chances at anything and you had to grab the first one that came along. You were young, so you would get by and not think twice about it. The Nissen hut did us fine, and we stayed there until Bob was born on 29 May 1949.'

By then it was time to move on, the hut with its semi-circular corrugated iron roof having more than served its purpose. Ken approached Abbey National about a mortgage for a semi-detached property at 12 Sheepfold Road in a housing estate on the far side of Guildford. On 21 January 1950, the building society offered an advance of £1,630, Ken agreeing to a monthly premium of £6 14s. 1d. (£6.70p). It was a considerable sum at the time, but it was a major step forward for the young family. 'This was our first proper house,' recalled Norah. 'There might not have been central heating or anything like that, but after what we had been through this was complete luxury. It was wonderful.'

Ken and Bert worked seven days a week. Their vision expanded to felling trees, sorting and grading them and selling on to sawmills. It soon became clear that the Honeysuckle Bottom yard was too small a premises for their plans.

The Ockham estate, a vast self-contained area close to East Horsley, was in the early stages of decline. When Ken and Bert heard that the lease on the former site of a small brickworks was available, they made a successful bid. It might have been an unprepossessing place, tucked away down a narrow wooded lane just off a minor road known as Long Reach, but in time this would become one of the most famous addresses in the world of international sport. For the moment, though, it was a rough and ready base with holes in the ground where the brick kilns had been. There were a few sheds and a bungalow close by the brick lane leading down from Long Reach.

A general mechanical engineer on the adjoining plot by the name of Charlie Gear would become well known to the Tyrrell family, as Kenneth Tyrrell recalled. 'Dad and Uncle Bert wanted to get into hauling timber. They had a wagon but had to work out a means of getting the timber onto it. One way was a system of ropes with a tractor to winch the trees onto the lorry. A better way would be to use a crane, but they didn't have one. They did have a Matador – a 14-foot-high tractor unit – and Charlie Gear built a crane on the back of it. He designed and made it himself – just the sort of thing he loved because he was very adept at doing ad hoc modifications.'

Urgent calls were going out at the time for pit props – balks of wood used to support the roofs of coal mines – the usual supply from Scandinavia having been halted by the war. There was a massive domestic demand for coal and the Tyrrells were flat out, Norah and Kenneth lending a hand whenever possible.

'Ken worked very, very hard to earn the money to buy a lorry,' said Norah. 'He enjoyed the timber business and he built up lots of contacts. He would go into an estate and buy what they called a parcel of timber. The estate would say they had an acre of trees which they wanted someone to cut down and take away. That would be a parcel. I used to go with Bert sometimes to do the measuring, running along a felled tree with a tape. Kenneth would help in the holidays.'

The company's finances were looked after by Eric Baker, an accountant who lived in a nearby house rented by the Tyrrells. As time went by, business showed no sign of diminishing, but with the entire operation becoming better organized Ken found more time to indulge in his favourite pastime – a vigorous game of football. He had joined Ockham, a team renowned for robust play rather than cup-winning skill. A piece in the *Surrey Advertiser* on 12 April 1952 summed up their approach. Under the heading OCKHAM MAN SENT OFF IN OWEN CUP FINAL, the report said: 'Park House School beat Ockham 3–1 in the Owen Charity Cup Final at Shalford. Ockham's 1–0 interval lead was ill-deserved for they had been on the defensive for most of the half. The game was marred by incidents which culminated in an Ockham player being sent off the field.'

This was strong stuff in a more genteel time. The same edition of the local newspaper also reported that Thomas Michael O'Rourke, 38, a labourer of no fixed address, had been charged with being drunk and incapable. In his defence, O'Rourke had told the court, 'I drink a lot, but persevered on Saturday and Sunday.' To prove it, he had had two pounds when he started out and just two pence left when arrested. O'Rourke was discharged with a caution. He got off lightly compared with the two youths fined 10 shillings (50p) after admitting to the heinous crime of riding on one bicycle at the same time. For those of a more responsible nature, the racing driver and garage owner Duncan Hamilton was advertising a 1948 Austin 8hp four-door saloon ('sun roof, pale green, brown leather, a very beautiful little car, 35 miles per gallon') for £615.

On the next page, a news story recorded an address to the local chamber of trade by Mr A Turner of the British Empire Cancer Campaign. He made the point that there would be alarm if a hundred people were killed in a train disaster and astonishment if it were to happen every day. But that was the reality of deaths caused by cancer. 'There is an extraordinary hush-hush atmosphere about this disease,' said Turner, before adding that doctors were confident of finding the cause and then the cure. In view of what would befall Ken Tyrrell, it makes poignant reading half a century later.

In 1951, Ken cut an imposing figure at 6ft 1½in when he turned out as centre-half for Ockham. Charles Hewlett played on the left wing and appreciated having Ken take command of the midfield. 'Ken was tall, not rawboned but a well-built chap for the job,' said Hewlett. 'He was a sort of Jack Charlton. I remember on one occasion we were playing Horsley – it must have been a cup match because Horsley was a bigger place than Ockham and they were in a league above us – and Ken's older brother Bert played right-back for Horsley. He was a stalwart of the team and, afterwards, you always knew you'd played Bert! I remember Ken saying to me, "Keep it up, Charlie! We're making the old bugger run round in circles!" That summed Ken up in many ways. He was considered to be a very useful player, a commanding figure on the field and a typical centre-half. He was wholehearted, and that seemed to apply to anything he took on.

'Ockham was in the Tillingbourne Valley League, in the lower reaches of village level. We were not pretentious. We were a reasonable village team and we got to the final of the cup on more than one occasion. It's been put to me that we were rather a hard team. I wasn't too much aware of that – but, of course, village football is rough and tumble at times, even if unintended.

'Our pitch had been under the plough for food production purposes in wartime. It was a pretty primitive place. We just had a cold standpipe outside and a shed, so after the game we would jump on our bikes, mud and all, and cycle home. Of course, the problem then was that half of the players' homes didn't have baths. So it was a bit rough and ready. But terrific fun.'

Hewlett's association with the Tyrrell brothers extended beyond the football pitch thanks to his work within the spare parts department of a Bedford dealer in Guildford. 'Bedfords were the predominant vehicles in the British army at the end of the war,' said Hewlett. 'There were a lot of them lying around. The Tyrrells had one and an old General Motors Chevrolet. They would come in looking for pinion bearings and suchlike. We would help each other out. With fuel in short supply, we were always glad of a load of logs. On one occasion, the Tyrrell lorry pulled up outside our house, right against the hedge, and before I could do anything they were chucking logs over the hedge – straight onto my wife's flower garden. I said to whichever one of them it was, "How much do I owe you?", and the reply came back, "Twenty-five bob [£1.25] to you, Charlie; anyone else, a quid." That was the sort of banter we had.'

The camaraderie was further encouraged by social events organized by the club. In July 1951 Ken agreed to go on a coach trip to Northamptonshire, just for a bit of fun with the lads. It would change his life completely.

2

Finding the Goal

Whatever troubles, if any, Ken Tyrrell might have been forced to endure in business, they were nothing compared to those being heaped on British Racing Motors. People talk about media pressure in the new millennium, but it was just as difficult and potentially damaging 50 years ago, a fact to which the beleaguered folk at BRM would have testified quite readily.

It has to be said, however, that the instigators of this jingoistic project played a part in their own downfall. It could hardly have been otherwise after encouraging the British public to contribute towards the building of a world-beating racing car and then proceeding to design the most complicated machine imaginable. More than 350 firms had committed themselves, but the original costs had quickly soared as the BRM directors faced the expensive reality of producing a supercharged V16 engine to power their car. They had not been helped by the struggle to return to normality in the immediate post-war years: the design of the BRM had been completed in 1947 but the parts were delivered at a trickle between April 1948 and May 1949. When the car was finally completed the following year, it had proved difficult to drive. Still, the shrieking V16 sounded glorious. When the pale green car was unveiled and driven up and down an airfield, the ground shook. Onlookers were stunned, and the press, on the basis of no firm evidence whatsoever, had immediately proclaimed that Britain finally had a car capable of winning Grands Prix. The problem was, the work had barely started.

The BRM made its race debut in August 1950. At least, it should have done. The car, still far from ready, was entered for a non-championship Formula 1 race at Silverstone, but a drive-shaft made of the wrong specification of steel snapped when the driver, Raymond Sommer, let out the clutch at the start. Spectators, whipped up by a booklet entitled *BRM, Ambassador for Britain*, cruelly tossed pennies into the cockpit as the stricken car was wheeled silently into the paddock.

Victory for the BRM in a minor club event at Goodwood raised hopes once again, and British fervour was wound up another notch a few days before the 1951 British Grand Prix when Randolph Turpin took the world middleweight title from Sugar Ray Robinson on a points' decision at Earls Court in London. In truth, that famous victory probably meant more to Ken Tyrrell than the prospect of seeing the BRM run at Silverstone. Certainly, he was prepared for nothing more than a good day out as he boarded the coach with his team-mates from Ockham. Later that day he witnessed history being made as Ferrari scored their first victory in a World championship Grand Prix, but he would never have believed that the wood yard from which he had just come would one day spawn blue racing cars capable of knocking Ferrari for six.

The BRMs, for there were two of them now, had at least managed to start, albeit it from the back of the grid after arriving at the last minute. But, in the hurry to complete the cars, the exhaust pipes had not been properly insulated and the drivers, Reg Parnell and Peter Walker, had been roasted. They were persuaded to continue after having their legs wrapped in soaked cotton wool and burn dressings. Parnell finished fifth. Unfortunately, he was no fewer than five laps behind the winning Ferrari.

For Ken Tyrrell that was a minor detail. He was intoxicated by everything associated with the day – the noise, the smell, the sense of drama. Sitting in the grandstand at Stowe corner, he was completely hooked, and it was one of the supporting races that had truly whetted his appetite for competition. As he watched the so-called 500 race, particularly the mid-field runners, Tyrrell had genuinely believed he could do as well, if not better, himself. The first seeds of a world-beating team had just been planted in that small corner of a Northamptonshire field.

The 500s were tiny single-seaters powered by 500cc motorcycle engines. These miniature racing cars, with their narrow wheels and spindly suspension, were the product of necessity in the immediate post-war years as Britain got back to its feet and motor sport fans looked for something suitable to race. There were very few cars around at that time, but motorcycles – and, more to the point, their engines – were in ready supply. It didn't take long for enterprising engineers to build a simple chassis to carry the single- and twin-cylinder engines in the back.

Charles Cooper and his son John were quick to spot their chance. Using the independent front suspension from two scrapped Fiat 500s, and joining it to a rudimentary frame and a 500cc JAP motorcycle engine, the first Cooper racing car was cobbled together. During the next decade, the Cooper Car Company would become famous the world over, winning the F1 championship after having started out manufacturing and selling these little 500s. Almost half of the 46 entries for the 500 support race at Silverstone on 14 July 1951 were Coopers. As the snorting machines made their way to the grid, little did Ken Tyrrell realize that the Cooper name was to play a major role in the next phase of his life. Neither could he have appreciated the significant influence due to be exerted at a much later date by a certain B C Ecclestone, the man at the wheel of Cooper-Norton number 20.

Bernie Ecclestone, having started from the middle of the grid, finished tenth, a few miles behind the winner, Stirling Moss, then aged 22 and on the cusp of greatness. But Tyrrell's eye was caught by the driver who started from the middle of the front row and finished a competitive sixth. The programme stated that Alan Brown, the driver of Cooper-Norton number 16, lived in Guildford. Tyrrell made a note of his name.

'He came to see me,' said Brown. 'I can't remember exactly when, but he asked if he could have a look at my car. I was with my parents, about a mile or so from where Ken lived. We had bought one of these six-car garages, a precast concrete thing. It was all very professional, and I think we impressed Ken generally. He was obviously very interested, and eventually he bought my car. I can't remember how much he paid.' Typically, Tyrrell could, many years later. 'I remember going to see him. I said, "I saw you race at Silverstone, sir. Can I see your racing car?" He showed me round his car in the garage and at the end of the season I paid him £500 for his Cooper and became a racing driver. Alan told me to take it to Brands Hatch, and if I couldn't lap within ten seconds of the record I was to sell it. But he didn't tell me that until after I'd bought it! I *just* made it.'

Tyrrell bought the car as a joint venture with Ron Stoneham, another amateur, and claimed his first outing was at Snetterton, which makes some sense since the opening 500 race of the 1952 season was on 31 May at this former airfield on the flat expanses of Norfolk. Unfortunately, the official entry list has been lost in the mists of time and Tyrrell's name does not appear in the rather incomplete records available. However, it is certain that he was part of a 42-car entry for the 500 International Trophy at Goodwood on 2 June. Because such a large number of entrants could not be accommodated in a single race, heats were laid on, the leading finishers in each heat – and the numbers varied from race to race – going through to a final. Driving car number 35 at Goodwood, Tyrrell qualified for his heat on the outside of the third row, which was four cars wide; Bernie Ecclestone was on the inside. History does not relate how Ecclestone and Tyrrell managed to retire and rule themselves out of a place in the final, but Goodwood, comprising the fast, curving perimeter road of the former Spitfire base close by the Sussex coast, was certainly a difficult track for a fledgling driver.

The unpainted car with its aluminium body panels and blue upholstery had been entered under the name 'R K Tyrrell'. Just over a month later, the Cooper was wheeled out again at Brands Hatch as an entry from 'Scuderia Guildbec', a racy combination which bravely mimicked the Scuderia Ferrari title and added a less romantic amalgam of Guildford and Beckenham, Stoneham's home town. It is not known where Tyrrell finished, the only good news being that he was not listed among the retirements.

The motorcycle engine formula continued to flourish; some 70 cars entered the Commander Yorke Trophy races at Silverstone on 23 August. The cream of 500 society was present, headed by Don Parker, Jim Russell and Stuart Lewis-Evans (whom Ecclestone would later manage when the talented Welshman progressed to Formula 1). And it was here that Ken Tyrrell first had his name added to the record books by finishing second in the 10-lap Junior Race, a prelude to the heats for the main event. He went on to be classified a fairly respectable 10th in Heat 2 and made it to the final, where he found himself among a long list of retirements, the strain of a colossal 63 laps taking its toll on fragile machinery running at maximum for most of the 101 mile event. Tyrrell's return to the airfield track on 20 September was even more disappointing when he crashed during the single 12-lap race.

The damage can't have been too serious because Scuderia Guildbec was out in force at Castle Coombe in Wiltshire a couple of weeks later. It was a sign of the open nature of motor sport in the fifties that Stirling Moss chose to enter this minor race, probably because he had nothing better to do. The prospective F1 star duly won his heat, Tyrrell taking a creditable eighth in the next and earning a place on the penultimate row of the grid for the final. The statistics merely relate that Moss won and Tyrrell finished outside the top six, but in so doing he presumably took his car home in one piece.

Moss and Tyrrell travelled north in October for the 25-lap King's Arms Trophy at Charterhall, another flat and featureless former airfield in the Borders region. Moss was beaten into second place by Eric Brandon, very much a 500 ace and Alan Brown's partner in their team, Ecurie Richmond. For Tyrrell the trip was made more than worthwhile with sixth place, an encouraging result on which to end the season.

Motor racing might have entered his soul, but it was in danger of exciting Ken Tyrrell a little too much. When the 1953 season opened he soon had his name down on the entry list for the Earl of March Trophy, a straightforward five-lap event at Goodwood. He qualified in the middle of the second row, lining up behind Brown (on pole), Moss, Brandon and Bob Gerard, a legendary name in pre- and post-war British motor sport. The race might have lasted a mere eight minutes and 53 seconds, but the exhilaration of the moment was too much for Tyrrell: he was the first, and probably only, retirement thanks to a crash. He probably didn't have time to notice that the former owner of his car won.

Dusting himself down, Tyrrell tried his luck north of the border once again. The effort was to be worthwhile, for he won a heat at the race meeting organized by the Scottish Motor Racing Club at Beveridge Park, near Kirkcaldy. Apart from Charles Headland, few of the English regulars were present, but local talent was out in force, names such as Joe Potts and Ninian Sanderson giving Tyrrell something to think about. The meeting was divided into two 'races'. Having won his heat for Race 1, Tyrrell chased Sanderson (later to win Le Mans) home in the final. He got his revenge with victory over the Scot when they ran in the same heat for Race 2, Tyrrell going on to score a fine win in the final by beating the much-fancied Headland, described by motor racing historian Doug Nye as 'a hard, uncompromising driver who tended to crash or win, with very little in between'. In later years, Tyrrell would recall that Beveridge Park drive as one of his best. 'It wasn't a big race, but it was very satisfying. I wasn't expected to beat Charlie Headland because he was quicker and much more experienced than me.' Saturday, 25 April 1953 was certainly quite a landmark for R K Tyrrell, racing driver.

Tyrrell Brothers, lumber merchants, continued to do well, mainly through very hard work rather than easily made money. The brothers' industriousness gave Ken enough spare cash to defray the expense of towing his racing car on a trailer to the various races without compromising the immediate needs of his family. Thanks to his background in the lumber trade, on the circuit Ken earned the nickname 'Chopper', and he responded by painting an axe on the flanks of his Cooper. Those trying unsuccessfully to pass him on the race track were of the opinion that the sobriquet had nothing to do with the timber business, one rival summing it up when he said, 'Ken always wanted to use the piece of road I was on at the time.'

Tyrrell continued to travel the length and breadth of the country, picking up place finishes and another victory in 1953. A seasoned campaigner now, he couldn't wait to get started the following year. He travelled to Kirkistown, a small circuit using a former wartime runway on a featureless part of the Ards Peninsula in Northern Ireland. Facilities were almost non-existent. The toilets comprised sack-cloth erected around a rudimentary arrangement. An elderly bus, parked by the start line, acted as race headquarters, and stood in for just about everything else. The first action of the day was to chase the neighbouring farmer's wayward cows off the track and remove the worst of their excesses from the racing line. Kirkistown might have been a rudimentary venue, but it was typical of the time.

More to the point as far as the racers were concerned, this was not only the first race of the 1954 season, it was also grandly titled 'The 500cc championship of Ireland' and attracted a small but quality entry. Tyrrell led the field on two of the 25 laps. Unfortunately, they were not the final two, but he had a lively scrap with Stuart Lewis-Evans and finished a close third, less than a second behind the winner, the now legendary Don Parker. As far as the Irish fans were concerned, this man Tyrrell from 'across the water' was obviously worth watching.

Certainly, you could not doubt the effort Tyrrell put in as he sat hunched over the wheel, mouth open, his large frame hanging over the side of the cramped cockpit while physically urging the little car through the bends. There were no corners whatsoever at the Brighton Speed Trial in September, so he leaned forward and kept his head low during the blast along the prom. For once running against the clock rather than wheel to wheel with fellow competitors, Tyrrell put his name in the history books that September when he lowered the class record for the measured mile to 29.62 seconds. Typically, no sooner had the weekly motor sport bible *Autosport* carried the report of Tyrrell's achievement than an issue a couple of weeks later published a picture of his Cooper spinning at Brands Hatch.

The Scuderia Guildbec partnership with Ron Stoneham having ended some time before, the R K Tyrrell entry was never seriously challenged on 5 May 1955 when Tyrrell won a minor meeting at Davidstow in Cornwall. Having braved the Irish Sea crossing the previous year, he then made plans to go further afield in the summer after entering a pair of races in Sweden. He got off to a bad start in the eight-lap Swedish Grand Prix at Kristianstad. After qualifying on pole ahead of a mixed entry of 18 cars, Tyrrell was posted as a retirement after just two laps of the four-mile track. The official reason given was 'engine', a fact which was dutifully reported in *Autosport*, along with the news that local drivers had cleaned up. One can only imagine a certain amount of straight talking from Tyrrell when he met the *Autosport* reporter a week later at Karlskoga, scene of the next race. The magazine certainly went to great lengths in the following issue to point out that Tyrrell had been struck from the rear by another competitor (Henk 'Hutchy' Hutchinson, a KLM pilot with whom Tyrrell had shared the front row), the blow fracturing a drive-shaft. In fact, it was more than a mere glancing blow, the impact having sent Hutchinson's Cooper cartwheeling down the track. But that was not the point. The apology finished: 'Ken's engine, prepared by Geoff Read, has not, in fact, missed a beat this season.'

Neither did it throughout the weekend at Karlskoga. The meeting was known as the 'Kanonloppet' (Cannon Races) thanks to Karlskoga being an armament centre for the manufacture of anti-aircraft guns. Ken didn't much care what the race was called when he saw that *Autosport*, on the page following the apology, carried the bold headline KEN TYRRELL WINS. The single-paragraph report said nothing about grid positions, but explained that Tyrrell had taken an immediate lead and had 'scrapped heartily' with Andre Loens before the winner at Kristianstad was forced to drop back with mechanical trouble, leaving Tyrrell the victor by 1.3 seconds from the similar Cooper of Colin Davis, the only other Englishman in the event. Just for good measure, Tyrrell also set the fastest lap at an average of 59mph. It would be his only moment of international fame as a racing driver.

Autosport's main report in the same issue covered the International Nine Hour Race at Goodwood. The comprehensive 10-page summary demonstrated the importance of sports car racing and its attraction to motor manufacturers. Aston Martin, very much to the fore on the international scene, had thrashed opposition from Jaguar and Ferrari in a race which fielded Mike Hawthorn, Tony Brooks, Peter Collins, Stirling Moss and other leading drivers. John Wyer, the shrewd team manager at Aston Martin, would have noticed the report of Tyrrell's win. Whether that was what persuaded him to offer Tyrrell a test drive is not certain, but Ken was not about to query the reason when he got the call. 'My drives in those two Swedish races probably earned me the test drive in a works Aston Martin that autumn,' he said. 'I'd never driven a car like that and I thought it was bloody marvellous. John Wyer told me that I had been quicker than Ivor Bueb [a leading driver] on the corner where he was timing, and that he'd be getting in touch.'

It came to nothing. Tyrrell's dream was swamped by an emotional backwash following the tragedy during the Le Mans 24-hour race the previous June. A collision between two cars had sent a Mercedes-Benz into the crowd, killing the driver, Pierre Levegh, and more than 80 people. Mercedes-Benz withdrew from motor sport at the end of the season, a move that placed Stirling Moss on the sports car market. Aston Martin snapped him up, and that was the end of Tyrrell's hopes for a works drive. As he put it, 'Moss became their number one driver and they didn't need a number six . . . so I blame Stirling for that!'

The year 1955 marked the height of Ken Tyrrell's career as a driver. He finished outside the top six in the support race at Silverstone's International Trophy meeting in May 1956, then entered a club race at Goodwood later that month but failed to start. His apparent lack of interest matched the fading appetite for 500 racing. The formula, having more than served its purpose, was beginning a slow but inevitable decline as Formula 2 blossomed and ageing Formula 1 cars became available. These were 'proper' racing cars compared to the funny little 500 machines with their rasping, snorting motorcycle engines. With typical ingenuity, Cooper Cars had led the way, first with front-engined F2 machines and then with the rear-engined chassis, which would ultimately take the firm from Surrey to the very top of world motor sport.

Tyrrell watched with interest. Having done all he could in his faithful 500, he took part in a few club meetings in 1957 at the wheel of Alan Brown's F2 Cooper, achieving nothing of note. As if trying to make up for lost time, in April 1958 he took a trip to the south of France and raced on a difficult but picturesque circuit on the streets of Pau, a sort of Monaco Grand Prix but without the brass knobs and high prices. Tyrrell was being managed on this occasion by Gerard 'Jabby' Crombac, a French Anglophile who was the continental correspondent for *Autosport* and a highly respected member of the motor racing scene.

'Alan Brown had lent his car to my partner Jean Lucas and he had finished second at Rheims the previous year,' said Crombac. 'I was a great friend of Alan and he took on Ken in the role of a sort of chief mechanic. He didn't actually do anything on the car but he looked after the logistics and so on. The idea was that Ken would drive one car and the other would go to people who could bring good start money. The first race on the continent was at Pau, and I was Ken's manager.

'In those days, there was a very good night-sleeping train from Paris to Pau and you could get compartments which interconnected with one another. So, we had a string of compartments; there was Alan and his wife Ann, Lucas and myself. I brought some champagne and brandy to make champagne cocktails – Mike Hawthorn had taught me how to make them. We had these throughout the evening and we arrived at Pau absolute wrecks. When Ken came to fetch us at the station, he was horrified! He wondered what he had got himself into.

'We put a friend, Nano da Silva Ramos, in the other car and he finished second. But Ken was a little lost because it was pouring with rain and, of course, this was a very tight track and he was more used to Goodwood and Silverstone.' Ken started from the middle of the grid and retired with broken transmission after 13 of the planned 50 laps. 'After the race, Ken came back to Paris with us,' Crombac continued. 'We went to a restaurant where they served trout *en papillote*. Ken was very much a rough diamond at the time and he complained loudly about having to pay whatever it was for "trout in a paper bag"!'

Tyrrell made his way back to England where, two weeks later, he planned to take part in the BARC (British Automobile Racing Club) 200, a first-class event for F1 and F2 cars on the perimeter road of the Aintree race course. The event was won by Stirling Moss, a timely follow-up to his thrilling victory in the Argentine Grand Prix where the Englishman had defeated the might of Ferrari and Maserati in his privately entered Cooper-Climax.

Apart from marking Tyrrell's first appearance in a major-league event, the race at Aintree was also notable for the re-emergence of B C Ecclestone, not as a driver but as the entrant of a brace of Connaught F1 cars. These British-built machines were not destined to be anything like as successful as their entrepreneurial owner in the decades to come. A similar cloud of failure hung over Tyrrell's effort that day: he started from the back of the grid, finishing 17th and last with crash damage.

Tyrrell decided to join forces with Alan Brown and Cecil Libowitz, the owner of a local engineering firm. Their collective ambition was to buy a pair of brand-new Cooper F2 cars, with Tyrrell taking part in the occasional race. That was the plan. The reality was to hit home at Tyrrell's next race, a fairly minor F2 event at Brands Hatch on 18 May.

The spring of 1958 marked the arrival in Britain of Bruce McLaren. A smiley 20-year-old from New Zealand, McLaren had won a Driver to Europe Award thanks to promise shown within the limits of his home environment. The deal was to put him into a works F2 Cooper, something he would handle with ease. But first it was deemed necessary by the Cooper family for Bruce to gain a bit more experience. He duly showed up at Brands Hatch. McLaren recalled the day in his memoirs. 'I was on the front row,' he wrote. 'I led off the line with 5500rpm on the clock and not too much wheelspin, when Ken Tyrrell went sizzling past in Alan Brown's blue Cooper. I didn't even know him and was perturbed that he should be going so much faster. I pulled up beside him at Clearways [the right-hander leading onto the pit straight] and he left me standing. I later found he was using second and third gears and high revs, while I had been using third and fourth. I managed to sneak by this puzzlingly quick car at the hairpin a couple of laps later and won the heat. In the second heat I piled on a few extra revs and headed Tyrrell into Paddock Bend and held the lead to the finish.'

Despite his still keenly ambitious plans as a driver, Ken Tyrrell was too pragmatic to allow a dream to cloud his judgement. He had just turned 34; McLaren, 14 years his junior, was obviously a faster driver. It was evident to Ken that he ought to be nurturing talent such as McLaren's, not forlornly attempting to defeat it. He took part in two more races in 1958 and achieved little of note. The time had come to stop messing about.

3

Discovering the Future

'Ken turned up on the doorstep. I wasn't in, but my father told me a big bloke – a bit rough – called Tyrrell had called and he wanted to talk to me. We met, and went down the pub. He offered me a job. That's how it came about. I was his first mechanic.' Strictly speaking, Alan Stait wasn't a mechanic. He was a machinist by trade, but he understood racing, spoke the language, knew what was needed to get the job done. That was good enough for Tyrrell. Stait being a machinist was a bonus rather than a hindrance.

Having decided midway through 1958 to run a car rather than race one, Tyrrell had taken a more proactive role in his partnership with Brown and Libowitz. He had needed a mechanic, and one of the first ports of call was only a mile away, just outside the village of Send. It was here that Connaught had been based before lean times had forced the sale of the cars to Ecclestone. Tyrrell had enquired about prospective candidates and Stait's name was put forward as a likely lad since he was now out of work. With Stait living in Guildford, it was a moment's work for Tyrrell to call in and use his infectious enthusiasm to extol the virtues of helping run a Cooper in Formula 2.

'I knew how to put a car together,' said Stait. 'I had never actually done it before – in fact, I'd never thought about it because I was a machinist – but I didn't think it would be a problem. It wasn't

Tyrrell Racing at this stage because it was still this consortium with Alan Brown and Cecil Libowitz. We were using a lock-up at Stoughton. It was quite a big one with a kind of workshop, but there weren't any facilities or anything like that. I remember, for example, that there wasn't a loo!'

The manner of Stait's first venture abroad, to France, was typical of the period: Ken used his Zephyr (a top-of-the-range Ford) to tow the Cooper on a trailer, Norah joining Ken, Alan and another part-time mechanic (also ex-Connaught) for the trip. At times it was a hectic schedule, never more so than at the end of the season when the plan was to enter the car in a Formula 2 race at Montlhéry near Paris and then move onto Casablanca for the Moroccan Grand Prix the following weekend.

That meeting might have been the final round of the 1958 World championship, but F2 cars were permitted to enter. With the organizers willing to pay good starting money if a local man was able to take part in Tyrrell's Cooper, it was a trip worth making. Unfortunately, the driver paying for the opportunity in France comprehensively destroyed the car by driving into the back of another competitor on the start line. 'It was very difficult if there was a shunt,' recalled Stait. 'If you knocked a [suspension] wishbone off in those days, the chassis was usually damaged as well. Not good. The chap who was driving the car at Montlhéry was obviously not very good judging by the damage caused. Because we had a wrecked car, Cooper had to fly in a chassis, bodywork and lots of bits to Le Touquet. We only had a few days to get down to Bordeaux. We reached Casablanca okay, but then we had to start rebuilding the car, almost from scratch.

'Ken had teamed me up for the trip with a South African who was working for Cooper. The bloke was totally useless. He was only interested in going along for the ride, and it made life very difficult. That was one of my worst-ever trips. When you have a job to do, and you know what to do, you want to get on with it. But it's no use being lumbered with someone like that. I had a go at Ken about it when we got back. I have to admit that sort of thing didn't happen very often. Ken was very reasonable about it, as he usually was, and that was the end of the matter.' Stait's efforts with the spanners were worthwhile, if only because the driver, Robert La Caze, came home third in the F2 category. Mind you, there were only four finishers in that class. At least the third place helped to defray the cost of a tin of paint.

Before leaving England, Stait had nipped into Woolworth's in Guildford and purchased some paint, a prerequisite of La Caze's deal, which called for the car to be in the colours of his home country rather than British Racing Green. Stait had simply set to and painted the bodywork by hand – a far cry from today, when the cars are stripped after each Grand Prix and resprayed completely under carefully controlled conditions; simply applying a fresh coat on top of the old one is out of the question since it means extra weight. Some teams spend several thousand pounds each time in order to have the right colour in a special paint. The cost of respraying three cars in readiness for one race today would have covered Tyrrell's expenses for the entire season in 1958.

Different times, too, for F1 reportage. Communications were so poor that the following Thursday's edition of *Autosport* did not carry a full report on the Moroccan Grand Prix – a significant omission considering Mike Hawthorn had just become the first British driver to win the World championship, even if he was driving for Ferrari rather than Vanwall, the popular British team favoured by Stirling Moss. The news section devoted a mere half a page to Hawthorn's triumph, with a note of apology explaining that the following week's edition would carry the full story. Sure enough, the 31 October issue not only ran a green cover, eschewing the usual red masthead as a sign of a British victory, but also devoted six pages to that final Grand Prix. Moss had done all he could by winning the race and setting the fastest lap, but once again he was relegated to the role of runner-up. Hawthorn's second place had allowed him to hold onto the title by a single point despite having won just one race compared to Moss's four. Consistency had counted for more than virtuoso performances spiked by unreliability.

Obituary notices were almost a weekly feature in motor sport publications of the day, and this issue of *Autosport* was no exception. Page three carried the sad news that Stuart Lewis-Evans had died of burns received after crashing his Vanwall on the 41st lap. The opening line said simply, 'The little man with the big heart has gone.' It made sad reading for Tyrrell since he had raced against and respected the talented Welshman. The loss of Lewis-Evans would have been a topic of discussion that week at the London Motor Show. Accidents were indeed a tragic part of the game, but an aspect racing people tended to gloss over with the simple caveat 'the throttle works both ways'. That much was true, and it will always remain so, but it was highly unlikely then that anyone would broach the subject of how to prevent fire in the first place, or suggest ways of offering a driver more protection. The death of Lewis-Evans? 'Lovely chap. One of these terrible things, ol' boy. By the way, have you seen the new Aston? Cracking good car.'

The Aston Martin DB4 was considered to be the star of the London Motor Show. Selling for £4,000 (including purchase tax), the 3.7 litre sports car was reckoned to be in demand, *Autosport* surmising that 'with 263bhp available, the performance cannot be less than sensational'. The average motorist was more interested in a two-seater Triumph TR3 at £699 or a four-door MG Magnette at £714 plus £358 7s. (£358.35p) purchase tax. Cars at the lower end of the market were standard in every sense, which was why heaters were on sale in the Earls Court stands priced at £15 each (plus 15 shillings [75p] for separate demister nozzles) but with 'free accessories and instructions for easy fitting'.

Ken Tyrrell remained loyal to Ford and his trusty Zephyr with its bench front seat and column gearchange. A keen motorist, he had fitted the four-door saloon with a Servais exhaust, a device with which the advertising assured drivers 'faster acceleration, smoother cruising and a saving in running costs. The smooth design of the

Servais manifold helps exhaust gases to escape with maximum speed and efficiency.' That was the general idea, but Tyrrell can't have been impressed by the blurb when the exhaust on his car refused to work properly. The Zephyr was serviced by Coombs of Guildford, where Alan Brown was the sales manager. A visit to their service department would be useful to Tyrrell for reasons other than fixing the exhaust. He was entertaining thoughts of going out on his own, but if he wanted to explore that particular avenue he needed to be looking for an extra pair of hands to assist Alan Stait. Tyrrell was tipped off about Neil Davis, a young mechanic working for Coombs who was reportedly interested in motor racing.

'The Servais exhaust system had developed a horrendous flat spot,' recalled Davis. 'I was given the task of sorting it out. When Ken came to collect the car, I went up the road with him to demonstrate that the problem was hopefully cured. He said he understood I was interested in motor racing and, when I said I was, we had a general conversation about what he was doing. Then he asked if I would like to help in the evenings because he only had one mechanic. I agreed. This was in 1958. At the end of that year, Ken said he was starting up his own team and I agreed to go and work with him full time.'

Tyrrell saw the timber yard as being the obvious place at which to establish his team. Since Norah could not yet drive and was commuting more and more often to Long Reach from the west side of Guildford, it seemed logical for the family to move out of Sheepfold Road and occupy the small bungalow in the yard. The team, such as it was, took up residence in one of the existing small sheds, but it wasn't long before space was at a premium. A solution was supplied by the armed forces. Stoughton Barracks occupied a sizeable piece of land close by Sheepfold Road, and word got out that the Women's Royal Armour Corps (WRAC) were due to replace the wooden huts there with more permanent structures. Tyrrell bought one large hut and charged Stait and Davis, along with next-door neighbour Charlie Gear, with the task of dismantling it and rebuilding it in the wood yard, where it would act as a workshop. It would also become the most famous shed in motor racing, this most humble of working environments ultimately producing some of the best racing cars in the world.

For the moment, though, Tyrrell continued to run with Alan Brown in Formula 2, before switching to Formula Junior. As ever, John Cooper had been swift to spot the commercial opening when Formula Junior was introduced in 1959 as a stepping-stone to F2 and F1. With the little 500cc racers having finally served their purpose, Formula Junior was seen as a more modern replacement, with one litre engines based on readily available production units. When it was agreed that Formula Junior would go international, Tyrrell automatically became a potential front-runner when in 1960 he offered to run a pair of cars for Cooper. He also confirmed an ability to spot driving talent.

Tyrrell was at the Cooper workshops in Surbiton when he met John Surtees. The name was already very familiar to Ken since Surtees was a dominant force in motorcycle racing; indeed, he was the 500cc world champion. Having done all there was to do on two wheels, Surtees was giving serious thought to competing in cars. Aston Martin and Vanwall had shown serious interest after Surtees had been immediately competitive during test sessions, particularly when his time around Goodwood in the Vanwall was bettered only by Moss. Typically, though, Surtees wanted to learn to walk before he tried to run flat out with the best in the world, so he went to Surbiton and ordered a Formula 2 Cooper-Climax for £2,437.

The only outstanding problem was the absence of a competition licence suitable for four wheels. Tyrrell happened to overhear Surtees' conversation at the workshops, and also happened to know exactly what was required to qualify for the licence: Surtees needed to take part in at least one club race, and conveniently enough Tyrrell had a Formula Junior car John was welcome to use. Surtees marvelled at his luck. In fact, it was a put-up job, the wily John Cooper having tipped off Tyrrell about the impending visit of a very

31

important prospective client whom the leading lights of motor sport were desperate to sign up. Ken had read the reports and heard the gossip, and didn't need a second bidding.

Their faith in Surtees paid off. On 20 March 1960 the Englishman qualified the brand-new and still unpainted Cooper on the front row for his first race at Goodwood and managed to lead on the opening lap. He finished second, but since he was beaten only by Jim Clark, another legend in the making, the result said everything anyone needed to know about the biker's potential.

Surtees agreed to do more races for Ken when his two-wheel commitments with MV Agusta permitted. That was often enough to allow Surtees to take a serious run at the 1960 Formula Junior championship, and along the way to appreciate the high stand-ard of Tyrrell's preparation. The irony was that Surtees would be denied the title thanks to consistent gearbox failures that had noth-ing to do with the work of Tyrrell and his meticulous mechanics, Stait and Davis.

The 1960 season was a busy one, Tyrrell running cars almost every weekend on tracks scattered across Europe. His team literally came within inches of tragedy at Aix-les-Bains in May when a tem-porary bridge spanning the road circuit collapsed and Keith Ballisat – a journeyman driver, later to become competitions director at Shell – spun Tyrrell's car in order to avoid piling into the wreck-age. The local police chief commended Ballisat's presence of mind. Several spectators were killed, along with the British driver Chris Threlfall, but the casualty figures would have been higher had Ballisat not taken urgent action. 'The incident occurred out of our sight on the far side of the circuit,' Alan Stait recalled. 'We didn't realize what had happened, and it was only when the drivers came back to the pits that we began to appreciate how serious it was. Keith's car was damaged, but by all accounts it could have been much worse.'

On the same weekend in Germany, the Nürburgring 1,000 kilo-metre sports car race had attracted the cream of international motor sport. An Aston Martin among the 67-car field was due to be co-driven by Henry Taylor, a farmer from Bedfordshire who was competent enough at the wheel to have received offers from privately entered teams in races such as this and in Formula 1. He had also cut his teeth in 500 racing, and he knew Tyrrell, the farmer and the timber merchant having raced wheel to wheel on many an occasion. Ken was keen to enter a car for the Formula Junior race supporting the Monaco Grand Prix a week later; he chose Taylor as his driver even though neither man had ever set foot in Monte Carlo.

'I was driving for Peter Whitehead at the Nürburgring,' said Taylor. 'We got back to the hotel and saw pictures on the television of the collapsed bridge at Aix. Ken was obviously right in the middle of it, and of course I was supposed to drive for him at Monaco the following week. I was with my wife, Peggy, and we decided to drive to Aix to see if we could help. We got there to find poor old Ken trying to sort out a considerable mess, what with the legal implications and one thing and another. When he had finished, Ken said he was just about skint. I said, "Don't look at me! I'm a farmer!" The idea of going to Monaco was an adventure for us both. I said I wasn't concerned about the money but that we should go down to Monte Carlo and see what we could do.'

There was no time to fix Ballisat's car, but John Cooper came to the rescue by arranging for Tyrrell to use a car normally hired out to local drivers. Because of the delays while the police took statements and generally went about their duties in the aftermath of the bridge failure at Aix, Tyrrell and Taylor were late arriving in Monte Carlo. Worse still, Ken discovered he did not have an entry. He turned to Gerard 'Jabby' Crombac for help. Crombac had entered a car for the F3 race, but his driver had been caught up in the bridge disaster at Aix. 'My entry was under the "Inter-Auto-Course" name,' he said with a grin. 'Originally, it had been known as "Intercourse", but when the British racing people heard what I had called my team, they were in hysterics and explained to me what it meant in English. Our French equivalent was nothing like that! Anyway, because a driver I was managing had crashed into the bridge at Aix, he didn't have a car to race at Monaco, but I still had an entry for him. Ken had not received the entry forms but he thought it was automatic. So he turned up with one car and, much to his surprise, the organizers said he had no entry. I said he could have mine, but the organizers said an entry could not be transferred. But if I wanted to enter Henry Taylor, that would be fine.'

Tyrrell and Taylor had the additional complication of having to qualify, which was easier said than done for a driver and entrant who had not seen the circuit before. They also had the drawback of a Cooper powered by a BMC engine: the four-cylinder unit was underpowered compared with the Ford Cosworth used by the favourites, Lotus. Still, as Taylor remarked, 'Having got that far, it was worth giving it a go, so off we went and, blow me, even with this horribly down-on-power engine, we ended up on the front row of the grid. That said a lot for the Cooper chassis. I remember saying to Ken that, since neither of us had enough to pay for the hotel, we'd got to bloody well do something in the race in order to win enough money to get us home! That's how bad it was.' Taylor had been beaten only by the works Lotus-Fords of Jim Clark and Trevor Taylor – no disgrace under the circumstances.

It was expected that the Scot and the Yorkshireman would race into the distance, leaving Taylor to fight off another Lotus driven by Peter Arundell. A top three or four finish would do nicely; a win, though still Tyrrell's ultimate aim in such a prestigious event, would be a bonus. Clark tore into the lead, Taylor losing ground during the scramble into the first corner, a tight hairpin leading on to Boulevard Albert 1er, which forms the start/finish straight for the Grand Prix today. In 1960, the track was no less difficult or tortuous, and Taylor made good use of the nimble Cooper chassis as he worked his way into third place. By the fourth lap, he had taken second from a Lola-Ford driven by Peter Ashdown.

Clark and Taylor were now in a race of their own, the Lotus holding a comfortable 10-second lead. That gap was cut in half when

Clark's engine began to misfire on lap 15. The Scot clung on to his lead, the engine seemingly clearing itself and allowing the Lotus to ease away once more. The predicted victory seemed assured, a second place for Taylor and Tyrrell beyond their wildest dreams. Then, with just five of the 50 laps remaining, Clark's Lotus came to a halt at the Gasworks Hairpin, a breakdown that was indicative of the Scot's appalling luck in Monte Carlo. Clark loved the demands of the street circuit but he would never win the Monaco Grand Prix. Taylor swept into the lead, Ashdown more than half a minute behind. Tyrrell went berserk.

'Ken was in the pits, shouting and screaming,' Taylor recalled. 'But he was not alone. Cooper, of course, had two cars [driven by Bruce McLaren and Jack Brabham] in the Grand Prix the next day. Their cars were garaged in a small side street, down by Portier Corner on the far side of the circuit. Every time I came down the hill towards Portier and the sea front, John Cooper kept running into the middle of the road shouting, "Go on, boy! Go on!" He was jumping up and down and waving his arms about the place. I was getting all this encouragement, but they didn't know that the poor old engine had run out of oil. I had enough to keep going on the straights but I couldn't get round the corners without free-wheeling. From memory, that had started just after I took the lead. Ken and John must have wondered what I was doing.' Crombac, on the other hand, did not know which way to look. Closely associated with Lotus, the Frenchman sat in Clark's pit and became more embarrassed by the minute as his entry – a Cooper, no less – led the race.

Taylor made it to the chequered flag. It was the first win for Ken Tyrrell as an entrant. And what a victory. The Monaco Formula Junior race was watched by the F1 cognoscenti; the winner received his prize from Prince Rainier. 'It really was the most exciting time for both Ken and me,' said Taylor. 'We had a lot of fun and picked up what we thought was the most extraordinary amount of prize money – about £3,000, I think.'

The following day, Sunday, Lotus made up for the disappointment experienced in the Formula Junior race when Stirling Moss won the main event and gave the English marque the first of many Grand Prix victories. Typically at that time, Moss had also driven in and won the sports car race at the Nürburgring the previous weekend, but there was no doubt that the result at Monaco was the one he cherished most. Moss was fêted that evening at the gala prize giving in the Hôtel de Paris – alongside the winner of the Formula Junior race. 'We automatically had an invitation to the ball,' said Taylor. 'I remember dancing with Princess Grace while Peggy danced with Prince Rainier. It was the most wonderful time, which I'll never forget – and neither did Ken. He always mentioned it in the years to come.' Crombac did not forget the occasion either: 'That night, "Chopper" invited me to the prize giving and he gave me a box of cigars. It was a wonderful evening – even though I lost my girlfriend because Stirling got interested in her!'

Taylor raced as and when he could. His name became familiar to British enthusiasts, particularly when he was associated with a promotional campaign for the latest electrical gadget – a portable record player. *Autosport* carried a picture of Taylor and Bruce McLaren staring fondly at a Dansette perched on the ramp of a racing car transporter. Today it looks as silly as a fridge being humped into a pub to keep the drinks chilled. The caption read: 'Racing drivers Henry Taylor and Bruce McLaren relax at Silverstone listening to "boogie-woogie" on the transistorized Dansette Diplomat portable record player.' The accompanying blurb explained that motor racing fans could take it to race tracks and listen to their favourite discs. As if, particularly when asked to pay £18 18s. (£18.90) – battery not included – for the privilege.

Taylor's relationship with Tyrrell continued to flourish when he won a tight contest at Albi in the south of France, a suitable reward for Ken's mechanics following a hectic programme after Ballisat destroyed the Monaco winner during a first-lap accident on the Crystal Palace circuit in south London. Even better was the fact that

Ian Raby, a rapid club driver, finished just behind Taylor in the second Tyrrell Cooper.

Encouraged by this, and the lure of big money, Tyrrell entered Taylor for the Monza Lottery, a flat-out charge on the famous autodrome near Milan. The only problem was that the Italian teams, having been soundly beaten at Monaco and elsewhere, were keen to win at home. Whatever the cost. One Lotus was prevented from starting because, according to the organizers, the car had 'dangerously low rear suspension'; other cars were considered 'dangerous' for similarly spurious reasons. Taylor made the front row for his heat, only to find that his car was waved off the grid because of an oil leak; a quick inspection by Tyrrell revealed that a leak existed only in the mind of the officials. Taylor resumed his position and finished sixteenth. Then the organizers stated that only the first 15 in each heat could race in the final, with the proviso that if any of those 15 couldn't compete, the next in line would move forward. Four cars dropped out. Taylor was still not allowed to start.

British organization, if not the weather, proved more equitable at Silverstone in October when Tyrrell entered the British Empire Trophy. With John Surtees in the running for the championship, Ken had taken the judicious step of providing the bike racer with a Lotus-Ford to improve his chances in the final races. For the Silverstone race, however, the organizers banned regular Grand Prix drivers, which ruled out Surtees, who had made his F1 championship debut at Monaco. The Lotus was entered for Taylor even though he had not driven the car before – or, more to the point, had not been allowed to drive it. 'Ken was very protective of John Surtees,' said Taylor. 'When Ken got hold of a Lotus, he wouldn't let me drive it. "No, no, you'll prang it, Henry," he'd say. "We'll leave it for John." The first time I was allowed to use it was in the British Empire Trophy. It went very well in practice and I was on the front row of the grid.'

Autosport solemnly reported the facts of the race. 'Taylor was about to race the new car for the first time,' explained the reporter, Martyn Watkins. 'At the drop of the flag almost every car paused as the rear wheels spun frantically in the wet. At the end of the first lap, Taylor's lead was something like six seconds – a fantastic demonstration of fast driving in the wet.' Well, not quite. In the days before television monitors, race reporters had to rely on what they saw from where they stood. Watkins was therefore blissfully unaware of a drama created by Taylor, one which had threatened to take out most of the field on the approach to Becketts corner on the far side of the circuit. Taylor explains what happened: 'The Lotus had a gear lever which, instead of going from left to right in the traditional manner as you went from first to fourth, went in the opposite direction. First gear was on the top right, with fourth at the bottom, on the left. It was okay when you were lapping on your own during practice because you could think it through. But when in the middle of a mob on the first lap, that was a different matter. On the flat-out approach to Becketts, I knocked it into bottom or second gear. It was pouring with rain, and the car went sideways, all the way to Becketts! I realized what had happened, but everyone behind me could see I was about to have the most glorious accident of all time and they slowed down. Funnily enough, at the end of the slide I happened to be pointing in the right direction for the corner. So I put my foot down, and away I went. I came round at the end of the first lap several seconds in the lead! Of course, in the pouring rain, if you are in front, you needn't worry. You've got it made, provided you don't do anything silly.' Watkins concluded his report: 'Henry Taylor set the fastest laps in the early stages of the race when the rain was at its heaviest, with a tour of 2m 4s at a speed of 84.97mph. It was undoubtedly his race – not only did he lead from start to finish, not only did he far outclass the field, his progress throughout was calm and unhurried.'

Taylor retired from racing a year later due to an eye injury; he moved to Monaco in 1973, where he runs a boat business. The British Empire Trophy takes pride of place in his office. 'Ken really was thrilled by that win,' he recalled. 'We went our different ways but we stayed close friends right to the end. He was always so professional, so sensible – and so enthusiastic! I wasn't in the least surprised when he went on to do so well.'

4

One-two, one-two

The 1960 season opened up exciting possibilities in Tyrrell's mind. The sixties had well and truly arrived, the dawning of a new era in which the world began to change fast. In January 1961 British football decided to leave behind the cloth cap, brilliantined hair days when a threat by players to go on strike brought an end to the draconian £20 a week maximum wage. Transfers of £50,000 soon became commonplace, and England and Fulham player Johnny Haynes became the first to receive £100 a week.

Motor racing remained in the gentlemanly era in which F1 teams bargained individually with race organizers for starting money and generally didn't make a fuss. Cooper had won two World championships in succession, Jack Brabham taking the double when he claimed five consecutive Grands Prix between June and September. The Australian would go on to greater things with his own team, but for Cooper 1960 marked the peak of achievement. Having stolen a march with the rear-engined concept, Cooper's advantage would soon be closed down as rivals caught up, and a change in engine formula for 1961 played into the willing hands of Ferrari.

Cooper needed to enjoy the benefit of healthy sales of Formula Junior cars, though track success remained hard to come by, thanks to Lotus and Ford Cosworth once again combining to make a more competitive package. Formula Junior was at the time being hailed as the most popular class of racing in the history of the sport, a claim that was easily understood as price tags of around £1,300 put the single-seaters within reach of amateur racers. Tyrrell spearheaded the professionals on behalf of the Cooper Car Company, titling his team 'Tyrrell Racing Organization', a grand British handle that summed up the boss's practical and systematic approach.

BMC had extracted more power from their 1100cc engine, but it was not enough to prevent Lotus from winning the first encounter of 1961 at Snetterton. A Tyrrell Cooper finished second, at the wheel Tony Maggs, a 24-year-old South African whom Ken had signed, along with John Love, a no-nonsense Rhodesian. Both men were keen to carve out a career in motor sport, and driving for Tyrrell in Europe was the perfect platform on which to display their talent. 'I had been really keen to go racing in Europe,' recalled Love. 'I got to hear about a chap by the name of Fitzwilliam who had just bought three Lolas, and I had been told he would be looking for drivers. I came up from Rhodesia, was introduced to Fitzwilliam and went across to Europe with him. He had about six or eight drivers lined up, so it was a bit of a Russian roulette kind of thing. We went to Monza and after a couple of runs he said, "I'll tell you what I'll do: you maintain and look after your car and you can race it." And that's what I did in 1960.'

Tyrrell first became aware of Love in 1960 during the race at Albi in France during which Ken's boys, Henry Taylor and Ian Raby, were given a run for their money by a driver whom the commentator excitedly referred to as 'Amour! Amour!' It was only later that Tyrrell discovered this to be a literal translation of the surname of a driver in a privately entered Lola. 'I was running third to Ken's two cars and I was screaming the hell out of this bloody Lola, just to keep up,' said Love. 'Apparently the commentator was getting really excited. A few weeks later, I was walking though the paddock at Brands Hatch when Ken came up to me and asked if I had a contract with Fitzwilliam. I said I was honour-bound but didn't really have a contract. So Ken asked if I would like to go to Goodwood and try one of his cars. I said I'd love to.

'I pitched up in my Mini Traveller and there were two glum-looking mechanics [Davis and Stait] leaning against the pit counter, with the car in front of them. They were probably saying to themselves, "Aw, Christ. Here comes another bloody colonial who's going to wreck our motor car." I saw Neil just recently [in March 2002] and I asked him if he remembered that. He said he did. I told him he had been a miserable-looking bastard with such a glum expression that he had hardly filled me confidence! We had a good laugh about that.'

Love went quickly enough to attract an offer of a couple of drives from Tyrrell at the end of 1960. Unfortunately, Love's commitment to race for Fitzwilliam threatened this opportunity to move his career forward. The way in which the matter was resolved says much about the method of going racing in the sixties. Today, the matter would have finished in court. 'I rang Fitz,' said Love. 'He said I was beginning to become known in Europe. I wasn't a big name or anything like that, but good enough to attract better starting money, and naturally he wanted to make the most of that. In effect, he was saying I was committed, even though there was no contract as such. So I said I would do those races for him but I would also like to do one particular race for Ken Tyrrell. It was agreed, and that's how I started to race for Ken.'

The relationship almost ended before it had begun. Their first race together was in August 1960 at Pescara on the Adriatic coast in Italy. This stunning 16-mile circuit ran from the coast into the mountains and back to sea level. Love was keen to make his mark. Too keen, in fact. 'There was this long straight along the coast, followed by quite a mountainous section,' Love remembered. 'I wasn't overconfident or anything like that, but I was trying fairly hard. Up in the mountains, I went through some straw bales straight into a bloody restaurant. At least I was close to a phone! I rang through to race control; Neil came on the other end. I said, "Look,

I've damaged the car." He wanted to know how bad it was. I said, "Well, let's put it like this. You're going to have to come and fetch me!" Ken wasn't too impressed, but I still got a contract to race for him in 1961.'

For that 1961 season Tyrrell had invested in a van capable of carrying two cars, with a third, if necessary, towed on a trailer; occasionally the effort would be split, one car racing in England, the other on the continent. Kenneth Tyrrell, about to celebrate his 17th birthday, would travel with the team during his school holidays. 'I remember going to Cesenatico in Italy,' he said. 'We had just the one car for John Love, so we went in a saloon car with a trailer on the back – just the three of us, John, Neil [Davis] and me. Tony Maggs was doing Goodwood, I think. I went along for the ride but I would do pit signals and stuff like that. Elsewhere, we had been having a hard time from Peter Arundell in the Lotus, but at Cesenatico we were up against Stanguellinis, which were Italian cars with front engines. We walked all over them. John was leading by miles when he developed a misfire. He came into the pits, and to this day I can see Neil wetting his thumb and forefinger and touching each spark plug in turn until he found the one causing the misfire. He quickly changed it and away John went. He finished third, I think.'

These were busy but happy times, Neil Davis and Alan Stait living on their wits in order to keep the cars running. 'We were racing all over Europe,' recalled Davis. 'Chimay, Rouen, La Chatre, Monza, Rheims, Stuttgart, Brands Hatch, Montlhéry. If they were fairly adjacent, we would go from one to the other which meant we could be away from base for five to six weeks at a time, doing the rebuilding as we went. I remember we had a shunt at Nogaro in France and the next race was in Sweden the following weekend. Alan Stait brought a car over from Dover, we met in Calais or wherever, did a swap, and he returned with the shunted one. John Love used to come in the truck with me on a number of occasions. He was very capable and would lend a hand. It was the same with most of our drivers; they were ordinary guys out to enjoy themselves, not pumped-up racing drivers taking everything far too seriously and missing the point of it all. There was no doubt that we were considered to be a top outfit. We did have a problem in the UK with the works Lotus team, but, other than that, the results speak for themselves. If John was first with Tony second one weekend, the positions would probably be reversed the next.'

Tyrrell scored three one-two finishes within the space of three weeks in May and June at Chimay in Belgium and at Magny Cours and Rouen in France. There was similar success in Scandinavia on successive weekends in August at Karlskoga (scene of Ken's victory in the 500 Cooper) and Roskilde. 'It was really hectic, but that was part of the fun,' said Tony Maggs. 'I had a little Mini for running around Europe but we would share driving the transporter, although John actually did more of that than me. When we were in England, John and I would flog up to Coventry in Ken's little Mini van, get the engines from BMC and bring them back. We had quite a lot of responsibility from that point of view. We didn't do that much mechanical work, but we did do a lot of the fetching and carrying. There was a great deal of team spirit. I would drive Ken's car and take Norah, and then we would swap. Norah helped out where she could, making tea and sandwiches, lap scoring and timekeeping, whatever needed doing. It was a very friendly, easy-going atmosphere. I can honestly say there was never a cross word between us.'

Tyrrell oversaw the operation and negotiated starting money. Rarely would he pick up a spanner – mainly because he didn't need to, thanks to the skill of Davis and Stait. 'Ken was always masterminding and overseeing; he was definitely in charge,' said Davis. 'He wasn't an engineer. He could organize and he knew when something wasn't right, but he couldn't put it right as far as the mechanics were concerned. You had to be honest with each other. You wouldn't cover anything up. You would pull the wool over Ken's eyes only once, and then you would be in trouble. He didn't bullshit. He was a straight-up man.'

Maggs also recalled that this uncomplicated approach of Tyrrell's embraced hotel rooms too, Ken's choice of basic accommodation setting a trend for which he would become notorious, even when taking part in Grand Prix racing a decade later. 'Everything was pretty basic then. From the team's headquarters to the cars themselves, they were straightforward compared to the highfalutin stuff you see today. The hotels were probably the cheapest, but that seemed to be an acceptable part of racing then. We had no fancy illusions of our own importance.'

Which was just as well on one particular occasion in France. The team, as usual, checked into a low-rent hotel, Maggs sharing with his wife, Gail. Ken and Norah had the room next door, in which a large wardrobe had been placed against the adjoining wall – such as it was. It was only when Norah opened the doors that she discovered the wardrobe was double-sided and served both rooms, but with the dividing panel missing. Worse still, a through-draught popped open the doors on the other side and revealed Mr and Mrs Maggs working at their relationship on the bed. Norah's Scottish upbringing prompted a gentle retreat and a quiet but firm instruction that Ken should stay away from the wardrobe, at least for the foreseeable future.

Norah knew how determined Ken could be, as did his mechanics. Davis had witnessed the lengths he could go to earlier in the year when they ran into engine trouble during practice for the race at Chimay. 'We were using local petrol,' he recalled. 'It was a bit dodgy, and we ended up with holed pistons. We tried lowering the compression ratio, but it was no good. Ken went off to phone Eddie Maher in the engine department at BMC. He came back and said, "Right, Neil. I want you to come with me. We're off to Zandvoort. The Dutch Grand Prix is going on up there and I've spoken to John Cooper who is going to let us have some fuel." So we set off through the night in Ken's green Zephyr. We met John Cooper in the early hours, loaded the Shell fuel in the boot and across the back seat, and immediately started back for Belgium.

'Dawn was just getting up as we charged into this Belgian village with a sort of zigzag in the middle. The road went from tarmac to cobbles. It was a damp morning. Ken was driving. We managed to scrabble round the first corner, but he spun the car in the middle of the second one. We had all this fuel on board; fortunately, we didn't hit anything. Just as we are gathering our breath and Ken is shoving the car into first gear, we spot this policeman with one of those tall hats. He's seen it all happen and his eyes are out on stalks. He grabs his whistle and starts blowing. Ken says, "We're not stopping!", lets out the clutch and we shoot off. We thought they might set up a road block, so I got the map out and we took a detour away from the main road. We reached Chimay just in time, put the petrol in the cars, and finished first and second. Ken liked that! That was the sort of man he was. He would drive all night if necessary just to get the job done.'

In October, the Tyrrell Racing Organization travelled to Montlhéry for their final race of 1961. Love won Heat 1, Maggs claimed Heat 2; the overall result, based on an aggregate of the two races, showed a dead heat. It was an appropriate summary of their season.

Maggs had sufficiently impressed John Cooper to earn an invitation to race alongside Bruce McLaren in the Grand Prix team for 1962; he would continue to drive for Tyrrell when his F1 commitments allowed, the New Zealander Denny Hulme, whose laid-back attitude outside the car belied tremendous speed when he was in it, acting as substitute. Hulme won several races for Tyrrell, a prelude to being snapped up by Jack Brabham's burgeoning F1 team, and then to becoming world champion in 1967.

Love stayed on board for another season, the hard work and nomadic existence appealing to the Rhodesian. 'It was great fun,' he said. 'Ken was always very good to us. In a way we were fighting for survival because we had to earn money to pay the bills and the cost of travel. Ken was very fair about the whole thing. The only aspect we were upset about was the lack of horsepower when compared with the Cosworths.

46

'I didn't mind lending a hand for whatever was required. I wouldn't be afraid to get stuck in; I had come from that sort of background. I had come from where I had to do all my own dirty work anyway; it wasn't anything new to me. I wasn't one of those guys that just pitched up in overalls and then buggered off to the bar afterwards. I enjoyed it, and I was interested in the cars. Neil and I made a good pair, actually. We'd have a box of tools and a few spares and that was it. We would make do.

'Like everyone else, I never, ever had a row with Ken. He was upset a couple of times when I pranged his car, he got a little bit glum, but we never had words. It wasn't that kind of relationship. I wanted to succeed and to win. I had no complaints, no regrets about it whatsoever.'

If Tyrrell and Love thought 1961 had been busy, the term took on a new dimension in 1962 when Ken continued his Formula Junior effort in Europe but also chose to run a team of Mini-Coopers in the British Saloon Car championship. Love took part in both series. 'Ken had written to me during the winter,' said Love. 'He pointed out that most of the Formula Junior events we did also had races for Minis and he wanted to know if I was prepared to do them as well. "It's extra pocket money," he said. "You get out of one car and into the other on the same day." I'd been used to doing that anyway so I knew that wouldn't be a problem. In those days you would drive a sports car in the morning and then a single seater or maybe a saloon later on. It wasn't like today.

'The BMC factory gave John Cooper two Minis and two for Ken. The works Coopers were for Sir John Whitmore and Bill Blyden-stein. Whitmore was considered to be the Mini king. I remember there was a meeting and they explained to me that there was one condition attached to me driving a Mini: I had to let Whitmore win. I said there was no chance. I wasn't prepared to do that because I went racing to give it all I'd got. So they suggested that we have three races and whoever was leading would be allowed to stay in front; the other guy would have to back off. I can't recall the exact score, but I won two or maybe all three of the races. Beating Whitmore was a bit of a feather in my cap.

'The Mini was unreal. I remember Silverstone, a race in pouring rain, and we were up against the Jaguars of Graham Hill and Jack Sears. Silverstone was a very fast circuit then but we would come through the final corner, Woodcote, side by side, lap after lap. In the Mini, in the rain, you just went into Woodcote flat out and went through the fast right-hander in one long old lurch! It was brilliant. We had such fun in those cars.'

Love won the British Saloon Car championship at his first attempt, but his year would finish on a difficult note that ended his chances of furthering his career. Ironically, it happened at Albi, the circuit where he had first attracted Tyrrell's attention. 'It was towards the end of that year,' Love recalled. 'I was behind Tony when he lost control. I had to avoid him and hit a wall on the outside of the corner. My arm was caught between the wall and the car and I ended up in Albi hospital. At around this time, it had been mentioned that I would have a Formula 1 test drive with Cooper or Brabham. Nothing was guaranteed, but the chance was there. Because of the broken arm, I missed my opportunity. Ken asked me back the following year, but I didn't want to do Formula Junior any more. I wanted to go further than that and I didn't fancy flogging round all those circuits again with a Formula Junior because you had to wring the necks of those cars to make them go. That just wasn't my thing. I had driven cars with a bit of steam and I fancied I wanted a car with more power. I decided to stay in South Africa and race there.'

Motor racing hit the front pages as a result of another accident in 1962: Stirling Moss crashed heavily at Goodwood and lay unconscious for four weeks. No one could be sure precisely why he had left the road and made no attempt to spin the car before spearing nose-first into a grass bank. The chassis, made of tubular frame, had folded around him. Moss was trapped for 40 minutes while rescuers attempted to cut their way through the wreckage. At 33, he was at the peak of his form, but he would never race again in top-level motor sport. He announced his retirement without having won the championship he had deserved several times over. Instead, Graham Hill became the second Englishman to claim the title when he won for BRM in 1962. It was an embarrassment of riches that season for Great Britain since Hill's main rival had been Jim Clark, the Scotsman's hopes draining away with the oil from the engine in his Lotus as he raced head to head with Hill in the final round. Few, though, were willing to bet against Clark in 1963.

Ken Tyrrell would see Clark at first hand when an unexpected turn of events led to his assuming his first role as a Formula 1 team manager. On 4 May 1963, John Cooper had a severe road accident when he managed to roll a twin-engined Mini prototype on the Kingston bypass. Tyrrell stepped in to assist John's ailing father, Charles, in the running of the Cooper F1 team at most of the Grands Prix that summer. Ken's Formula Junior team continued the now familiar round of racing through Europe, but was collecting fewer wins thanks to the Lotus-Ford combination being even stronger than before.

Sure enough, Jim Clark established a record by winning seven of the ten Grands Prix in 1963, and settled his first world title at Monza on 6 September. Six days later, a waif-like figure ran onto the pitch for the first time at Old Trafford to play for Manchester United. George Best was only 17, but with his outrageous talent, long hair and gently rebellious way, the Belfast boy would epitomize the excitement of the Swinging Sixties. Ken Tyrrell was about to play his part in the phenomenon by opening the door for another young Celt and creating a partnership which would take them both to greatness. In fact, he would go one better. Best didn't score in that League game against West Bromwich Albion, but Tyrrell's boy took the place apart almost from the moment he first slid into the cockpit of a single-seater racing car.

5

No Bloody Idiot

John Young Stewart had no desire to drive single-seater racing cars. His dream was to race an E-type Jaguar or the awesome Ferrari GTO, fast cars with a roof and a passenger seat. Single seaters – 'proper racing cars' – were beyond his modest ambition.

When all was said and done, Stewart was only a petrol pump attendant at the family garage in Dumbuck. The difference was, he wanted to be the best petrol pump attendant and run the cleanest, most efficient forecourt in Dumbartonshire. It was that wish to work to the best of his ability which would ultimately see Jackie Stewart become recognized as the best racing driver in the world. For the moment, though, the idea of racing for Ken Tyrrell seemed as fanciful as flying to the moon. He barely knew who Tyrrell was. As young racing fans do, Jackie had converted a school jotter into a scrapbook into which he stuck clippings from newspapers and motoring magazines, each of the fuzzy black and white pictures identified by Stewart's spidery writing. 'Alan Brown's Coopper at Speed' said one caption; 'A Graet Thrill' said another. Apart from capturing the sense of excitement, Stewart's handwriting also demonstrated his problems with dyslexia. Not that anyone, least of all the hapless sufferer, was aware of such a debilitating handicap in the 1950s. Only in later years would Stewart begin to understand the problem – probably around the same time he realized that in the background of one of the yellowing pictures was a certain R K Tyrrell at the wheel of his Cooper 500.

Stewart had met Ken briefly in the early 1960s. Following his success with John Surtees, Tyrrell gave a trial to Bob McIntyre, a Scot and another world-class motorcycle racer who owned a 3.8 Jaguar he had bought from the Stewart garage. He was a good friend of the family and quickly appreciated Jackie's love of speed, McIntyre frequently taking the bouncy wee lad to bike test sessions on a hill at Glencoe in Argyllshire. In fact, McIntyre became Stewart's role model, even more so when Jackie was asked to accompany him to the test session with Tyrrell.

'It was at Goodwood,' Stewart recalled. 'Bob asked if I would go with him because he didn't know anything about car racing. Jimmy, my elder brother, raced cars, and even though I hadn't raced anything at that time Bobby knew I was such a big enthusiast that it would be worth taking me along. That was the very first time I saw Ken. It was a big deal for me. It was the same Ken I was to get to know so well: the same flat cap; the same walk; the same jacket – everything. He was totally in charge and typically to the point. He gave Bob a test, but Bob didn't meet up with what Ken thought was acceptable. And that was it. Bobby didn't get the drive. He was an artist on a bike – the first man to lap the Isle of Man at 100mph – but Surtees had more experience on four wheels and could make the switch. Bobby couldn't. End of story. We went back to Scotland.'

Scotland went into mourning in August 1962 when McIntyre, one of the country's favourite sons, was killed at Oulton Park in Cheshire. Stewart was stunned, but it did little to dampen his ardour for motor sport. He had turned 23 and begun to race, mainly in club events north of the border, his natural ability standing out in the midst of fairly ordinary competition. It was not long before the offer of a drive with Ecurie Ecosse came along, Stewart believing he had reached the height of personal ambition with the Le Mans winners from Edinburgh. In fact, he had barely started along this particular road. A visit to Goodwood with the Scottish team's sports car would change everything. Even though Stewart spun and finished second in the race, he had put the Ecurie Ecosse Cooper on pole position and had the measure of the fancied opposition until that moment of over-enthusiasm. Robin McKay, the manager of Goodwood and a shrewd judge of talent, made a mental note.

When the tragic news came through at the beginning of March 1964 that Timmy Mayer had been killed in New Zealand, McKay knew that Tyrrell, who had planned to run the talented American that season, would be looking for a replacement. 'I had a phone call from Robin,' said Tyrrell. 'He told me this chap Stewart had been going round Goodwood in an Ecurie Ecosse sports car and he had looked very good. I paid attention because I knew McKay was a good judge of this sort of thing. So I rang Jackie's brother and asked if he knew what Jackie wanted to do: did he want to potter around in amateur racing, or did he want go further than that? Jimmy said he was pretty sure Jackie wanted to go further, so I said there was a test drive on offer if he was interested.'

Stewart was both flattered and perplexed, for the Tyrrell offer represented a major step forward. Formula Junior had been scrapped to make way for Formula 3, and Tyrrell's F3 car would be much the same as the previous Formula Junior model, but it was a single seater, and Stewart had not so much as sat in one before. 'I really had no desire to drive single-seater cars,' Stewart said. 'I would have given anything to drive for someone like John Coombs or Equipe Endeavour, the big names of the day in British motor sport, and race a 3.8 Jaguar or an E-type or a Ferrari GTO. That was my total ambition. I honestly didn't think single seaters were something I could ever do. I had absolutely no interest in that direction.

'My brother said I had to call Ken Tyrrell. I didn't know what to do, so I phoned Jimmy Clark, whom I'd got to know really well. I would stay on Jimmy's farm in the Borders quite often, and Helen [Stewart's wife] and I would go to motor club dances and so on. In 1963 I had won something like 16 of the 23 races I had entered, and it had been in a myriad of cars: Tojero Jaguar and Cooper Monaco sports cars, a Lotus Cortina, a Marcos GT car, all sorts. I was the Club Racing Driver of the Year. For 1964, I was going to continue with Ecurie Ecosse and top teams such as Coombs and Red Rose Motors. I really didn't think it could get any better than that. So I asked Jimmy for his opinion. He said, "If you are going to go motor racing in a serious way, then you've got to get into single seaters. And, if you're going to make the step, then Ken Tyrrell is the best man to go to." So I phoned Ken and said I would like to give it a go.'

Stewart drove the 430 miles to Goodwood on his own. Tyrrell's van and immaculate racing car, overseen by Neil Davis, were parked in the grass paddock. Tyrrell and McKay were present, as was Bruce McLaren who, unknown to Stewart, would set a performance yardstick by completing a few laps in the same car. And, as if by chance, John Cooper was also hanging about, seemingly passing the time of day. 'I was so naive!' recalled Stewart. 'The whole thing seemed incredibly "big time" to me. Never having sat in a car like this before, even if I had been three feet from the steering wheel it would have felt okay. I knew Goodwood well. But that was all I knew. I thought the car was powerful, but the thing that really impressed me was the way it was so responsive. After everything I had driven before, it was like an F16 fighter plane compared to a 747. This car was alive! Ken told me just to drive round and get to feel comfortable. I never even thought about doing a fast lap time or going quicker than anyone else.'

That was not the way it appeared to those watching from the pits. Stewart was soon on McLaren's pace. When he went quicker still, Tyrrell called him in. 'I had done exactly what was asked, so I was surprised when Ken said, "I told you to take your time." I knew Bruce had already been out to make sure the car was running properly and was set up for the circuit. I didn't even know he was setting a time. I had no idea about any of that. It never entered my head that I had to go as fast as him in order to look good.'

Because he had travelled to Sussex on his own, Stewart did not have an ally in the pits, ready to pass on word of how the assembled company could hardly believe the evidence of their stopwatches. Stewart was called in once again and asked to get out of the car. McLaren climbed on board, ostensibly to check the car over; in fact, with Stewart having unwittingly redefined a fast time for the day, McLaren was out to set the record straight. As far as Stewart was concerned, the Grand Prix driver was being incredibly decent in making sure the car was up to scratch. 'Bruce was like a god to me. He'd won Grands Prix, and here he was with his smart Bell crash helmet, a state-of-the-art piece of kit compared to my Herbert Johnston, which was basically the sort of hat worn by polo players! Bruce was so sophisticated. A superstar.'

He was also slow. When Stewart returned to the track, he once again beat McLaren's best effort without realizing it. Tyrrell, Cooper and the rest were acutely aware of what was happening. This little Scottish chap with the chirpy accent was incredibly gifted. 'It was obvious,' said Tyrrell. 'When Jackie went quickly straight away Bruce, being the nice chap that he was, said, "This is ridiculous!" and got back in the car and went quicker. Then Jackie went faster still. While all this was going on, John Cooper was out watching at one of the very fast corners, the first one after the pits. He came rushing back and said, "You want to get that boy signed up quick!"' In the years to come, Ken would be hailed as a talent spotter extraordinaire. He would destroy that notion in typically blunt fashion. 'On that day,' he would say, 'if you couldn't see Jackie was a future champion, then you were a bloody idiot.'

'When I came back in,' said Stewart, 'they told me I had been faster than Bruce. That was news to me. I have no recollection of looking at the lap times on a clipboard to see what I had done. I had just driven the car, feeling more and more comfortable with it every lap. It was a fantastic wee car. I loved every minute, and Bruce was really nice about it when we had finished. Ken asked me if I wanted to talk about a drive. I said I did. So we got in our cars and went back to Hook House.'

Ken and Norah had recently moved out of the bungalow in the

timber yard and into a three-bedroomed cottage about a mile away which had been the home of the chauffeur working for the owners of the main house, 'Tyrrells Wood'. The name was coincidental, but rather than cause confusion Ken and Norah chose to name their cottage 'Hook House' after the nearby Hook Wood. Its situation on rolling hills was idyllic, the view right across to the Berkshire Downs completely unspoiled. Stewart was even more impressed as he followed Tyrrell's car along the winding gravel drive. 'This was big time for me, everything about the day,' he recalled. 'Bear in mind that Helen and I probably had £50 between us. I was working in a garage and we had rented an apartment. We had nice furniture, but because I would never have anything on hire purchase we had no money at all. So here I was in this lovely house owned by Ken Tyrrell. I had just driven one of his cars and he wanted to talk to me about a contract to become a professional driver. You can see why all of this was a very big deal.'

Tyrrell offered the Scot two options: Stewart could have a retainer of £10,000 with the proviso that he signed a contract giving Tyrrell 10 per cent of his income over a period of at least five years; or he could agree to a retainer worth £5 (the minimum figure allowed to make the contract legally binding) and receive 50 per cent of the prize and bonus money. All of this was in a different financial league to anything Stewart had ever experienced. In an interview a few months earlier, Jackie had explained how he had made ends meet as a club racing driver. 'I went, for example, to a race with my E-type Jaguar at a meeting at Rufforth, about 265 miles from my home. A hotel was out of the question, so to keep expenses down I left at five a.m. that day, drove down, raced and drove home the same day. My day at Rufforth netted me between £25 and £30, so if I could keep doing that I was very happy.' In the space of a couple of hours, then, Tyrrell had not just moved Stewart's financial goal posts, he had taken them clean out of the park. The start of the 1964 season was only a matter of days away and Stewart had to give Tyrrell his decision by the following morning.

'Ten thousand pounds!' said Stewart. 'That was a *huge* amount of money. But I was thinking, "There's something I don't know here!" I was trying to work out Ken's agenda. If he was willing to give me £10,000, there had to be more money in this game than I had realized. On the other hand, there was something of a gamble in opting purely for prize money. Formula 3 promised to be very competitive indeed, but because I had other drives arranged in sports cars and touring cars for which I would receive expenses, I knew I would make something there. I was still working in the garage too on a wage of about £22 a week. I was living in an apartment in Helensburgh, so I figured I could get by. I called Ken and accepted the £5 retainer. That was the start of it.'

Things had moved with great speed. Mayer had been killed while practising for a race at Longford, Tasmania, on the last day of February; Stewart tested the Formula 3 car on Monday, 9 March; and five days later he found himself racing at the first major European meeting of the season at Snetterton. The test, typically, had been kept secret by Tyrrell so the main point of discussion in *Autosport* was the fact that Tyrrell had entered at all (in any case, the deadlines at the weekly motor sport magazine meant the preview of the race had been written before Stewart and Tyrrell had concluded their deal). It was described as 'controversial' to have the Tyrrell Racing Organization take part in Formula 3. 'This class of racing', thundered the editorial, 'is supposed to be for the up-and-coming drivers and not works or semi-works equipes.' Tyrrell was undeniably in the latter category since, once again, he was racing with cars loaned by the Cooper Car Company and powered by engines supplied free of charge by BMC. Still, Stewart could be described as an up-and-coming driver – as he was about to demonstrate.

Stewart claimed pole position and destroyed the opposition in the pouring rain. His lead at the end of the first lap was so great that Alan Stait, watching from the pits, was caught completely by surprise. 'The cars left the grid, and there was a bit of a wait for them to come round at the end of the first lap. Only one appeared, and that was Stewart. We thought, "There's been a big shunt!" And then the rest came through in a bunch. He had pulled out an absolutely amazing lead in just one lap, so much so that John Cooper was jumping up and down shouting, "Slow him down, boy! Slow him down!"'

Thanks to his share of the prize money, plus bonuses from Shell and Dunlop for using their products, Stewart's first pay packet came to £186. Proof that he had made the correct contractual decision would come in the following 13 races: Stewart won 11 of them. Such success fuelled the discontent over the Tyrrell team's presence in Formula 3. In fact, it was Tyrrell who had become irritated, since the constant carping in the press had given the impression that the Formula 3 races were mere club events when in Tyrrell's opinion they were international and therefore worthy of the appropriate prize and start money. In an interview in *Autosport*, Tyrrell turned the tables on his critics: 'The view that Formula 3 is only club racing has given promoters the opportunity to put on an international race for negligible starting money.' The reader could imagine him thumping the table as he warmed to his theme. 'This has been followed up by fuel companies not paying bonuses. After all the press comment, they have taken the view that since this is only club racing, it is of no interest to them. In this country, the prize money has become ridiculous, especially considering the poor start money. A fair fee for starting should be £75 for the number one car and £60 for the second car. Overseas, the prize money is so much better. And at Monaco the Formula 3 prize money is higher than Formula 1, although there is no starting money whatsoever.'

The less serious side of motor sport was never far away. A later edition of *Autosport* covered the International Trophy at Silverstone and reported that BBC Radio's pit lane reporter, John Bolster, had been spotted in the British Racing Drivers' Club tent 'enjoying a splendid breakfast – champagne and cornflakes'. It wasn't so much the story that raised a smile – Bolster, with his plummy accent and deerstalker, was an extrovert character – more the fact that it was placed on the lead news page alongside an item about the latest Formula 2 engine from BMW. The report on the non-championship race revealed an epic finish as Jack Brabham, at the wheel of one of his own F1 cars, snatched the lead from Graham Hill's BRM at the last corner. As for the Formula 3 race, it almost went without saying that it was a Stewart benefit, Jackie followed home closely by his team-mate Warwick Banks.

It was to be tough luck for Banks that he should make it to the Tyrrell team in the same year as Jackie Stewart. The 25-year-old from Lincolnshire had been chosen on the strength of his performances in club racing, particularly after scoring 13 wins at the wheel of a Turner sports car in 1963. 'I was out in Australia when Ken got in touch through some mutual friends and asked if I would come and have a test drive,' he recalled. 'It was a call very much worth pursuing. Ken was something of a hero in those days as a team manager; driving for him was exactly where I wanted to be. It was a bit unfortunate that Jackie should be in the team at the same time! Jackie was always very commercially minded and professional. I don't think I was any less professional from a driving standpoint, but from the commercial outlook Jackie knew what he was about from the word go – and he still does. I was probably a bit more like Jim Clark in that Jimmy wasn't terribly commercial; he did it mainly because he enjoyed driving, and I took the same view.'

The Monaco F3 race on 10 May was the fifth of the season for Stewart and unquestionably the most prestigious. It was his first brush with continental opposition, and he wiped the floor with them. At the end of the second and final practice session, held just after dawn on the Friday morning, Stewart was two seconds faster than anyone else. He won his heat as he pleased and took the lead on the third lap of the final. Reporting in *Autosport*, Bill Gavin wrote: 'Stewart proceeded to draw away in his characteristic relaxed style, the stopwatch being the only indication that he was going so much faster than the rest of the field.' Halfway through the 24 laps, the Scot's lead amounted to 13 seconds. He maintained that gap and got to meet Prince Rainier and Princess Grace. It would be the first of many visits to the most famous podium in motor sport.

Tyrrell's attention had been divided between Monte Carlo and Monza, where Banks had been racing in the Vigorelli Trophy on the Thursday of that week. Ken had got more than he bargained for when he flew into Milan to keep an eye on the other half of his operation. 'I had gone to Monza with Neil in Ken's Series III Zephyr,' said Banks. 'We had finished practice when Ken flew in and joined us in the evening. Neil suddenly doubled up and said he would go and have a lie down for a while. He eventually returned and tried to eat something, but couldn't. He didn't feel at all well. Ken called the doctor, who took a look and said Neil had a bit of indigestion and there was nothing to worry about. But Ken wasn't happy. He looked at Neil, looked at the doctor, and said, "I want him in hospital – now!" So Neil was taken off. Ken and I had dinner and then decided to go and see Neil. I think he was in the local convent. When we asked to see Neil, they said we couldn't. He was on the operating table. He'd had a burst ulcer. If Ken hadn't done what he did, Neil would have died. It was typical of Ken's intuition. Neil and I were sharing a room and he probably would've passed out in front of me!' Banks finished third at Monza, then dashed to the airport for a flight to Belgium. Tyrrell was running the works Mini-Cooper effort there, and a class victory at Zolder would be the prelude to Banks becoming the outright winner of the European Touring Car championship. At least it made up for constantly having to play second fiddle to Stewart in Formula 3.

A race on a superb road circuit at Rouen on 28 June was a typical example, Stewart and Banks finishing one-two. On this occasion, Banks was lucky to be in the race at all. His story of finding a fix for a technical problem not only highlights the simplicity of a racing car in 1964, it also exposes the complete lack of safety features by today's rigorous standards. 'My car was misfiring badly during practice and we just couldn't find the cause,' Banks recalled. 'On race morning, we took the F3 car onto a public dual carriageway near the circuit and belted up and down, but the misfire was still there. Everything that could be changed had been changed, but to no avail. There was a fuel line running from the tank at the front of the car to the carburettor at the rear, and it passed through the cockpit, resting on one of the chassis members as it did so. I sort of idly picked up the pipe, and the misfire stopped. That's when we realized it had been lying on the hot water pipe, which was causing the fuel to vaporize. Typically, it wasn't touching the pipe on Jackie's car! So everything was okay for the race and we finished first and second again. I remember Jackie and I went to the bank on Monday morning and picked up £850 – which wasn't bad going in 1964!'

Banks would have his day when he won at Brands Hatch in August. Stewart, rather uncharacteristically, spun while trying to wrest the lead from Brian Hart, a talented privateer who 25 years later would build the engines to power Tyrrell's F1 cars. Despite the minor indiscretion, however, Stewart's name was on everyone's lips. He had already enjoyed an F1 test drive with Lotus and would soon sign for BRM, his future in Grand Prix racing assured. The Tyrrell Racing Organization had done its bit.

'I couldn't have asked for better,' said Stewart. 'The preparation was absolutely top class; I could see that from the moment I first arrived. Having said that, it wasn't immaculate! The back of the truck was . . . well, everything was in the back of the truck! It wasn't like walking into the sort of F1 truck you see today where you could almost eat your lunch off the floor. I wouldn't have known anything different in those days, but the main thing was that it was very efficient. You could feel it; you knew you were with the best outfit, and that was thanks to Ken, the epitome of the team manager.

'He was also my tutor. He would talk me through things like gear ratios and ask questions such as, "How does it feel like this, and like that?", and you had to explain it. It was a learning curve that embraced everything. Norah was there all the time, doing the timing and getting the food and just being around. We would go out together for dinner every night. It was a real family atmosphere. We were staying in terrible hotels, rooms with bare bulbs and rats running around. I can remember throwing shoes at them in one place. But it was a terrific education. He would pretty much leave the actual running of my race to me. There was one occasion at La Chatre in France, for example, where I had a problem at the start and had to come through the field with no clutch – which wasn't easy because La Chatre had a first-gear hairpin. The signalling was on a long straight, and Ken was out there with his mouth open, waving like mad. You couldn't miss him! I came through to finish second. Apart from Brands Hatch, it was the only time I didn't win in 1964.'

Stewart's rise was so rapid that he began Formula 2 racing (for a semi-works Lotus team) halfway through his first season of F3, and made his F1 debut in a non-championship race in South Africa during the European winter of 1964–65. For 1965, Tyrrell had plans to compete in F2 as well as in F3, Stewart being signed, along with John Surtees, to drive the former while Banks continued with F3 for the time being. But having had the upper hand in 1964, the latest F3 Cooper-BMC was off the pace thanks to a rise in competitiveness in cars powered by the latest Ford. Banks, however, did win one race in 1965 – thanks largely to the British spring weather. 'It absolutely threw it down,' he recalled. 'This was the International Trophy meeting at Silverstone. I remember it extremely well. We were outclassed when the Ford engines got their act together and I was eighth on the grid. Ken came up to me before the start and said, "You can win this." I said I thought he was joking. But, right enough, everyone seemed to lose control in the lashing rain and terrible conditions, and I won.

'That was our last race together. I decided there was no point in carrying on. But there was no ill feeling. It had been a great privilege and a pleasure to drive for Ken. He was very fair, and your money always arrived on time. If he said something would happen, then it did happen. We never had a cross word – perhaps because one was too much in awe of him. He would always have the right answer and take the wind out of your sails! He was a great guy, but I knew it was going to end at some point. We were on borrowed time with the BMC Formula 3 engine, and when the Ford screamers were finally sorted out we just couldn't compete.'

Fortunes in Formula 2 were little better, the BRM engine in the Cooper proving uncompetitive on the rare occasions when it was working properly. Tyrrell's best result was one second place. The Cooper Car Company was paying the price for concentrating on Formula 1; Ken knew it was time to move on. After a decade of loyalty to the cars in British Racing Green with two distinctive white stripes down the nose, Tyrrell, that archetypal Englishman, was about to try something French. When it was a matter of winning races, patriotism came second to competitiveness. And if you'd turned your back on this next car then, in Tyrrell parlance, you'd have been a bloody idiot.

6

'Parlez-vous F1?'

'Towards the end of 1965, Ken came back from a trip to France. He came straight up to me and said, "You're going to Paris – and it's not for a holiday."'

This was a bolt from the blue for Neil Davis. There was no connection whatsoever between the Tyrrell Racing Organization and France, apart from the fact that the team raced there, albeit without much success in 1965. Nonetheless, Ken had made the trip to Paris for the French Formula 2 championship prize giving. 'Jabby' Crombac, the journalist who had helped Ken and Henry Taylor secure their entry at Monaco in 1960, introduced Tyrrell to an imposing man by the name of Jean-Luc Lagardère. It was to be one of the most crucial introductions of Tyrrell's life.

Lagardère was the general manager of Matra Sports, the competition department of Engins Matra, a major aerospace and missile manufacturer. Matra had become involved in the motor industry almost by default. The firm's founder, Marcel Chassagny, had been friendly with René Bonnet, the owner of a small concern making racing cars and a road-going coupé named the Djet. When Automobiles René Bonnet went out of business, Chassagny bought the assets and Lagardère was put in charge. He had been quick to spot the importance of image, particularly when trying to sell the smart little Djet. Plans were laid to build a Formula 3 car, and it was a measure of Matra's pragmatism that this predominantly French firm had no hesitation in using the British Ford engine, simply because it was the best.

That principle was also applied to the car itself. There would be no compromises. This may have been Formula 3, a comparatively minor class of racing, but aerospace construction would be brought to bear on the chassis. It would make the difference between a good car and a really great one. It was a complicated and expensive process, but Matra lined the box-sections on either side of the cockpit with polymer resin, thus providing a seal which allowed the fuel to be carried without the use of rubber bag tanks. The benefit here was that bulkheads providing additional strength could be placed inside the box-sections, a method of construction ruled out by bag tanks. The result was a racing car with previously unheard of levels of structural rigidity and precise handling. The only thing Matra lacked was a star driver.

'At the time I was organizing all the F2 races in France,' said Crombac. 'I watched Matra with interest from the beginning, and when they won with Jean-Pierre Beltoise in F3, that spurred on Lagardère. He wanted to go F2 but realized his team was inexperienced; Beltoise wasn't a top driver because of the effects of an arm injury during a sports car race. So he asked me to suggest a good English team with good engines, drivers and infrastructure. Matra, he said, would build the chassis.'

Lagardère had witnessed Tyrrell's struggles with the Cooper and he knew that Ken had the services of Jackie Stewart for Formula 2. Stewart, having won his first Grand Prix for BRM at Monza in September 1965, was a highly respected name. Crombac moved in to bring the two sides together at the prize giving. 'We just talked over a drink,' recalled Tyrrell. 'Lagardère said they were coming into racing and I had no idea who they were. I had no idea they were a rocket company and a missile outfit. He said they were determined to do well and that they had won at Rheims in Formula 3 that year. I didn't even know that! I said to him, just in passing – I really wanted to get away – "The first thing you want to get is a good driver!" Lagardère replied, "You've got a good driver. Can't we do something together?" I really wanted to get away, but agreed to talk some more over dinner while waiting for my flight at Orly. I really didn't think much about it. Then he said, "Why don't you come over and see what we are doing?" He more or less talked me into it.'

Tyrrell duly made the trip to the Matra Sports factory at Velizy, on the outskirts of Paris. It was a tatty place, but Ken was immediately impressed by what was going on inside. 'So Ken came back and said I had to go to Paris,' recalled Davis. 'We sent an engine and gearbox by freight and I flew into Orly, where I was picked up by a guy called Gerard Ducarouge [later to become the designer of Ligier and Lotus F1 cars]. We went to Velizy and began the process of installing the engine and gearbox.'

The next step was to get Stewart behind the wheel. Tyrrell had already spoken to the Scot, and the response was not promising. 'I called him and said I had done a deal with Matra. He said, "A what? A Matra? Are you stark raving mad?" In fact, I hadn't actually done a deal. I had said it was subject to the car working and they'd agreed to send it over to Goodwood.' The Formula 3 car, with a BRM Formula 2 engine in the back, was flown into Gatwick on board a Bristol freighter, an aircraft owned by Lagardère thanks to his additional role as a transporter of race horses. 'This was *Star Wars*!' Stewart recalled. 'Not just the fact that this was an aerospace firm, but that they were flying the car into Britain! Believe me, in the mid-sixties this was a helluva big deal. The boys picked up the car and took it to Goodwood for me to try. Ken was the one who saw the potential in Matra; he was impressed by their engineering. And immediately I drove the car, I knew it was sensational – so surefooted. This was a car of integrity and precision. It was pure quality. There was no question that Ken and Matra were on to something.'

Ken agreed to run two cars in Formula 2 in 1966 for Stewart and Jacky Ickx, a rising star from Belgium. Ickx would also race a Tyrrell-Matra in Formula 3. However, the Matra chassis might have been superb, but in Formula 2 guise with the wretched BRM it lacked performance. Brabham, on the other hand, might have produced an inferior chassis made of old fashioned (compared to the Matra) tubular construction, but it was powered by a Honda engine, for which there was no match throughout 1966.

At the end of the year, *Motor Racing* published a track test of the Tyrrell-Matra F2 car. The tests, a regular feature of this monthly magazine, were carried out by John Blunsden, a respected journalist who knew how to drive a racing car. The Tyrrell-Matra test was run at Brands Hatch, and Blunsden was impressed from the moment he arrived.

'My track testing in those days brought me into contact with many different cars, some of which, shall we say, were better prepared than others. But with Tyrrell, you knew the car would be properly screwed together and immaculately prepared. That was certainly the case. By the time I arrived, the car had been unloaded and warmed up by Neil Davis. The test was the only thing on the programme that day, yet Ken was there as well. It was typical of his attention to detail.

'From the moment I first left the pits, it was immediately apparent that this was a lovely car to drive. I went through my usual routine of having two stints, the first to get used to the car before coming in and having a think about it. Then I would go out again and begin to push hard. Ken was on the stopwatch, but he wouldn't let me see the lap times. I was really getting to grips with the car in the second stint. It was feeling good, and then Ken gave me the "in" sign. I thought the car needed refuelling, so I duly came in.

'Ken gave me a bit of paper. It was a list of my times, and it showed they had been coming down lap after lap, which is what would have been expected. But then one was slower than the previous lap. For Ken, that was a sign that the driver had reached his level and was maybe becoming untidy. It was time to bring him in rather than risk having the car stuffed in the bank. I felt I could have gone a bit quicker, but I had no argument with Ken's logic. It was typical of his complete professionalism.'

Blunsden's story referred to the car being unloaded from an impressive transporter – Tyrrell had moved on from the small van with two cars shoehorned inside. This new vehicle, the size of a bus, was purpose-built. In fact, it should have been a bus, travelling the streets of Havana, but the ship taking the chassis to Cuba had sunk in the Thames estuary. Tyrrell had been quick to spot a possible bargain. 'It was one of several Leyland chassis that had gone down with the ship,' said Davis. 'They had been recovered eventually and Ken discovered that these vehicles were to be auctioned at Barking in Essex. Ken and I went along, and after about three or four of them had been sold, Ken said he reckoned it was a cartel and we had no chance of buying anything, so we went back to Ockham. After a while, Ken made some enquiries in order to discover who had bought these buses. He called the guy. I don't know whether this man had suddenly begun to wonder what he was going to do with all these buses, but the upshot was that Ken bought one of them for the same price the guy had paid for it. From memory, I think it was about £1,200.

'There was no chassis as such; it was more or less a frame. I rang Leyland and the person I spoke to said we had bought a pig in a poke because we would never be able to build anything on it. So we got Tiverton bodybuilders to come up from Devon and take a look. They said it would not be a problem. It was explained that they would construct big sides so that it would be stressed like a normal vehicle. Of course, we had to overhaul it because the thing had been full of seawater. A lot of the parts, wheel bearings and things like that, needed to come off and be replaced because they had become pitted. The engine was flat and mounted beneath the vehicle. We removed the sump and everything looked fine inside – presumably because the oil had preserved it. We overhauled the brakes too, and when we were finished it was as good as new. And, thanks to Tiverton, we had a vehicle designed purely for carrying racing cars and working on them. It was state of the art.'

That said, not much had improved at Ockham. The Tyrrell Racing

Organization continued to work from the small collection of on-site sheds. Davis, although promoted to chief mechanic, presided over just two other mechanics – Keith Boshier and Les Shepherd, who was starting his second season before returning to his native Australia. Alan Stait, now married and preferring not to travel, had joined the fledgling McLaren team, with whom he could follow his original trade as a machinist.

Still, change was afoot, particularly when it came to the Formula 2 rules for 1967. A step up from 1000cc to 1600cc ruled out the Honda engine. The Ford BDA became the thing to have, and Ken made sure he was first in line, even though the four-cylinder engines cost £2,500 each. With the Ford BDA on board, the Matra F2 car really was a winning proposition. Sure enough, Stewart and Ickx between them won seven races that season; unfortunately, a flamboyant Austrian by the name of Jochen Rindt won nine on his own. Rindt's extrovert style in a Brabham-FVA was one of the highlights of the season; the other was the performance of Ickx at the legendary Nürburgring in Germany on 6 August.

Because the track measured 14 miles and the cars appeared just 14 times, the organizers of the German Grand Prix allowed F2 cars to bolster the entry. This twisting, plunging leviathan of a circuit was perfectly suited to the nimble Matra and a driver of Ickx's bravery, and he stunned the F1 world by recording a lap time of eight minutes 14 seconds. Had the F2 cars not been forced to start the race from the back of the grid, the Tyrrell-Matra would have been on the front row, between the Brabham of Denny Hulme (who went on to win the race, and to become world champion) and the BRM driven by none other than Jackie Stewart. Ickx continued to cause havoc during the race itself, charging his way into fourth place before his suspension broke, the F2 machine unable to cope with the numerous crash-landings and the extra ballast called for to make life more 'fair' for the F1 cars. Stewart, meanwhile, had stopped with transmission trouble. The first thing he did on his return to the pits was advise Tyrrell to slow Ickx down before the Belgian killed himself.

'That performance was absolutely fantastic,' Tyrrell recalled. 'I had first been impressed by Ickx when I came across him during a touring car race in Hungary. The occasion stood out in my mind because Jacky was very young. He always looked younger than he actually was, so he looked 17 but was probably 19 or something. He was driving a Lotus-Cortina, something broke – the front suspension, I think – and he came in with the front wheel falling off. But he was so calm and collected. There was none of this usual business of continental drivers waving their arms in the air and shouting, he simply came in and told them what was wrong. That impressed me. So I asked him if he would like to drive for me, and he said he would. That performance at the Nürburgring was incredible. I never told drivers to go faster or slower. All I would do was give them information on the race situation and leave it to them. They knew what to do. Ickx would sometimes get a bit erratic and I would just signal the word "head". He knew just what I meant – "use your head".'

Apart from Ickx, the talk of practice had been the stunning pole position performance of Jim Clark, who was almost ten seconds faster than anyone else. The Scot then set a new lap record for the race from a standing start on his first lap. He eventually retired with broken suspension, but his performance had been no surprise, least of all to Ken Tyrrell. Clark was at the wheel of a Lotus 49, an elegant car which had made its debut a month before. But it was not so much the beautifully simplistic lines of the Lotus that drew Tyrrell's attention as the engine that powered it.

Grand Prix racing had undergone a change of engine rules at the beginning of the 1966 season. The advent of the three-litre formula had prompted Colin Chapman, the mercurial founder and boss of Lotus, to cast around for an engine for his new car. With the help of Walter Hayes, the Director of Public Affairs at Ford of Britain, Chapman had persuaded Ford to invest £100,000 in a brand-new engine, designed and built by Cosworth Engineering in Northampton. The Ford DFV, as the V8 was known, would set new standards

69

and be the backbone of F1 for the next decade, but Tyrrell's interest in the new engine was driven by more than a mere concern for the well-being of Grand Prix racing.

The Lotus-Ford had made its debut at the Dutch Grand Prix at Zandvoort on 4 June 1967. Tyrrell had travelled to Holland specifically to see the new package. Despite the fact that it had run no more than a few miles in testing, Graham Hill put the Lotus on pole position. Jim Clark, who for tax reasons could not travel to Britain, sat in the car for the first time during practice and qualified sixth. Hill led easily until the engine failed after 11 laps, Clark moving forward more or less to win as he pleased. It was a dream debut, one that helped crystallize a thought in Ken Tyrrell's mind. 'It was bloody obvious,' he said. 'You had all this rubbish everyone had been using and here was a proper engine. It was being done by a company I had the greatest respect for. As soon as I got back, I sent off a telegram to Cosworth ordering three of these DFV engines. It was, in some ways, a strange thing to do. First of all, they were £7,500 each and I didn't have the money! And secondly, they were not being offered for sale. Tongue in cheek, I wanted to be the first in line if they were going to become available. I would worry later about how to put the deal together.'

The significant point was that Tyrrell had just initiated a move into Formula 1. Attempting to secure a supply of engines was only the start. He would need a driver, and he would need a car. The timing on just about every count would prove to be perfect.

The success of Matra in Formula 2 and Formula 3 had made the French government aware of the prestige to be had from international motor racing. At the same time, the formation of a state oil company, to be known as Elf, introduced a major player for whom motor sport would also be the perfect vehicle on which to create a dynamic image. In January 1967, Elf and Matra had agreed to co-operate on the building of a Grand Prix car and engine, the French government stepping in a few months later with £800,000 to help fund this ambitious project, one which in some respects was almost too ambitious. Lagardère of Matra was aware that the design and building of a potentially complex V12 engine would not be the work of a moment. His engineers, and those who understood the technicalities, could see the pitfalls, but the French public, whipped up by the media in BRM-like fashion, could not. Still, when Tyrrell approached Lagardère with a proposal to run a Matra with a DFV engine, the pragmatic Frenchman saw the wisdom of having a second string to his bow. The potential deal became a certainty when Tyrrell explained that he could persuade Jackie Stewart to drive the new car.

Stewart was ripe for the plucking. His third season with BRM was filled with frustration, the British firm having failed to learn lessons from the past by designing another 16-cylinder engine for the three-litre formula. As ever, the engine was late, Stewart making good use of the less powerful BRM V8 to win at Monaco in 1966. When the 16-cylinder – designed, for good measure, in a complex H-configuration – finally arrived, it was heavy and unreliable. Stewart struggled with the unwieldy car in 1967; nonetheless, his efforts had not gone unnoticed. Tyrrell was not the only team owner with future plans for the Scot.

'The H16 BRM was bloody awful,' Stewart remembered. 'I had been with Graham [Hill] for the first year, but then he had gone to Lotus with the promise of the Ford DFV. I was left holding the BRM baby. The car was so bad that all the BRM drivers were going at the same speed. By that I mean you couldn't use the car to find an advantage. You had to go to circuits such as Spa or the Nürburgring before there was any difference. Elsewhere, you weren't able to hustle the car, and I found that very discouraging. I was getting tired of it because we sometimes had to use the 2.2 litre V8 in order to be even remotely competitive simply because the H16 wasn't getting the job done.

'In the meantime, I had been talking to Ferrari. I had told Enzo Ferrari that I wanted to drive for Ken in Formula 2, but Ferrari didn't like that idea because he had his own F2 car. I also wanted part of the Ferrari painted blue, and he didn't think much of that idea either! But we were talking.

'Ken had come to Zandvoort to see the debut of the Lotus-Ford. I remember he was very vocal about the DFV. He kept saying, "That's the future, that's the future!" He was talking about going into F1 and he placed an order with Cosworth. He had this idea of putting the DFV in a Matra, and I knew he was talking with Jean-Luc Lagardère, who is one of the biggest industrialists in France now. He was big then in my mind, and I was very interested in Ken's plans and the suggestion that I might drive for him. That's when I told Ken I had asked Ferrari for £20,000.

'I went for a second time to Ferrari and agreed a deal for 1968. I shook hands with the Old Man [Enzo Ferrari]. Not long after that, when I was at Enna in Sicily for a F2 race, Jacky Ickx asked if I was still talking to Ferrari. It transpired that Ferrari had told him I was asking for the world and they had offered Jacky the drive, provided he agreed that weekend. He asked me what he should do. I told him to accept because I was not going to do the deal any more. There was a big row between Ferrari and me after that. But that was when I decided to go with Ken.

'In a way, it was a relief, because I was frightened of Ferrari. I had followed the sport closely over the years so I knew all about the politics associated with the team. I had got to know Fangio quite well, and he used to tell me how terrible Ferrari was to work for because of the politics. In my own simple way, I only wanted to be looking ahead and never over my shoulder. I just had an un-comfortable feeling. It was quite different with Tyrrell. I knew and trusted Ken implicitly. It was very positive because I knew we would be pulling together.'

Tyrrell soon overcame the small problem of finding the £20,000 necessary to pay his driver. Ford had made it clear to Lotus that the supply of engines would be on an exclusive basis only for the first year. From 1968, the DFV would be readily available – a clever move that ensured Ford full coverage in F1 since customer engines of this quality would be in short supply. Equally, Walter Hayes (now vice president, Ford of Europe) could see the benefit of being associated with Ken Tyrrell, Matra and Jackie Stewart. Ken played the latter card to the full when looking for funds to pay his driver. 'Ken said he had heard Jackie Stewart was going to Ferrari,' said Hayes. 'Well, that was like bringing the British Empire – or the Scottish Empire, or whatever – to an end if Stewart went to Ferrari. We couldn't possibly have that.' Tyrrell had struck the right note. 'I had tremendous assistance from Walter,' Tyrrell admitted. 'I said, "Look, I've got a bloody good chassis here and surely you want such a good engine in more than one chassis?" I didn't know that Lotus had been told their deal was exclusive for just one year. I said that I thought I could get the money, but I wanted someone to stand beside me. Walter said he would see that the money was made available. So he provided the £20,000 I needed for Jackie on the understanding that when I got sponsorship I could give it back. That was bloody good! It meant I could go ahead and do the deals and say I had Stewart as my driver.

'Dunlop were really struggling thanks to Firestone giving them a hard time, and they had no decent runners in F1. I had always been with Dunlop, and they had some very successful tyres in Formula 2, so Jackie and I went to see them. Jackie was instrumental in this; we always did our deals together. There was never any jiggery-pokery. Jackie knew what was going on as well as I did. We said we wanted a lot of money for what we needed to do. Dunlop, as I hoped they would, explained that they had been at the top in Formula 1 and didn't want to go out at the bottom. If they were to go out, they wanted to do it as winners. They agreed to provide the money. I was able to pay Walter back. We were away.'

Tyrrell was going Grand Prix racing. Elf agreed to co-sponsor the new team, which would operate under the name 'Equipe Matra International'. These days, such a move would be a momentous event worthy of press conferences and elaborate launches hosted by television personalities who know even less about motor racing than

half the invited audience. In 1967, it was barely a matter of conse-
quence. *Motor Racing*, almost as an aside, mentioned that Ken
Tyrrell was entering the big league; for the team itself, the move was
a natural progression, nothing more.

The Tyrrell operation remained very much a family affair,
Kenneth Tyrrell taking his wife Sandy to races in between fulfilling
his role as a pilot of Tridents for British European Airways (later to
become British Airways). 'I remember Sandy and I went with Neil,
Jackie and Jacky to a European championship Formula 2 race at
Rouen in 1967,' said Kenneth. 'Sandy and I were the pit crew,
and Neil was the mechanic. I was dumbstruck because I was in the
presence of at least two of the greatest drivers ever. One evening,
going out to dinner, there were about eight of us in the same vehicle.
I was steering, Jackie was changing gear and Jimmy Clark and the
mechanics were in the back. Dad had to go off somewhere else with
Ickx, but that was the sort of thing you would do quite regularly.
Amazing when you think about it now.'

'When it came to moving into Formula 1, I don't remember it
being a particularly momentous decision,' said Norah Tyrrell. 'I
don't think I was that impressed with the whole thing. But then Ken
was not one to be daunted by objections! He knew what he wanted.
It just happened, and I do recall going up to Cosworth to pick up
an engine and taking a cheque with me. Looking back now, it was
a huge step, but at the time it just seemed to evolve. Of course,
Formula 1 was different then. No sponsors, no motorhomes, nothing like that. Just the same guys and the same truck, but a different
racing car.'

As far as Neil Davis was concerned, one day simply merged into
the next, one job following another. 'We had gone to the German
Grand Prix in 1967 with the F2 car for Ickx,' said Davis. 'There was a
plate on the bottom of the chassis to bring the car up to the weight
limit, but the car was never designed to carry the extra load, what
with leaping over all those jumps and being pushed to the limit by
Ickx. But we did a couple of races like that, and the next thing I

know we are taking delivery of a Ford DFV at the end of the year and Ken says we're going F1 racing. "Oh, okay, Ken." I mean, that was it!'

The engine was shipped to Paris for installation in the first F1 Matra-Ford, which in effect would be based on the F2 car. Known as the MS9, Matra saw this as a test vehicle, and the French were concerned when Tyrrell made noises about racing it in the opening round of the 1968 championship, the South African Grand Prix at Kyalami on 1 January. Their misgivings were reflected in the state of the car when it carried out a brief test at the Montlhéry circuit, the bodywork painted in a coat of unattractive light green primer. The ballasted F2 car was also on hand, the suggestion from Matra being that this should be used for the first race while the F1 car was properly sorted. Tyrrell and Stewart would have none of it. They would race the MS9; it was the only way to learn.

'The only problem,' Davis recalled, 'was that the F1 rules required the car to have a starter motor, and we didn't have one on the MS9. It was extremely difficult to do, but we managed it thanks to Matra designing brackets and fitting universal joints. It was all a bit of a rush in order to get the car ready to catch the boat to Cape Town, from where it would be taken by train to Johannesburg. Meanwhile, we went back to Ockham and prepared to fly out.

'So, the Tyrrell Grand Prix team arrives for its first race. We have two cars, one of them a brand-new F1 car, and four people! There's Ken, myself and two mechanics – Max Rutherford and Roger Hill. Our spares, such as they are, consist of a few bits and pieces scraped together at Matra and put in boxes. We didn't bother with the F2 car – Jackie only did a few laps in it – and concentrated on the MS9 F1 car. It was overheating madly. The car didn't look good in the first place thanks to this khaki primer, but we made it even worse by cutting the nose to try to get more air into the radiator. It looked a right mess.'

Ungainly it might have been, but Stewart put the Matra-Ford on the front row of the grid. Better than that, he took charge on the first lap, the Matra leading the best Lotus, Brabham, McLaren and Ferrari could offer. But it didn't last. An oil cooler, fitted in haste, soon split and the engine ran out of oil. A point, however, had been made; Equipe Matra International had arrived. It had been a headache for Davis and the boys in more ways than one. 'We put up a good show, considering the limited amount of people and the little amount of time we had to prepare the car. But it seemed a natural step. There wasn't the pressure like there is today. If we had run out of bits, we would have asked the boys from McLaren or whomever. They would have helped us out, and at the next race we would have returned new parts. It was that sort of situation.

'Normally there would not be much time for socializing thanks to there just being four of us, but in South Africa there was a slightly unusual situation in that there was a day off in the middle of it all and Paddy Driver, a local racer well known to everyone in F1, threw a party at his house. Max Rutherford didn't go for whatever reason, but Roger, Ken and I went along. Mike Hailwood [legendary motorcycle champion and a good friend of Driver] was in charge of the temporary bar in Paddy's garage. Mike worked out that the bigger the gin and tonics or whatever, the less time people would spend going back for more. The drinks were in tumblers, I remember. You can imagine the effect.

'Time slipped by very quickly. At some stage after midnight, Ken said he wanted to go. I hadn't seen Roger for a while, but I eventually found him in the field which was acting as a car park. He was not in the car we had hired. There was a Mini parked alongside. Both doors were wide open and there was Roger, across the front seats with his head out one side and legs sticking out the other! We threw him into the back of our hire car and Ken drove us home. Roger and I woke the next morning with thumping headaches, and we had to go to work. It was awful. It was one of those "That's the last time I'm ever going to do that!" situations.'

At least there was to be peace and relative quiet for the small team during the following weeks. In a move reflecting a dedication and attention to detail that would characterize the team in years to come, Tyrrell stayed on at Kyalami for a fortnight of relentless testing. At the end of it, the replacement engine was, to quote Davis, 'smoking like a dog', and Stewart had completed 1,361 miles of running, 156 of his 534 circuits under the lap record. Moreover, Equipe Matra International had learned numerous lessons. Now they were ready to get serious with the first proper Grand Prix car, the MS10.

7

Hold the Champagne

'The final entry list for the Race of Champions has been published, with one important addition: Ken Tyrrell has decided after all to run his new V8 MS10 Matra-Ford for Jackie Stewart, and as Jackie has recently decided to take up residence in Switzerland, this will be his last race in England for some time.'

Autosport, as ever mixing court and social, carried this taster for the European season opener at Brands Hatch on 17 March. In 1968, non-championship races were an important part of the F1 structure. Tyrrell's sojourn at Kyalami apart, testing was not the grinding preoccupation it is now. Non-championship events were seen as exploratory sessions, a chance to exercise machinery and personnel in race conditions without the threat of losing championship points. Besides, Brands Hatch was within easy reach of McLaren, Brabham, Lotus, Cooper, BRM and, of course, Tyrrell. Ferrari was the only team on the entry list operating outside England, but it was a measure of the importance attached to the Race of Champions that the Italians had entered no fewer than three cars. Tyrrell had just one, the first MS10 having been delivered a few days before. Official practice would provide Stewart with his first opportunity to drive it.

He was not impressed. The MS10 handled badly. Stewart had to fight the car in the corners and struggled to prevent it from wandering alarmingly on the straights, but he managed to wrestle the Matra-Ford onto the outside of the front row, joining Mike Spence's BRM and the pole position McLaren of Bruce McLaren. This was the first outing for McLaren's new car too (also using a Ford DFV), and the New Zealander was about to enjoy a far more successful debut than Ken Tyrrell and Jackie Stewart.

McLaren was listed in the official programme (price two shillings and sixpence, or 12½p) as car number 1, with Stewart driving number 15. Adult spectators were charged £1, children five shillings (25p). An additional 15 shillings (75p) secured a grandstand seat, and true enthusiasts could part with another £1 to gain admission to the sloping paddock, where they could see the Tyrrell Racing Organization transporter (now painted French blue) disgorging the MS10 and watch the three mechanics carry out preparations along-side the truck. The schedule on race day included events for Formula Ford (a recently introduced nursery series for single-seater drivers), saloon cars and sports cars. The 50-lap Daily Mail International Race of Champions was scheduled to start at 2 p.m.

McLaren won the princely sum of £500 for leading from start to finish, the first time the New Zealander had won at Brands Hatch since the day 10 years before when he had trounced Ken Tyrrell and triggered a new phase in Ken's life. A team owner now, Tyrrell was unlikely to get rich on the £60 prize money for finishing sixth. Stewart had held second place for some time, but his game effort to keep the car on the road could not prevent a gradual fall through the field before a lengthy pit stop brought respite as the mechanics sorted out a problem with the brake and clutch pedals.

The back section of the official programme carried an advert for the BOAC 500. This prestigious round of the World Sports Car championship was due to be held at Brands Hatch on Sunday, 7 April 1968, a date that would become seared in the minds of motor sport folk around the world. The advertising blurb claimed that Jim Clark would be driving a new Ford sports car. If only that had come to pass. Instead, he travelled to Germany for a Formula 2 race at Hockenheim. On the fifth lap, while holding a distant eighth place, Clark's Lotus left the road on a fast curve, probably because of a slow puncture. The subsequent impact with the trees killed the Scotsman instantly. Tyrrell and Stewart, along with the rest of the motor racing community, were stunned. Clark was so good that he seemed indestructible. The message taken on board by Clark's colleagues was: 'If it can happen to Jimmy, it can happen to us.' With Clark gone, the world of Formula 1 was looking for a new king.

But winning the championship was the last thing on Stewart's mind, not just because of the work to be done on the Matra MS10, but because he simply did not think that way. 'I was never really sure I was good enough to be world champion. I never, ever thought I was better than everybody else. I knew, because I was doing well, that I was quite good. You know how people say that they have to believe they are the best before they can perform? Well, that was never my philosophy. I always thought somebody else was better and I had to try harder to beat them or get myself into a position where I had some sort of advantage. So I didn't go into F1 with Ken thinking this was my gateway to being world champion. And I don't believe Ken was thinking about winning the Constructors' championship either. His attitude was: "This is the best engine. We've got a good car, so what do we have to do next in order to compete against the likes of Ferrari?" He would rub his hands together in the way he did, and say, "This'll be good for us. Let's go racing!" I really think the championship was too much of a dream for him at that time.'

Such a thought would have been expunged further from his mind at the end of April when Stewart crashed during practice for a Formula 2 race at Jarama in Spain and broke the small scaphoid bone in his right wrist. He would be out of racing for several weeks. Stewart had been setting quick times and knew the circuit well, a double irony because the Spanish Grand Prix was due to be staged there a fortnight later and Tyrrell had been delivered a new chassis, the latest MS10 a much improved version of the car Stewart had fought so gamely at Brands Hatch.

Matra's own car, the MS11 with its V12 engine, had been coming on apace too, the testing carried out by Jean-Pierre Beltoise. Since the MS11 was not yet considered ready for racing, Beltoise was the obvious stand-in for Stewart in Spain. He proved it by holding a strong second place then snatching the lead at the very moment wisps of smoke began to appear from the back of the car. Beltoise was called in when the wisps became serious-looking blue plumes. A pinched oil pipe was diagnosed and fixed, by which time several laps had passed. Beltoise eventually rejoined to finish fifth, and last. Nonetheless, the promise was clearly evident.

Monaco was next, but Stewart remained *hors de combat*. With Matra due to give the MS11 its debut, Beltoise was not available. Tyrrell overcame the difficulty by hiring Johnny Servoz-Gavin, a dashing Frenchman with long blond hair and a massive amount of natural talent. Servoz-Gavin was sensational during practice on a street circuit made even more treacherous by the occasional shower. Sliding the light blue car at will, the Frenchman powered his way onto the front row of the grid to take a place alongside Graham Hill. The old master had won this race three times; the young pretender had barely sat in a Formula 1 car before. Tyrrell and Stewart repeatedly advised caution; 80 laps was a long way on this difficult track, and the race would not be won on the first lap. Servoz-Gavin nodded, then clipped a barrier while leading on the opening lap. Tyrrell's reaction is not recorded. Stewart could scarcely wait to get behind the wheel again for the next race at Spa Francorchamps.

He wore a plastic support on his lower arm and wrist, but the discomfort caused by the steering during practice forced a couple of pit visits so that he could have his thumb bound as protection against the cutting action of the brace. This did not prevent him from taking a place in the middle of the front row, though, between the Ferraris of Chris Amon (on pole) and Jacky Ickx. Stewart spent two-thirds of the race engaged in a furious battle with Denny

Hulme, the Matra and the McLaren passing and repassing as they scrapped initially for fourth place, which became third, then second, then a fight for the lead when the cars ahead dropped out. With ten laps to go, Stewart came round alone, Hulme having stopped with transmission failure. The Matra was half a minute ahead of Bruce McLaren, and the team began to think the unthinkable. The feeling that they might win this classic race on a classic circuit intensified as the laps ticked by and Stewart maintained his lead. The pits at Spa Francorchamps occupied a downhill run from a hairpin. At the end of the penultimate lap, Stewart rounded the final corner and coasted into the Tyrrell pit. He was out of fuel with 8.7 miles to go.

'We had extra fuel tanks on the car,' recalled Neil Davis. 'According to the calculations from practice we should have had enough fuel on board, but Jackie had been having difficulty getting out of the pits because the engine had a flat spot which didn't clear until the car got going. Ken had said to turn up the fuel metering unit a couple of notches to get over this problem, and that turned out to be just enough to make us run out of fuel. Jackie barely managed to get into the pits, where we refuelled him and got him going again. I'll never forget that Dick Jeffrey, the Dunlop manager, had already brought champagne into the pits. Ken went absolutely ballistic! "Don't you ever effing bring champagne in here again!" he roared. "Get it out!" We were absolutely devastated. Our maiden Grand Prix win was there for the taking and it just slipped away. Everyone was in the back of the truck – Mrs Tyrrell, everyone – and we were all in tears. It really was no consolation that Jackie finished fourth and scored our first points. We should have had nine points for the win, no question. Everyone was absolutely drained.'

Despite Stewart's speed and commitment, he disliked Spa, not because of the ill fortune visited upon him on that June afternoon, nor because of the supreme challenge presented by the road circuit sweeping through the Ardennes. His objections centred on the fact that there was insufficient back-up for a driver in terms of safety features and medical support should something go wrong – which it did frequently at such a high-speed track lined along its length by natural hazards. And Stewart could speak from experience. Two years earlier the race had started on a bone-dry road, but halfway round the lap the cars had run into a rainstorm of such devastating proportions that several spun off the road. Stewart was among them, his BRM finishing in a ditch, the Scotsman trapped by the stove-in side of the car, the ruptured tank spilling fuel into the cock-pit. As Graham Hill and another driver worked feverishly to release Stewart, they did so in the knowledge that the wreck could burst into flames any second. Worse was to follow. The nearest trackside medical centre amounted to nothing more than a tent where little could be done for Stewart's broken shoulder, cracked rib, petrol burns and heavy bruising. When an ambulance finally arrived, the driver managed to get lost – twice – while traversing the bumpy back roads en route to hospital.

Stewart had since been energized into a campaign of safety aware-ness. It was to be an uphill struggle. The race he had just lost was a case in point. Brian Redman had crashed when the suspension broke on his Cooper just as the young British driver hit the brakes at more than 170mph. The car not only vaulted the barrier, it hit parked cars and caught fire. The marshals were quickly on the scene, but a comment in *Autosport* that some were seen smoking cigarettes while dousing the flames illustrated that there was a still long way to go.

In the same magazine, the editorial made a timely and well-reasoned call for the introduction of a substantial roll-over bar behind a driver's head. These were mandatory, but the required specification was so pathetic that a young British club driver, a married man with a baby daughter, had been killed outright at Silverstone when he rolled his Formula Ford and the roll-over bar was bent back and flattened. The editorial made a plea that stout roll-over bars should be compulsory, 'in all types of club racing'. The implication was that the roll-over bars on F1 cars were perfectly adequate. In 1968 they might have looked that way, but by today's standards they were completely useless since the driver's head was usually level with the top of the bar, in some cases protruding above it. That very point was illustrated on the cover of *Autosport*, a picture of McLaren on his winning way at Spa not only showing the flimsy roll-over bar but also the absence of a seat harness.

McLaren's first Grand Prix win in his own car had moved the New Zealander into third place in the championship. Stewart was 14th thanks to the three points earned at Spa, but 21 points behind the leader, Graham Hill, who had won at Monaco and in Spain. Significantly, though, two drivers on the championship table were dead: Jim Clark, killed on 7 April, and Lodovico Scarfiotti, who had died on 9 June during a hill climb in Germany. In between, on 7 May, Mike Spence of BRM had lost his life during practice at Indianapolis. The season was not halfway through, yet the period around the seventh of each month was beginning to take on an unspoken and spooky significance.

The Dutch Grand Prix was scheduled for 24 June, previews for the race at Zandvoort noting that the fifth round of the championship was wide open. Stewart arrived in the seaside resort with some trepidation, for the plastic support for his right wrist would be more of a handicap on the twists and turns of Zandvoort than it had been on the faster expanses of Spa. Stewart kept his running to a minimum on the first day, Friday, and didn't go out at all on Saturday when light rain meant the final practice would have little bearing on grid positions. He had already done enough to qualify on the second row of the 3–2–3 grid, but he didn't hold out much hope since his wrist had become badly swollen. His only saviour would be the slower and less physically demanding pace if it rained.

On race morning, Stewart's prayers were answered. On a fine day, Zandvoort could be a glorious place for a race as the cars swept through sand dunes that provided superb natural grandstands, but on this occasion it was a miserable spectacle as wind from the North Sea carried low cloud and drizzle. The rain relented half an hour before the scheduled 2.30 p.m. start, only to dash everyone's hopes shortly afterwards and make the choice of wet-weather tyres *de rigueur*. In Tyrrell's case, the Dunlop rain tyres, with an extra-wide drain channel cut in the middle, would be the team's ace card. That and the consummate skill of John Young Stewart.

By the end of the first lap, he was in second place, chasing the Lotus of Hill. By the end of the fourth lap, the Matra-Ford was in the lead, and there it would stay for the next two hours and 40 minutes – for that's how long it took to complete the 90 laps, or 234 miles. Today, Grands Prix either run to a maximum of 198 miles or two hours, whichever comes first; in 1968, endurance counted for just as much as speed. There were no scheduled pit stops, just a relentless afternoon of running on a track made even more slippery by wind-blown sand and oil dropped by cars less solid than they are today. Yet after 60 circuits Stewart had lapped the entire field – or at least the 10 survivors from the original 19 starters.

After the disappointment of Spa, Ken and the team said nothing. Dick Jeffrey of Dunlop kept the champagne out of sight. Patrick McNally, the *Autosport* reporter, had a fine view of the finish from the press tribune in the grandstand opposite the pits. 'Ken Tyrrell and his crew waited with bated breath as Jackie Stewart completed his final lap,' he wrote. 'It was only when the blue Matra-Ford hove into sight that they let themselves go. It is difficult to imagine anyone who deserved victory more than Jackie, and one couldn't help but feel pleased for Tyrrell too, for his car has always been a potential victor and now at last it has actually won – a car, one must remember, which has only been in Grand Prix racing for six months. Stewart's victory makes him now second overall in the championship.'

Jeffrey finally uncorked the champagne to celebrate Dunlop's first win in two years, the débâcle with the bubbly at Spa having been forgotten. Despite this momentous achievement for the little team from Ockham, it was greeted with typical Tyrrell understatement. 'I really don't remember it being a wild celebration or anything like that,' recalled Stewart. 'We were delighted, of course, and the British newspapers carried big stories the next day. Television coverage hardly existed, certainly nothing like it is today. But once we had finished with the champagne, it was rather like winning in Formula 3. Okay, that's done, now let's get on. We knew we were fast and we knew we were competitive. It was just a question of winning when the time was right. That was the way it seemed to me. Ken felt much the same.' France, however, was in full celebration mode. Not only had Stewart secured victory, the works Matra V12 of Jean-Pierre Beltoise had finished second after a powerful drive through the field. The influential French sports daily *L'Equipe* carried a headline that proclaimed THE DAY OF GLORY HAS COME; this was, after all, the first French victory of note since motor racing had restarted after World War Two.

The next race happened to be the French Grand Prix. The road circuit at Rouen was besieged, but the French were roundly beaten. The Belgians, however, were happy: Jacky Ickx scored a brilliant maiden victory, thanks largely to having set up his Ferrari for rain, which began to fall only moments before the start. When the drizzle later became a deluge, Ickx was home in a boat in every sense of the expression. For Stewart, the struggle on dry-weather tyres became a hopeless one when Ickx began to lap a full twenty seconds faster. There was no alternative but to abandon fourth place and stop for wets, and this was 30 years before scheduled pit stops for fuel and tyres lasted fewer than 10 seconds thanks to a team of 20 mechanics operating with well-practised efficiency. In 1968, there were three Tyrrell mechanics. It took them almost two minutes to work their way around each wheel, a seemingly time-consuming operation, but one in which Tyrrell was yet again breaking new ground. This Grand Prix was the first occasion on which an air gun was used to remove wheel nuts, a feature which would become as commonplace in F1 as wielding a spanner. The stop was in fact not as costly as it might have been since the field had become strung out and others were stopping too. Stewart lost just one place, and by half distance he was up to third, where he would stay for the rest of the afternoon, the race this time lasting for a mere two hours 25 minutes.

Hill had failed to finish, leaving the championship wide open with the Lotus driver just eight points ahead of Stewart and Ickx. It was the perfect situation for the British Grand Prix at Brands Hatch. Hill took pole, Stewart's only consolation for struggling into seventh on the grid being that Ickx was a further five places behind. All that hard work by Hill looked like being undone when a typical British summer's day brought thick black clouds that threatened to unleash their load on the Kentish circuit. When reports came through of a downpour five miles away, the grid went into a panic – one deliberately started by Ken Tyrrell. With about eight minutes to go, umbrellas went up in the spectator enclosures and Ken ordered the Matra to be raised on jacks and wet-weather Dunlops fitted. This was the signal for a mass chattering of air guns as rivals followed suit. Then, with a couple of minutes remaining before the off, Tyrrell quickly ordered the return of dry-weather rubber just as the umbrellas began to come down. The grid was in complete disarray.

In fact, the rain would hold off, vindicating Tyrrell's decision, which allowed Stewart to move into fifth place on the first lap. But as the race progressed the nervous handling of the car, combined with occasional but ferocious bumps, began to take their toll on the Scotsman's injured wrist. By the time he had completed the race, Stewart was sixth, two laps down on the winner, Jo Siffert in a privately entered Lotus. The good news for Stewart was that Hill had retired with a broken drive-shaft while leading; the bad news was that Ickx had finished third to move ahead of Stewart on the championship table, and Hulme had closed to within two points after bringing his McLaren home in fourth place.

Once the celebrations and ceremonies had been completed, the F1 circus decamped to Graham Hill's country cottage on Lord Brabourne's estate in Kent. A large marquee and bar saw plenty of action, the mood set by a dummy poster for the London newspaper *Evening News* whose headline read GRAHAM HILL SHOCK, referring to the rakish Englishman's retirement from the race.

Underneath, someone had added 'shaft trouble again'. The following day, Sunday, the scene shifted to a cricket ground at Mersham, near Ashford, for a charity match between a Grand Prix XI and Lord Brabourne's Xl. His Lordship's side included HRH Prince Charles, who was sent packing to the pavilion thanks to a neat catch by Bruce McLaren. Unusually for Jackie Stewart, he missed both social events. 'I was totally exhausted,' he remembered. 'Having to drive the car on those bumps, with the plastic cast on my arm, really took its toll. I think I slept for something like 18 hours. I was so drained.'

Once Stewart had recovered, he thought of recent events and the sadness that continued to envelop the motor racing fraternity. Clark, Spence, Scarfiotti had gone in the space of three months. Then, at the French Grand Prix, Frenchman Jo Schlesser had been killed when his Honda crashed and caught fire. That was on 7 July. The next Grand Prix would be on 4 August, as close to the dreaded seventh as anyone wanted to be. Worse than that, this race would be at the Nürburgring, the most dangerous circuit of all. It was not something Stewart wanted to talk about, but it was in his mind nevertheless. Despite his misgivings, Jackie Stewart would race on a track that was in the most lethal state imaginable and produce a drive Ken Tyrrell would rate as one of the greatest he had ever seen.

8

Total Madness

'This business of the seventh of the month,' said Jackie Stewart. 'It wasn't mentioned as such, but I can tell you that everybody, and I don't care who they were, felt very twitchy. In those days we were a very tight little group travelling round together and the loss of a driver was always felt very badly. In that summer of 1968 it seemed an endless succession of sadness, one funeral after another. You couldn't help but wonder who would be next, particularly at a place like the Nürburgring.'

In motor racing terms, the Nürburgring was the equivalent of the Grand National course, filled entirely with hazards as perilous as the old Becher's Brook. Anyone conquering this circuit experienced a sense of achievement that had no equal. Not only had you won, you had also survived. One hundred and seventy-six corners per lap, plunging, rising, dipping, twisting, curving, waiting for the slightest mistake. With the best will in the world, a track of this size and scale was impossible to marshal to the standards expected then, never mind the infinitely more stringent values of today. It was simply too long and, in parts, too remote. Travel round the track in a road car with Stewart and he would point to small fir trees beyond the barrier on the fast uphill run to the Karussell corner. 'Except they're not small trees,' he would say, 'they're the tops of very tall trees. Go over there and they'll never find the car, let alone the driver.' Comparing other circuits with this place was like suggesting a hike across Dartmoor was as hazardous as the Normandy landings.

Writing about the circuit a few years later, Stewart explained his reluctance to bring Helen to this particular track. 'I always try to discourage her from going to the "Ring". It can be a very difficult place for a racing driver's wife. The worst thing about it is the eight-minute wait before your car comes round again. In the event of a breakdown or a small accident, she could have sat in the pits for three quarters of an hour wondering what had happened, with everybody looking the other way and saying maybe it's nothing – but all the while wondering.'

The Nürburgring was not a place to be treated lightly, not even when the sun shone and the majestic surroundings made the circuit look inviting. When Stewart arrived on the day before practice began in August 1968, it was raining. And it would continue, almost without letting up, for the next three days. This, he didn't need to be told, was the Nürburgring at its most forbidding, and a lap in his hire car merely deepened the pit of his stomach. 'Actually,' Stewart recalled, 'the conditions during that lap were the best they would be all weekend, but of course we didn't know that. At the Nürburgring, you always lived in the hope that it would be better the next day.'

That was the philosophy adopted the following morning, Friday, when the circuit was opened for official practice. The layout of the track incorporated a short loop around the pits, which meant drivers could make exploratory runs without having to complete the full 14 miles. Visibility was down to 200 yards and Stewart decided not to venture onto the long circuit, preferring to use the loop to bed in his tyres and brakes in the hope that the weather would improve. It was a tactical mistake, the only one Stewart would make. Those drivers who had completed a few laps of the circuit proper found it to be dry in places, and their lap times would turn out to be the fastest of the entire weekend. By the time afternoon practice was due to start, conditions had deteriorated so badly that the officials decided to scrap the session. Still, there was always Saturday.

It was no better, but because he had not recorded a time, Stewart had no option but to go out and complete a few laps. In fact, he was the fastest of the day, but the time was nowhere near the pace set by those drivers who had been adventurous the previous day. Now more than ever, Stewart hoped the rain would abate. In dry conditions, he would have a difficult enough time overtaking those ahead, but in the wet, in the impenetrable mist and spray? He didn't want to contemplate it.

On race morning, there was no alternative. The grey and the gloom continued to seep through the forest and sap enthusiasm. Given the limited amount of practice, the organizers agreed to lay on an extra practice session, the times counting for the grid. Stewart did not want any part of it. 'Ken said I should go out. He argued that I would find out where the rivers of water were, and it was better to discover that now than during the race. Of course, he was correct, and when I went out I found the conditions to be absolutely terrible. It was raining heavily, the fog was pretty bad in places, and that just made the problems normally associated with driving at this circuit even worse than usual.

'On most circuits you can see where the pools of water are lying, but at the Nürburgring, with the hedges and trees, you couldn't see that far ahead and you would arrive over a crest and go into a river that felt several inches deep and was maybe two or three feet wide. The car would immediately aquaplane and go out of control. I came back to the pits and said I didn't think we should practise any more under those conditions. Really, we shouldn't have raced, but the drivers were not united in those days. We had not formed into a strong enough group, and even though few of us liked the idea of racing under those conditions, we didn't have a collective voice to say no.'

And all the time, lurking in the background, was the spectre of the season's history and the approach of the seventh of the month. It was not a subject Stewart contemplated raising with Ken. 'I wouldn't have mentioned it, because what could Ken have done about it? At that time, I was the only person who knew about how to deal with such situations, particularly with undertakers and so on. I had been through it a lot. I knew they had to have a zinc- or a lead-lined coffin. There were only certain airlines which would carry a coffin, and it had to be a cargo plane. There were only about two European undertakers who knew how to do things properly. I had all their phone numbers. So when it came to a reluctance on my part to go out, there was no ill feeling. Ken could sense what was going on.

'In those days we used to stay in a family hotel, in the nearby town of Daun. I had also taken a room in the Sport Hotel beside the track because there were no motorhomes in those days and I always liked to have somewhere to relax. That's where Ken came when he wanted me to go out and do those laps. In many ways, he felt it more than me because you can imagine what he would have to go through if, after my objecting, something happened to me out on the circuit. I was right, but so was he. There was no shouting or cajoling. Ken was very firm. It wasn't "I want", it was, "Jackie, this you have got to do. I don't like the idea of it – but you've got to do it." There's no suggestion that I would ever have said no to Ken. I would have put my point, but there was never any doubt in my mind about who was the boss because it was his team. If it had been an issue of serious gravity as far as I was concerned, I had the muscle to refuse, but it was never something I did for the sake of it. It was a case of deciding what there was to lose and what there was to gain. In this instance, there seemed to be so much more to lose.

'So we did it. I was very lucky in the respect that I was very compartmentalized – I was able to shut out any worries and focus completely on driving the car. I did a quick lap. It wasn't a case of going round saying, "Well, screw you, I'm going to go slowly." I did a hard lap as if it was a racing lap, but I was lucky all my life in that I was able to compartmentalize. This was a job that had to be done. Ken always knew that if I was talking safety, it didn't mean I would drive slowly. He knew I would do what was necessary, just as he accepted the other business of safety had to be considered as well. But it was as if that was another piece of paper, as if to say, "Okay, we've dealt with what needs to be done in the car, now let's have a look at this."'

The feeling of trepidation intensified as the rain got heavier. The start was delayed, but there was no chance of a reprieve as the drivers walked to the grid spread out in front of the main grandstand. The place was packed, the open enclosures opposite the pits a heaving mass of dripping umbrellas. Quite what they expected to see was difficult to say since the cars would swirl past a mere 14 times, but at the Nürburgring you knew anything could happen. There was always the feeling that you were witnessing something special. Anyone who dared to race there deserved your patronage. And your profound respect. Not least on a day like this.

When the West German national flag fell, Jacky Ickx, starting from pole position, spun his rear wheels excessively and Stewart almost drove up the pit lane in his efforts to get alongside the Ferrari. He managed it, despite the wheels of the Matra becoming stuck momentarily in a drainage gutter. At the first corner, Stewart found himself in third place behind the Lotus of Graham Hill and Chris Amon's Ferrari. But third might as well have been 33rd. 'I couldn't see anything,' Stewart recalled. 'I mean, nothing at all. Zero. The spray was absolutely incredible. I couldn't see the car in front, and you were literally driving blindly into this wall of water. I tried to get out of the spray and go up the inside, and that way I could see a little more clearly. I knew I simply had to pass Chris and Graham as quickly as possible. I managed to pass Amon on the downhill run to Adenau Bridge – in fact, one of the most difficult parts of the circuit. I can't remember how I did it, but I know I was relieved because until then I didn't think I had ever been more frightened while sitting in a racing car. Even in the dry, your car took off at least 13 times – this was before they improved the Ring a few years later – and the whole thing was just a drama from start to finish. So when you added rain and fog – well, it was indescribable.

All you could do was try to keep the car halfway under control. It was like a juggler in a high wind with lightweight balls.

'From the moment you left the back of the pits and headed out, you had no way of knowing if someone was catching you. Normally, on a shorter circuit, your pit board would give you the gaps so you always had a pretty good idea of what you needed to do to keep the guy behind at arm's length. But not here. I wanted to make the gap bigger every lap. So having passed Chris, I was then very keen to get ahead of Graham before we reached the start/finish area. I figured that if I could get ahead then I could open out a lead since he would be struggling along in my spray. There were hedges running along both sides of the Tiergarten Straight before the pits, and I knew the spray would be hanging around for some time because of that.'

Stewart pulled off the perfect move and caught Hill by surprise at the exit of Schwalbenswanz, a long and tricky banked curve. Now he had the 170mph Tiergarten Straight to himself. 'Even then it wasn't that easy. There was a very fast kink in the straight but the apex was just over a hump. There was a sign warning of a low bridge and after that sign there was a gap in the hedge. When you glimpsed that, you knew you had to lift off the throttle slightly and expect the kink. It took some courage in the dry, but in the wet . . .'

There was silence in the start/finish area, save for the occasional strident tones of the public address system as word came through from various parts of the circuit. Unlike a normal venue where com-mentators dotted around the track could talk the leaders through each lap, there would be long periods of hush at the Nürburgring, a weird feeling for a race track. All that could be heard in the pits was the splashing of rain and muffled conversation from the enclosure opposite. Ken Tyrrell and his mechanics could only stand and wait, their imaginations trying vainly to picture the impossible conditions as their man raced on. Or so they hoped. Tyrrell-Matra number 6 could have been in a hedge for all they knew. The nine minutes seemed an eternity.

'It was awful,' said Neil Davis. 'There should never have been a race, but once they started then you knew you were in the lap of the gods to a great extent. We knew the Dunlop rain tyres were the best, and that would help, but there was much more to this race than that. When the field went off the grid in a cloud of spray, we ducked through the pits and watched them come along the back loop before disappearing off into the country. Jackie had started from sixth on the grid and he was already into third place as he went past the back of the pits. Then we waited a long, long time. Finally, we heard this engine. Out of the mist came our car. Then nothing. Nobody else. We thought there must have been a mighty shunt somewhere. But no! Suddenly the rest of the field came through.'

Stewart was eight seconds ahead – a massive margin at such an early stage. After two laps, he was a colossal 34 seconds in front, the Scotsman driving with a combination of intuitive brilliance and concentrated bravery on a track which was changing its complexion by the lap. 'Elsewhere, you might expect to win races by 30 seconds,' said Stewart, 'but even when the pit board told me I was one minute 20 seconds ahead – a hell of a cushion – there was no question of backing off. Because this was the Nürburgring, the thinking was that if something went wrong you had to allow enough time to limp back. So you had to press on.'

It was a prescient move. During the final laps, the Tyrrell-Matra's throttle began to stick open. It was the last thing a driver needed at any circuit, but under these conditions, at this track, it was Stewart's worst nightmare. 'I remember that clearly,' recalled Davis. 'The Ford DFV engine had these peculiar throttle spring plungers. We had extra springs fitted on ours, but when they got wet and dirt on them, they seized up. Instead of expanding, they stayed closed and dropped out. Jackie ended up driving by flicking the ignition on and off because he wasn't sure if the throttle was going to shut properly when he lifted his foot off the pedal. It wasn't returning because these springs had dropped out. To drive round there like that was quite magical, quite magical.'

There would be no respite for Stewart. As he completed the 13th and penultimate lap, his heart sank when there was no sign of an official to indicate that this horror might be brought to a premature end. Stewart pressed on, knowing another 14 miles of hell lay ahead. 'I honestly thought they would stop the race,' he said. 'It had really started to pour and the track had become even more treacherous than before. You would suddenly be confronted by rivers which had not been there on the previous lap. At one point, I entered the third-gear corner at Wippermann and suddenly lost control in a deep river running from left to right. I was sliding sideways across the track, but somehow the tyres found some grip and I managed to regain control. Graham, who was some way behind by now, arrived at the same spot eventually and spun.'

At the end of the last lap, Stewart was four minutes ahead and in a different league from the rest. He had parked, vacated his car and was waiting on the rostrum by the time the third man appeared out of the gloom to take the chequered flag. Jackie was accompanied by Ken and the rest of the bedraggled team.

'You had to stand out in the rain and signal, there was no alternative,' said Davis. 'We were absolutely soaked, but you don't notice when you've won, particularly seeing your car come home first in a race like that. There was a tradition at the Nürburgring where they would weigh the winning driver and give the equivalent amount in chocolate to an orphanage. We filled up Jackie's pockets with tools and weights. The organizers were a bit shocked when this wee Scotsman tipped the scales at something like 18 stone!'

But the wee Scotsman had far weightier things on his mind as he thought again about the day of the month and its historical overtones, and he wasn't alone. 'We just wanted to know if there had been any serious accidents,' said Stewart. 'We heard that Vic Elford had crashed, and the first thing everyone asked was, "Is he all right?" In fact, he was. And the amazing thing was that, despite the truly appalling conditions, no one was badly hurt.

'Even now, I can remember every corner of that circuit as it was then. It had been an ambition of mine to win at the Nürburgring, and to do it under such horrifying circumstances made it something special – certainly something I can look back on now, from the comfort of my fireside, and savour. But really, when you think of the conditions we raced under that day, it was madness. Total madness.'

9

The Big Man

François Guiter was a big man, softly spoken but with a quiet, commanding presence. To perceive his slightly benign look as a sign of a pushover, a foreigner in Formula 1 who knew nothing about the sport, was to make a serious tactical error. Guiter arrived on the scene in 1968 and his influence on international motor racing would be immense. His initial dealings with Ken Tyrrell led to a huge row, but it was the last disagreement between the two in a remarkable relationship which would last for 11 years.

Guiter was the head of promotions for Elf, the French state petrochemical company. It has long been thought that Elf stood for Essence Lubrifique Français, but in fact it was a marketing term designed to present a pleasant and sympathetic image (the computer had also thrown up the word 'Elan', but this was rejected because of its use as a brand name elsewhere). Elf had been launched through a clever campaign in France during 1967. The company had bought a ready-made network marketing under the Caltex brand name and Elf began the softly, softly promotion by painting the Caltex stations white. After a hiatus, these filling stations sprouted red dots, accompanied by advertising proclaiming, 'The red dots are coming'. Then, overnight, Elf decals suddenly appeared to complete the fresh, young image of the new fuel company. Guiter, brought on board to promote the company, was into his substantial stride.

'I was in charge of the launch in 1967,' said Guiter. 'Basically, Elf was a technical company run by engineers. They were very good at what they did – deep sea drilling, and so on – but they didn't know how to go about marketing their company. They said they wanted to become associated with products for automobiles and be involved on the technical side. So I was wondering what would be a link between the technical aspect and the general public. We made a big survey and it came up with one answer: motor racing. The problem was that at that time France was nowhere in motor racing. Apart from the success of Alpine in rallying, there was nothing. We needed to look at Formula 1 and something that would be a potential winner. At the same time, Matra was looking for a way to demonstrate their technical ability. Everything they had done – making arms and so on – had been secret, but they had also come to the conclusion that motor racing was the answer. They had already made a Formula 3 and a Formula 2 car. It was obvious for Elf to join with Matra. We decided on a four-year contract, which was very rare at the time. We announced it at the Monte Carlo Rally and said we would win in Formula 3, then win in Formula 2, and in the third year win in Formula 1. For the fourth year, we would win Le Mans. Everyone laughed.'

The French motor racing authorities quickly became familiar with Elf, and Monsieur Guiter in particular. Elf's first race with Matra was at Rheims, a spectacularly fast road circuit in the Champagne region of France. The track at Rheims was the province of 'Toto' Roche, a rotund gentleman whose speciality was to stand in the middle of the track before the start of a race, drop the flag when he felt like it, then run (as best he could) for his life. The miracle was that no driver had yet knocked him down, though several had done their best to come close. Rheims was also the territory of BP, the swathe of green and yellow paint along the concrete pits marking a long-standing association. The difficulty was obvious to everyone but Roche when he leased a pit box to Elf. 'We hired this pit, and of course the first thing we did was paint it in the white, blue and red of

Elf,' recalled Guiter. 'That seemed the normal thing to do. The next morning, we arrived to find it had been repainted in BP colours! So we painted it Elf again. Then we waited that night, and when they came with their BP paint – we box! Toto Roche came and shouted, "What are you doing? We have been with BP for years!" I said, "We don't care! If you sell something you should respect that and the people you are taking the money from!" Our pit stayed in Elf colours after that.'

The Formula 2 contract between Tyrrell and Shell in 1967 proved more difficult to circumvent, but Elf were already eyeing the following year and Tyrrell's advance to Formula 1. The Tyrrell-Matra had carried Caltex identification during the first race in South Africa, but once in Europe small Elf logos were to be seen on the flanks of the blue car. It was not until the Nürburgring in August that Elf came on board to a greater extent, and that resulted in a clash of wills. 'My first contact with Ken was at the Nürburgring,' recalled Guiter. Then he paused, a smile playing on his lips. 'Ken had not put the Elf stickers on the car because our fuel was late arriving. That was true, but we were upset by this and there was a big argument between us. A very big argument! But we reached agreement, the stickers went on the car, and Jackie won the race. We became the best possible friends after that.'

Their burgeoning relationship was helped even further as the 1968 season headed into the final quarter. Stewart retired with engine failure after leading briefly at Monza, and then finished sixth in Canada. There were two races left, and thanks to a terrifying moment with a fuel churn, Ken came close to missing them both.

The penultimate round was held at Watkins Glen, a challenging track set in rolling countryside in the Finger Lake region of New York State, an area which became even more beautiful at the time of the race thanks to its autumnal hues. Watkins Glen was popular with the team principals because the organizers paid more prize money than anyone else. The mechanics also enjoyed being there thanks to the camaraderie encouraged by the Kendall Centre – in effect, a long barn with a central isle which allowed spectators to see the teams at close quarters while the mechanics worked on their cars. Luckily for Tyrrell and everyone else, there were few spectators present on the day before practice.

'The teams were side by side in stalls, almost like a cattle market in the nicest sense,' said Neil Davis. 'I was over at Lotus, borrowing some bits and pieces, when I turned round and saw a huge orange ball of flame where our team was. Ken had been using a five-gallon churn to add petrol to one of the cars. Fortunately the tanks were nearly full and Ken was adding the last little drop when the whole thing erupted in an inferno. Ken dropped the churn, partly on fire. McLaren were next door, and very fortunately Mike Barney, one of their mechanics, immediately grabbed a dry powder extinguisher – a huge contraption on iron wheels – and put the whole thing out in a matter of seconds. Thanks to his quick reaction, we were saved from . . . well, it didn't bear thinking about. There were full open churns dotted here and there, and cars with fuel in them; the whole place could have gone up in no time at all. As it was, the heat alone had damaged wiring and lights in the ceiling. Ken was very, very lucky. No one to this day knows exactly what caused it. One of the local policemen told us that the area was well known for static electricity. The batteries were out of the car because they were being charged, but Ken had been wearing a nylon shirt, so we could only suppose that a static spark had set the whole thing off. Once we realized everyone was okay, the problem then was that everything was covered in white powder. We worked halfway through the night to replace all the cables, hoses, injector pipes, the throttle cable and various other bits and pieces on the car. We had a local painter come in and touch up the bits that were damaged by the fire.'

Johnny Servoz-Gavin might have finished an excellent second at Monza – a result that turned out to be one of the few high points of his career – but, in an age when race-by-race driver deals were more relaxed, he was not entered for Watkins Glen. In the aftermath of the fire, this was fortunate, since it gave Stewart the use of two cars.

In the event, Jackie chose the undamaged chassis, and led from start to finish. Such a clear-cut win put Tyrrell into an unbelievable situation for a novice F1 team: Jackie Stewart would go to the final round in Mexico City with a chance of winning the World championship.

'Obviously, we hadn't come into the season thinking we were going to win the championship,' said Stewart. 'After winning the race at Watkins Glen, I went across to California and spent some time in Los Angeles with [film director] Roman Polanski. It was the perfect way to relax, although again I wasn't sure that we were thinking endlessly about winning the championship. Still, we had a real chance; Ken knew that and I knew that, because we had all the right things in place to allow us to do it. I was up against Denny [Hulme] in the McLaren and Graham [Hill] in the Lotus – very tough competition. I knew that Graham in particular would be difficult to beat because the Lotus 49 was a fantastic racing car. But we also knew our car was quick and it would come down to a bit of luck and whatever happened on the day.'

The Magdalena Mixhuca circuit in the outer suburbs of Mexico City was considered to be one of the best of its kind. A banked 180-degree curve threw the cars onto the finishing straight and into a clever mix of corners throughout the flat circuit's 3.1 mile length. With mountains in the distance and a sports park on the infield, the attractive setting was rounded off by pits and garages that were far in advance of anything to be found on the 12-race calendar.

'We were staying in a hotel in the centre of the city,' Kenneth Tyrrell recalled. 'It was a lovely place and each room had a little sort of mini pool. But a gin and tonic cost about £1.50, which was huge money then – and you know how fond Dad was of his pre-prandial G&T. He was outraged! So Mum said, "We're not having this!", and went out and bought a bottle of gin and some tonic from a local store.'

Ken had need of a restorative drink on the Saturday night. Practice had been satisfactory enough on Friday when Stewart set third fastest time, but it all went wrong on the second day. A broken drive-shaft not only punctured a tyre but also wrecked part of the suspension and the rear wing. Aerofoils had grown in size and popularity during the year, developing rapidly from upward-curving rear bodywork and small plates on the side of the nose to flimsy, suspension-mounted devices which shook and vibrated alarmingly, high above the back of the car. But since everyone had them, you had to follow suit in these pioneering days of discovering the true value of downforce and aerodynamics. And in Tyrrell's case, the rear wing was another item that needed replacing.

More serious was the fact that there were only two cars present, but on this occasion Servoz-Gavin was scheduled to race the second one. Following the incident with the drive-shaft on his regular car, Stewart took over Servoz-Gavin's chassis (the one which had been damaged in the fire at Watkins Glen) during final practice and set his best time of the weekend. So far, so good. The problem arose when Stewart decided he felt more comfortable in his regular car. Assuming it could be repaired, he would race it, but the rules of the day dictated that his grid position would be governed by the best time set in that particular car. It meant he would start from seventh on the grid instead of fifth. Hill and Hulme would start from third and fourth respectively. Stewart decided the gamble was worth taking; 65 laps (202 miles) was a long way to go in a car in which he did not feel comfortable. As ever, Ken did not interfere, leaving the decision entirely in Stewart's hands. As Jackie sat down to ponder how he would get past Dan Gurney's McLaren and the Honda of John Surtees on the third row, Ken went off for a gin and tonic.

The city was still recovering from hosting the Olympic Games a few weeks before, an event made more remarkable than usual by the exploits of the athletes at altitude. Bob Beamon's long jump had been too long for officials to measure with their latest, supposedly sophisticated equipment; the use of a conventional tape indicated a colossal jump of 8.90 metres, shattering the world record by 55 centimetres. The thin air at 2,250 metres above sea level aided the destruction of records across the board.

The Olympians might have struggled in the heat, but the motor racing people had few complaints when race day dawned fine and warm. Any worries about Stewart's grid position were soon dispelled when he completed the first lap behind Hill's leading Lotus and the Honda of Surtees. It was a good start for Stewart, but not good enough if he was to take the title. Hill was ahead by three points, with Hulme the outsider, a further three points behind Stewart. The mathematics said that all three could tie on points if Hulme won with Stewart finishing second and Hill coming home fourth. But perhaps the most significant statistic at this precise moment was the one which said Hill would become world champion if he finished first or second, regardless of what Stewart and Hulme achieved, for Hill was leading the race.

Stewart moved into second place on the next lap. By lap five he was in the lead, but not for long. The Matra and the Lotus ran nose to tail, Hill diving to the front once more on lap nine. The championship looked like being a fight between these two, and a lap later it became a certainty when the rear suspension broke on Hulme's McLaren and spun him out of fourth place.

championship calculations were upset slightly when the dark blue Lotus of Jo Siffert came charging through the field, the Swiss very annoyed and anxious to make up for a terrible start from pole position. Siffert, driving for the private entrant Rob Walker, had delighted the F1 world by winning the British Grand Prix, a result as significant as a Minardi driver finishing on the podium today. With the bit between his teeth, Siffert overtook the Matra, and then the Lotus. Hill was not unduly worried of course, since second place would be good enough, and even if Stewart did demote Hill to third that would be insufficient to give Jackie the title.

It became marginally more serious for Hill when no sooner had Siffert taken the lead than a broken throttle linkage sent the blue car into the pits. Now Hill was leading with Stewart poised directly behind the Lotus in its red and white Gold Leaf colours. The game of cat and mouse continued for 13 dramatic laps, Stewart shadowing Hill's every move. Would he pass him? *Could* he pass him?

The question became irrelevant on lap 38, when the gap between the leaders suddenly extended to five seconds. One lap later it was 15 seconds. This was not part of the script. Gradually, Stewart fell down the order as the Matra appeared to stutter and misfire. 'We were actually being caught out by Matra's unique system of fuel tanks,' said Davis. 'Because they didn't use bag tanks like everyone else, the inside of the monocoque [chassis] was rubber coated and the fuel carried directly inside. This was done during the construction of the car, and when they had finished the excess rubber grunge was drained out. We had gone all year without any trouble, but during this race some little balls of rubber had managed to get into the fuel system – and they more or less stopped the car. Jackie struggled round to finish seventh. We were devastated, but it was basically our fault because this was something we should have checked beforehand.'

Stewart might have thought he had chosen the wrong car when Servoz-Gavin breezed past him to take fourth place ten laps from the finish, but then the Frenchman's engine suddenly blew in a spectacular manner, leaving Tyrrell with a £2,000 repair bill to add to his misery. Hill, meanwhile, raced to victory and his second world title. In the end, Stewart was 12 points behind in second place. He was left to ruminate on what might have been had he not been forced through injury to miss two races, and had the car not run out of fuel at Spa.

'Well, that's true,' Stewart agreed, 'but we didn't spend long thinking about it because, when all was said and done, we had enjoyed a fantastic first year together; better than any of us could have hoped for. In any case, it was nice to be voted top driver in various awards at the end of the season. That said a lot. But I always felt that, in a way, I wasn't yet ready, as a person, to win the championship. Graham was just so much better at it than I was. He was a good after-dinner speaker and he knew how to handle everything associated with being the champion. Compared to Graham, I was the young lad! In any case, he had been my team-mate when we were at BRM and we were great friends. It was actually very valuable for me to go to all the events and listen to him speak and just see how he dealt with everything; 1968 was a good understudy year, and I don't think I would have done the championship justice the way he did. I had got the kudos that I wanted with these various awards and I was also number one in the *Autocourse* annual's assessment of the season. These were the sort of things a driver could be proud of.'

For their part, Elf were equally delighted. Ken Tyrrell had vindicated the decision by Elf to spread their support and go with the British team, particularly as the works Matra V12 had collected a mere eight points compared to 45 for the Tyrrell Matra-Ford. Elf had also managed to usurp Shell and support the Tyrrell F2 team in 1968. Stewart took three wins in this category, but that was a mere footnote to victory in the European Formula 2 championship for Jean-Pierre Beltoise in the works Matra. With the French firm having won a Formula 3 title in 1967, François Guiter's bold prediction was on course. And on the evidence of Tyrrell's debut showing in Formula 1, few were willing to bet against Elf and Matra taking the World championship in 1969, especially when the new season's model was unveiled. The motor racing cognoscenti thought the MS10 was good, but their conception of a very fine racing car was about to be blown away by a superb example of the genre.

10

Absolutely Champion

For an aerospace company, Matra had been remarkably slow on the uptake. Wings and aerodynamics had become the motor racing buzzwords during 1968, but the French firm's collective mind appeared to have been on other things. Apart from worrying about making their own car and V12 engine competitive, there had been unrest, general strikes and student protests over social and working conditions throughout France. The future seemed far from certain.

As the racing season ended and the political situation became calmer, Matra took a hard look at what was required for 1969. The first thing was to accept that the Matra V12 was better suited to sports car racing. The second was to concentrate solely in F1 terms on Ken Tyrrell and his Matra International team. And the third was to design and build a new car, the MS80.

The significance of this major design rethink was to be considerable. These days, teams would not consider entering a season without having a new car at their disposal; at the start of 1969, Matra was the only manufacturer to have gone to such trouble. The rest – Lotus, McLaren, BRM and, to a lesser degree, Ferrari – were happy to make do with revised versions of their existing chassis. It was to be a serious error on their part, one that would become evident as soon as the Matra MS80 broke cover at the end of February. Here was a car that incorporated the many lessons learned in 1968. Its bulbous form was a departure from the cigar-shaped norm, the removal of the fuel from high tanks to the sides and centre being just one benefit of a chassis making the most of the first advances in aerodynamic thinking. As before, the Matra remained unique in its use of the structural fuel tank system which improved the car's rigidity and did away with the use of bag tanks. Matra had used this system in the knowledge that bag tanks would become compulsory in 1970, thus rendering the MS80 obsolete at the end of the year; they had gone ahead regardless, such was their faith in the technical advantages of the design. Their confidence would prove well founded.

Initially, Ken Tyrrell applied the brakes to such enthusiasm. The MS80 was tested briefly at Montlhéry before being shipped to South Africa and the first race of the season. Stewart drove the new car for a few laps but, since little was known about it, Ken opted for the safe option and chose to race a pair of MS10s. With the works Matra F1 effort having been shelved, Beltoise switched to Tyrrell, leaving Servoz-Gavin to concentrate on Formula 2 and the European championship, which he would duly win in the Tyrrell-entered MS7.

Ken's caution proved typically astute. Stewart led all the way at Kyalami, the MS10 with its high wings fore and aft proving too much for Hill's Lotus in second place. Stewart repeated his dominance during the Race of Champions two weeks later at Brands Hatch, but the difference this time was that he used the MS80. Bruce McLaren, watching from trackside after his car had broken down, was staggered by the ability of the MS80 to ride the bumps and put down the power from the latest version of the Ford DFV. Even with a single rear wing, the new Matra was proving to be fast and efficient. The irony was that much of the aerodynamic thinking incorporated in the car was about to be made redundant by potentially disastrous events at the next Grand Prix on arguably one of the most spectacular circuits ever used for Formula 1.

Montjuich was too good to be true. Located in Barcelona's largest park, the 2.35 mile track used public roads, starting from the highest point outside a vast stadium and corkscrewing to the bottom, sweeping past the royal palace and then gathering pace through very fast uphill curves on the return leg. The view from the top was stunning, but spectators and most certainly the drivers had no time to take in the profile of the magnificent city spread below for it was at this point that the track went through one of the most frightening sections of all. As the drivers blasted past the pits in top gear, they crested a rise and immediately plunged downhill towards a very tight left-hand hairpin. Not only did the cars become airborne just as the track curved gently to the right, the drivers had to position themselves perfectly for the slope that followed and then engage in vicious braking and swift down-changing. At times, the frantic activity could be too much for the spectator to take in. With steel barriers lining either side of the road, the race was not for the faint-hearted. It was certainly the last place to have a mechanical failure of any kind, but that was precisely what happened in the race. Twice, in fact. Involving cars from the same team.

If ever the high-mounted wings were going to look dangerously fragile, it was here at Montjuich. Though they were aerodynamically sound in theory, the same could not be said for the slim supports attached to the front and rear suspension. They looked perilously frail, particularly when the cars became airborne at 170mph and thumped onto the track at the top of the hill. On the ninth lap, Hill's rear wing buckled as he flew over the jump, the sudden loss of down-force proving predictably disastrous: the Lotus went out of control and smashed into the barrier. Miraculously, Hill was unhurt, his main concern to determine exactly what had happened. One glance at the collapsed wing told him all he didn't want to know. The problem now was that his team-mate, Jochen Rindt, was leading the race and Hill feared a similar failure. Word was sent back to the Lotus pit, but it was too late. The same thing happened as Rindt crested the rise for the 20th time, his car bouncing off the barrier on the left and careering straight across the track before crashing into Hill's wreckage and turning over. Hill was on hand to help pull a bruised and battered Rindt from the cockpit. Again, the wonder was that the driver was not gravely injured, particularly considering that no mechanic, no matter how hard he tried, could wriggle into the badly bent chassis once it had been returned to the Lotus factory.

In the midst of this wreckage and confusion, the race continued unabated. Chris Amon comfortably led Stewart for the next 36 laps until the Ferrari engine failed without warning. It was typical of the New Zealander's wretched luck, and on this occasion Stewart was the beneficiary, the Tyrrell-Matra MS80 cruising to an easy maiden Grand Prix win.

As Stewart stood on the podium, officials from the governing body's sporting arm, the Commission Sporting International (CSI), were already preparing a response to questions about the future of high-mounted wings. The general consensus among the teams was that they should be banned, but Ken Tyrrell would have none of it. He alone was running a car designed specifically with the high wings in mind and his advantage would be seriously eroded, if not wiped out altogether, if the wings were removed at a stroke.

Meanwhile, Rindt wrote a letter to *Autosport* from his home in Begnins, Switzerland, where he was convalescing. He left no one in any doubt about his opposition to aerofoils. 'My accident in the Spanish Grand Prix has been the biggest one so far,' he wrote. 'Through a lot of luck and safety precautions taken by the Spanish organizers, nothing serious happened. I was happily driving round the fastest bend on the track when my wing broke and changed its downthrust into reverse. The back end of my car started flying, and I nearly flew over the double guard rail on the left. Can you imagine what would have happened if the car had flown into the crowd?' Showing remarkable prescience, Rindt went on to describe the difficulties involved when running in close company. 'The wing obviously works via the airflow over it and this situation changes rapidly if you happen to follow another competitor; he has the full use of the wing and you yourself have to put up with the turbulence created by his car. You cannot pass him because, after getting near to him, your wings stop working and you cannot go quickly. This fact spoils racing to quite a large extent.' Rindt could have been talking about racing with the sophisticated aerodynamics of today.

In May 1969, the teams headed for Monaco knowing that confrontation would be hanging in the air. The race organizers, the Automobile Club de Monaco (ACM), spoke to every entrant before the start of practice, asking if they would agree to run without aerofoils. When all but Tyrrell agreed – Ken pointing out in words of one syllable that the ACM was not in a position to enforce such a decision, and if they did he would lodge a formal protest with the governing body which would result in the Monaco Grand Prix losing its championship status – the cat was firmly set among the pigeons. Time was ticking by, and the ACM had no alternative but to allow the cars to run with wings on the first day of practice, Thursday. Meanwhile, club officials were busy rounding up as many members of the CSI as they could find in order to convene a meeting that evening. Five representatives – among whom, significantly, there was no British delegate – invoked a safety clause empowering them to make a change to the rules with immediate effect. Aerofoils (but not nose wings) were banned forthwith.

Tyrrell was furious, but his hands were tied. 'He really was very angry,' Stewart recalled. 'There were several "froth jobs" with anyone who would listen! He wasn't getting a lot of sympathy from the other teams; they saw it as a way of making us less competitive. But the thing that really annoyed him was the arbitrary manner in which the decision was taken. It offended his sense of right and wrong.'

Thursday's practice times, with Stewart leading them, were declared null and void. The teams had to start from scratch, and a gaggle of strangely naked cars took to the track early on Friday morning. At first, the times were about a second a lap slower, but once the final practice session on Saturday had finished, Thursday's times had been beaten – with Stewart once again leading the way.

That improved Tyrrell's mood, as did an impressive third-fastest lap for Beltoise in the second MS80.

The Grand Prix got off to an encouraging start as Stewart took an immediate lead. It began to look as though he might win his third Grand Prix in succession. By lap 20 (quarter distance), Stewart was almost half a minute ahead of Hill's Lotus, with Beltoise third. Then, within the space of a couple of minutes, both blue cars were out with identical drive-shaft failures. Ken's team was nothing if not consistent. With Hill going on to win the Monaco Grand Prix for a record fifth time, the gap to Stewart at the top of the championship table had been reduced to three points.

If aerofoils were no longer in fashion, then four-wheel-drive most certainly was. This was the latest avenue of technical innovation in Formula 1 as Lotus, McLaren and Matra hurriedly prepared cars in the hope of finding a performance advantage. A five-week lay-off (the Belgian Grand Prix had been boycotted by the teams after a row over inadequate starting money) gave Matra enough time to have the so-called MS84 ready in time for the Dutch Grand Prix on 21 June. It also allowed the CSI to get its act together and define more clearly the ban on aerodynamic devices. In simple terms, the rear wings would be limited in size and position, thus doing away with the ridiculous high-mounted aerofoils.

Stewart briefly tried the four-wheel-drive car during practice at Zandvoort but found little to write home about thanks to his efforts being hampered by a fuel pick-up problem. Besides, the MS80 had been good enough to put Stewart in the middle of the front row between Rindt and Hill. The fact that he was not on pole did not bother Stewart unduly. 'Pole was not the big deal it is now,' he said. 'In those days, practice was enormously long and the object was to have a car that was driveable for the whole race. You've got to remember that there were no pit stops and you had to think about how the car would feel with a full load of fuel at the start compared to how it would feel a couple of hours later. The other difference was that there was overtaking as a result, so pole was not the be-all and end-all that it is now. Ken and I shared the same opinion about the car being driveable in the race, so we did a lot of heavy and mid-race fuel loads during practice and we would finish practice with a car that could do the whole race very well rather than being a sprint special. Ken was very clear on this. "You've got to finish," he would say. "If you do that, then you'll be in a strong position." Sure enough, when we finished in 1969, it was usually first or second. So, starting from the middle of the front row at Zandvoort, with a car which I knew to be in good shape, was exactly what we both wanted.'

The wisdom of the Tyrrell philosophy was amply demonstrated in the race. The Lotus pair led initially, Stewart moving into second place after a few laps, the Scot (or 'the long-haired Scot' as the media referred to him, in deference to his trendy coiffeur) perfectly positioned to take the lead when Rindt's Lotus broke down. Stewart was never troubled for the rest of the afternoon, his third win moving him clear of Hill (who had also retired) on the points table. This was becoming a habit, one which was summed up perfectly by Simon Taylor's post-French Grand Prix *Autosport* editorial two weeks later: 'It isn't really news that Jackie Stewart won another Grand Prix for Matra last Sunday; or that he was fastest in every practice session, earning pole position by the margin of 1.8 seconds; or that he went straight into the lead at the drop of the flag and pro- ceeded to pull out a lead at something like two seconds a lap; or that he now has more than twice as many championship points as his nearest rival. However, it was rather fitting that it was the French Grand Prix that should have seen such a Matra triumph, rivalling only their Stewart/Beltoise one-two at Zandvoort last year [1968]. Matra may be using British engines, British tyres, a Scots driver and a brilliant British team manager, but there can be no doubt that on most circuits and in most conditions the French chassis is the most competitive. It was Ken Tyrrell's finest hour.'

The back pages of the same issue carried an advertisement for the RAC British Grand Prix at Silverstone on Saturday, 19 July. The blurb talked about Formula 1 coming to the fastest circuit in the country. Admission to each of the two days of practice would be 10 shillings (50p), and this would rise to £1 on race day. For an extra 50 shillings (£2.50) spectators could have a grandstand seat, and a further 30 shillings (£1.50) would gain admission to the paddock, where they could virtually rub shoulders with the stars. The advertisement was titled, 'The Race of the Year!'. For once, the copywriters were on the mark. It would turn out to be one of the best races ever seen.

The light-blue Matra International truck edged into the gravel paddock on the Wednesday afternoon after the three-hour run from Ockham. Three cars were unloaded – two MS80s and the four-wheel-drive MS84. By today's standards the place was a mess thanks to the Silverstone organizers having made a half-hearted attempt to clear the rubbish left over from a club race the previous weekend. The three cars were parked on the gravel with litter and debris all around. A few wheels were stacked here and there with each mechanic's rather battered fold-up toolbox open and ready for business. The transporter was parked alongside with a white Ford transit nearby, the rather ropey-looking van being used to ferry wheels and tyres to the Dunlop compound and backwards and forwards to the pit lane. The transporter and cars might have been parked directly behind the pits, but there was a chest-high fence separating them from the pit lane. This was in the days before garages, and it was necessary to manoeuvre each racing car to a collection area at the far end of the paddock, from where they would be released onto the track and into the pit lane at the appointed hour, the procedure being reversed when practice had finished. Nobody complained. This was the way it worked in 1969.

Matra International was the yardstick. Apart from their impressive transporter, each of the six mechanics was dressed in smart light-blue overalls and a tartan cap and went about his business with the minimum of drama. Tyrrell and his team might have been a model of quiet efficiency, but the same could not be said of Lotus when the red and gold truck eventually arrived to disgorge a handful of cars and nothing but discontent. Colin Chapman had become passionate about his four-wheel-drive car, the Lotus 63, so much so that he had sold the faithful 49Bs Hill and Rindt had used with such success. A row between Chapman and the drivers (particularly Rindt) led to the hasty return of the 49s and the farming out of the unloved 63s to a hapless test driver, John Miles, and the Swede Jo Bonnier, who watched in dismay as the competitive 49B he thought he had just purchased was taken back 'on loan'. Since Gold Leaf Team Lotus was perceived to be Tyrrell's main rival, the frosty atmosphere played into Stewart's hands. Or it should have done. As things turned out, Ken's team would have troubles of their own.

Practice started off on a positive note when Stewart was fastest at the end of the first session on the Thursday morning. Lotus did not appear at all. A further sign of the era's relaxed nature came when Graham Hill cheerfully agreed to complete a few laps in a Brabham, the team's regular driver, Jacky Ickx, having found himself delayed at Brussels airport. It was the equivalent of Michael Schumacher taking a Williams for a spin on behalf of an indisposed Juan Pablo Montoya. The scenario became even more bizarre when a nonplussed Ickx finally arrived, climbed into the car, and was 0.4 seconds slower than Hill.

Matters became more serious on Friday, particularly when the two-hour session in the afternoon had the added attraction of a financial bonus. The *Daily Express* was offering £100 at the end of each half-hour for the quickest lap in the preceding 30 minutes. It looked to be an easy £400 for Tyrrell. Stewart ventured out at the beginning of the first half-hour, set a very quick time, then retired to the pits from where he watched with wry amusement as the rest tried to deny Tyrrell his first £100. The lap of 1m 21.1s was good enough, and Stewart continued to demoralize the opposition at the beginning of the second period by producing a lap of 1m 20.6s, which would turn out to be the fastest lap of the weekend. But, as events were about to prove, it would be of no use to Stewart when deciding his grid position.

With £200 in his pocket, Tyrrell decided to put the next half-hour to good use by sending out Stewart in the MS84. This proved little, other than the fact that the four-wheel-drive car was a couple of seconds off the pace. Stewart returned to the MS80 for the final few minutes of the third period, his target a 1m 21.4s set by Rindt. He really went to work, sliding the blue car through the quick corners that dominated the circuit. Rindt's time looked as if it was about to be savaged as Stewart rushed under the *Daily Express* bridge at 175mph aiming for the long and very fast Woodcote corner at the end of the lap. With his usual precision, even at these speeds, Stewart placed his right front wheel on the edge of a kerb at the apex of the corner. Little did he realize that the concrete there had started to break up. The front wheel flicked a jagged piece into a vertical position and it promptly punctured the right rear tyre. From being in total control, Stewart instantly became a passenger. The Matra spun across the track and the outside grass verge before thudding heavily into the wooden sleepers opposite the pits. Almost before anyone had had time to register what had happened, Stewart had flicked off his belts and was out of the car, gesticulating at marshals to warn approaching drivers of the hazard on the inside of the corner. The session was stopped and the car removed, the Tyrrell mechanics recognizing immediately that the Matra, with its broken rear suspension and dented chassis, would not be fit to race the following day.

The dilemma was obvious. With the rules requiring a driver to race the very car he had qualified, Beltoise was asked to hand his MS80 to Stewart while the MS84 was made ready for the Frenchman to qualify. With just over 30 minutes remaining, all thought of £100 bonuses went out of the window. Stewart had a job to do, particularly as there was no time to adjust the driving position and pedals on Beltoise's car. It was a mark of the Scotsman that he nevertheless recorded a lap of 1m 21.2s, good enough for the middle of the front row; Beltoise struggled round in 1m 31.2s to join Bonnier at the back of the 17-car grid. Rindt, meanwhile, had taken pole position with a lap of 1m 20.8s. Despite the setback and near miss for Stewart and Tyrrell, all was set fair for the battle to end all battles.

From the moment the starter dropped the Union flag, Stewart and Rindt were in a class of their own. On the first lap alone they were more than three seconds quicker than the next man, Denny Hulme; by the end of five laps they had destroyed the lap record, Rindt leading Stewart by less than half a second as both men drove on the absolute limit every inch of the way. Stewart took the lead on lap six and immediately set another fastest lap. He improved on this time two laps later, but when Rindt went quicker still on lap nine and again on lap 11 the gap between first and second place was a mere three-tenths of a second. Hulme and the rest were 15 seconds and a different world away.

They drove nose to tail, sometimes alongside each other. The pace was breathtaking as the Matra and Lotus swept through the wide, fast curves. Between laps eight and 15, Stewart recorded either a 1m 22.2s or a 1m 22.3s. Rindt covered his every move, a lap of 1m 22.1s taking him on to the Matra's gearbox as they came to lap Beltoise, struggling along with the four-wheel-drive car. There followed a moment of confusion, Stewart diving to one side of the Frenchman, Rindt to the other – and the Lotus came out in front.

They were among the backmarkers now, but the gap between them was never more than half a second. On and on they went, lap after lap, the times never varying by more than a tenth of a second. It was a truly mesmerizing contest between two of the fastest men in Formula 1. 'It was the cleanest race you could ever wish for,' said Stewart. 'Jochen and I were good friends; we saw a lot of each other where we lived in Switzerland. I trusted him on the track and he trusted me. If one of us got alongside, the other allowed enough room. But you knew he would attack again given the slightest opportunity. We were absolutely flat out all the way. It was an incredible race.'

On lap 38, close to half distance, Rindt and Stewart scythed through a tense five-car battle for fifth place, Rindt making the most of it and extending his advantage to three seconds. But the Tyrrell pit was keeping Jackie informed as he prepared another attack. It came on lap 57, Stewart raising his pace to cover the 2.9 miles in 1m 21.3s, the fastest lap of the race. He did it again on lap 60. The gap was just over a second. The third-place driver, Ickx, was more than a minute behind. No one noticed the Brabham. No one cared. The crowd of 100,000 was transfixed by the battle for first place, the red, white and gold car towing the blue one in its wake as they averaged 129mph lap after lap. Rindt knew Stewart was about to have a go. So did the spectators, poised either on tiptoe or on the edge of their seats. An hour and 18 minutes seemed to have passed in the twinkling of an eye.

Then the race and Rindt's car fell apart. An end-plate on the rear wing of the Lotus had come adrift, and every time the Austrian flung his car into the right-handers that peppered Silverstone, the errant piece of metal rubbed on his left rear wheel. Stewart, meanwhile, was ready to pounce, lining himself up as they rushed down Hangar Straight at 175mph and snatching the lead as they braked for Stowe. As Stewart completed lap 62, Rindt darted into the pits to have the offending part torn off. The stop took 34 seconds, enough to have Rindt rejoin in second place, but out of contention. The feeling of anticlimax was massive. Stewart immediately dropped his pace and cruised to his fifth Grand Prix win in six races.

As the F1 circus decamped to Mill Hill for the traditional party hosted by the Hills, it almost went unsaid that only the most exceptional circumstances could deny Stewart and Tyrrell the championship. When Stewart finished second to Ickx at the Nürburgring two weeks later, he required just a single second place at any of the remaining four races to secure the title.

Stewart duly obliged in the best possible way on 7 September at Monza by winning a thrilling slip-streaming battle; a mere one-fifth of a second covered the first four finishers after 230 miles of wheel-to-wheel racing. Typically, this victory came about more as a result of judgement than luck, Tyrrell and Stewart having thought the whole thing through. Shunning the use of a rear wing in the interests of speed on this flat-out circuit, Stewart also employed a long fourth gear with the final sprint to the flag in mind. Beltoise, on the other hand, opted to run a rear wing, which gave him better braking and more stability as the leading pack arrived at Parabolica, the final corner. The Frenchman outbraked everyone to take the lead, but then ran slightly wide, allowing Stewart and Rindt to slip inside. It was between the Lotus and the Matra as they accelerated side by side towards the flag, the act of changing from fourth to fifth just enough to drop Rindt back by 0.08 seconds at the line.

Dick Jeffrey of Dunlop now had every excuse in the book to break out the champagne. This championship owed just as much to the efficiency of the tyres as the speed of the car and the skill of the driver. As ever, Tyrrell remained low key and kept the celebrations to a minimum. 'We had come to expect nothing more from Ken,' Stewart remarked with a chuckle. 'It didn't change a single thing. I mean, he didn't go and buy himself a new jacket or anything like that!' Mechanic Roger Hill agreed. 'It was pretty typical of Ken. To be honest, I can't remember anything about a celebration. Obviously we were really pleased to have won the championship – it was a sort of official recognition that we were the team to beat – but there was no wild partying or anything like that. We packed up and got on with the job. It was the way Ken worked. He was very, very good at keeping everyone's feet on the ground. And by doing that he managed to get everyone to pull in the same direction all the time. When you're working as a team, you can't have three or four groups pulling in different directions. So Ken's way of working ensured that never happened. It was the same with Mrs Tyrrell. She was always worried about us, be it a mechanic, a truck driver or Ken. She kept an eye on everyone, particularly if you weren't well or something. That and Ken's attitude just kept this feeling of family within the team. Yes, sure it was nice to win, but Ken was always looking round the corner to see what was coming next.'

And well he might. Unbelievably, the reigning world champions were about to find themselves without a car for the coming season, the result of a most bizarre set of circumstances, even in a business already noted for its moments of profound uncertainty. The Tyrrell Racing Organization was about to go from nirvana to nightmare in a matter of months.

11

A Heap of Scrap

Three weeks after winning the championship at Monza, Jackie Stewart flew to New York to appear on *Today*, a high-profile TV show. All seemed well with his world as the trendy sportsman with his smart clothes, sideburns and collar-length hair chatted easily about his season and the forthcoming United States Grand Prix. Inside, however, Stewart was worried. This race, plus the final round in Mexico, would be his last with the Matra MS80. Stewart and Tyrrell knew that would be the case since changes to the technical rules for 1970 required Matra to build a new car, one that was likely to be even better than the MS80. The point was, Stewart would not be driving it.

Matra was about to be taken over by Simca, and it had been made clear by their parent company, Chrysler, that a Ford engine in the back of 'their' car would be as unwelcome as a can of Coke at a Pepsi-Cola convention. Stewart and Tyrrell were urged to run a Matra with the V12, but the former's doubts were confirmed when he tested the Matra engine. 'I drove the Matra V12 at Albi in France on the day after we had a Formula 2 race there,' said Stewart. 'It felt good, but it just didn't feel like a racer. It was driveable but it felt too calm; there was no bite to it. The Ford Cosworth engine was kind of raw by comparison. It didn't have a lot of smooth edges when it came to feeling the engine work. The vibrations in the car were coarse, yet there was a solid feel to them. It felt robust. The Matra sang more sweetly, but that's not what you wanted. It was like a soprano, but you knew that the baritone was stronger. It got there slowly and comfortably whereas the Ford DFV was surging in each gear, really wanting to go with some urgency. It confirmed my doubts about using the V12, even though we knew [using the Ford DFV] would mean having to look elsewhere for a chassis that almost certainly would not be as good as anything Matra was likely to produce. But without a competitive engine, the best car in the world is going nowhere.'

Stewart and Tyrrell had made a rod for their own backs. Neither Lotus nor Brabham fancied selling a car to a team which was likely to use it to give them grief on the race track. BRM was willing to provide a chassis, but, like Matra, would not contemplate having it powered by anything but their home-grown engine. Ferrari, of course, was out of the question, but there was the thought that Stewart could race for McLaren since Bruce McLaren was thinking about reducing his driving commitment in F1. In any case, there was a clash across the board since Stewart and Tyrrell were with Dunlop and the rest were contracted elsewhere.

If Stewart thought the prospects looked bleak, the situation was about to get even worse when he travelled north from New York to Watkins Glen. On his arrival at the Glen Motor Inn, Stewart was called to Tyrrell's room. Ken told Jackie that the Dunlop board of directors had just decided to withdraw from racing and therefore could not support the Tyrrell team in 1970. 'It was a total and complete shock,' said Stewart. 'I was stunned, and so was Ken. We had built up a tremendous relationship with Dunlop and won the championship together. We couldn't understand the decision because Dunlop had gained so much, and would continue to do so, in terms of publicity from our association. But the point was, it was October, and the competition had already sorted their plans for 1970 with Goodyear and Firestone.'

Stewart and Tyrrell went to work, using all the powers of persuasion at their disposal. At the end of a two-and-a-half-hour meeting in England, they came away having persuaded the Dunlop directors to approach the board and attempt to reverse the decision. Two days later, Stewart and Tyrrell learned that they had been successful. The funding was back on stream, but there was not yet a car on which to lavish it. Ken was hoping for a last-minute reprieve from Matra, but in his heart of hearts he knew it was a forlorn wish.

The situation had not improved by January 1970, although by this time a new name had entered the frame. March Engineering had been founded at the end of 1969 by an ambitious consortium comprising Robin Herd, Alan Rees, Graham Coaker and Max Mosley – who would later become president of the sport's governing body, the FIA – all of whom had been involved in motor racing in various capacities. They astounded the racing community with audacious plans that included building and racing cars in Formula 3, Formula 2 and the CanAm sports car series in North America. But the claim that March would enter a team in Formula 1 was more difficult to believe, particularly when they offered to make their F1 car, the 701, available to whoever wished to buy one. Tyrrell was a prime candidate. For March, having the world champion on board for their maiden season would be a priceless endorsement of their product.

The truth was, Tyrrell's options were being reduced to virtually zero as the first Grand Prix beckoned. He began discussions with Mosley, a barrister and former racing driver whose sublime skills in court had not been mirrored on the track. Mosley had decided he would be better at selling cars than driving them, but his astute business brain would not allow him to accept Tyrrell's offer of £6,000 for an F1 car Mosley felt was worth £9,000. Even though time was getting tight, Tyrrell would not budge. Mosley, realizing that Ford would not want to lose Stewart to a rival engine manufacturer, gently nudged the American giant into agreeing to make up the £3,000 shortfall. Now it was certain that Jackie Stewart would drive a March-Ford in 1970.

So, too, would Chris Amon and Jo Siffert in the works cars. Then

March pulled off another extraordinary coup when they persuaded the STP Oil Corporation in America to sponsor a March for the reigning Indycar champion, Mario Andretti. The motor racing world was deeply impressed. Taking a more pragmatic view, Stewart felt March had bitten off more than it could chew, but those doubts were to be supplanted by more serious worries once he had actually driven the car.

Stewart kept a diary throughout 1970 and the entries became more despairing by the day. On 16 February, following the first test with the March 701, Stewart wrote that the car wouldn't go any faster despite all manner of adjustments. Five days later, he referred to the car as being 'nothing to rave about', particularly when it could not get close to the lap times established with the MS80. 'Both Ken and I feel the problems are inherent to the car's design,' he wrote. 'These are not the sort of things you can overcome through suspension tuning. So we're stuck.'

That might have been so, but the world at large was not to know about the car's shortcomings, particularly when March 701s filled the first two places on the grid for the opening race of the season in South Africa. Stewart was on pole. 'Quite surprising really' was to be the height of his enthusiasm for a car he continued to find very difficult to drive; he considered himself lucky to finish third behind the Brabham-Ford of Jack Brabham and Denny Hulme's McLaren-Ford. Not even a win in the non-championship Race of Champions would change Stewart's opinion as the blue car darted and bucked on the bumps of Brands Hatch. Similarly, a win in the Spanish Grand Prix at Jarama on 19 April would prove almost embarrassing as the March phenomenon gathered a momentum it didn't really deserve. Even though Jackie had led from start to finish, Stewart and Tyrrell knew the win had partially fallen into their laps thanks to the opposition being either uncompetitive or unreliable, Tyrrell's usual excellent preparation paying off on a day when only five of the 16 starters had reached the end of the race. The second Tyrrell-March, driven by Johnny Servoz-Gavin, had finished fifth.

With Beltoise having returned to the works Matra team, Ken had given the talented French youngster another chance in F1. For reasons which were hard to pinpoint, Servoz-Gavin's performances thus far in 1970 had had none of the wonderful flair displayed during his admittedly short-lived debut at Monaco two years earlier. When he crashed and failed to qualify for the next race – at Monaco, of all places – Servoz-Gavin told Ken he was quitting. With immediate effect. Unbeknown to Tyrrell, his driver had sustained an eye injury when struck by a branch while taking part in an off-road event during the winter. The sight in his right eye had been impaired, and private hopes that it would make a full recovery were dashed when his vision continued to prove troublesome, particularly while racing. He went on television and was prepared to admit that driving a racing car now frightened him. The charismatic Frenchman walked away and the motor racing community never saw him again.

Stewart, meanwhile, added further to the March legend when he qualified on pole, alongside Amon's similar car, and led for 27 laps until ignition trouble intervened. He watched the final laps of the Monaco race knowing that his championship lead was about to disappear as Jack Brabham headed for victory, Amon's March having retired when a bolt dropped out of the rear suspension. Stewart and Tyrrell had seen their fair share of drama in motor racing, but even they were amazed when the normally astute Brabham locked up his brakes on the approach to the very last corner and nosed into the straw bales, leaving Rindt's Lotus to nip through and take a victory no one expected. Brabham recovered to finish second, but even with the loss of three potential points the Australian now led Stewart in the championship.

Ken and Jackie were giving a lot of thought to finding a second driver. Since the end of the liaison with Matra, Tyrrell no longer ran a Formula 2 team, but the series remained popular among the drivers. Stewart raced a Brabham for John Coombs, the Guildford garage owner, and Ken joined him at an F2 race at Crystal Palace in south London to check out the promising young talent. Tyrrell had the names Clay Regazzoni, Emerson Fittipaldi and Tim Schenken on his list. When he discovered that the first two were committed elsewhere and Schenken had yet to gain enough experience, Tyrrell paid closer attention to a handsome Frenchman with penetrating dark eyes and, much more importantly, a raw but natural speed.

François Cevert had been making a name for himself across Europe. This son of a wealthy Parisian jeweller had won the 1968 French F3 championship for Tecno, and the Italian marque had given him an F2 drive the following year. Jackie witnessed his potential at close quarters when Cevert led the first heat at Crystal Palace before Stewart found a way through; he was too busy squabbling for the lead in the final to notice Cevert's impressive form as he held a superb fourth place until an over-enthusiastic Emerson Fittipaldi bundled the Tecno into the wall. But Tyrrell had seen enough, and Cevert was asked to test a March soon after. Apart from his latent ability, there was the additional bonus that Cevert was French, a fact that would please Tyrrell's sponsor, Elf, and the oil firm's motor sport director, François Guiter.

To the surprise of many, Elf had opted to stay with Tyrrell despite the split between the English team and Matra. Guiter had absolutely no doubt about continuing his company's support. 'Jackie did not like the Matra engine, and this was no surprise,' he said. 'The engine was good for Le Mans, but not Formula 1. We followed Ken because we trusted him. It was that simple. And, obviously, Jackie was one of the very best drivers and it was very good for Elf to be associated with him. The March was not a good car and yet they won a Grand Prix. It did not matter how! Elf made the most of the publicity. We were very happy to stay with Ken.'

Stewart's was the lone Tyrrell entry for the Belgian Grand Prix at the beginning of June. It was a measure of the Scotsman's commitment that he put the recalcitrant car on pole at a circuit that continued to frighten the drivers more than they cared to admit. Stewart was again vocal in his condemnation of the absence of safety

facilities on the eight mile road course, describing it and the Nürburgring as the two most dangerous circuits in the world. He freely
admitted he did not wish to leave Geneva and go to race at either
track simply because he could never be sure he would return home.
But when the time came to pull on his crash helmet, Stewart closed
his mind to the doubts at the same moment as he shut his visor.

Regardless of what his driver might have been doing out of the
cockpit, Tyrrell knew Stewart would deliver once the stopwatches
were running. And at Spa in 1970 he did so in spades: the Tyrrell-
March was two seconds faster than anyone else, a truly astonishing
margin. No sooner had that been accomplished than Stewart was in
the thick of a meeting of the members of the Grand Prix Drivers
Association (GPDA). It was a heated affair, summed up by Jackie
with a note in his diary to the effect that he was baffled by the lack of
prudence shown by one or two drivers, particularly Ickx, who was,
of course, Belgian and a huge fan of his home circuit and all its
inherent dangers. 'Jacky has an image that is the direct opposite
to mine,' wrote Stewart. 'He has short hair, I've got long hair; he
wears three-piece suits, I go mod; he talks about risks while I talk
about safety.'

Stewart also had to contend with the fact that Ken, despite trusting his driver implicitly, was occasionally concerned about his being
unnecessarily affected by the extra-curricular activity. 'It's true,'
Stewart confirmed. 'Ken used to get on to me about working on the
safety thing and getting too excited and pushing not to race on
certain tracks such as the Nürburgring. He always thought that it
would have taken something out of me and weakened my potential
performance. He was always worried that it would happen, but he
later recognized that it never did. And he could never understand
why!

'In that respect, we were quite similar. Ken had had his front
teeth, shall we say, rearranged after some accident or other when he
was racing. When he got excited and was giving you what-for, you'd
get this froth job when he'd come close to foaming at the mouth.

But the point was, even the worst froth job and telling off wouldn't in any way impede his appreciation or his care for that person. He would give the most enormous rattle to your cage and he'd do it in a very graphic and expressive manner, yet you would still remain good friends. With a lot of people, if you ever fell out to the level that Ken quite often did after verbally attacking you or abusing you, you would have said, "Right, that's it! You go off and do your own thing and I'll do mine." But that was never a consideration Ken would have had. He saw my behaviour to be rather similar to his in that he would feel terribly strongly about something and yet, once he had said what he had to say, it was finished. But his feeling was that he had to say it – quite categorically, most times! So when I was doing my thing, particularly on safety, he was prepared to put up with that because he had come to realize it wasn't affecting my performance.'

Safety was rapidly becoming a sensitive issue. Stewart led the Belgian Grand Prix briefly before retiring with engine failure. He was glad of the chance to get away from the place at the end of a week of hugely mixed emotions. A few days before Spa, the motor racing world had been stunned by the news that Bruce McLaren had been killed during a private test session at Goodwood. Immensely popular, the New Zealander had, like Jim Clark, seemed a safe, responsible driver who was quick without putting himself or anyone else at risk. But fate takes no consideration of common sense. While thundering down the back straight at 180mph in his orange 7.5 litre CanAm M8D, the rear bodywork had become detached and McLaren's beautiful racing car had suddenly become a horrible projectile, flinging itself into a marshals' post and kill-ing the driver instantly. The fact that it happened on a Tuesday, a time when no one expected to be assailed by tragedy, merely added to the sense of shock and grief. And there was worse to come, if such a terrible thing can be qualified in this way, two weeks later at Zandvoort in Holland.

Piers Courage had also been an early retirement at Spa, his de

Tomaso-Ford having stopped with low oil pressure. The 28-year-old Englishman was seen as a future star, particularly by his entrant, Frank Williams. Courage and Williams had built up a tremendous rapport even though they came from opposite ends of the social spectrum: Courage, the scion of the brewing family; Williams, brought up by a single mum in the north of England but just as passionate as Courage about cars and motor racing. Williams had tried his hand at racing but his enthusiasm had frequently got the better of him and he did considerable damage to his cars and his bank balance. Far better, Williams reasoned, to buy and sell this and that in order to raise the money to run a small team. The rapid rise to Formula 1 had been extraordinary, Williams barely pausing for breath as Courage's speed and flair bolstered the dream that this small outfit could one day win races. It was only natural, therefore, that Frank Williams should see Ken Tyrrell as a role model and a modest hero.

'I remember seeing Ken, I think it was in the paddock at Silverstone in 1964,' Williams recalled. 'This was at the time when he was running that unbeatable Cooper F3 team with wee Jackie and Warwick Banks. I was acting as a "gofer" – go for this, go for that – helping out people where I could and trying to raise money in the process so that I could race a fairly old Brabham. I managed to do about half a dozen races, so I was in racing, but more on the nuisance fringe than anything else. Like everyone else, I followed Ken's progress with keen interest, and by 1969–70 there was no question that he was the top. I considered him to be my role model from the point of view of running a team. But I also admired his relationship with Jackie and I was trying to emulate that with Piers.'

Williams and Courage had been having a frustrating time thus far in 1970. Their car, built by the Italian company de Tomaso, had proved difficult and unreliable, the combination failing to finish a single race. But in Holland things were looking up when Courage qualified ninth and then broke free from a mid-field scrap to run in seventh place during the race. A points finish looked to be a possibility until lap 23, when a thick column of black smoke changed everything. Going through the fast sweeps at the back of the circuit, Courage had run wide at 140mph, crashed into a bank, hit a post and overturned. He perished in the subsequent inferno. Williams was completely devastated. The F1 circus rallied round and, once again, it fell to Jackie Stewart to take care of the arrangements to get rid of the wreckage and help officials establish just what had gone wrong. Two days later, Stewart and Tyrrell attended a memorial service for Bruce McLaren at St Paul's Cathedral. The day after that, they travelled to a small parish church in Essex to bury Piers. It seemed completely irrelevant that the Tyrrell-March had finished second the previous Sunday and put Stewart back on top of the championship.

But the show would go on. It seemed trite to say so, but Bruce and Piers would have wanted it that way. Had they been around, they would have been eagerly joining in conversation about the latest phenomenon from the stable of Colin Chapman to arrive in F1. Apart from the first two laps, the Dutch Grand Prix had been led from start to finish by Jochen Rindt in a Lotus 72. This car set new standards in the manner of Chapman's Lotus 49 in 1967 and Tyrrell's Matra MS80 in 1969. Alongside the March 701, the wedge-shaped Lotus 72 was a red and white sliver of speed compared with a blue brick on wheels. It looked likely that Stewart's championship lead would be short-lived. 'The March really was a very unattractive car to drive in every respect,' Stewart recalled. 'It wasn't elegant to look at and it certainly wasn't smooth and elegant to drive. You were just on the edge of everything all the time. But that's what it took to make it go fast – and it was fast if you did that. But at Zandvoort we realized we were just no match for the Lotus. The 72 was on a different continent. There was no comparison. Added to that, Brabham was in better shape with his new car, the BT33. We were simply up against it, and, to be honest, we had done well to get that win in Spain and even to get as far as leading the championship halfway through the season. But we were under no illusions.'

As if to compound the impending misery, on 11 June Stewart received an unwelcome, if not entirely unexpected, 31st birthday present when Dunlop formally announced their planned withdrawal from racing at the end of the season. This time, there would be no going back. The announcement merely accelerated plans being hatched in secret down in the Ockham wood yard.

Meanwhile, the racing went from bad to worse, Stewart's efforts in France and Britain hampered by a troublesome electrics control box that kept him out of the points. Cevert had joined the team in Holland, where he had retired with engine trouble; he followed this with 11th place at Clermont Ferrand and a creditable seventh at Brands Hatch. In between these races, Stewart had been commuting across the Atlantic to take part in the CanAm series, and honouring his F2 commitments. With the recent tragedies, things began to take their toll. 'I returned to Geneva exhausted,' Stewart wrote in his diary on 21 July. 'My energy and drive were in a state of collapse. I feel almost lost, I don't have a heart, there is no will to race or do anything. When I sit, I'm glued to my seat. At times I'm actually dizzy. My nights are fitful. I awoke this morning with my fists clenched, and I have no idea what to do about it. Never before has this happened. The doctor would probably tell me I'm overworked and prescribe tranquillizers. I wouldn't take them. I called Ken. I told him how I'm feeling, everything I'm going through, and asked what he thought I ought to do. Very predictable. He told me I have to handle it on my own.'

The high ambient temperature of Hockenheim in late July did not help Stewart as he continued to wrestle with the car in preparation for the German Grand Prix. His struggle in the race was brought to a premature conclusion, the engine failure doing Stewart more than one favour as he made a quick escape. By early evening he was in London with Helen; together, they watched the world go by in Hyde Park. This unexpected opportunity for relaxation allowed him the time to ponder his life, to compare the respective values of the world outside with the sometimes false existence of a top racing driver. Suddenly, he found all his problems were put in perspective. This positive period of introspection soon banished all the listlessness and lack of energy.

There was no such resolution with the car. At least Stewart felt more able to deal with its problems as the circus moved to Austria, where Tyrrell's drivers were forced to retire with mechanical trouble. Stewart's championship was history, but at least he was in a healthier frame of mind. Then came the Italian Grand Prix at Monza, where the monkey thudded onto his back again.

During practice on the Saturday, Rindt's Lotus crashed as he braked from 180mph for the Parabolica. The car turned sharp left and smashed into a steel barrier, the impact tearing off the front suspension and bulkhead. Rindt was gravely injured by the seat-belt buckle – a terrible price to pay for not wearing the crotch straps that would have prevented him from 'submarineing', or being pulled down into the cockpit. But Stewart knew none of the details; he, along with the rest of the pit lane, had merely been told that Rindt had crashed. One official even went so far as to say that Rindt was okay and had spoken on the telephone from the marshals' post.

Stewart went immediately to the medical centre and was thrust into a scene of appalling chaos as spectators and photographers crowded around the ambulance carrying medical people working feverishly on the seriously injured driver. There was no system of control, no obvious person to speak to. It was Italian mayhem at its worst. One look at the horrifying scene in the ambulance was enough for Stewart. Now he had to stay calm and take care of Rindt's wife Nina, as well as informing Chapman and Bernie Ecclestone, Rindt's manager and close friend, that the situation was extremely serious. Then he had to find Helen in the midst of this dreadful pandemonium on a hot afternoon.

When Stewart finally got back to the pits, Ken was waiting for him. He didn't need to ask about the outcome; Stewart's face said it all. 'Right,' said Tyrrell. 'Hurry up and get in the car. There's only fifteen minutes left and I want you to get a good time before the session stops.' Stewart pulled on his flameproof balaclava and helmet, but the emotions of the moment suddenly swept over him, the awful acceptance of the fact that his close friend was almost certainly dead. Pulling himself together, Stewart slid into the cockpit of the March. 'Again, I started to cry,' he wrote. 'I tasted salt. I sat there and people tried not to look at me and I knew there was nothing I could do to stop the crying, so I went out. And as soon as I got going, it stopped. I was all right. I ran four laps and came in on the checker and my last lap was the fastest I had ever done at Monza and the fastest I would do that weekend. It was said that I was trying to hurt myself, that it was suicidal. But it wasn't. It felt the same as any other lap.'

Stewart later understood why Ken had told him to get into the car, that it had been a result of the understanding between the two men. 'I knew I had to get in the car and go out,' said Stewart. 'That's where we had an amazing relationship. We were so close that it was one of those hand-rubbing things where Ken was being firm, and leaving no doubt in my mind. There was no drama. Ken must have been aware that I was concerned because Helen had to go with Nina to Milan, and he must have realized I knew there was no hope for Jochen. All sorts of people came up afterwards and said, "Ah, you just didn't care, did you?" That's not me at all. It was just a very clean, good lap, and it was the best lap I did. If Ken was around now – and he should be, by the way – he would say that it was another Nürburgring in the sense that he didn't force me to go out but he and I both knew it had to be done. Some people might have expected me to go out and do a "regulation" lap and then come in, park, go away and sit down somewhere. But Ken wouldn't have expected that. I knew, once he said it was time to go out, that I would deliver for him. If he had thought I had been so upset that it would have been really negative, I think he would have taken another view. But he didn't, and it never occurred to me that I shouldn't go out. We actually had a chance of winning that race, even in the March! I drove what I thought was a pretty good race. I was out of touch with the leader but nevertheless finished second.'

As Stewart beat a hasty retreat to the airport and a friend's waiting Lear jet, his mind was on the well-being of Nina Rindt and Helen. There was, however, some good news to consider. Very good news, in fact. There were still three races remaining and it was pretty certain Stewart would never need to drive the dreadful March 701 again.

12

Let's Do It Ourselves

'I was riding into Guildford with Ken one day and I was saying what a heap of rubbish the March was,' recalled Neil Davis. 'I said I couldn't understand why we didn't build our own car. Surely we could do better than this? Ken was very secretive about everything. He paused for a few seconds. Then he said, "I want you to keep this to yourself, Neil. I'm thinking of building my own car." That was the start of it.'

Tyrrell's hand had been forced by the shenanigans a few months before, at the beginning of 1970. It seemed ridiculous to Ken that the future plans of the reigning world champions should be dictated by what they could – or, in most cases, could not – buy from other manufacturers. The alternative was for Tyrrell to build his own car. It was a route he did not particularly want to take since it would mean more worry and an end to the convenient arrangement whereby a partner such as Matra would take care of all the concerns about designing, building and repairing the chassis. But the plain truth was, Tyrrell had no option.

The wood yard would make a suitable location in more ways than one. Ken had bought the land and the two cottages on it for £15,000 on 25 March 1970. The wooden shed would make a reasonable workshop, and the natural screen provided by the trees would help maintain the secrecy Tyrrell felt was vital. The most difficult question for the moment would be finding a designer for the car, someone preferably without a high profile on the F1 scene. Tyrrell was not interested in a freelance; he wanted a designer who was in a position to stay with the project full time. Typically, he had in mind someone whom he thought might make a suitable candidate even though this man had never designed a car in his life.

While working with Matra on the four-wheel-drive MS84, Tyrrell had met Derek Gardner, a studious Englishman who specialized in transmissions. Gardner knew a bit about racing thanks to his involvement with Lotus and their four-wheel-drive Indy cars, plus, of course, the Matra F1 car. The MS84, in fact, had raced four times in the hands of Beltoise and Servoz-Gavin in 1969, scoring a point for a sixth place in the Canadian Grand Prix. Initially, Gardner had felt that four-wheel-drive would be better than conventional rear-wheel-drive, but he subsequently changed his mind when, as he put it, 'the four-wheel-drive car started asking more mechanical questions than we were ever to find answers for'. Nevertheless, Gardner's association with Matra meant Tyrrell already knew enough about the man's methodical approach. He also knew Gardner's home phone number in Leamington Spa.

'I had a call from Ken, asking if we could meet somewhere to discuss something I might be interested in,' Gardner recalled in an interview with Eoin Young of *Autocar*. 'We met at a little pub on the Thames at Henley, somewhere we reckoned was halfway between Leamington Spa and East Horsley. Ken, fairly typically, came straight to the point and asked if I thought I could design a Formula 1 car. He said he didn't want an answer straight away. But the one provision Ken made was that no one, but no one, was to know anything about this.

'I spent some time considering whether I could design a Grand Prix car; then, having decided that I could, I wondered whether I should! I knew what the answer would be before I started my deliberations, but I had to convince myself. I finally agreed and left my existing job.

'Since secrecy was imperative, I set myself up with a "cover" as a private engineering consultant and had stationery printed to that effect so that I could order parts and have machine work carried out without raising any suspicions or having my project connected in any way with the Tyrrell Racing Organization. My anonymity at that stage was an important asset, although I had in fact already established contact with several of the accessory firms while I was at Ferguson Research working on the four-wheel-drive systems, so I wasn't exactly a stranger.'

Gardner converted an upstairs room at his home in Parkland Avenue into a design office, setting up shop with a drawing board, a desk and a few filing cabinets. Having never designed a car before, he was starting with a clean sheet of paper in every respect. The enormity of the task began to sink in when Gardner saw one particular edition of *Wheelbase*, a BBC motoring programme. 'It was all about the new March project,' he recalled. 'There was Jackie whistling round Silverstone with the new March at a time when I was deep in the throes of my own design, unable to ask advice from anyone except Ken on points that puzzled me. I watched Jackie and the March, and there seemed to be no way that I could compete with this sort of thing when I was a one-man band working from home.'

Gardner studied photographs of existing F1 cars and carried out his own investigations on suspension design and car dimensions. In his opinion, the McLaren M7 (as raced in 1969) was the ideal format, but in the end Gardner's creation began to look like the MS80 – no surprise, perhaps, considering his involvement with Matra and the fact that the MS80 was considered to be so good. The truth was that Gardner had set out to design a wedge-shaped car (as the Lotus 72 would be on its first appearance six months later), but the impossibility of finding space for the requisite amount of fuel meant an evolution towards the Coke-bottle plan of the MS80.

Having established a rough idea of the shape of the car, Gardner asked a local firm of joiners to make a mock-up of the cockpit section, to which he added bits of aluminium, cardboard and chicken wire, spraying blue paint on what had become known as the SP (Secret Project). Now the time had come to have an engine and gearbox mounted on the back. This would involve letting a few more people in on the secret, as well as Gardner having to make a great personal sacrifice. Since there was no room inside the house for the mock-up, Gardner had to use his garage – which meant selling his pride and joy, a Mark VI Bentley, because he could not bear the thought of this pristine classic car standing outside, exposed to the elements.

'A couple of weeks after Ken had talked about doing his own car,' said Davis, 'he told me to take a Ford DFV and a gearbox up to Derek's house in Leamington Spa – "but don't tell anybody!" I met Derek in what you might call a pretty standard sort of a house. He took me into the garage, where we unloaded the DFV, and there was this wooden chassis. He was a very methodical man, Derek; a very nice man, very clever with it.'

By now, Stewart was also in on the secret. Ken had mentioned the idea to Jackie at the first race in 1970, in South Africa; the next step was to have the driver sit in the mock-up of what would be his car. The cloak-and-dagger arrangements continued. 'Jackie was doing some testing with the Formula 2 car at Goodwood,' said Gardner. 'During a lull, he jumped into a private plane and whistled up to Coventry. I met him at the airport and drove to my house, which was about 10 minutes away. He tried the mock-up for size, checking on pedal positions and generally tailoring the car to his own requirements. Only Jackie could drive that first car – anyone bigger simply wouldn't have fitted! My daughter, then aged six, was a great Stewart fan, but neither she nor the neighbours knew that a Grand Prix car was taking shape at number 23, or that Jackie had been to the garage to try it for size!'

This ought to have been a pivotal, highly involved moment for Stewart. He was reigning world champion, yet here he was, stealing into Warwickshire on a weekday and slipping into a domestic garage to try out the nucleus of a car that would need to win more races and, hopefully, at least one more title. And he couldn't mention a word about it on pain of a Tyrrell froth job. 'Ken was a private man,' Jackie said. 'He only told me what he needed to tell me initially. It's not that he didn't trust me; he just didn't want to put me in an awkward position. The way his mind worked was like this. If I had something to tell Ken that was confidential, he would rather I didn't tell him. I would say, "Ken, I'm going to tell you something and we've got to keep it a secret," and immediately he would say, "Jackie, I don't want to know." "But I need to tell you." "No, Jackie. I'd rather not know!" If something got out and he was one of the few to know about whatever it was, he just didn't want to be in that position. It was a responsibility he didn't want to take. He felt the same for other people. That was the story of his life. The fewer people who knew, the better. Even in later years when I was doing the Stewart-Ford, he wouldn't let me tell him anything. In fact, he didn't want to come to the launch of our new car. "No," he said. "You don't want me there. How can I be there? You are a competitor. You can't have me having a look at your car. I'm not going on the turntable." He did come to the launch, but he never went near the car. His integrity in things like that was second to none.

'But getting back to the Secret Project, I had absolutely no doubt about going along with it. This was what we had to do. Derek was a modest man, very quiet and certainly not extravagant in the use of his words. Even at such an early stage, I liked the look of the car and what he was trying to do. The MS80 concept was very sound, with the weight in the middle of the car. Of course, designing it was one thing, building it another. But even then there was absolutely no doubt in my mind. I had such confidence in Ken and the people he had gathered around him. They weren't extrovert or gregarious people. Neil [Davis] was a quiet, dedicated guy who had been with Ken from the start. Roger [Hill] was tremendously solid, as were people like Max Rutherford, Roland Law [joint chief mechanic] and Roy Topp [specialized welder]. Terrifically secure and decent people. I mean, even when you talk to them today and ask questions about something in the past, the answer is likely to be, "Sorry, can't tell you anything." Just like Ken!

'It was as if each team cloned people in the image of the leader. At Lotus, for instance, there was a guy called Andrew Ferguson who walked like Colin Chapman, behaved like Chapman. Same with Peter Warr, the Lotus team manager; he was another Chapman in the making. At Tyrrell, the people working there probably didn't think of themselves being like Ken in that respect, but because of the culture he developed and encouraged, everyone was much the same. There was no single individual who would have developed a high profile. It just wasn't like that in the Tyrrell Racing Organization. I had a solid belief in what they were doing. If Ken said it was going to be okay, then it would be okay. Anyway, I always knew that if it failed, I could always drive for someone else. But that was never at the forefront of my thinking. There seemed every reason to believe that this was worth a shot.'

By June, Gardner had finalized his design and the first metal was being cut, Tyrrell having found a specialist sheet metal works about five miles away in Old Woking. The owner, Maurice Gomm, was of course sworn to complete secrecy. Much of the machining was carried out by another small company in the same area. Gardner used the wind tunnel belonging to the mechanical engineering department of the University of Surrey, where he devised a nose with a flat, blade-like front with a swept-back opening beneath to take in the cooling for the radiator. Bit by bit, the parts arrived at the wood yard for final assembly of what would be known as a Tyrrell 001. The date circled on the calendar was 22 August, a week before the Monza GP and the day of the non-championship F1 Gold Cup at Oulton Park in Cheshire.

By the beginning of August Stewart was making visits to the wood yard for seat fittings. 'The car is being constructed at our workshop in Surrey,' he wrote in his diary. 'The shop itself is un-believable. A timber yard with a road going through it, a driveway really, on which you could lose a Mini in the huge potholes. Ken's office, where he normally does his lumber business, has a tree going right up through it, and the place is usually a shambles. You can't believe that, right here, in the corner of some English wood, is housed the organization responsible for some of the finest racing cars in the world, the home of the MS80 Matra, the 1969 championship car, and now the Tyrrell-Ford.'

Sure enough, some people could not believe it. Eoin Young, who lived not far from Ockham, had called in one day to see Ken in connection with a book Young was writing on Bruce McLaren. He was having a cup of coffee with Norah Tyrrell in the office when he asked if there was anything interesting going on in the workshop. Norah, thinking on her feet, assured him there was nothing happening because the cars had not yet returned from the last race. Had Young walked the 50 yards to the shed, he would have stumbled on a major story.

The build programme was in full swing that summer, Ken becoming increasingly nervous about word getting out. 'Roland [Law] stayed back at the factory for those few months when we went to the races,' said Davis. 'We were still only about 12 people in total in those days. We then built the monocoque [chassis] in the lower shed and the fabrication department was in there as well. The car was assembled and built in the wooden shed. Roy Topp was the welder/fabricator, and we had three sheet metal workers. All the wishbones and everything like that were made in there.'

As time raced on, the mechanics were sometimes flown straight back from a Grand Prix by private plane in order to allow more time in the workshop. Such apparently luxurious treatment naturally prompted curious looks and smart remarks, but no one guessed just what was going on. At least no one except Eric Dymock, the motor sport correspondent of the *Guardian*, and even he could not be 100 per cent sure. 'It was almost by accident,' Dymock recalled. 'It was an obscure connection, someone who knew someone who said that Maurice Gomm was building bits for a racing car. I started asking around. Max Mosley confidently assured me that it would be impossible for Ken to build a car without March finding out about it! But I kept asking until I found one or two people who wouldn't say that it was *not* happening. Then I ran the story.'

Under the headline STEWART SET TO DRIVE NEW TYRRELL-FORD, Dymock wrote: 'Jackie Stewart, the world champion racing driver who has been having an unsatisfactory season with his March racing car, may soon have a new one. His entrant, Ken Tyrrell, is believed to have an entirely new car under construction at his small Ripley, Surrey, workshop. It is expected to appear for the Oulton Park Gold Cup race on August 22.' Dymock went on to describe, with commendable accuracy, how the car would be a conventional two-wheel-drive with a body shape like the Matra MS80. Dymock also noted that the fact that Tyrrell's World championship team had felt they had to resort to building their own car at such a late stage in the season was a blow to the prestige of March. 'This was published during the week [beginning 10 August] of the Austrian Grand Prix, and I met Ken on the plane [out there],' Dymock added. 'He gave me a right froth job! He said I was making a terrible fool of myself. But the more cross he became, the more I knew I was probably on the right track. It was to be the only decent scoop I ever had!'

Eoin Young read the story and immediately spoke to Ken. 'You don't think I would be silly enough to build a Formula 1 car, do you?' came the quick retort. Young wasn't so sure, and he became decidedly curious in Austria when Tyrrell appeared more serious than usual. Young noted that Ken was behaving strangely, wearing his spectacles all the time while pacing up and down the pit lane, taking a close look at all the cars. 'I was always under the impression that Ken's interest or knowledge in matters technical exceeded my own by only a very small margin,' Young wrote in his *Autocar* column. 'And I know very little about technical things.'

The day after the Austrian Grand Prix – Monday, 17 August – all was revealed. The great and the good of motor racing were called to Dagenham Motors in London's Regent Street where the drapes were

142

removed from the royal blue car, the first to emerge from the wood-shed at Ockham. It had cost Tyrrell £22,500, including the engine and gearbox. More importantly, 001 weighed a hundred pounds less than the March 701. On that basis alone it was money well spent, the journalists present in the Ford showroom agreeing unanimously about the high standard of preparation.

If Gardner was shy about speaking before such an influential audience, which included the top brass from the Ford Motor Company, then he was even more worried when the time came a few days later for 001 to run for the first time at Oulton Park. Tyrrell, in his usual plain-speaking way, had made it clear that if the car was not quick enough it would soon be parked in the Donington Racing Car Museum, alongside the four-wheel-drive Lotus 63 and other celebrated motor racing failures. Gardner's sense of anxiety was not eased when rain drenched the parkland circuit and an electrical problem meant the engine would not start. The first test was postponed until six a.m. the following morning, the day official practice was due to begin.

In the unlikely event of Gardner having any doubts about the ability of his driver, they were quickly dispelled when Jackie took his designer for a lap of the circuit in a Ford Cortina. 'The track was still damp and there were leaves and twigs everywhere from an overnight storm,' Gardner recalled. 'I have never had a drive like it. He was sitting there, chatting away, telling me when he would be changing up to third in the racing car, then fourth, and going downhill he would be braking here, and aiming for that, and I was sitting there petrified. There seemed to be no way, Jackie Stewart's abilities notwithstanding, that the Cortina would stay on the road. I could see the next day's headlines already. We were approaching the right-angle right-hander at Old Hall, with the car sideways at a good 45 degrees and the track wet and all those leaves, and he was still chattering away. Then a rabbit popped out in front of us in the middle of the road. Without altering course or chat, he reached out and peeped the horn, the rabbit shot back again, and we made it through the corner. I've never forgotten that. It really restored my sense of relative values.'

Some of motor racing's chattering class not in Gardner's privileged position that morning had begun to murmur that Stewart was beginning to lose his touch. The Scot soon put the lie to such nonsense by lapping Oulton Park four seconds quicker than anyone else – at the wheel of the unloved March. Jackie was in the 701 because the team was still experiencing difficulties with 001. The back-up car was also good enough to set a second-row time in the dry. 'We had a fuel metering problem,' said Davis. 'Because it was so cold, the metering unit seized up. We took the unit out of another engine and fitted it, but all of this meant we didn't get much running. Fortunately, they let us use the covered scrutineering area because otherwise we would have been working in the grass paddock.'

Even though it meant giving up his front-row position, Stewart elected to start the Tyrrell from the back of the grid in recognition of the fact that he had not qualified the new car. The purpose of the weekend was to learn as much as possible about 001, and they couldn't do that with it parked in the truck.

Stewart made a storming start, but came charging into the pits at the end of the second lap, grass and debris in the radiator duct providing evidence of a trip across the grass caused by a jammed throttle. 'It was one of those things that happens when you have a new car and you are in a rush to get it finished,' said Davis. 'There was a panel which was used to get a rubber fuel tank into the monocoque. The throttle cable ran across the top of this hatch, and unfortunately the cable had become jammed between the hatch and the side of the monocoque and that had stopped it from working properly. We put some tape over the hatch to stop the cable going down the inside. Away he went, and broke the track record.'

In the end, an engine failure brought the debut to a premature end, but a point had been made. John Surtees won the race in a car bearing his own name. Jochen Rindt crossed the line in second place, pulled up sharply at the exit of the first corner, vacated the Lotus, grabbed his bag from a marshals' post and sprinted across the field to a waiting plane. It would be the last his British fans would see of the colourful Austrian. Fewer than two weeks later he would be beginning his fateful attempt to qualify for the Italian Grand Prix.

Tyrrell took 001 to Monza, but various problems led to a decision to race the March, Stewart finishing second but still deeply upset after the horrific events of the previous day. He couldn't wait to be done with Monza and move on to Canada and the next race at St Jovite. Tyrrell had booked the circuit for two days of private running before the start of official practice. It was to prove a testing time as a succession of niggling problems limited the running and stretched everyone's patience. To make matters worse, the car was handling badly and the lap times were four seconds off an acceptable pace. By the time practice got underway, the mechanics were exhausted, as Stewart noted in his diary.

'They've had too many months of day and night working with no time off,' he wrote. 'They've followed this regimen to the sacrifice of their homes, their families, and in some cases their health, and the strain is beginning to show. Not only have they had the enormous responsibility of preparing a car for the world champion – preparing it well and safely – but they've also had to build the Tyrrell, a car which all along we've known was a gamble. Now they've come to Canada, suffered a time-change problem, and after no more than four or five hours' sleep plunged straight into changing an engine [on the Tyrrell, following a failure during the second day of the test] and getting the two March cars ready for the first day's practice. And there have been consequences. Today, a spanner was left in the cockpit of my car, down by the pedals – something that should never happen and could have caused a dreadful accident. I was annoyed, really angry, and when they fished it out I merely looked at Ken and said nothing. Everyone knew it was bad, a mistake which could have hurt someone, and there was no point in saying anything. Yet it's the kind of thing that shows we're not where we ought to be, and of course it adds considerably to the strain.'

Stewart himself was contributing to the pressure by considering a future that might not include the Tyrrell team. Matra would have signed him on the spot for 1971; there were others – BRM and Brabham, for instance – who were willing to talk. Whether he would have gone that far will never be known; certainly the team's problems continued. On the third and final day of practice a wheel worked loose on the Tyrrell. Stewart reverted to the March to establish a time, all the while waiting for the Tyrrell to be fixed. With 10 minutes remaining, and the wheels torqued extra tight, 001 was ready. Stewart lit the back tyres as he powered from the pits and set off on a five-lap run, the last one – which had as much to do with the driver as improvements to the set-up of the car – good enough for pole position. As ever, Stewart made it seem easy. The Tyrrell-Ford looked to be a winner. Observers on the sidelines didn't know the half of it.

Stewart continued to paint a rosy picture during the race when he tore off into the lead and pulled away by a second a lap. For 31 laps this went on. 'The car was extraordinary,' said Stewart. 'On pole and comfortably leading the race – it was like taking sweeties off the kids. And this was at St Jovite, a demanding circuit, a driver's circuit. You had to have a car that worked, and we'd finally got the Tyrrell sorted. Which was just as well because there were some quite tricky places at St Jovite, and I remember exactly where the car failed.' A front stub axle broke, a fundamental failure that sent Gardner packing. 'I rushed back to England and in the space of seven days I redesigned the wheel upright and axle,' Gardner said. 'Jack Knight Developments worked non-stop, and when I packed my bags and headed back to North America for the United States Grand Prix, my luggage included two completely new front uprights.'

Such frantic efforts were made worthwhile when Stewart qualified 001 on the front row and once again led the race, this time for 82 laps. Then, teething trouble of a different kind raised its head.

'Jackie was leading by quite a margin,' said Davis. 'Unfortunately, there was a tie wrap which was too close to the exhaust. It melted and let one of the oil pipes rub on the exhaust pipe, which slowly burnt through the oil pipe. It started smoking, but Ken didn't want to bring the car in because he wanted to put up a show for the following year. So he let Jackie carry on, but Chapman was jumping up and down saying our car was creating a hazard and it should be black flagged and taken out of the race. Eventually the matter was settled when the engine ran out of oil and blew up. But, once again, a point had been made.' The race was won by Emerson Fittipaldi in only his fourth Grand Prix. There was a double, if slightly muted, celebration for Lotus since Fittipaldi's impressive drive also ensured that Jochen Rindt became the first posthumous world champion.

That left the final race in Mexico at the end of October, which would be a nightmare of a different kind when enthusiasm got the better of the spectators and they climbed over the barriers to sit on the edge of the track. 'That was a complete débâcle,' Stewart remembered. 'I went round with Pedro Rodriguez, who drove for BRM but was the local hero. The police were with us and we were saying, "Please, go back. Go back." The people were lovely, they did exactly what we asked and went back. We returned to the car and rode off, then I looked in the mirror and it was like a sea we had just opened was closing down again! We had made no difference at all. We went back to the organizers and said, "Look, it's never going to work; we can't race like this." And they said, "You have to race. I promise you, if you don't race, that crowd are going to come and burn the pits down and the cars." So we raced – and it was ridiculous. I was in third place behind the Ferraris when I hit a dog. This didn't actually have anything to do with the crowd problem because there were always dogs roaming around the track in Mexico. I hit this poor dog – it was a big one, a mongrel Alsatian. At 140mph it felt like an elephant when I suddenly hit it. The impact destroyed the monocoque.

'So that was a very unfortunate end to the season. But we had been very encouraged. Apart from those difficult couple of days in Canada, the car was giving back messages that said it had what was needed to get the job done. I felt I was not going to be entering into a relationship that was going to see me on the back foot all the time. This was a good car, no doubt about it. It was good because most of the teams were using the same engine and there wasn't much to choose between the different tyre companies. So, this was a level playing field, and the Tyrrell was showing well. I also had confidence in everybody working on the project. It was a good feeling, encouraged by the fact that Ken was in charge. He was such a practical man. His great strength was his almost mundane thinking process – such as why should we have something that is not going to do a race distance? Okay, somebody might be slightly faster, but we are going to win by solid engineering, and being strong and reliable as well as competitive.

'Looking back, such a performance from a new car should have been surprising, but because of the group of people that were around at the time it was no big deal. There was an immense modesty about the whole thing; you could call it naivety, but Ken was never a naive man, you couldn't call him that. Modest, yes, and he retained that all the way through. I had got to the stage in my career where I was rounding off my skills. I felt I was going to be at my peak, and I knew there was no need to fear failure with the Tyrrell project. We were ready to go.'

13

Back to Unbeatable

'When I returned to Tyrrell, I found there had been absolutely no change. It was like going back 10 years. At McLaren, we'd had proper toilets, a shower, nice washrooms, hot water and so on. When I was at Tyrrell before, there was a galvanized tank under a waterspout coming from one of the buildings. It was used for washing your hands. That was still the case in 1970. It literally was comparing a factory with a wood yard.'

Alan Stait had rejoined Tyrrell as a machinist while Ken was building 001. Tyrrell's first mechanic had moved on to McLaren a few years earlier, but Stait believed that Bruce McLaren's death in June 1970 would spell the end of the company – a misjudgement if ever there was one. Nonetheless, he was happy to be reunited with his old boss, even if the facilities at the Tyrrell Racing Organization – or Elf Team Tyrrell as it was now known – remained spartan.

There could be no getting away from the fact that this *was* a wood yard. Six dark green timber lorries bearing the legend 'Tyrrell Bros. Ltd' on each door were ranged along one side of the rough ground. Immediately at the end of the potholed entrance road stood Ken and Norah's former cottage on the right and a small low-roofed building on the left. This was the office, with the toilets attached, one door of which was locked and only Norah Tyrrell held the key in deference to this being the Ladies. Which was just as well, because the Gentlemen's remained, by all accounts, extremely basic. A lean-to shack with a chimney stood on one side of the toilets. In the background, an open-sided timber cutting shed with a tin roof housed a miscellaneous collection of lorry parts and rusting agricultural equipment. These so-called buildings in a wooded glade in Surrey were the production areas for bodywork which would become the most photographed in the motor racing world. It barely made sense then, never mind when recalling such basic facilities a couple of decades later.

It was also the workplace of Keith Boshier, another local man who had joined the team as a mechanic in 1967. 'I got the job in much the same way as everyone else,' he recalled. 'I had just finished my apprenticeship with a BMC dealer in nearby Godalming when I saw an advertisement in the *Surrey Advertiser* for a mechanic. It was typically Tyrrell, of course – none of your block adverts, just a little one tucked away on the page. I went to Long Reach and looked down the drive into the wood yard and thought, "No, this can't be it." But of course it was, and once I had talked to Ken I thought being a motor racing mechanic was too good to be true.'

Boshier had started off with the Formula 2 team in 1967, and after two seasons of F1 he decided he would prefer to be home-based rather than rushing around the world to the Grands Prix. 'When work began on the first Tyrrell in 1970,' Boshier continued, 'I started doing the bodywork. The original car, 001, was mainly aluminium. I said to Ken that we should be making the body out of glass fibre, and eventually that's what we started to do. I began in that tin shed by the toilets, doing the nose and the seats and bits and pieces. In early 1971 I was moved into the cutting shed. "It's just temporary," I was told. It had windows with no glass, just plastic sheeting. "Don't worry," they said. "It's not worth putting in proper windows because you're going to have a workshop soon." I was to be in that cutting shed for 27 years!'

Derek Gardner, meanwhile, had joined the team full time and set up his drawing office in a Portakabin next door to the wooden hut.

Activity in that ex-military building, and the machine shop along-side, gathered pace as the team began to build a second car, 002, the Tyrrell boys making the actual chassis this time rather than relying on Maurice Gomm. The other difference was that this car was four inches longer in order to accommodate Cevert, who towered over Stewart – which, some might say, was not too difficult.

When seated in the car, however, Jackie Stewart remained the biggest man on the race track. Yet the pundits were predicting a walkover for Ferrari in 1971, particularly as the Italian 12-cylinder cars had come good and, with Jacky Ickx and Clay Regazzoni on board, won four of the last five races in 1970. The word was that the Ford Cosworth V8, about to go into its fourth full season, had passed its best, that Tyrrell, now without Dunlop, would struggle initially during a new relationship with Goodyear.

Ken addressed the latter point by arranging a lengthy test session with 001 at Kyalami in January 1971. Testing may be an integral part of every F1 team's schedule today, but in 1971 it was still another useful novelty being pioneered by Tyrrell. It was also the cause of much activity for the small workforce. Stewart ran one DFV for 986 miles before it was shipped back to Northampton, proving the reliability of the Ford Cosworth beyond all doubt. The car, mean-while, continued to run like clockwork for another 500 miles until a pebble jammed between the accelerator pedal and mounting bracket, causing the throttle to jam open and the car to badly damage a front corner as it rammed an earth bank. This added to the workload at Ockham as 002 neared completion and the first race of the season beckoned them back to South Africa.

It seemed the pundits might be right when Mario Andretti won for Ferrari. In fact, it was a lucky first win for the American in F1 since Denny Hulme's McLaren-Ford had run into trouble. Having said that, Stewart was fortunate to finish second and collect six points, the handling of the car less than perfect due to a wrong choice of tyres. The fact that this was the first finish for a Tyrrell car was offset by Stewart's disappointment with his performance and the sight of Cevert's new but badly damaged car being brought into the pits on the back of a truck. The Frenchman, struggling in the heat, had been running in seventh place when perspiration stung his eyes at an inopportune moment; the blue car careered into the wire-mesh catch-fencing on the outside of a corner. More late nights were pencilled in at Ockham.

The schedule over the next few weeks was a hectic one. A non-championship race in the United States had been sandwiched between two in England. When Ferrari claimed two of them and a 12-cylinder BRM won the other, the writing did appear to be on the wall for the V8 DFV. Added to which, Goodyear was losing the battle as Firestone made it four wins in a row. Then, in mid-April, came a proper race on a proper circuit: the Spanish Grand Prix at Montjuich Park, Barcelona.

It was hard to believe, but this race marked the first anniversary of Stewart's last Grand Prix victory. The chances of ending the drought seemed even more remote when the statistics showed Goodyear to be struggling without a win over an identical period. It became a cast-iron certainty in the minds of the pundits when Ickx put his Ferrari on pole, with Regazzoni's similar car alongside and the V12 Matra of Chris Amon on the outside. Stewart was on the inside of row two, so what chance for his eight-cylinder DFV in powerful company such as this?

Still, the Tyrrell-Ford was reliable, Stewart having finished all three non-championship races on the podium. A third car, 003, had been built for him in time for Spain, but would it be fast enough? Jackie knew that, on a driver's circuit such as this, it probably would be, provided the handling was exactly as he wanted. Initially, that seemed a tall order, as Gardner recalled. 'The calendar was so crowded and we had to spend so much time repairing damaged cars that we hadn't done much basic development. When we got 003 to Barcelona, we changed everything – the suspension geometry, the car's ride height, the lot.'

This work was done on the Saturday morning. In keeping with

the manner of working at the time, practice for each race was held at the organizers' discretion, unlike today when the same precise schedule is rigidly enforced for every Grand Prix no matter where it is in the world. In Spain, practice was held in the early evening on Thursday and Friday, leaving the teams a third session at the same time on Saturday. Rain during final practice meant Friday's times would count for the grid, but, worse still for Stewart, he had no way of knowing whether or not the changes made to the car had been successful. Nonetheless, he was quickest in the wet, a fact that helped tip the balance towards taking a gamble and running the new set-up for the race. If they were wrong, then Stewart would have a struggle on his hands for 75 laps of one of the most spectacularly demanding tracks in the world. The only certainty in Stewart's mind was that the Ferraris were not at their best with a full load of fuel. He had to get into the lead as soon as possible and build a cushion against the inevitable attack later in the race. It was a tall order given the experienced hands spread across the grid in front of him.

Ickx shot into the lead, but by the time the pack had crested the rise immediately after the start and dived towards the hairpin at the bottom of the hill, Stewart had already dealt with Amon and Regazzoni. He then chased after the leader, and within a couple of laps he was on the tail of the Ferrari, probing Ickx's defences as the Belgian struggled with the handling. Towards the end of lap five, Ickx ran wide very slightly as he came through the fast corner leading on to the pit straight. Stewart lined himself up and began to squeeze alongside as they headed at 175mph for the top of the hill. With absolutely no room for error, the cars became airborne briefly before crashing onto the road with full force, both drivers hard on the brakes, but with Stewart on the inside line for the left-hand hairpin. It was an exceptionally brave but necessary move. Within a lap, Stewart was one second ahead and pulling away.

By half distance, Stewart's lead had extended to 8.5 seconds, the gap increasing all the time until there were just 20 laps remaining. With the Ferrari now free from its earlier weight penalty, Ickx went to work. The Belgian equalled his pole position time and reduced the deficit to 6.2 seconds. Stewart responded by dipping below his best practice effort, but Ickx kept coming: 4.4 seconds, then 3.5. Cevert, who had started from the middle of the grid, was running in seventh place when the leaders came to lap the Frenchman with 13 laps to go. By the time the Tyrrell team got round to advising Cevert to let Jackie through while perhaps not being quite so accommodating for Ickx, the leading pair had rushed past, such was the intensity of their battle.

The blue car and the red car were on the absolute limit, the tension increasing further when a backmarker unintentionally delayed Stewart and his lead dwindled to 2.8 seconds with exactly 10 laps remaining. Two laps later and Stewart went faster than Ickx's pole time. The gap was 3.9 seconds. Ickx gave one final push, setting the fastest lap of the race – an incredible one second faster than pole – and edging to within 2.4 seconds of the Tyrrell, but that was as close as he would get. Stewart was too experienced to make a mistake now. When they crossed the line, the Scotsman was 3.4 seconds to the good. It had been a superb contest to match the splendid surroundings. Stewart had just given the Tyrrell marque its first win, and he had been made to work for it.

'It's interesting looking back on that race now,' Stewart said. 'A motor sport magazine recently ran a list of 100 Great Drives and a couple of mine were included. But not this one, which is one I think I would have chosen. Montjuich was a very difficult race track, and on top of that we weren't as well prepared as we could have been. The 1971 season had not started as well as we would have liked and we had the additional problem of having the new car, 003, at Barcelona and I hadn't even run it before. Certainly, it wasn't as good as I would have wanted. Montjuich was quite a bumpy circuit and the car was going light in a lot of places. Those long left and then right curves leading on to the pit straight were very fast and very spectacular – as was, of course, the crest of the hill at the end of the pit straight. Very quick places, very quick. To say the least, I pulled a fairly significant move on Ickx to take the lead! That was what I would call a proper race, and to win there for Tyrrell for the first time was a very good result. No question about it.'

The pundits paid due tribute, but the feeling persisted that the 12-cylinder teams were going to have their way. After all, only two V8s had finished in the top six, Hulme's McLaren-Ford almost lapped in fifth place. It was agreed that Monaco, the next round of the championship, might suit the more nimble V8, but overall the Cosworth was becoming obsolete. In the meantime, there was a non-championship race to be run on the flat expanses of Silverstone, and that, for sure, would be 12-cylinder territory.

True enough, Amon put his Matra on pole, but the 12-cylinder entry had already been weakened by Ferrari's last-minute withdrawal due to labour unrest at the factory (usually a handy euphemism for simply not wishing to be bothered with such a race during the busy championship season). The wisdom of writing off Stewart and Tyrrell was put into question when the combination led the first heat from start to finish, but then it all went wrong. Starting from pole for the second heat, Stewart got only as far as the first corner, Copse, where a stuck throttle caused the car to plough straight on and cannon into the grass bank, directly below a television camera. The pictures showed Stewart immediately flicking off his belts and climbing quickly from the cockpit. A swift glance at the front of the car was enough to tell the Scot that the team would have even more work on its plate in order to have 003 repaired for Monaco in a few weeks' time. It was a worrying thought for Stewart since the most prestigious race on the calendar had generated a diary full of social and business commitments. The last thing he wanted to worry about was not having his latest car.

A crew from ABC Television travelled from the United States to Monaco to make a programme on Stewart and Tyrrell. In addition, Jackie would be accompanied throughout by Roman Polanski as the filmmaker produced a movie entitled *Weekend of a Champion*. It would turn out to be a most revealing documentary, although it was perforce unable to show the drama in the cockpit as the race unfolded.

During practice, everything seemed in order as Stewart set the fastest time on Friday morning, the only one of three sessions to be run in the dry and therefore good enough to give Tyrrell one of the most important pole positions of the season. If Stewart did not make a mistake and the car ran reliably, then in theory this race should be his. Assuming, of course, it didn't rain. On the third weekend of May 1971, there was no guarantee of that. Monaco was experiencing its worst bout of late spring weather for some time, and the practice sessions had already told Stewart that the Tyrrell and its Goodyears were hopelessly off the pace in the wet.

It was with some trepidation that Stewart pulled back the curtains of his room in the Hôtel de Paris on Sunday morning. It was not raining, but by the time Jackie and Helen emerged from the back door of the hotel and set off for the pits, the mountain peaks dwarfing the principality were already lost in dark cloud. Wearing off-white overalls and carrying his helmet bag, Stewart made regal-like progress down the hill, waving to the packed balconies and pausing briefly to sign the occasional autograph for course workers.

His car was ready and waiting in the pits, Ken having helped Roger Hill push the blue number 11 from the garage in the side street opposite. Cevert's car was also in place, along with a third chassis, 001. Only Matra and Ferrari had gone to the similar trouble of bringing a spare car to Monte Carlo – another small sign of Tyrrell's professionalism and attention to detail. Such a precaution is now *de rigueur*, the leading F1 teams bringing a back-up car for each driver at Monaco.

Stewart felt he was not so well prepared. He had not been sleeping well, and instead of winding down during the period before the start he found himself being distracted by irrelevances. He was startled, therefore, to find himself walking towards his car without having donned his second layer of flameproof underwear. By the time he had adjusted his attire in the open pits and calmed himself down, Stewart was ready to make for the grid, where Hill and Roy Topp were waiting to help strap him into the cockpit.

Tyrrell, meanwhile, was flitting back and forth between Stewart on the front row and Cevert in 15th place on the penultimate row. For one driver, it was a case of aiming for a win; for the other, it was a matter of surviving 80 laps of a race track that would severely punish even the smallest error. Tyrrell told Cevert, much as he had done Servoz-Gavin three years before, simply to pace himself and bring the car home. The race and the championship points would look after themselves.

Cevert was the second retirement. The first, Graham Hill, proved that Monaco is no respecter of reputations as the five-times winner dumped his Brabham into the wall on lap 2. Five minutes later and Cevert limped into the Tyrrell pit, his left rear wheel showing signs of heavy contact with something solid.

Stewart was not about to make the same mistake – at least, not if he could help it. Despite leading the race by five seconds, Stewart had known he was in trouble from the start. During the single warm-up lap, the front brakes had locked more often than they should. A quick investigation by the mechanics discovered that a joint on the brake balance bar had come unwound, but there was no time to fix it. Stewart would have to tackle the race with virtually no rear brakes. For an average driver, it was an invitation to slide straight into a wall on the first lap; for a driver of Stewart's calibre, it was an opportunity to demonstrate his deft touch. Apart from the occasional puff of smoke from the front Goodyears, particularly under braking when going downhill towards Station Hairpin, the opposition had no hint of his problem.

Not that there was much of that on this particular day. The Ferraris, BRMs and Matras gradually disappeared from Stewart's rear-view mirrors. It was only when Roger Hill's pit board indicated that Ronnie Peterson's March had moved into second place just before half distance that Stewart knew he might have a problem. He maintained a 16-second lead and responded instantly to the young Swede's every move, the prospect of a battle in the closing stages evaporating when Stewart added another 10 seconds to the gap and then focused on nursing the Tyrrell home.

The intense concentration required during nearly two hours of relentless effort took its toll when Stewart was sick in his helmet. But he was there to take the chequered flag, and then to grab a welcome drink from Roger Hill as he headed towards the royal box. As he cleaned himself up with the aid of his flameproof balaclava, Stewart looked exhausted, his shoulder-length hair lank with sweat. Soon, he was almost lost inside a vast garland. The cup was his.

Tyrrell, meanwhile, was down in the pit box, rubbing his hands, organizing the packing up and thinking about the next race in Holland. When Stewart finally returned to his team, very satisfied with his afternoon's work under such trying circumstances, he was not exactly swept off his feet. 'It was so typical Ken,' said Stewart. 'From a personal point of view, this win was better in some ways than Barcelona. Knowing that the brake balance bar wasn't working and then being able to bring the car home without making any mistakes, particularly in the early laps with a heavy fuel load, that was most satisfying. So I rushed back to the pits to get a little pat on the back, and there was Ken, rubbing his hands, pacing about, his attitude almost being, "Look, I'm sorry, I've got no time for you. We've got to get this place packed up." There wasn't even a "well done" or anything like that. It was a case of, "Hang on, Jackie . . . er, Roger? Could you just get that into the truck and then would you take care of the fuel?" And on like that. Quite incredible. But that was Ken. That was the way it worked. And looking at the way the team operated as a family unit, you have to say it worked very well. There were no big egos in the Tyrrell camp!'

Which was just as well, perhaps, because the team was in for a serious drubbing on the Zandvoort track. This time, on race day, the rain really did come and Stewart's worst fears were realized when he spun out of third place early in the race and spent the rest of the afternoon trailing unhappily around at the back of the field. He finished 11th, five laps down on the winner, Ickx.

'That was a nightmare,' Stewart recalled. 'We were right out of it. Firestone runners filled the first eight places. I was really, really pissed off because just keeping the car on the road was a major miracle. The man in charge of the Goodyear racing division was a guy called Fred Gamble. He left the race before the end! I was keen to get away too, and I remember standing at Schiphol airport and having one of those strange feelings that someone was watching me. It was a weird feeling. So I went behind some shops and came round the other side – and there was Fred, standing behind a pillar, trying to see if I had gone! We've laughed a lot about it since, but I was hard pressed to see the funny side when trying to drive the car!'

Cevert had endured an equally miserable race. After tangling with another car and spinning into the sand, the Frenchman had had the car pushed back onto the track, and he had continued in last place. The incident had damaged part of the suspension, though, and the left-rear corner suddenly collapsed, fortunately not on one of the faster parts of the circuit. When Cevert finally returned on foot to the pits and Tyrrell discovered the cause of the trouble, he gave his driver a dressing down. Cevert was told in no uncertain terms that if a similar thing happened in the future, he was to come into the pits and have the car checked before continuing. No race result was worth such a risk.

Stewart was leading the championship as July dawned, but Derek Gardner was aware that the 12-cylinder engines might come into their own on tracks with long straights, places such as Paul Ricard and Silverstone, which were next on the calendar. To that end, Gardner introduced a rounded, full-width nose to reduce drag and improve speed. In fact, it did little for the latter but, coincidentally, improved the handling. Thinking of the engine too, he experimented with a box placed on top of the engine with an inlet in clear air, high above the driver's head, the object being to force the air into the DFV and increase performance. According to Tyrrell, however, the airbox had not been high on the list of priorities when it came to testing.

'We introduced it during a test at Zandvoort when Cevert was doing the driving,' he said. 'We had been carrying the thing around for several weeks and never actually got around to putting it on the car! So, François went out, did one lap and came straight in. He said, "It's tremendous! Amazing! I'm getting 200 or 300 revs more out of each corner." So I said, "Hang on! For Christ's sake don't do a complete lap! First of all, you go out now and confirm what you think is happening. If you are getting more power or revs, don't do a complete lap; lift off for part of the lap and when we signal you to keep it going, keep it going down the straight and we'll see what it gives you at the end of the straight. But never do a good lap time." That was the problem, of course. Most things you do to improve the car are visible and your rivals will have it for the next race. Anyway, François confirmed what he had first thought, so we took it to the next race, which was the French Grand Prix at Paul Ricard, and waited to see if it was going to give us the advantage we thought it might.'

It did. In spades. Stewart put the Tyrrell on pole, led all the way, set the fastest lap and won by almost half a minute – from Cevert. The opposition was devastated, so much so that there was muttering about an oversize engine and illegal fuel in the Tyrrell. There had to be something! A fuel sample was found to be completely legitimate. Ken Tyrrell's grin became even wider. The airbox permitted the Tyrrell to run as fast as the Ferraris and the new nose allowed it to handle even better than before. It was as simple as that. The technical breakthrough was confirmed when Stewart ran away with the British Grand Prix on 17 July in arguably one of the most boring F1 races ever staged at Silverstone. But that merely increased the frustration of the losers. It was not until the fuel was checked yet again and Stewart's Silverstone engine was sealed and taken for examination – and declared to be under the 3000cc limit – that the doubters were silenced. For Tyrrell, such an unusual amount of fuss was the ultimate accolade.

Stewart led the championship by 23 points, but it was predicted that Ickx would close in thanks to his mastery of the Nürburgring, scene of the next Grand Prix. Instead, there was a total collapse of the Stout Party when the superior handling of the Tyrrell left the Ferrari standing, Cevert adding to the demonstration by giving Tyrrell another one-two. Ickx had crashed while trying to keep up, and Regazzoni's Ferrari had finished third, a full mile behind the blue cars. Stewart's championship lead had grown to 32 points with four races remaining. It was almost a formality.

In fact, Stewart would clinch the title while coming to a halt on three wheels, Ickx having retired his Ferrari from the Austrian Grand Prix on 15 August a few laps before Stewart struck trouble. A drive-shaft failure, caused by incorrect heat treatment, had spun the Tyrrell off the road. It was an unfortunate way to secure a championship since Ken was immediately preoccupied with what had gone wrong. 'He didn't like that sort of thing, not at all,' said Stewart. 'Mechanical failure was his biggest fear as a constructor; it was always a big issue with Ken. If his drivers were hurt, or worse, he felt that very heavily. I had very, very few mechanical failures with Ken, but he was always on top of that, always worrying quietly about it.

'I remember a mechanic leaving a spanner in the footwell of a car at Goodwood. It got tangled up with the pedals. I got to a left-hander where you needed to back off, but the throttle stayed open because the spanner had got behind it. It had also jammed itself behind the brake pedal, so I was on full throttle and couldn't press the brakes. I shut off the engine and went straight across the grass, rejoining the circuit again on the straight. In the end, the bumps caused the spanner to suddenly untangle itself. Ken was absolutely livid, and the guy was dismissed immediately. Ken was really heavy on that, but only if there was a degree of carelessness rather than unintentional error. You certainly don't intend to leave a spanner in the works, but in this case it was done through a lack of diligence. A design error would not be carelessness; you were doing it for the best, and that would be different.

'Ken didn't apologize because he didn't have to – and I wouldn't have expected him to. My relationship with Ken was such that I didn't actually require an apology. You could tell by his demeanour just how he felt. There was no need for him to say any more.'

As soon as the championship was won, Gardner began to think about 1972. To that end, an experiment with repositioned radiators caused a problem for Stewart in the Italian Grand Prix at the beginning of September, although Cevert almost won it in a slipstreaming dash to the line – just 0.18 seconds covered the first four cars – where he was classified third. Stewart scored his sixth win of the season in Canada and led the final race at Watkins Glen until tyre trouble forced him to drop back to fifth. For that cash-rich race, Ken had entered three cars for the first time, Peter Revson joining the team. The American didn't last long in his home race, but Cevert rounded the season off brilliantly for Tyrrell by scoring his maiden win and helping Ken pocket $50,000. Here was final proof that the Frenchman had rapidly matured into a world-class driver, and that his car was the best in the field. It was a remarkable achievement for Elf Team Tyrrell in their first full season as a constructor based in a Surrey wood yard.

Ever mindful of a handy excuse to put on a race and make money, the wily John Webb, the promoter at Brands Hatch, quickly organized a Rothmans World Champions Victory Race for 24 October. Even though the F1 season was officially over, the race attracted entries from Lotus, BRM, Surtees, March, Brabham, McLaren and, of course, Tyrrell, with cars for Stewart and Cevert. The programme (20p) carried an interview with Ken in which he paid tribute to the team and downplayed his role in their success. 'Everybody working for the team is an exceptional person in his own right,' said Ken. 'Everybody is keen for the cars to do well. It's not just a job for them, but something rather special. I suppose if I've done anything at all, it is getting these people together. That has been my contribution.'

It was difficult to believe, but Elf Team Tyrrell amounted to no more than 19 people. To prove it, the programme saluted the achievement by listing them:

Ken Tyrrell: Managing Director
Norah Tyrrell: Secretary/Timekeeper/Lap Scorer
Derek Gardner: Design Director
Neil Davis: Works Manager
Roger Hill and Roland Law: Joint Chief Mechanics
John Bullock and Michael Coyte: Racing Mechanics
Roy Topp: Specialized Welder
Keith Boshier: Mechanic – glass reinforcing panels, etc.
Ken Sykes: Mechanic – general
Peter Turland: Toolmaker – sheet metal worker
John McKenzie: Pattern-maker – sheet metal worker
Alan Stait: Machinist
Robin Coleman: Transporter Driver and Racing Mechanic
Richard Over: Driver – general
Colin Dickson: Metal Worker and Welder
Andrew Smalley: Apprentice
Eric Baker: Accounts

All told, the race meeting was a fine way of paying tribute to them, and a substantial crowd turned up at the Kent circuit on a blissful autumnal morning. The day got off to a jocular start when Ford organized a race for team managers and owners in identical Mexico saloons. Tyrrell, looking rather sheepish in shining new overalls, duly appeared in the paddock, where Jackie presented his boss with a helmet bearing the symbol of an axe with 'Chopper' emblazoned on the sides in large letters. In a rowdy 10-lap event, the team principals set a poor example for their drivers by indulging in bumping and barging tactics which would have no place in any racing school. Jack Brabham crossed the line first, Tyrrell having been elbowed down to 12th place. He blamed his pit signaller, a long-haired Scot whose name he had momentarily forgotten.

The day continued with a Formula 3 race, led by Patrick Depailler, a young Frenchman who would later become a vital part of the Tyrrell team, perhaps sooner than Ken expected. For the moment, however, attention switched to the 40-lap main event, one which promised an interesting contest since pole position was held by Jo Siffert's BRM, with Peter Gethin (the winner of the Italian Grand Prix) alongside in a similar car and the Lotus of Emerson Fittipaldi on the outside. Stewart, in trouble with the circuit's many bumps, was on the third row with Cevert, more than a second slower. The mild, windless day continued – perfect conditions for a motor race without the usual pressure of a Grand Prix.

Things came to a desperate end after just 19 minutes. A spiral of black smoke from the woods at the back of the circuit signalled the return of motor racing's greatest fear. Siffert, who had made a poor getaway from pole, had just moved into fourth place when the BRM suddenly left the road on the fast approach to Hawthorn Bend, a sweeping right-hander at the top of a hill. The Swiss driver suffered a broken leg but perished in an inferno that was poorly dealt with because, a subsequent inquest revealed, the fire extinguishers were inadequate.

The race was stopped immediately and a day of celebration quickly turned into one of great sadness, for Siffert had been a popular racer, one who never gave of anything but his hard-charging best. The teams packed up and went home, Tyrrell's wonderful season – he had won the Drivers' and the Constructors' championships – having ended on the worst possible note. It was not the last time Ken and his team would experience such mixed emotions when they least expected it.

14

Ulcers to the Ultimate

'I didn't pick up the World championship trophy at the prize giving in Paris,' said Stewart. 'We didn't have private planes then, and I was doing something else at the time. But the truth was I was really run down, and didn't fully appreciate why.' Stewart was still in the dark as to the true state of his health when he won the opening race of the 1972 season in Argentina on 23 January, the day his father died. Stewart was on top form in Buenos Aires, but the sad news from Scotland was to be a more telling indicator of the difficult times ahead.

Stewart and Cevert were quick again during testing and practice in South Africa at the beginning of March, but both were plagued with mechanical trouble in the race. Worse was to come in Spain when Cevert had a misfire and Stewart, unaccountably, spun into the barrier and punctured the radiator on 003. A fortnight later at Monaco, scene of his perfect drive 12 months before, Stewart was strangely off form, struggling into eighth place on the grid and spinning yet again during a wet and difficult race. It was obvious that all was far from well with the world champion.

'I spun at least once,' Stewart recalled. 'Okay, the conditions were bad, but not that bad. I just couldn't get it together. Maybe the wet-weather Goodyears weren't that great, but there was no getting away from the fact that I wasn't where I should have been. I had a stomach ulcer that was bleeding, but I was unaware of it. Or at least I wasn't reading the signs. I was energyless and run down. When I closed my eyes, I was seeing stars all the time. Even after my disappointing performance at Monaco, I never remember Ken saying, "God, I wish you'd done better than that." He didn't ask if there was anything wrong because that was down to me. I decided to go for a medical, and that's when I realized I had a problem. There was no alternative but to miss the next Grand Prix.'

Ken asked Brian Redman to take Stewart's place. Redman was a world-class sports car driver but with a limited amount of F1 experience. The Lancastrian couldn't make up his mind, so Cevert became Tyrrell's sole entry at Nivelles in Belgium where he finished second behind the Lotus of Emerson Fittipaldi. The Brazilian was rapidly emerging as the pretender for the crown, particularly as paddock scuttlebutt had written off Stewart as a spent force. 'A lot of people really believed that was the end of me, that I was having some sort of breakdown,' said Stewart. 'They were citing the fact that I had been far too busy, and I had been rushing about the place dealing with safety issues, doing commercial appearances, breakfasts, lunches, tours round the tracks and work for Elf, Ford and Goodyear. And I had also been driving in the CanAm series in North America. Ken didn't like that, but he didn't say anything so long as it didn't seem to be affecting me. Now, this was different. I just had to back right off. But I was ready to come back for the French Grand Prix [on 2 July].'

Derek Gardner and the team had been busy producing 005, a completely new car. The most obvious difference was the slab sides and an altogether more stubby appearance, thanks to the 005 being lower and shorter than its predecessor. Cevert was entrusted with the initial test, which was successful enough to prompt Ken to let the Frenchman have the car for his home Grand Prix at Clermont Ferrand. Perhaps carried away by the sense of occasion, Cevert stuffed the new car into the crash barrier, damaging the front badly enough to have 005 withdrawn from service. Cevert had not escaped lightly either: pain-killing injections were necessary to cope with an injured hand. Meanwhile, 002 was made ready, Stewart taking the faithful 003 for his comeback while a third Elf Team Tyrrell entry was given to Patrick Depailler for an F1 debut in front of his countrymen.

Stewart immediately scotched rumours of his impending demise by setting third fastest time on this challenging road circuit. Amon was fastest in the Matra and looked to have the race sewn up when the perennially unlucky New Zealander picked up a puncture. This came as little surprise to Stewart who from an early stage had spotted the flinty stones flicked onto the track as drivers cut corners. The Scot steered a cautious course, and when Hulme's McLaren dropped out, Stewart found himself in the lead and on his way to win number two. 'Ken and I had talked about this before the race,' said Stewart. 'Typically, Ken had said to take great care and just go for the finish, and I agreed with him. That was volcanic rock with edges like razor blades. It was so tempting to cut those corners and I knew the stuff was going to be kicked onto the track.' It was Depailler, in fact, who collected a puncture. Cevert produced a gritty drive to finish fourth.

Stewart had finished almost half a minute ahead of Fittipaldi, but second place was enough to keep the Lotus driver 13 points clear at the top of the championship table. Fittipaldi extended his lead by winning at Brands Hatch, positions reversed as Stewart finished second and dropped 16 points behind the Brazilian. Ken Tyrrell's immediate concern was the damaged cars being unloaded from the back of the blue transporter at Ockham. Stewart had crashed 005 during practice (he relied on 003 for the race) and Cevert had spun off at Paddock Bend. Damage to 002 had been modest, but was made much worse when Peterson, having his own private accident, spun at the same corner and collided with the abandoned Tyrrell.

There was to be no respite for the team. Two weeks later the truck returned from the Nürburgring with a damaged 003, Stewart having tangled with Regazzoni's Ferrari on the last lap. Stewart was furious, not only because he was attempting to take second place at the time on a day when Fittipaldi had retired, but also because Regazzoni had barged the Tyrrell off the road as Stewart came alongside. 'I was very upset about that collision. It was the first time I'd had anybody weave in front of me all the way down the back straight. The collision, part of the way into the final lap, was entirely his doing. There were not many places that gave you the space you needed, but the final bend on a downhill section was one of those. His behaviour – in those days, anyway – was out of order, but I was so annoyed that no one disciplined him. I went to see the officials afterwards but they weren't interested.

'On the very rare occasions when I was involved in an incident like that, Ken would let me get on with it. He would sympathize, but that would be it. He wasn't there to fight my case. I might have lost a possible six points for the team and myself, but as far as Ken was concerned, what was done was done. If I wanted to sort something out with the officials or the other driver, then go ahead.'

Determined to have a shot at reducing Fittipaldi's lead, Stewart elected to race 005 for the first time in Austria on 13 August. A problem with vibrating front brakes had been cured by mounting the discs by the wheels rather than inboard on the car, as had been the popular trend. All seemed well when Stewart shot through from the second row to take the lead from Fittipaldi and Regazzoni, the blue car pulling away. Just before half distance, however, the handling of the Tyrrell went awry and Stewart gradually dropped down the order to finish out of the points in seventh place. A win for Fittipaldi more or less assured the Brazilian of the title with just three races to go.

Stewart's crew were puzzled by the vibrations and handling problems encountered in the race. There was nothing obviously wrong, not even during a subsequent test session at Silverstone. It was not until the front-left tyre, the same one that had been used for the race in Austria, was finally changed that the problem ceased. It was then discovered that the inside shoulder of the tyre had worn unevenly.

Such a thing would never occur today because of the automatic tyre changes during pit stops; even if a car could run non-stop from start to finish, the tyres would be returned immediately to the supplier. A team would never consider running the same tyre again during a test, any more than Norah Tyrrell would have contemplated reusing a tea bag when brewing up in the back of the truck.

Fittipaldi duly settled the championship in style by winning at Monza, both Tyrrells having retired. 'The thing I remember about that day was the attitude of the Italian crowd,' Stewart recalled. 'In those days, you walked to the grid, where the car would be waiting. I came out of these big gates, and everybody was standing up to applaud me as I walked onto the track. With that towering concrete grandstand, I have to say it really was quite impressive. So, we come to the start of the race – and my clutch breaks on the line and I go nowhere. And now they're all whistling and booing! That's when, as a sportsman, you suddenly realize the fickle nature of the crowd. As far as I was concerned, my only worry was that no one was going to slam into me from behind. But the crowd didn't care about that!'

The Tyrrell team came back with a vengeance in North America, Stewart winning in Canada on 24 September, Cevert then backing up his team-mate to give Ken the lion's share of the cash at Watkins Glen as the Tyrrells finished first and second. Depailler, drafted in for this final round, gave a good account of himself as he moved from 19th place to seventh at the finish. As the curtain came down on the season, the three blue cars arrived back in the pit lane in formation. The grandstands rose in applause. Tyrrell remained very much the yardstick, even after a year which by their rapidly increasing standards had been difficult. 'Yeah,' said Stewart. 'Four wins. A bad year, right enough!'

The *Autosport* review of the season named Stewart as the top driver; Michael Kettlewell, editor of the prestigious *Autocourse* annual, also made Stewart number one in a Top Ten Drivers assessment. So much for the Scot having lost the plot. Talk of retirement was quietly forgotten. Forgotten, that is, by everyone but the man himself.

There was no sign of anyone throttling back at Ockham. Work had commenced on a proper facility, ostensibly for the maintenance of the timber trucks. Sure enough, the fleet of green lorries was still there, although never used, the timber business having been gradually reduced in size before Ken sold his interest to his brother Bert, who eventually moved the company to smaller premises in the neighbourhood. Ken had put a price on the vehicles and anyone who wanted to pay was welcome to them. Unfortunately, no one wanted to pay, so they began the process of slowly rotting away, grass and weeds sprouting between the chassis members. 'It was so typical of Ken,' said Keith Boshier. 'He would set the price – let's say £3,000 – and even if someone came along and offered £2,950, Ken would say, "No! Sod it. The price is £3,000. If you can't pay it, I'm not interested." So they sat there for ages. In the end, I think he had to get someone to come in and tow 'em away!'

Tyrrell was more generous when it came to looking after his staff, setting new standards by making sure the race mechanics had time off by flying them to and from the races rather than making them travel by road. Ken's professionalism also extended to the hardware, Tyrrell the only team to go to the trouble of taking a spare car to the first race of the 1973 season in Argentina. In fact, the back-up (003) was never used, Stewart and Cevert relying on the latest-generation Tyrrell 005 and 006 with further small modifications. They finished practice on the second and third rows of the grid respectively, seemingly a confirmation of the order of seniority and potential within the team.

But not for long. Cevert had been maturing rapidly, learning at Stewart's right hand and putting the advice and lessons to good effect. There were no team instructions within Tyrrell, Stewart's superior speed and racecraft having naturally settled such issues. But now Cevert was ready to go, and he meant to prove it from the off.

As the field charged towards the long right-hander at the far end of the Buenos Aires autodrome, a blue Tyrrell moved to the front. It wasn't Stewart. A lightning start by Cevert had taken him past his team-mate and alongside Regazzoni's Marlboro BRM and Fittipaldi's John Player Special Lotus. Calm as you like, the French-man snatched the lead. Regazzoni was having none of it and retook the Tyrrell, but Cevert was not to be shaken off. When the Firestone tyres on the BRM began to lose their edge, Cevert was back in front, Stewart, meanwhile, having gradually moved forward to make it a Tyrrell one-two. But rather than challenge his team-mate, Stewart defended him by holding off a resurgent Fittipaldi, the Lotus driver doing everything possible to find a way through but to no avail. It was only when a slow puncture caused Stewart to back off that Fittipaldi was able to take second place, and eventually the lead. Nonetheless, second and third was a good start to the season for a team with what was now arguably the strongest driver pairing in the field.

Brazil joined the championship trail with a race at São Paolo in February, but the Tyrrell proved a handful over the twists and bumps of Interlagos. Nevertheless, Stewart threw himself into the challenge of hounding Fittipaldi, the Tyrrell driver finishing an exhausted but worthy second. Cevert was just as tired after coming home 10th, thanks to a stop to change a punctured tyre and a struggle with handling aggravated by suspension trouble.

Anyone still doubting Stewart's commitment, even after such a gritty drive in Brazil, was to be convinced during practice for the next race in South Africa. A chafed brake line sent fluid everywhere but towards the brake calipers just when Stewart needed them most. With virtually no stopping power at the end of the 175mph straight, Stewart spun the Tyrrell through three layers of wire-mesh catch-fencing before it slammed into the concrete wall lining the outside of Crowthorne Corner. The left-hand suspension front and back was destroyed and one of the stout fence poles made a nasty dent in the chassis. The damage could have been much worse, but even so, it would be a struggle to repair the car before race day.

Stewart immediately took over Cevert's car and set 16th fastest time. Cevert, with no qualifying time to his name, had to start from the back.

The chances of a Tyrrell victory seemed slim, particularly with the usual suspects – Fittipaldi (Lotus), Hulme (McLaren), Regazzoni (BRM) and Peterson (Lotus) – occupying the front rows. And just for good measure, they were joined by a young South African making his F1 debut in a McLaren. Jody Scheckter, although destined not to finish after running as high as fourth, made a big impression that did not go unnoticed by Tyrrell.

Ken was banking on his cars at least running reliably and picking up points. The mechanics had managed to straighten out the damaged car for Cevert's use, but Stewart added to the workload by having them change the rear suspension on his designated car to a configuration he had not tried before. The odds might have been stacked against Tyrrell, but Ken was too experienced a campaigner to draw early conclusions. In motor racing, anything can happen. On Saturday, 3 March 1973, it most certainly did.

A multiple collision at Crowthorne in the early laps resulted in Mike Hailwood's Surtees ramming the spinning BRM of Regazzoni. The BRM caught fire, and Hailwood bravely dragged the semi-conscious Swiss free from the burning wreck. In the confusion, no one noticed that Stewart had been on a charge, the revised rear suspension having transformed the car – into a race winner, as it turned out. Stewart breezed past the opposition as if it was standing still. By lap seven he was in the lead. No one would get close for the remaining 72 laps.

The drama was not yet over. Peter Revson, who finished second, claimed Stewart had overtaken his McLaren at a point where yellow warning flags were still being waved at the scene of Regazzoni's accident. Initially, the stewards threatened to throw the Tyrrell driver out, but a protest brought nothing more than a reprimand, Stewart claiming that the overtaking move had been completed before the yellow flag. Given his relentless pursuit of better track safety, it did indeed seem unlikely that Stewart would have entertained even the slightest risk to either himself, fellow competitors or, more importantly, track workers at the scene of the fire.

Cevert, meanwhile, was running but not classified after a pit stop to change tyres punctured by the accident debris, plus further stops to attend to a problem with the fuel mixture. It had not been the Frenchman's weekend, a fact confirmed the following Monday when, in a virtual repeat of Stewart's accident, Cevert crashed at Crowthorne when a brake pipe chafed during a tyre test. The mechanics were nothing if not busy and needed the brief respite while the battered cars were flown home.

Stewart was to take a hard-earned win on 8 April when a non-championship race at Silverstone was run in sleet, but by now Ken Tyrrell had things on his mind other than the vagaries of the weather and the next round of the World championship in Spain. Lunch with Stewart in a private club in London answered a question that had begun to quietly bother Ken. 'I took Ken and Walter Hayes to Marks Club in Charles Street, which was one of the best eating houses in London,' said Stewart. 'I told them I planned to retire. It was the first Ken and Walter had heard of it. Ken said something along the lines of, "Well, if that's your decision, then how do we deal with it?" I said I wanted to race for the rest of season but I had wanted to give Ken a chance to sort something out. We agreed that nobody would discuss it. Nobody was to know. Not even Helen.'

Certainly there was no sign of impending retirement when Stewart pushed hard at the end of April in Barcelona; he might have won had brake trouble not intervened. A somewhat lucky win for Fittipaldi consolidated the Brazilian's lead in the championship. There was further proof of Stewart's willing obligation to himself and his team when the F1 circus gathered three weeks later at Zolder, a new venue for the Belgian Grand Prix. Right from the start, the track surface proved inadequate for the job, the drivers at one point threatening to withdraw their labour rather than crash their expensive machinery. Stewart was at the forefront as usual, his sometimes strident views prompting a few seasoned cynics to remark that the Scotsman should simply shut up and drive. Which, when the organizers failed to address the problem, is precisely what he did. And he won. On a day when wrecked cars lined the track, Stewart did not put a foot wrong, steering clear of the gravel and broken tarmac fringing the racing line. Even better, Cevert, after leading and spinning off, recovered to give Tyrrell a one-two finish. Fittipaldi finished third, his championship lead shrinking to seven points.

Monaco was next, and Stewart walked it. In one of the most convincing displays among many, the Scot toyed with a late challenge from Fittipaldi and reduced the gap to three points. Stewart had led most of the way, but not on the first lap when Cevert surprised everyone – not least his team-mate – by charging through from the second row of the grid. In true Monaco style, he paid the price for his enthusiasm by hitting a kerb. The subsequent pit stop dropped the Frenchman to the back of the field, but by cleverly latching on to Stewart, who was one lap ahead, Cevert made the most of back-markers dutifully moving out of the leader's way, a two-car Tyrrell train passing through. Such insouciance not only indicated Cevert's supreme confidence, it also earned him fourth place. By now Ken had no doubt that this was the man to replace Stewart as his leading driver and potential champion.

Cevert continued to create the right impression by qualifying on the front row, ahead of Stewart, and then finishing third in Sweden in mid-June, Jackie following behind in fifth place. With Fittipaldi having retired, the championship remained delicately poised. Positions were to be reversed in France when a collision between Fittipaldi and Scheckter cost the Lotus driver at least second place and helped promote Stewart to fourth after the Tyrrell had stopped to change a punctured tyre. That placed Stewart at the top of the table, one point ahead of Fittipaldi, second place for Cevert in the race good enough to make it two Tyrrell drivers in the first three in the championship. But if Scheckter was arguably the innocent victim of Fittipaldi's enthusiasm in France, there was to be no question about the South African's part in a colossal accident two weeks later at Silverstone.

Ronnie Peterson had scored his long-awaited first win at Paul Ricard, and the quiet Swede travelled from France to Britain knowing what was possible. Sure enough, he put his black and gold Lotus on pole position with Stewart just behind him on row two, alongside the second Lotus of Fittipaldi. Peterson was the bookie's favourite. Stewart had other ideas.

A pace car – something of a novelty in F1 – led the 28 starters for one slow lap, the field pausing at the exit of Woodcote, the very long and fast right-hander leading on to the pit straight. When the starter dropped the Union flag, Stewart shot through from fourth on the grid and lined up behind Peterson as the field swept into Copse Corner and on through Maggotts, swinging left towards the long right-hander at Becketts. Typically, Stewart had been thinking this through beforehand. Becketts was the one place where over-taking might be possible if the leading driver could be taken by surprise. Peterson was about to be taken by surprise.

Stewart didn't appear to brake. In one sweeping move, the Tyrrell darted alongside the Lotus and powered through the corner with such apparent ease that Peterson was seen to shake his head in dis-belief. Hammering home the psychological advantage, Stewart drove the rest of the opening lap on the very limit. The blue car shot under the *Daily Express* bridge and swept through Woodcote in one long, glorious drift, the Tyrrell dancing uneasily on the ripples in the track surface. It was one of the most thrilling of the many tingling sights created by that corner. It was also to be the last. Woodcote had been causing palpitations among officials for some time. Scheckter was about to write it into history.

Trying to emulate Stewart while holding on to third place, Scheckter slid wide at the exit, put a rear wheel on the dirt and spun to the right. He managed to reach the pit wall without being touched, Cevert among those to squeeze through, but the impact sent the McLaren rolling backwards as the remaining cars rushed out of Woodcote. All at once, the track became a swirling mass of wreckage as wings, wheels and bodywork flew in all directions. Miraculously, there was only one minor injury.

The race was stopped while the track was cleared. Stewart knew he had it all to do again as the race would be restarted using the original grid positions. As Peterson sat on the pit wall, Stewart walked casually by. 'You know about Becketts now, Ronnie,' he said with a chuckle. 'I'll have to try somewhere else this time.' Peterson smiled weakly.

In fact, the Lotus driver would have the last laugh. An attempt by Stewart to take the lead, this time into Stowe corner, ended in disaster. The Tyrrell's gearbox had been giving trouble occasionally, and it chose this moment to play up. The transmission locked and sent Stewart spinning into a cornfield on the inside of the corner, the resulting damage forcing a long delay in the pits and an eventual 10th place. The only good news was that Fittipaldi had retired.

Stewart's lead was extended to 10 points by the end of the Dutch Grand Prix on 29 July, but he was to care little about that, or the fact that his 26th victory had exceeded the record established by Jim Clark. The race had been marred by the death of Roger Williamson, a promising young English driver. What irritated Stewart in his capacity as safety campaigner was the needless nature of the tragedy. Williamson's March had overturned and caught fire. He was still alive, but trapped, and there was insufficient manpower or equipment at the scene to save him. It was yet another tragic wake-up call for the sometimes complacent officials.

Just to add to the tension, the next race was at the dreaded Nürburgring. As ever, Stewart locked away his emotions once he pulled on his crash helmet and closed the visor. He dominated practice and the race, leading all the way with Cevert a car's length behind throughout the 14 laps. As in Holland, where Cevert had also trailed home his team-mate, Stewart had gone at his own pace – that is, just slow enough to win – but there was no doubt in his mind that Cevert had been fast enough to win on each occasion. The pair of them had driven faultlessly, and Stewart would long remember their performance that sunny day at the Nürburgring, a classic circuit and a place to savour when driver and car were as one. At any other time, however, it was a nightmare. Only Stewart, Tyrrell and Hayes knew that Jackie had just finished with it for good.

The championship was almost a formality now. Fittipaldi's troubles had been such that Cevert had overhauled the Brazilian for second place on the table. The Austrian Grand Prix on 19 August made little difference to the placings, Stewart finishing second after the luckless Fittipaldi lost the lead when a fuel pipe broke with six laps to go. With 24 points separating the two, Monza would surely settle it once and for all. Stewart needed only to finish third or higher to be sure of his third world title. In the event, he finished fourth, but that was enough. And the way he did it marked the drive down as one of the finest of his career.

The weekend started badly for Stewart when a cholera immunization made him feel ill, the car almost reacting in sympathy by behaving strangely on this super-fast track. On race morning, when the engine in Stewart's car dropped a valve, there was no reason to believe he was going to finish the day as champion, particularly since he was starting from the third row of the grid. Furthermore, eight laps into the race he suffered a puncture and the pit stop dropped him to 20th, deep among the backmarkers. The comeback was the stuff of legends, Stewart slicing through the field. By lap 20 he was 11th; the same distance again and he was sixth, pulverizing the lap record as he went. When he came to pass Cevert in fourth place, the Frenchman did not hesitate to let him through. No one was going to stop the wee Scot on a day like this. He only finished fourth because Revson's McLaren was so far ahead.

'People refer to that drive as being worth a place in the top 100,' said Stewart. 'Yes, it was a very good race because it was actually tough to do well at Monza. It was such a simple circuit that everyone was flat out for most of the way and it was hard to find an advantage. So, under the circumstances, I did well, particularly after stopping to change a tyre. You've got to remember that wasn't done in six seconds in those days! But, yes, it was a good way to win the championship.' Tyrrell would always list that drive as one of the most impressive he had seen. 'People talk about Jackie and his performance at the Nürburgring in 1968, and rightly so, but Monza was exceptional too. The point is that you needed a different type of talent for these two race tracks. At Monza, we hadn't been all that good in practice, but after the pit stop to change the wheel Jackie went faster than he had gone in practice. He went like hell! It was fantastic, an incredible performance. His attitude seemed to be that he was effectively out of the race, so he just got stuck in and drove.

'I remember Mike Hailwood saying to me that Jackie had passed him going into the chicane at the back of the circuit, and when Mike came out the other side, he couldn't see Jackie. He thought Jackie must have had a big shunt because there was no sign of him! Mike was very impressed by that.

'I said to Jackie afterwards, "So, what about practice when the car didn't do this and didn't do that and understeered and the engine was no good and all of that?" And he just said, "I dunno! I just drove as hard as I could and really enjoyed it." It was a wonderful drive. Quite superb.'

The one certainty was that the entire team could now enjoy the final two races, at Mosport Park in Canada and Watkins Glen. Depailler had been invited to drive a third car, but the mildly chaotic Frenchman proved he was often his own worst enemy by breaking a leg while motorcycling in the mountains near his home. Chris Amon, without a drive, accepted the offer.

The Canadian Grand Prix was confused thanks to the entire field making pit stops halfway through when the rain ceased and the track began to dry. Stewart added to the muddle by forgetting Tyrrell's precise orders and coming into the pits before he was given the all clear. With Amon's car already occupying the pit, Tyrrell waved Stewart back out again. He eventually received his dry-weather tyres and rejoined to finish fifth. But Stewart's problems were nothing compared to those of Cevert. The Frenchman's pit stop had gone according to plan, Cevert immediately getting into a battle with Scheckter for third place. Then the two cars touched, Cevert slamming into the crash barrier head on. The front of the car was destroyed, but Cevert was more intent on destroying Scheckter as the two drivers abandoned their respective wrecks. Marshals had to intervene. It was only when he had calmed down that Cevert realized his ankles were hurting badly.

Plans were immediately put into action to have a new car built for Cevert in time for Watkins Glen a fortnight later. This was a Grand Prix no one wanted to miss. It would be Stewart's last race – a fact which continued to remain a secret, even though the media was buzzing with speculation – and also his 100th Grand Prix. The team had always done well at Watkins Glen, Jackie winning in 1970, François in 1971, and Jackie heading home the one-two finish in 1972. Above all, the Finger Lake region in autumn was a delightful place to be. Elf Team Tyrrell could hardly wait to get there. When it was all over, they could scarcely get away quickly enough.

15

A Terrible End

'It's hard to believe now when you think about Grand Prix drivers with their own jets and so on,' said Stewart, 'but, in between the two races in North America, François, Helen and I went, along with the mechanics, like a group of tourists to see Niagara Falls.'

Among the small band was Jo Ramirez, who had joined the team at the beginning of the previous year to work on Cevert's car. Ramirez, familiar with Formula 1 and international sports car racing, nevertheless found working with Tyrrell to be a unique experience. 'I had been with one of the top teams in sports cars but I wanted to get back to F1,' he said. 'I had asked Ken about a job and he said to call in at the factory. Don't forget, the team had just won the championship in 1971. I couldn't believe it when I arrived in the wood yard for the first time. I remember thinking, "They did all that – from here? Impossible!" But it was the people rather than the place. I quickly discovered the fantastic atmosphere, and, working with someone like Roger Hill, I learned so much. He was a very clever guy. And there were people like Keith Boshier, who was such an artist with the glass fibre. And Butty [Peter Turland], who made the chassis. It was an incredible team, a very close team. If someone had a problem, then everyone would stop what they were doing and get into it. Nobody needed to say the word; everyone was there for you. And that was because of Ken and the way he worked.'

Ramirez had watched Cevert mature through the difficult season in 1972 and blossom into a self-assured driver, ready to win the championship. 'The fantastic thing was the adoration François had for Jackie,' Ramirez recalled. 'He looked up to Jackie and quickly realized he could learn so much. In some ways it worked against him. At the Dutch Grand Prix in 1973, for example, that was the start of the dream period for us when Jackie and François finished first and second there, and then at the Nürburgring a couple of weeks later. But the point was, Jackie was leading at Zandvoort, and as he accelerated out of Tarzan hairpin he missed a gear. François nearly hit him, but he pulled alongside and then lifted off. Jackie recovered and away they went, still first and second. I was helping François out of the car at the finish when Jackie came straight over and said to him, "What did you do that for? It was your race. I made a mistake. You should have taken the lead." And François said, "But Jackie, that's not the way I want to win. I want to beat you fair and square. So long as you're around, I'm happy to sit behind you." That's the way he was.'

If the drivers of today would scoff at such a refusal to win at all costs, they would be appalled at the concern and affection shown by Cevert at Monza, the race where Stewart clinched the title. 'That was amazing,' said Ramirez. 'During the warm-up on race morning, Jackie had an engine problem and we had to change it for the race. Ken was asking about the engines available in the truck and I said we had the one that François had used during the Austrian Grand Prix. It had been fresh for that race and we knew the oil consumption and the water temperatures were okay. So Ken said to go ahead and put it in Jackie's car because the engine was a known quantity and, typically, he didn't want to take any risks for this race. François was always interested in what Jackie was doing, and when we told him we were putting in the engine he had used in Austria, he went mad. "No! No!" he said. "You can't do that. That engine was a dog, absolutely hopeless. You can't give Jackie that engine for such an important race!" He went straight to Ken and said the same thing, but Ken wouldn't have it. The engine went in because we knew it was reliable.

'So the race started, and, as you know, Jackie had to make that pit stop because of the puncture and rejoin at the back of the field. He smashed the lap record over and over again as he came through the field and passed François along the way. After the race, François did not seem as happy as usual. I knew exactly what was on his mind. Eventually we talked about it, and he just could not believe that Jackie had gone so quickly with an engine François knew was not good. Jackie had passed François and left him standing. He was absolutely stunned. He was happy for Jackie but sad for himself because he wondered if he could ever do something like that. François needed a bit of reassurance. Once he accepted that Jackie had the experience and that he, François, was getting better all the time, then he was okay.'

Certainly, Cevert had put Monza to the back of his mind when he went to Canada. It disappeared completely from his thinking in the immediate aftermath of the crash with Scheckter. 'The top of the steering wheel on François's car was completely bent,' said Ramirez. 'The front of the car, down by the pedals, was bent right over. François had been braking hard but, at the last moment, he must have pulled his feet back. Had he not done so, he would have been very badly injured. As it was, his ankles were badly bruised. I remember going to the hospital and looking at his shoulders; the safety belts were marked on his skin like they had been painted in red. It had been a big impact. As I say, he was so fortunate his injuries were not a lot worse. We were quite happy to carry him around during the trip to Niagara. It was a lot of fun being together like that.'

The team dynamics of the time were summed up by Derek Gardner. 'Ken is very good to work with, he's a professional. He does have fixed views on certain aspects but he is always open to see the other side. He can be very forceful; if he thinks he is right and you are wrong, or he thinks you don't know, then he can be very forceful. But if it's a matter of engineering or design, it's my decision, but obviously we have to agree on policy. I consider Ken knowledgeable from an engineering point of view; he has had so much experience of racing cars and he has seen so much and he's remembered so much, to the point where if you think of an idea, he will probably say, "Well, so-and so tried that and this happened." But, undoubtedly, Ken is an organizational man. He does get the best out of people. There are other teams who call themselves teams, but at Tyrrell we are a team because we work together.

'Having said that, it is every man to his own. Jackie is a driver, I am an engineer and Ken is the manager. It works beautifully – or it seems to. With Jackie, for instance, he is not an engineer and it is his lack of engineering knowledge which is actually useful in the way we work. He will tell you exactly what the car is doing, paint a very vivid picture so that it's as if you are in the car. He will then expect you to be able to do something about it. If you try something, he will then tell you what effect it had. François tends to be a little more technical – not a great deal, but he likes to understand these things. I think he could be very good in that area. It works very well with Jackie and François.'

Gardner was obviously hoping that both drivers would be staying with the team for 1974. Even though it was autumn 1973, teams were only just beginning negotiations for the following year, a preoccupation that these days engulfs teams almost before the new season is underway. The specialist magazines continued to discuss whether or not Jackie might retire, but the tentative tone of the articles confirmed that Stewart's secret had remained intact. No one outside the triumvirate knew; not Helen, not Cevert.

'That was beginning to prove a bit tricky,' said Stewart. 'Drivers weren't signed up by August/September as they are now, but by Canada [the week 17–23 September], teams had started to approach François and he didn't know what to do. He had obviously become very hot property and he saw the trip between Mosport and Watkins Glen as a good time to ask my advice.

'Because he had injured his ankle during the race in Canada, he couldn't walk very well. We had a big Ford Galaxie and I put him in the back of that and off we went to Niagara. I had to carry him on my back like a child to see the falls! We drove on to New York, stopped overnight there, and then went to Bermuda. We stayed in some sort of club and all of us shared a bungalow. It was good, because François could get into the water and work his ankle, as well as having massages and the treatment he needed.

'When he started talking about his options for 1974, I couldn't tell him I was retiring. All I could do was say I didn't think he should go elsewhere. I said he should have one more year with Tyrrell. I explained that I was not planning to race for ever. I said I didn't know when I was going to retire and that he needed one more year with me. He would get a lot of podium finishes and win the odd race, then he would be number one and world champion – and I had absolutely no doubt that he would. But I just couldn't tell him to hold on because he would be number one sooner than he thought. I told him what not to do rather than what to do. Of course, I was going to tell him immediately after the race anyway, so it was all going to become very clear.'

Stewart had clearly been having discussions with Tyrrell about Cevert's future, although one of Ken's suggestions caught Jackie slightly off guard. 'Ken said he thought François should win at Watkins Glen – my last race!' said Stewart. 'That assumed we would be in a dominant position. Ken said François had finished second to me three times and it would be a really nice thing if I were to let him win at Watkins Glen. It's true that we had been first and second at the Nürburgring, but I was never stretched. We had such a cushion over everybody else. When you get into a rhythm that is comfortable – round the Ring it's not exactly comfortable, but you know you are not pushing to the limit – you don't feel pushed. I always thought François must have wanted to win, but he didn't have the speed to pass me. It would have been a struggle for him. But, having said that, he could have done it if he had wanted to. I told Ken all that. He was obviously thinking about who could be number one in 1974, and I said he had to have François. Ken said, "It would be your biggest gesture ever in motor racing – your 100th Grand Prix, and all you need to do on the last lap is come down the front straight, just back off and let him through." I said it was a lot to ask in my last race – *if* we were in that position. But it was a serious consideration for me because another win – I had already got 27 and the record – wouldn't mean that much really. I had already done what I needed to do. I was definitely giving it some thought.

'Looking back now, the point is that there was this openness in the team. There was nothing, no issue I would have been frightened to talk to Ken about, and there was nothing I would have expected him to be nervous about when talking to me. That didn't mean to say that either of us would not have been hurt by harsh comments, but we weren't afraid to voice them. Still, as far as Ken's suggestion was concerned, events were to overtake us in the worst possible way.'

The approaches from rival teams (Lotus, for certain) added the final touches to Cevert's belief in his own ability. If nothing else, he would try to end the season on a high note. Starting with pole position at Watkins Glen.

The first day of practice, Friday, was held in cool conditions. Peterson was fastest, with Stewart a couple of tenths behind the Lotus and Cevert third quickest. There was a mood of calm assurance about the Frenchman. 'He was not over-confident,' Stewart recalled, 'but he was quite cocky, like a young fighting cock, in fact; a good-looking one as well. He was a perfect specimen, a really great character. He was utterly charming, tall, and a wonderful classical pianist for good measure. When it came to driving, he genuinely thought he could do well at the Glen.'

There were to be two sessions on Saturday, the final day of practice. It was warmer than the previous day and lap times began to tumble, Peterson remaining the quickest. Cevert improved to fourth fastest. With a couple of minutes of morning practice remaining, Cevert knew there was more to come. It would not be a problem.

Helen Stewart had arrived in the pits and taken up position on a makeshift seat on the pit counter. As Cevert sat in the car, preparing to go out, Helen took a picture. Cevert looked up and saw her. 'He gave me a wave,' said Helen. 'Then he shut his visor, blew me a kiss and off he went. That was the last I ever saw of him.'

Not long after, the pits and track adopted the eerie silence that comes when cars unexpectedly stop running for no obvious reason. In the days before on-car cameras and full coverage of each and every lap, there was no way of knowing what might have happened. It could be a car broken down in a dangerous place; it could be an engine failure dumping oil on the track; it could be a minor accident; it could be much worse. An uneasy feeling crept along the pit lane as, one by one, the cars returned. A few were missing, including all three Tyrrells – Stewart, Amon and Cevert.

'I was out on the track at the time,' said Stewart. 'Just after the start of the lap, the track went downhill and then uphill to an esses where the road went right and left over a crest. There was debris everywhere, and I could see blue bodywork. Chris [Amon] was standing by the side of the track and I thought he'd had the shunt. I asked if he was okay and he signalled that it wasn't him. He had obviously stopped and got out to see what had happened. Then he pointed to the wreckage of François's car. I could see there were other drivers, including Jody Scheckter, going to see if they could help. I got out and went over.

'It had been a massive accident, just the worst kind you could imagine. The car had hit the barrier on the right, ricocheted across, hit the barrier on the opposite side and then turned upside down along the top rail. It was absolutely horrible. François was still in the car, but I could see from the scale of the accident and his condition that there was absolutely no chance he had survived. I left the scene and got back into my car to return to the pits.

'I was angry, very angry, about the whole sport, the whole thing. One of my regrets is that I didn't stay with François. I don't think anybody dies immediately. Okay, that may seem a ridiculous thing to say when the ferocity of the accident is on such a scale, but I just felt as if I should have taken his helmet off, or done something. Anything. Just stayed there a bit longer. To this day, I regret not doing that.'

Word spread quickly. There had been a bad accident at the esses. One of the Tyrrells was involved. A sponsor of the Lotus team was filming in the pits and caught an anxious Colin Chapman meeting his team manager, Peter Warr, hurrying back from race control.

'Who is it?' asked Chapman.

'Cevert,' said Warr.

'Is it bad?'

'Very bad.'

Chapman turned, and then paused. 'Aw no!' he exclaimed to no one in particular. 'Bloody hell! Cevert . . .'

The rest went unsaid. Here was a driver entering his prime, poised to go on to greater things. Now it seemed he was yet another fatality in a seemingly endless roll call of wasted talent. It was doubly hurtful since the season was close to an end, yet this perfect autumnal morning had produced more horror on a grand scale. The F1 personnel were numbed, none more so than the members in the Elf Team Tyrrell uniforms.

'I remember that feeling,' said Ramirez, 'that dreadful feeling when the noise level drops and the cars that were running come into the pits very slowly. And your car is not among them. There was a truck leaving the pit lane to go to the scene of the accident. I went to jump into the back of the truck and Jody [Scheckter], who had just returned to the pits, shouted to me. "Don't go!" he said. "Don't go!" I knew then. My heart sank completely.'

As Stewart drove into the pit lane in the sister car of the one he had just seen torn apart, his mind was numb, but bitter experience told him there was work to do. 'By the time I got back, everyone had already been told that it was a horrendous accident. I'm sure that Chris had already said that François could not possibly have lived. Ken asked me the same question, and I said I couldn't believe he was still alive. Then Ken said, "But you can't say that for sure, can you?" I said that I couldn't, and that was when I got more concerned about it and thought maybe I should have still been there. And it was made worse because nobody came and told us officially.

'We had a little caravan out the back. Edsel Ford [great-grandson of Henry Ford] and his wife-to-be, Cynthia, were there and we were just hanging around, not really knowing what to say. When we went out to start practice again, it was announced on the PA that François had died. We had a minute's silence.

'Nobody wanted me to go out, but I did. They all thought something had broken and it wasn't a good idea to expose ourselves to another potential breakage. I was very clear on that one; I went out and went quite quick – and had exactly the same thing happen at the same place in the esses. The difference was, I was in a higher gear than François. It was like approaching a second-gear roundabout in a road car. If you use third, the car feels slow and lazy, but in second, the car is all excited and the deceleration is aggressive. That was the difference between our two cars. He was in fourth and I was in fifth. Added to which, François would have been at the top of the rev range in fourth, whereas for me it seemed better to use fifth even though it was slower on the exit. That allowed me to execute the corner more smoothly – as long as I was right. If I got it wrong, it would be slow as hell. But I had enough confidence to do it. It wasn't that we were using different ratios; we had already been through one day of practice, so the car was set up. In my mind, fifth gear was the one to use even though it was a slight compromise. You would go into a right-hander, then a left and over the top into another right which led on to a straight. You were accelerating very fast, all the way through. So, by the time you went over the top, the car was on tiptoes, very light. Then it would dig in. There was a bump just over the hill, and when the Tyrrell hit it, because it had a very short wheelbase, it would torque [flick] to the right. So when it happened to me, my car was less nervous and more docile. I was able to deal with the problem.'

Whether out of respect, shock or for technical reasons, no one went faster in the afternoon session. Ken decided to withdraw his cars from the race, leaving empty places in fifth and 12th spots where Stewart and Amon would have been.

'François had gone off as usual, full of life and smiles,' Roger Hill remembered. 'When he didn't come round again there was that strange feeling that something was seriously wrong. You didn't need telling. We just knew there was a problem. It is very difficult to deal with the aftermath of something like that, but Ken gathered us all together and we just got on and did it. But having said that, we knew it could be dangerous – and it still is. One has to recognize and understand that side of the problem. You realize before you start that this sort of thing could happen, so you are mentally prepared – but only more or less. François had been such a lovely guy. It really shook us very badly.'

Tyrrell had to come to grips with the worst accident ever to affect his team. The wrecked car had been taken to a garage in the village of Watkins Glen. Someone would need to check it over. 'Ken asked Roger, Roland and me if we would go and take a look,' said Ramirez. 'We needed to know if anything had failed on the car and caused the accident. I have never seen anything like it. The mess . . . it was just awful. Parts of François were still there. It was just so horrendous. I was physically sick. Also, the other very difficult thing was to then go to François's room and collect his things. That was heartbreaking. Just terrible.'

'Ken was very upset – everyone was,' said Stewart. 'I can't remember anything specifically. I remember Ken being there when I got out the car, and then I remember us talking before I left the track. I remember Helen had already gone back to the Glen Motor Inn, and that's when I went to the room and told her that I wasn't going to race again. That was the first time she had known about it, but we agreed that we should stay and go to the race out of respect for François. But I don't remember Ken being in any way outwardly emotional about it. I wasn't as emotional as I had been when Jochen died; that affected me more and I don't really know why. Not just because of the circumstances. There was a big vacuum over a period of time.

'I can't remember how we got home from Watkins Glen. I do remember that the funeral was in Paris, and then we went to the family burial ground. We were standing round the tomb with the coffin, which was a large American one, big because of the airline requirements. Unfortunately, the coffin wouldn't go in the tomb. Nobody had thought of that. So we had to do what was left of the service right there, and then turn round and leave. It was one of those terribly bizarre things that happen – and this was happening at the worst possible time.'

The loss of Cevert affected everyone in the team and the entire Tyrrell family, from the oldest to the youngest. 'It was just awful,' said Kenneth Tyrrell. 'Sandy [Kenneth's wife] and I weren't at Watkins Glen, which somehow made us feel so helpless. We had spent a lot of time with François that year. He would come over to the factory for a seat fitting or something, flying his own private aircraft. He used to land at Fairoaks, which is not far from Ockham. He would say, "Let's go for a trip!" and he would fly Sandy and I and Claire [5] and Adam [3] to the Isle of Wight where he would land and then play with the kids on the beach. Just wonderful moments.' 'You'd just melt when you saw him,' Sandy added. 'It was his eyes! He was a real ladies' man. He was absolutely dishy. A real charmer.'

As the specialist magazines paid full tribute to Cevert, some carried mention of Stewart's rumoured retirement. The following Sunday, Ford organized a press conference at the Carlton Tower Hotel in London, where Jackie confirmed the rumours. There was a mix of emotions: relief that Stewart had finished his career without drawing a drop of blood; sadness among the mechanics that the wee man would no longer be around to take their workmanship to the limit on the race track. 'It was more than that,' said Keith Boshier. 'You'd do anything for Jackie, absolutely anything. He was so good at motivating people and he always took an interest in everything that was going on around him. I remember him at a race meeting going up to the bloke with the saucer outside the loo and chatting to him. What was in that for Jackie? Nothing. But he would do it, just as he would know all the tyre fitters, all the trade people, and remember their names. If you were sick, he'd come to see how you were. You wouldn't see any of the other drivers doing that. But, yes, it was also what he did in the car. We got to the stage where we knew when we went to races that if you went without a problem, you were pretty well going to win. That's just how it was.'

An era had ended. Ken Tyrrell knew things would be different from now on, but he had no idea that in terms of superb endeavour his team had just scaled the final peak. Slowly at first, but inexorably, it would be downhill from here on.

16

Starting Over Again

The events at Watkins Glen were covered in Eoin Young's diary column in *Autocar* with as much dignity as anyone could muster under such terrible circumstances. Young knew from bitter experience just how difficult it would be for Tyrrell and his team. The New Zealander had come to England as Bruce McLaren's secretary, ghosting his friend's column for magazines worldwide as well as becoming a partner in the original McLaren racing team. Deciding he would rather write about gossip than generate it and then attempt to hide it from fellow journalists, Young became a freelance writer. It was with painful professionalism that he had carried out his duties while penning Bruce's obituary in June 1970.

Young covered F1 worldwide and the CanAm scene in North America, a rigorous schedule that was eased by his landing a job as public relations consultant for Gulf Oil, who sponsored McLaren in both series. In truth, Young was more of a maître d' than a heavy PR person, choosing the more acceptable path of pouring a glass of wine and allowing the writers to make up their own minds in their own time about Gulf and the company's role in motor sport. It worked perfectly, until Gulf pulled out of CanAm racing at the end of 1973.

'Tyrrell phoned me up in November,' recalled Young. 'He said, "Gulf is out of racing – and you're out of a job." I said I didn't think it was quite that bad. Ken asked if I wanted to do the same sort of thing for Elf, and I said I didn't know. He said, "I asked you a question! Do you want to do the same thing for Elf?" When I sort of grunted in the affirmative, he said, "Right. You're on the first flight to Paris in the morning, you have a meeting with François Guiter at 11 a.m. and you are going to have lunch with him." I went, had lunch with Monsieur Guiter, we shook hands, and that was it for the next however many years.' It was to be the start of the first F1 motor sport hospitality unit to be set up specifically for journalists, arguably one of the most successful there has ever been, due in part to the welcome nature of the venture and Young's cheerful largesse. Guiter, meanwhile, would look on approvingly from the sidelines. This was part of his marketing strategy, another first for Elf and Tyrrell.

'I had no preconceived ideas about the sport,' said Guiter. 'I had not been to a motor race before. I came from TV and cinema, but when I started in F1 I could see big possibilities. We put a camera on the car – of course, in those days it was a big camera, nothing like you have now – and we invited a lot of key television people to see F1 through the film we had made. You also have to remember that, in France, Monaco was the only race we could watch live on television, and I think it was the same in many European countries. So we were giving F1 as well as Elf a lot of exposure.

'We were fortunate that, when we came into F1 in 1968, it was the first year when commercial sponsorship was allowed on the cars. By the time we got to the first Tyrrell with the large nose, we had put big Elf stickers on the car. I remember once at the British Grand Prix, the BBC came to us and said they would not televise the race if we did not take off our "giant" stickers. We said we didn't care. We said, "You are just one country and there are many others who will televise it." We heard nothing more; the BBC went ahead and televised the race!

'So all of this was creating fantastic exposure for Elf. I was a marketing man, and I brought a new approach. It was easy because, really, F1 was about gentlemen in tweed drinking whisky. Few people had thought about how to use motor racing. And one of the things we did was to feed the press at the races. There had been very little for them to eat, so we set up something at Ken's motorhome. He didn't always like that, but it worked. We had Young to look after things, and everyone seemed very happy.'

A more important question for the media was the identity of the Tyrrell drivers for 1974. Educated guesswork had already led to Jody Scheckter being the first choice. In fact, Ken had been at work before the fateful weekend at Watkins Glen had begun. The layout of the chalets at the Glen Motor Inn was perfect for allowing drivers to slip in and out of various rooms for secret assignations with team owners. Tyrrell had met Scheckter on the morning of first practice. 'He was told he would be a member of a two-car team but that he wasn't to ask any more questions because there would be no answers,' said Tyrrell, who obviously had an advantage over Scheckter in that he knew Stewart was about to retire. But Tyrrell's carefully orchestrated plan was shattered 24 hours later.

'Starting afresh with two new drivers was like beginning in Formula 1 all over again,' Tyrrell remarked. 'When I signed Jody, the first thing I had to tell him was that we didn't expect to win the World championship in 1974. I said he was not supposed to win Grand Prix races for me yet. I wanted one World championship point from him in the first race in Argentina and two from the next one in Brazil. If he could maintain that upward trend through the season then it was not unreasonable to expect him to win a Grand Prix later in the year.'

There might have been no pressure to go out and win the championship but, nevertheless, driving for Elf Team Tyrrell and sitting in Jackie Stewart's seat was a daunting prospect for Scheckter. 'It's going to be bloody hard,' he said at the time. 'I would really have liked a year under Jackie or someone who could have taught me. Now I'm going to have to feel my way for myself. Everyone relies on me now and I've got to put my mind to make sure of things like packing my gloves and overalls and visors and stuff like that. If I forget something now, it isn't just a nuisance. It could ruin a day of testing for me. The whole factory is hoping I will do well. I'm very much aware that Jackie was such a professional and now they're getting a guy with not much experience. I know Ken says he's not expecting a lot in this first season, but I'm still following in the path of the best driver in the world.'

A few weeks after signing Scheckter, Tyrrell brought Patrick Depailler on board to drive the second car. This was even more of a gamble since the Frenchman had competed in just two Grands Prix – and he arrived for his first seat fitting on crutches. It was just as well that Depailler was the opposite of the muscular Scheckter since the mechanics had to lift him in and out of the cockpit. Depailler knew how fortunate he was to be given the chance after the leg injury had forced him to miss the final two races of 1973. As he described the cause of the two fractures to his left leg, it became clear there was a worrying moral to the story, one which indicated that this carefree soul from Clermont Ferrand would never change. 'Every time I ride my bike, I'm like a crazy man,' he said. 'But, because Ken offered me a drive, this day I was riding very slowly, very prudent, but because of this I was not concentrating enough and I rode into a tree! So maybe I should keep going fast.'

That would prove difficult once he was out of plaster and on the race track. The Tyrrell, with its short wheelbase, would be a nervous and difficult car for two novices, their struggle emphasizing Stewart's complete mastery of the machine and exacerbating the loss of Cevert and his burgeoning talent. When Scheckter and Depailler qualified 12th and 15th in Argentina in mid-January, it seemed that things would never be as they were – at least in the short term.

Depailler managed to pick up points for top-six placings in Argentina and South Africa at the end of March, but Gardner was flat out on a brand-new car, one which would be more forgiving. Scheckter received the first 007 in time for the Spanish Grand Prix on 28 April and promptly scored his first World championship points with fifth place. When he followed that up with third in Belgium and second in Monaco, it seemed that Tyrrell's request for a possible victory later in the season might come sooner than expected. Incredibly, Scheckter completed the numerical sequence by scoring his first win at the next race in Sweden. Even better, Depailler finished second. The Tyrrell pair had been untouchable at Anderstorp, and no one could say exactly why. It was only June, and it seemed Elf Team Tyrrell had never been away.

Behind the scenes, however, Ken had been keeping his young drivers in check. In an interview at the end of the 1974 season, Tyrrell described how he had planned two different strategies for his drivers at Monaco. 'Patrick had done a very good practice time and was on the second row of the grid. We didn't know at that stage that he would have a problem and would not be able to start in his proper race car. So we were actually talking to him about the chances of winning the race. The plan was for him to make as good a start as he could, try to get in front on the first lap and then to win as slowly as he could. It would be up to Patrick to decide how he got to the front, depending on the starts made by the drivers ahead of him.

'With Jody, I gave different instructions altogether. He had qualified further back and I told him that if he finished this race and also managed to be in the first six, then that would be a tremendous achievement, especially if the race was as competitive as we thought it might be. Our instructions were for Jody to keep it on the island, don't touch any kerbs or guardrails, and to finish the race. Since this was his first visit, it was essential that he got the experience of an entire Monaco Grand Prix behind him, not just the first 10 laps. It was a question of trying to make sure that he was better prepared for next year, not still green in terms of this race.

'Jackie has been very helpful,' Tyrrell continued. 'He sat in on some of the meetings and he was able to give a lot of good advice, especially to Jody who has had little or no experience on some of the European circuits. Jackie warned him about overdriving during the early laps, which he said people seem to do at Monaco for some reason.'

Scheckter had obviously paid attention as he drove superbly to take that second place. The flow continued after Sweden as Scheckter finished fifth in Holland and fourth in France. The British Grand Prix was next, and Tyrrell took the short journey to Brands Hatch with the thought that a podium place at the very least would be on the cards. It would turn out to be much better than that.

It had been a strange season thus far with no team in particular taking the initiative. Ferrari, with an impressive new car and now under the control of Luca di Montezemolo, had not been consistent. Niki Lauda had won his first Grand Prix in Spain and had followed that with a victory in Holland, but overall the heavily reorganized team had yet to gel. McLaren had won a couple of races; Lotus, Brabham and Tyrrell had claimed one each. The British Grand Prix was wide open, and another wild card was thrown on the table when Tom Pryce, a prodigiously talented Welshman in his first season, put his black Shadow on provisional pole at the end of the first day of practice.

In the background could be heard the first rumblings of a political machine that would ultimately steamroller and dominate the F1 scene. For years, the teams had been negotiating individually with race organizers. Bernie Ecclestone had reappeared in F1 as the owner of Brabham, and he had quickly realized that the teams would be better off bargaining collectively. The Formula 1 Constructors' Association (F1CA, soon to be renamed FOCA) had been formed and had given organizers grief in 1973 by asking for more money. The organizers, in turn, had banded together to form Grand Prix International (GPI) and naturally resisted the demands. The GPI crumbled when, one by one, the organizers did separate deals with F1CA. It was the beginning of a new era, masterminded by Ecclestone.

At Brands Hatch, the 34 drivers entered for the race were more interested in finding a place among the permitted 26 starters. This never looked like being a problem for Tyrrell, particularly when Scheckter qualified third and Depailler 10th. Jackie Stewart, now in action as a TV commentator and a pundit at pre-race briefings on behalf of Elf, thought the race would be a fight between Lauda and Scheckter – an interesting prediction which appeared to ignore Peterson's Lotus on the outside of the front row.

The British Grand Prix marked a step forward in safety as the drivers were asked for the first time to complete a parade lap rather than follow the familiar practice of moving forward from a dummy grid to the starting grid proper, a procedure which had caused more problems in the past than it had prevented. The system worked well, particularly for Lauda, who made a perfect start and shot into the lead. Significantly, though, Peterson dropped to fourth, and it was Scheckter who gave chase. There seemed nothing the South African could do about Lauda as the Austrian maintained a steady eight-second advantage.

Further back, however, there was the first hint of trouble when John Watson pulled into the pits with a punctured tyre on his Brabham. Small, flinty stones had been flicked onto the track at various places, and within a few laps five more cars had stopped with similar problems. Lauda was untroubled, and remained that way until there were about 20 laps remaining. Then he began to feel the Ferrari squirm a little as he went through left-handers. The eagle-eyed Stewart quickly spotted the problem and told viewers to look for a dip in the profile of Lauda's right-rear tyre. Stewart was certain Lauda had a slow puncture.

He then described the Austrian's predicament: should he stop and lose the lead while changing tyres – an operation that in 1974 would have the car at rest for at least 15 seconds – or should he risk trying to reach the finish? Lauda chose the latter. It looked like paying off until five laps from the end when Scheckter, sniffing victory, snatched the lead. To the Tyrrell team's delight, that was victory number two in a season in which little had been expected.

Since the race was on a Saturday, there was time for celebration.

Ken and Norah had recently left Hook House and moved to the Old Rectory, a delightful detached property next door to the church in the nearby village of Clandon. As it was just over an hour's drive from Brands Hatch, it was the perfect place to host a party. 'We had extended Hook House and we really liked it there,' said Norah. 'The only reason we thought about moving was because we now had grandchildren and I wanted a swimming pool. There was no flat ground at Hook House, and Ken also wanted a tennis court. So, Ken found the Old Rectory and we fell in love with it. We were to be together there for 27 years.

'We had been having post-race parties at Hook House, flying in the Elf people by helicopter and so on, but there was a lot more room at the Rectory. When we won Brands Hatch, I wasn't at the race because I believed that these parties never work unless the hostess is doing a lot of work. So, everyone came back after that race. We had a marquee on the lawn; it was really nice. And great for the team after all the uncertainty at the beginning of the year.'

When he finished second in Germany and third in Italy, Scheckter found himself one of five drivers with a chance of the championship as this topsy-turvy season drew to a close. By the time the final race at Watkins Glen came round in October, the contenders had narrowed to three, and Scheckter was still one of them, albeit the outsider. In the end, Emerson Fittipaldi took his second title and seven different drivers had won races. The fact that Scheckter had been among them was more than Tyrrell could have hoped for, although Depailler, his season peppered with accidents, clearly had some way to go. In between crashes, however, the Frenchman had demonstrated that he was quick. He simply needed firmer guidance from Tyrrell.

The same could be said for Ken's youngest son, Bob. Having been to London University to read Spanish, Bob had no idea what he wanted to do at the end of it, the situation not being helped when he went for various interviews but failed to land a job.

'At that age you don't know that your dad knows the right

answers, you know it all yourself,' said Bob. 'I went to three interviews for management trainee courses and I wasn't getting any
offers. They all wanted to know what my father did, and I said he
ran a F1 team. So when they asked if I was interested in the team,
I said I was and that, who knows, one day I might go into the business. Looking back now, it was a stupid thing to say! I was talking
it over with Dad and he wanted to know what they were asking
at the interviews. When he heard what I had been saying, he
exploded. "For Christ's sake, don't tell them that!" Next interview,
I got the job!

'I went to work for Turner and Newell in Rochdale. I loved going
up there. There was no way I could join the family business with Dad
then. There wasn't room for anyone else; it would have been awful!
Kenneth had been more involved in going to the races than me. I
remember standing around during test sessions when Jackie was
driving and going to some of the races, and I remember only two
family holidays – there might have been more but I honestly don't
remember them. One was near Poole in Dorset and the other was a
pretty awful place in Majorca. That was it! The rest of the time was
spent racing. I used to drive vans for the team for holiday money in
the summer, delivering stuff to Cosworth and bringing engines back.
But to work for Dad full time would have been the pits!'

Kenneth Tyrrell was always the more likely of the two boys to join
the team, but by 1974 he was a fully qualified pilot, flying Viscounts
for British European Airways. Bob, however, did eventually enter
the business, and François Guiter was largely responsible for it. 'I
don't quite remember how it started,' said Bob. 'Guiter said to me at
a race somewhere that a lot of money could be made by selling team
merchandise. You couldn't buy a Tyrrell jacket then. Dad didn't
wear one, none of the mechanics did. They had overalls, but there
were no uniforms. Dad had a cloth cap! I don't think he was
involved at all. Guiter just said, "Why don't you do it?" I said I
didn't know anything about it, but he said Elf would give me £5,000
to help get it up and running and I had to do the rest. So I took a

week off work and we set up a stand at Monza. By Saturday, we had sold out. We had no stock left! I thought, "This is good!" I handed in my notice. I might have known very little about T-shirts, but Dad knew even less. It was worth trying. My wife Alison and I went to all the races, selling the gear, and we got a proper stand. It started to do really well. Other teams caught on, and eventually there were dozens of small shops at the race track.'

The Elf Team Tyrrell branding went down well at the end of February 1975 in South Africa where Scheckter was preparing for his home Grand Prix on 1 March. It was to be a dramatic few days. Scheckter crashed during final practice while trying to improve on his second row grid position. It was a major accident at the same section of track where Peter Revson had been killed during a test session the previous year. The difference this time was the newly installed catch-fencing the wayward Tyrrell had used to dissipate its speed, Scheckter eventually coming to a halt without actually hitting the barrier that had caused Revson's fatal injuries. Scheckter was able to return to the pits, where he told Tyrrell the car was not too badly damaged. 'I said I thought it was still possible to make it a runner. Ken later said I would make a lousy insurance assessor. He said it was like a man with one leg as a runner.'

Overnight, the mechanics, led by Roger Hill, built up the spare car, incorporating the most up-to-date bits and pieces that were still salvageable from the wreck. There would be an hour's running on race morning, enough time to have the car sorted for the Grand Prix. At least there would have been had the engine not seized four laps into the session. Once again, Hill and the crew had it all to do. Engine changes normally took four hours; they had only three available before the start.

Rather than stand around and get in the way, Scheckter returned to the Kyalami Ranch for lunch. On the way back to the track, the door of his helicopter flew open. The pilot dealt calmly with the situation, quipping that it was a hot day and they needed the fresh air. Scheckter wondered what on earth could happen next.

A perfect start catapulted the South African into second place between the Brabhams of Carlos Pace and Carlos Reutemann. Scheckter was still feeling his way with the car, but on lap three he decided it was good enough to have a go at taking the lead. No sooner had he done it than the brake pedal became spongy; he would have to pump it for the remaining 75 laps. The chances of holding on to the lead seemed slim. When Pace could no longer mount a challenge, Reutemann took over, closing down the gap on the Tyrrell. Scheckter pushed as hard as he dared. Reutemann responded. This continued for an hour and a half, but when the finishing line came Scheckter crossed it three and a half seconds ahead.

'When I won my first ever Grand Prix in Sweden the previous year, I figured that was going to be the most memorable win in my career,' Scheckter wrote in his column in *Autosport*. 'It wasn't until I stood on the winner's rostrum at Kyalami that I realized how proud I really felt about winning my own country's Grand Prix. Before I left South Africa to race in Europe, I didn't have an ambition that said one day you've got to come back here and win the GP. All I wanted to do then was to be able to come back and run in the GP. I'm not an emotional person, but I don't mind telling you that there was an enormous lump in my throat up there on that rostrum. I feel really proud to have made history for my country as the first South African to win at home, but the sad thing is it's only my name that will go down in the record books, because it was truly a classic example of a team effort. Ken, Derek and Roger and the mechanics really did a fantastic job picking up the trail of rubble I seemed to be leaving behind me and creating something raceable out of it. Jackie Stewart, who was there doing the radio commentary, reminded me that in 1973 he had tossed his car into the fence and ruined it in practice and Roger and the boys had rebuilt it and he'd gone on to win the race.'

Unlike 1973, however, this was to be the team's only victory in 1975. Scheckter finished joint seventh in the championship, more than 40 points behind the winner, Lauda. It was indicative of a mixed season for Tyrrell, competitive at some races, off the pace in others. Depailler had fewer accidents and set the fastest lap at Monaco, but otherwise his best result was third at Kyalami.

In his column on 16 October, Scheckter said he had considered offers to go elsewhere but had decided to stay with Tyrrell. 'It hasn't been a brilliantly successful year,' he wrote, 'but it's a good team and I believe that the measure of a really good team is its ability to stick together during the bad times as well as the good times. Ken runs the best team in motor racing, and I'm delighted to be staying on with him.'

A few weeks later, Tyrrell confirmed that he would keep Depailler for a third season. The news broke during a test session at Silverstone. The interest, however, centred not on the fact that the Frenchman would continue with the team but on what sort of car he would be driving. Once again, Ken Tyrrell was about to confound the motor racing world with one of the best-kept secrets yet.

17

Two Too Many

Motor sport writers had been aware that something was in the air. In early September 1975, speculation suggested that Ken Tyrrell was thinking of entering three cars in 1976, the third being run under a separate sponsorship deal, much as McLaren had done in 1974 with two Marlboro cars for Emerson Fittipaldi and Denny Hulme, the additional entry for Mike Hailwood having been sponsored by Yardley. Sure enough, Ken had entered a third car at Watkins Glen for Michel Leclere, but that was normal practice at the end of the season, a means of trying out new talent. The fact that Leclere was French also pleased Elf.

Autosport proved to be the most astute when the news pages suggested that the story was really about the car rather than the driver or the number of entries. 'Apparently,' said one item, 'the car is so technically advanced it's as revolutionary as the Cooper was in the late fifties. "Where did you hear that?" chuckled Ken. "If it's that revolutionary, you'll have to wait an awful long time before you see it."' It was a typical piece of stonewalling by Tyrrell. The media would have to wait no more than a fortnight.

On 22 September, members of the press were invited to a function room in the Heathrow Hotel. François Guiter led a party of French journalists, the Elf boss wearing a wry smile as they boarded a coach with four steerable front wheels for the short journey from the airport. 'I said it was funny, some of the things the English did with their vehicles,' Guiter remarked with a grin. His colleagues, puzzled at first, were about to understand the reason behind Guiter's subtlety.

A new car sat under a sheet, and the profile suggested it was a fairly normal racing car; a bit long, perhaps, but with a bulge on top where the airbox should be and four semi-circles at each corner. Tyrrell, Gardner, Depailler and Stewart mounted the stage. On cue, Neil Davis and Roland Law began to pull back the wraps. Nick Brittan, one of the most astute motor sport columnists of the day, described what happened next. 'The disrobing started from the back and was dramatically slow. The Ford Cosworth engine was revealed to a barely discernible grunt. The conventional cockpit aroused nothing but studied disinterest. Then came the first sight of the first small front wheel. You could hear the slight suck of air from the hundred-odd people in the room. Then the sight of the second set of mini wheels, and the slight suck turned into an audible rush of wind. Then silence. But real silence, for five seconds. It was the silence of disbelief. It was broken by nervous laughter. Then poorly supported applause. (Very difficult to clap with a glass of Elf champagne in your hand.) The expression that will remain etched on my mind for a long time was that of Frank Williams. Pure, honest, unadulterated, total disbelief. Eyes glazed. Jaw hanging open.'

The audience had come face to face with the first six-wheeled F1 car. And no one had known anything about it. 'I really don't know how we managed to keep that quiet!' said Neil Davis. 'We must have had 30 or 40 people involved and they were from ordinary walks of life – mechanics, fabricators, sheet metal workers – and I just don't know why they kept it secret. We had to have special small wheels and brakes made involving outside contractors. And then there were the special tyres. Yet the word never got out. Absolutely amazing. Ken had asked everyone to keep it secret and they did what he asked them to do. It was typical of the loyalty he inspired.'

Gardner had been thinking along these lines for some time thanks to earlier work with four-wheel-drive projects and the technical problems they entailed. 'Then we found ourselves in the seventies and in a strait-jacket,' he told *Motor Sport* magazine. 'Almost every-one out there had the same engine, the same gearbox, the same tyres; we needed to find a way out, we needed to find an unfair advantage – and the six-wheeler was it.' A popular theory was that the benefit of having four tiny front wheels was a massive reduction in the car's frontal area. Gardner explained that the size of the huge rear wheels put paid to that supposition. The main gain was in the absence of aerodynamic lift created by the standard front wheels; the smaller the wheels, the better the aerodynamics would work.

Gardner told the press at the launch that the six-wheeler – or 'Project 34' as it was known – was a concept for research purposes which might or might not have racing applications. Winter testing would prove that the car definitely had a racing application when it was consistently faster than its four-wheel predecessor. Critics pointed out that the P34 could hardly be otherwise since the 007 design was becoming long in the tooth.

It was not all plain sailing. Gardner, worried that the drivers might be unable to see the front wheels, had portholes cut in the cockpit sides to help to place the car while cornering, as well as to keep an eye on the condition of the tyres. The windows also allowed spectators to see the drivers at work, a benefit which was lost when Scheckter and Depailler, who soon became accustomed to the car's narrower front, stopped using them. When the windows were removed and spectators complained, Tyrrell responded by saying he had asked for their opinion through Eoin Young's column in *Autocar* and editorials in other magazines. 'We got 15 letters,' Tyrrell said with a snort. 'Forget it! Okay, so that means that people don't write to their MPs and complain, that it's too much trouble to put pen to paper. Perhaps everyone would have liked to see all the cars that way, but how were we to know? Fifteen letters is pretty pathetic. So we said we wouldn't bother. It wasn't that important anyway.'

The brakes, however, were a bigger concern. The drivers were finding it difficult to stop at least one of the four front wheels from locking before the others, but that did not prevent Tyrrell and Gardner from entering a P34 for the Spanish Grand Prix, the fourth race of the 1976 season at the beginning of May. The car was entrusted to Patrick Depailler, who immediately justified the decision by qualifying third, 11 places ahead of Scheckter's 007. Having done that, Depailler then underlined Gardner's worries during the race when he retired with brake trouble after just one-third distance.

Even so, the potential was there, a fact confirmed two weeks later in Belgium when Scheckter finished fourth in his first outing with a six-wheeler. It got even better at the next race in Monaco when both Tyrrell drivers finished on the podium, Scheckter second and Depailler third. Critics were forced to eat their words. Newspapers and magazines reported that Elf Team Tyrrell appeared to be on a roll, but not even the wildest optimist could have predicted what would happen next. Moving on to Anderstorp in Sweden in June, Scheckter claimed pole position and led Depailler home to a one-two. It was an extraordinary result at the same circuit where the Tyrrells had dominated two years earlier. And, once again, no one really knew why.

That much became evident as the rest of the season went by and the results began to slip down the scale of significance. The blue cars led races and the drivers finished on the podium six times, but never again would they get close to the heights experienced in Sweden.

Gardner put it down to Goodyear (understandably, perhaps) concentrating on development of the standard front tyres for Ferrari and McLaren as Niki Lauda and James Hunt fought an enthralling battle for the championship. This was the year of Lauda's fiery crash during what would be the last Grand Prix on the Nürburgring, followed by the Ferrari driver's remarkable recovery and a return, his head swathed in bandages, at the Italian Grand Prix a few weeks later. Showing a similar resolve not to be beaten despite a serious points deficit, Hunt clawed his way back with wins in Canada and at

Watkins Glen. Significantly, Tyrrell had put him under pressure on both occasions; Depailler might even have won at Mosport had a fuel line not broken and sent fumes into the cockpit. The instant he crossed the line, just six seconds behind Hunt's McLaren, Depailler immediately pulled onto the grass and slumped in the cockpit. Once helped from the car and taken to the medical centre, the doughty Frenchman was soon back in the Tyrrell caravan explaining how he had been on autopilot during the final laps. Seven days later, Scheckter led 41 of the 59 laps at Watkins Glen. Unfortunately for Tyrrell, Hunt was in front on the last of them when the chequered flag was shown.

An interesting sign of the times had occurred during an unofficial practice session on the Wednesday before the race. Scheckter, having agreed to join the Wolf team for 1977, asked Tyrrell if he could try one of the cars entered by Walter Wolf for the US Grand Prix. Ken agreed. Scheckter, wearing his overalls with Elf patches (the Wolf ran on Fina fuel), climbed on board and expressed himself satisfied after lapping within a second of the time established by Depailler in the P34. There would be as much chance of such a thing happening today as there would of seeing a Tory minister sitting among the Labour backbenchers during Question Time in the House of Commons. And it wasn't as if this was an end-of-term feeling associated with the final race. There was still one round to go.

Hunt's victory in the United States ensured that the fight would go to the wire in Japan at the end of October. Atrocious conditions prompted Lauda to decide that there was more to life than taking unnecessary risks; his withdrawal from the race, coupled with Hunt's third place, was enough to give the Englishman the title by a single point at the end of a championship fight which had done much for the profile of Formula 1.

Almost unnoticed on that grey, wet day, Mario Andretti won his first (of many) races for Lotus, and Depailler took second; had it not been for a puncture, he might have won. It was ironic that a tyre should have given him trouble because, ultimately, the rubber on the P34 would cause its downfall. The small front tyres had been improved, but not enough to stay on the pace. The situation was about to get much worse.

In an interview in March 1977, Ken showed little sign of remorse over Scheckter's exodus to Wolf. 'Jody is an unusual driver in that he went well on occasion but gradually became overshadowed to some extent by Patrick,' he said. 'That was something of a surprise because, generally speaking, Patrick had not been rated very highly and one wouldn't have thought that he could have been in front of Jody on so many occasions. So, you have to say that Jody was something of a disappointment, but I have always felt – and still feel – that he could be world champion in the right car. Maybe we didn't provide him with one. I'm not sure what the right car should be. But I have great respect for his talent and he has the right make-up to be a world champion.'

Tyrrell put his finger on the problem when he referred to the car. Scheckter was even more blunt in later years when discussing the P34. 'It was a rubbish car. I never agreed with the two fundamental concepts behind it. People talk about Tyrrell being technically quite good in those days, but I never saw it that way. Ken was a very good team manager, but at that stage they had started to fall behind technically. There's no question, when I signed for Tyrrell in late 1973 it was the team to be with. They had won championships and races in the short time before, but the unfortunate part was that François Cevert was no longer there, so we started with two young guys, Patrick and myself. I think that made Ken look at the whole thing in a different light, and it was perhaps not the best thing to do. Everyone said that Ken was the guy who calmed me down. The trouble is, it's difficult to say whether he did that too much or whether I was going to do that anyway.

'But the thing that stood out was that Ken and Norah were the most ideal pair I have ever met. A beautiful couple. I remember when we were in Brazil and in all sorts of trouble with the car. We were having a debriefing, and I was so outrageous, spitting blood and really letting fly. Suddenly, in the middle of the debriefing, Ken said we would have to excuse him because he had to go and see Norah and make sure she had a lift back to the hotel. I couldn't believe it! The cars were terrible, and Ken was concerned about Norah! I mean, I would have kicked my wife out and made her wait until I was finished. But that said everything about Ken and Norah, certainly the most wonderful couple I ever knew.

'Still, Ken could be very hard when he needed to be. It worked both ways. I had many failures with the P34, so many in fact that I came to England, had a meeting with Ken and told him I couldn't drive the car any more. I was scared because it was breaking all the time and he had to do something about it.'

Because of the refusal to hide his feelings, there were those at Ockham who were glad to see the back of the South African and his lack of enthusiasm for the P34. Those who were sorry to see him go were more than consoled by the signing of Ronnie Peterson, one of the fastest drivers of the time. Depailler, meanwhile, continued to revel in his ability to chuck the six-wheeler around, so much so that team members entered the new season with high hopes. At least, some of them did.

Twenty-five years on, Neil Davis continued to cherish an evocative memory of the P34. Mounted on the chimney breast in Davis's living room, a black and white picture shows Depailler in full flow, the four tiny front wheels on opposite lock as the Frenchman powered with typical extravagance through a corner. 'That was taken during a winter test at Paul Ricard in France,' said Davis. 'I'll never forget it. Ken rang me from the circuit and said he wanted me to go over to the bookmaker's in Woking and put £500 on Patrick to win the championship. I thought, "Blimey, that's not like Ken. He must know something!" Apparently, Patrick had smashed the lap record. The car was a lot bigger, but he was really flying. So I put the £500 on for Ken – and £25 for myself!'

Tyrrell was not alone in his enthusiasm. The news pages of

Autosport on 16 December 1976, under the heading DEPAILLER
STARTS TO FLY, carried the following story about the test at Paul
Ricard: 'Depailler was sensational in the latest Tyrrell P34. The car,
aerodynamically much sleeker than the earlier six-wheeler, eventually flew round in a sensational 1m 46.4s (compared to the previous
best of 1m 47.6s for Hunt's McLaren), the quickest ever set by an F1
car at Ricard, and beginning to nibble at the late Mark Donohue's
times in the CanAm Porsche four years ago. This is remarkable
when one considers that Ricard features a mindless mile-long
straight and the Porsche was giving around 1200bhp (compared to
465bhp for the Tyrrell). Patrick said the new car was very much
easier to drive through the quick corners than had been the case
with the older one.' Small wonder Tyrrell placed his enormous
wager. Sadly, it would be money down the pan – not that you would
have known it judging by a neat brochure produced by Eoin Young
extolling the virtues of the team and marking the arrival of a new
sponsor to join Elf.

Just a week or so before that *Autosport* article, the specialist press
had carried the news that, following the withdrawal from F1 of the
American-owned Penske team, First National City Travelers Checks
were switching their support to Tyrrell. Most of the money coming
in to Tyrrell from the US bank would be used to establish a research
and development department at Ockham. This was a major step
forward, not just for Tyrrell but for motor racing in general. Dr Karl
Kempf, a 27-year-old scientist formerly working on race tyre
research with Goodyear, had been signed by Ken. The American's
brief was the construction of a mathematical model for the P34 and
the putting in place of electronic instrumentation on six-wheelers
run by the development team. The installation of a computer at the
factory was seen as ground-breaking. These were revolutionary
times in F1. News also broke later in December that Hunt and
McLaren were to try a radio link between the car and the pits.
Today, of course, computers and radios are as essential as brake
pedals and steering wheels.

Young's glossy brochure, on a neatly folded sheet of A3, also explained that the team continued to operate more as a family than as a high-pressure business group. 'Ken Tyrrell heads the team of 30 who design and build the cars and race them all over the world,' said the blurb. 'His wife Norah looks after lap scoring and timekeeping, and son Bobby handles a marketing operation selling exclusive Elf Team Tyrrell racewear. The family atmosphere pervades the team of mechanics and car-builders. Roger Hill is chief mechanic, Roland Law is production manager and Neil Davis is works manager. The team also comprises two designers (in addition to Derek Gardner), a computer analyst, six mechanics who travel to all the circuits, two mechanics who prepare the test cars, five metal workers, three machinists, two glass-fibre specialists, a gearbox specialist, one van driver, two truck drivers and four administration staff.'

The brochure went on to explain that the P34 had become more aerodynamic thanks to a sleeker body shell and a slightly narrower track. In theory, this was the way to go; in practice, the inability of the front tyres to match the rest of the car would ultimately cause its downfall. Goodyear continued to focus development on the four-wheel cars. The result was that the rear tyres supplied to Tyrrell were state of the art, but the front tyres were metaphorically going nowhere. The discrepancy was reckoned to be as much as two seconds a lap, a hopeless scenario which upset the balance of the car to such an extent that not even Peterson, for all his brilliant reflexes, could cope. The front of the car simply did not want to go into any corner presented to it.

Changes to the front track made little difference, and resulting problems with the brakes meant modifications which brought more unwanted weight. In 1977, Depailler notched up just three podium finishes in 17 races; Peterson would have to make do with a third, a fifth and a sixth. It was the first year in which Tyrrell had failed to win a Grand Prix since the inception of the F1 team. Such a public failure would prove too much for Gardner. At Monza, in September, he left the team, turning his back on F1 for ever. It was a sad departure for a gentle, gifted man who had achieved a great deal in a very short time. It was also the end of the P34.

'I have no regrets,' said Tyrrell. 'It was an exciting project. We didn't make the decision to build the six-wheeler that easily. Derek wanted to build it several years before and I didn't think we were sufficiently experienced as manufacturers to cope with it. When we had to replace 007, I gave Derek the go-ahead to build the prototype and to explore the possibilities. It looked good, and we ended up having one of the most successful "first-year" cars ever built. But we didn't develop the car in the way we had hoped we would. That was quite obvious from the results, and for reasons some of which were known to us and some unknown. But I don't regret it for a minute.'

Peterson returned to Lotus for 1978 after a deeply disappointing season. 'Tyrrell was a team I'd always wanted to drive for,' he told Alan Henry of *Motoring News*. 'I'd wanted to for a long, long time. Their organization is very good and I reckoned that the six-wheeler would not only be very good, but it would also be reliable. But it was neither. It was no advantage at all. First of all, it was too heavy and, secondly, it was incredibly unreliable. I didn't see the chequered flag that often [in 1977]. By the time we got to Long Beach, a circuit on which it should have been great, I realized the whole business was hopeless. From then on, it didn't improve at all. In Argentina it was so hot in the cockpit that neither of us could drive the thing comfortably for more than three laps. We were almost dead in the car and fell off during the race through sheer lack of concentration.'

'I did regret Ronnie leaving,' said Tyrrell. 'It was one of the most disappointing things of 1977 because Ronnie had been a driver I had always wanted to have on the team. Unfortunately, he came to us in a year when we didn't have a competitive car. It was a great disappointment for him and for me. It was even worse for Ronnie than for Patrick, because Patrick had been with us for four years and he was entitled to expect one bad season! I felt very sorry for Ronnie

213

because he tried very hard all the time but the results were not what anyone wanted.'

François Guiter, for one, was sad to see the end of the P34. 'A car with six wheels! It was fantastic for Elf!' he exclaimed. 'We received a lot of publicity from this during the two years. In fact, there was a lot more to it than that. When the car first raced in 1976, it had a yellow stripe on each side. This was because there was a plan to use a Renault engine. It was Ken, in fact, who helped persuade Renault to use a turbocharged engine in Formula 1.'

Considering Tyrrell's resolute stance against turbos in later years, there is an amazing irony in the fact that he had been instrumental in bringing these forced induction engines into F1 in the first place. The rules had allowed for the turbocharging alternative ever since the introduction of the three-litre formula in 1966, but none of the manufacturers had taken up the option in the belief that a 1.5 litre turbo would never be a match for a normally aspirated three litre, particularly one as efficient and simple as the DFV. Compared to the uncomplicated Ford V8, a turbo with its inherent hardware and plumbing and cooling problems would be a nightmare. Renault began to think otherwise, thanks, in part, to Ken Tyrrell.

'Jabby' Crombac takes up the story. 'Guiter had to show results to his management at Elf. He knew Matra was not in a winning position, and eventually he had to give up Matra because of Renault. There had been a big row at Le Mans, on the Elf balcony, between the management from Matra and the management from Renault. Matra were doing well with the V12, but Renault, with their Gordini V8 in the Alpine, were not. Obviously, the Elf people were only interested in the Matra because the Alpine was in the doldrums, and the Matra and Renault people nearly had a fight! Renault went to Elf and said, "You are a state company like us; you must give up Matra otherwise you will lose the contract you have for Elf to supply all new Renaults with oil and so on." It went all the way up to Georges Pompidou, who was prime minister. He voted in favour of Renault.

'Renault was doing well in rallies, but Elf wanted to continue circuit racing. They were no longer with Matra after 1970, so they had to have something. Also, Guiter was wonderful in his support for French drivers, and they wanted to continue that. Elf paid for Renault's engines. They had produced the V6 sports car engine, and obviously the next thing for Renault and Elf was F1, but they didn't know which type of engine to go for. One view was to add three more cylinders to the two litre V6 and make it a three litre. Another idea was to work on a turbocharged engine because they already had experience of that with the Alpine rally car.

'They decided Ken should make the choice between the two. He came to Paris and listened to the arguments from both sides. He said that if Renault made a three-litre engine it would never be better than the Cosworth V8, but if they tried something new – in other words, turbocharging – it would take some time but perhaps they might find it to be successful. If it failed, well, they would be forgiven for at least trying something different. So Renault and Elf decided on the turbo, which means Ken was the godfather of this engine.

'The other thing to remember is that everyone knew Renault would be unable to make a very good chassis – at least to start with. But, because they were close to Ken, the deal was that he would use the turbo. Hence the yellow stripe on the P34.'

The arrangement did not materialize because Ken was not totally convinced by the turbo. His doubts were confirmed in July 1977 when the first Renault F1 car made its debut in the British Grand Prix and retired after 16 laps with a blown turbo. But that was to be merely the first faltering step in a long haul to success, not so much for Renault, but for the era of turbocharged engines.

For now, Tyrrell was preparing for another season with the faithful Ford Cosworth V8. First, though, he had to find a replacement for Ronnie Peterson, someone capable of joining Depailler to race hard in the next Tyrrell, a car that would have two wheels fewer than its spectacular but doomed predecessor.

18

Can't Catch Up

Didier Pironi must have wondered just what he was getting into. It was a dull, cold morning in November 1977 and he was standing in the unprepossessing car park at Ockham, staring at the building that housed the team he wanted to drive for. It was just after 8 a.m. and employees were beginning to arrive, some in beaten-up machinery, others in cars which had been lovingly cared for. The car he needed to see most, Ken Tyrrell's Ford Granada, was not present. Pironi was asked to come back in an hour. What to do? Ockham was hardly the centre of Paris.

The contrast between the former wood yard and Pironi's home city could not have been more extreme. Neither could the difference in cuisine as he arrived at a small transport café a few miles away on the A3. Ham and eggs, washed down by lemon tea and paid for with a crisp blue five-pound note, filled in the time, Pironi admitting that his appetite was not keen, such was the importance attached to the forthcoming interview.

Pironi was a perfect example of the Elf schooling system, the Frenchman having worked his way through the junior ranks, winning championships and the prestigious Monaco Formula 3 race the previous May. Tyrrell had witnessed that and much more in his role as one of the judges in the annual Elf competition for young drivers. Now it would be a case of dotting the 'i's and crossing the 't's. Or so Pironi hoped.

'I think we go now,' he said, suddenly rising from the Formica-topped table and freeing himself from the grease-laden air. Twenty minutes later, the Tyrrell car park was almost full as Pironi climbed from his rented Ford Escort and walked, briefcase in hand, to reception. A few minutes later, he made his way down the narrow windowless corridor with its emulsioned and lightly soiled plastered walls to the door at the end. A familiar gravelly voice from within responded to the knock. Pironi opened the flush-panelled door and was immediately confronted by Ken Tyrrell, rising from a high-backed leather chair which seemed to dominate the stark office. With his boyish looks, Pironi looked for all the world like a pupil about to be interviewed by the headmaster.

The analogy seemed perfect when Pironi finally emerged and tried but failed to maintain the ice-cold poise that would become his hallmark. 'To drive for Tyrrell is . . . fantastic! Fantastic!' he enthused. 'They are the best. No question.' Before he could say anything further, he was ushered next door to the workshop for a seat fitting in a car designed by someone who had gone through the same interview process some seven months before.

Maurice Phillippe had joined Tyrrell on 1 May. His credentials were impressive. A former design draughtsman with De Havilland, Phillippe had worked at the right hand of Colin Chapman during the halcyon days of the Lotus 49 and 72 before spending time on the Indycar scene in North America. He had signed up with Tyrrell as a consultant, later assuming the role of technical director on Gardner's departure. 'I discussed what we should do for 1978 at great length with Maurice,' said Tyrrell. 'He was of the opinion that the complications of a six-wheeler were such that it would be a fearsome task to try to get the front suspension geometry right when dealing with four wheels instead of two. Also, Maurice felt that by having a car which was, shall we say, "unusual" when compared to the rest, you never really knew where you stood. You could never be certain whether you had any advantage. The other aspect Maurice was keen on pursuing was designing a car that was simple for the mechanics to service. So, we opted to go back to a more straight-forward design.'

Tyrrell 008 was unveiled amid much heaving and grunting. A launch was organized in the beautiful surroundings of nearby Clandon Park, but the plans went awry slightly when it was discovered that the front door of the Palladian house had never been designed to accept a racing car. Particularly the P34, which would form part of a background display in the imposing entrance hall. To the mounting horror of Aubrey Parnell, the hapless caretaker, a group of strapping mechanics manhandled the bulky machinery sideways through the expensive woodwork and onto the polished marble floor, upon which one of the cars deposited a serious amount of oil. It was worth the trouble. The French press, flown in and headed as usual by François Guiter, were much taken by this piece of typical English charm. As for the local media, there were pragmatic questions to be asked about the presence of not one but two French drivers in this most British of teams.

Typically, Tyrrell came straight to the point. 'If there was a British driver who was good enough and had the same support from British industry which Didier has in France, then I'd sign him up. But there isn't. What on earth is a company like BP doing, for example? I mean, *British* Petroleum! It would be perfect if they had a schooling system like Elf. But they don't. The French boys have been able to get into Formula 2 with Elf and, in fact, seven of them have become champions. The British boys have not had this opportunity. They are scratching around to find the money. They need £150,000 or so for Formula 2, but because they can't put a deal together they are at a huge disadvantage. So we have two French drivers, and we are very happy with them.'

The Tyrrell transporter left Ockham at 6 a.m. on Wednesday, 23 November, six days after the announcement, and headed for the shakedown test at Silverstone. It was so cold that Depailler had to keep running to the loo between outings of no more than half a dozen laps. The Ford DFV proved reluctant to start first time. During one of the silences, Tyrrell leaned into the cockpit.

'Patrick, d'you remember the first time you drove the P34?' he asked.

'Yes, it was 'ere.'

'That's right,' said Ken, before flashing the familiar toothy grin. 'And you spun at Becketts. Remember?'

'Sorry, Ken, I can't 'ear you,' Depailler replied, looking up, his smiling eyes saying everything about the true quality of his hearing.

Depailler didn't spin that day, but reported that at pace he could see the rear wing vibrating in his mirrors. Other than that, the car seemed good. But there was a long way to go.

Tyrrell had no reason to change his mind about employing French drivers when Depailler finished third in the opening race in Argentina on 15 January 1978, and Pironi collected his first championship point at the next round in Brazil. It got better still in South Africa, where Depailler was part of a thrilling battle for the lead with Peterson's Lotus, the Tyrrell eventually losing by a whisker. Another podium position followed at Long Beach in California. Then, in the first week in May, came Monaco.

'Maurice more or less brought 008 to us because it was already drawn for another project he had been working on before he arrived,' said Roger Hill. 'He was a very different character to Derek. He was more hands on and he would make some wonderful sketches of any little mod he wanted to do. You didn't need a proper drawing because the sketch was just brilliant. I think some of the guys have kept some of them because they were little works of art.

'Anyway, he needed to do a modification when we were in Monaco. The car had these long radius rods; there were two of them running back to each rear wheel. They started buckling for some reason, and because there was a day off between the two practice days at Monaco, Maurice was able to fly back to England and have much larger ones made. He brought them back to Monaco, we fitted them to 008, they stopped bending and the car just went like hell after that.'

Depailler made a stunning start from the third row and shot into second place behind the Brabham-Alfa Romeo of John Watson. After tangling with Carlos Reutemann's pole position Ferrari at the first corner, Niki Lauda sorted himself out in the other Brabham and closed on the leaders. For 37 laps it looked like being a three-horse race, Depailler's blue and white Tyrrell sandwiched between the red Martini-sponsored cars. Then Watson, struggling with a brake problem, disappeared into an escape road. Now Lauda gave serious thought to taking the lead, but Depailler remained completely unflustered, and eight laps later he received respite when a puncture forced Lauda to make a pit stop. The Austrian, the reigning world champion, then began a storming comeback into second place, but Depailler was home free.

After a season without winning, Ken and the mechanics jumped onto the track and welcomed Depailler's first F1 triumph. To round off the day, Pironi claimed an excellent fifth place after resisting relentless pressure from the Arrows of Riccardo Patrese for an hour and 58 minutes. It was to be the highlight of the season. Four seasons, in fact.

The general trend to come was summed up during successive races in the late summer. Pironi's car had been damaged in Austria and it took his mechanics, Harold Mendel and Colin Denyer, every available minute to have it repaired in time for loading onto the truck in time to leave for Holland at the end of August. Mendel stayed at home that weekend (his wife was giving birth), his place taken by Roger Finnis, drafted in from the development team. The spare car was under the care of Roger Coombs and Richard Gear, with Roger Hill in overall command. The truck crew, John Lucas and Ian Hunter, provided additional help, along with Mick Brown, a factory hand taking his turn to attend a race meeting.

The Tyrrell transporter was now an articulated truck hauled by a

Ford Intercontinental; the Leyland bus chassis that had served the team for 10 years had literally belched its last puff of diesel smoke the previous season. Ian Hunter had suffered two nightmare trips as a result. 'The Leyland had a separate starter switch and it would stick down occasionally,' he recalled. 'On top of that, the engine had begun to stall quite often for some reason. I was on my way to the Swedish Grand Prix [in June 1977] with the six-wheelers on board, pulled up at a set of traffic lights rather quickly and the engine stalled. I pushed the starter button, got the engine going, but didn't notice that the button had stuck down. I drove for ten miles or so before realizing. I released the button and turned the engine off with the truck still going, and bump-started it because now the starter wouldn't work. I drove onto the ferry and got towed off when we got to the other side.

'When I finally reached Anderstorp after one or two dramas, I phoned back to England and asked them to bring out a starter motor. Roger [Hill] said not to worry, he'd fix the starter. I took the motor off the truck and gave it to Roger – and he couldn't fix it. That's how bad it was. So we got the local Leyland agent out. He couldn't fix it either. Since it was going to take too long to get a replacement, we had to find a way of getting the truck back to England. The Leyland guy made the starter work by poking a balldriver inside the motor and pushing one of the contacts forward. But you had to lie under the truck to do this! It was the only way to start the engine.

'Leaving Anderstorp, there was always a mad dash to catch the ferry. One of our trucks had already left, but I waited behind to get the two cars on board after the race. It was a big rush, but everything was fine until I reached a set of traffic lights where someone shot the red coming the other way. I had to pull up very quickly – and the engine, of course, chose that moment to stall. The truck was straddling this junction and I had to get out, crawl underneath with the balldriver and begin poking it into the starter motor. By the time I had finished, the traffic was jammed in all directions. I *just* managed to make the ferry.' Hunter nursed the truck back to Ockham, where a new starter motor was fitted.

The next race was at Dijon in France. It would be the last for the trusty Leyland. 'We had just left Dijon and it broke a piston,' Hunter said. 'I had a damaged racing car on board which they needed to get back to England very quickly. A guy called Roger Chalk came by in the Ensign truck and offered to give us a tow. We couldn't tow it off our rigid truck because there was nothing substantial to fix it to, so there we were, the articulated Ensign truck towing the Leyland with a piece of rope! You have to have an air supply for the brakes, so we got out one of the air bottles used for the wheel changes in the pits and put that in the cab, on the seat. It had a regulator on it and a tyre inflator and a pipe going out of the window and on to the brake cylinder so we could pump the brakes up. So we drove along, watching the gauge, and when the pressure dropped I would blow it back up again.

'After snapping the tow rope several times, we got to Paris just as dawn was coming up. The thought of tackling the Peripherique like this was a non-starter. I tried the engine. It started, and ran very roughly on five cylinders. We'd had to remove the half-shafts while towing because the Leyland had an automatic gearbox. These had to be refitted so that I could drive round Paris. By the time we reached the other side, the engine was well and truly on the boil. We bought a proper wire tow rope from a French truck driver and continued to Le Havre. Once we had struggled off the ferry in Southampton, we were met by a tow truck with all the correct gear – proper air lines, a big rigid tow bar and so on. I was towed all the way from the coast to Ockham – at 25mph. That was the worst bit of the journey because we had just done 300 miles in France on the end of a piece of rope at 55mph! It was, to say the least, an eventful swansong for the old Leyland.'

In August 1978, Hunter and Lucas enjoyed a trouble-free run to Holland in the Ford articulated truck. They were helped throughout the weekend by Mark Green, a 17-year-old working during his school vacation. Green was known to the team, and his reputation as a hard worker had got him the much-prized part-time job. Ken had a firm ruling on the question of youngsters wishing to become F1 mechanics. His daily post regularly contained requests from enthusiasts wishing to act as 'gofers'. None of them was considered. The set procedure was best illustrated by 23-year-old Steve Leyshon who, along with Bob Skene, worked on Depailler's car.

Leyshon had written to the team while still at school and was advised to serve an apprenticeship in the motor trade. Steve duly learned the basic mechanical ropes with a Ford dealer in Cardiff, and when he wrote back to Tyrrell he was asked for an interview. Much to Leyshon's surprise, he was offered a job on the usual trial basis of one month followed by a further probationary three month period. Eight months after joining, Steve was selected to travel to the 1977 South African Grand Prix. Just over a year later, he could claim to have tended the car that won the Monaco Grand Prix.

'That was the final cherry on the cake,' said Leyshon. 'Looking back now, the whole period was like a dream come true. Ken was the straightest-talking person I've ever met. He had a way of telling you something that made you listen, even if you didn't want to. You knew exactly where you stood with Ken.

'I'll never forget Bob Skene and I were on the receiving end of one of his froth jobs one day at Brands Hatch. After practice, you would remove the fuel that was left in the car and give the figures to Ken so that he could work out the consumption. We made a good team, Bob and I, since we were a sort of Celtic Fringe, Bob being from Aberdeen and me from Cardiff. We got on well – too well on this occasion. I was pumping and Bob was pouring; I thought he was counting and he thought I was counting. When we realized that neither of us knew the exact number of gallons, we tried to work it out. I wrote down what we thought should be the numbers and gave the notepad to Ken. He went away, and when he eventually came back the notepad flew from one side of the garage to the other. He went mad! Later that night, he made sure I went with him to dinner and nothing more was said. He'd had his say and that was it. Everything was done and dusted. Now, let's have dinner.'

Any chance of a repeat of the Monaco win in Holland disappeared when Depailler retired with an engine problem. At least his car was still in one piece; Pironi had been involved in a massive accident on the first lap, the Frenchman having collided with Patrese's Arrows. More than 200 hours' worth of effort by the mechanics to get the car ready had been wiped out, the Tyrrell having been hit from virtually every angle as it slammed into the crash barriers. Two weeks later, the Tyrrell truck returned to Ockham with not one but two damaged cars, Pironi and Depailler having been caught up in a multi-car collision on the first lap at Monza. This incident became much more serious when the hugely popular Ronnie Peterson succumbed to his injuries. It was a shocking blow to motor sport in general and Team Lotus in particular, one which took the joy right out of Mario Andretti's first World championship.

Peterson had been the perfect team-mate for Andretti, and they dominated the 1978 season in a car which had set new standards. Apart from looking sinister and sleek in the black and gold John Player Special colours, the Lotus 79 had introduced an aerodynamic phenomenon known as 'ground effect'. This effectively harnessed the passage of air beneath the side pods and pulled the car towards the ground. It immediately established a new agenda in design centres throughout the motor sport industry. Maurice Phillippe's office was no exception, and the Tyrrell 009 was the end result.

There was just one snag, and a major one at that: the new car did not have a single scrap of sponsorship identification on its flanks. After ten very successful and happy years with Tyrrell, Elf had pulled out. Coincidentally, First National City Travelers Checks had gone too. It was a major blow to the team, though neither Ken nor Bob Tyrrell realized at first just how serious it was.

Bob and his wife Alison had become more deeply involved with the marketing of team gear, this branch of the business having moved up several gears since those first tentative outings with one small stand at the races. 'Originally, we were just involved with Elf France,' said Bob. 'Then other countries joined in and we started getting orders from Elf places all over the world. These were serious numbers – 5,000 jackets at a time. We used to make sure the deliveries came in when the team were away at the races. Alison and I would pack them up – that's how I got a bad back!

'I was not involved at all with sponsorship; Dad did the deals with Elf. In those days, you didn't have a marketing department or anything like that. If you had a sponsor, you looked after him and you didn't go round trying to fill up the rest of the space on the car. It was a case of, "Everything's all right because we've got a sponsor and that's all we need to do." The merchandising was providing a good supplement and the six-wheeler had created a fantastic market, but obviously, none of this was a substitute for proper sponsorship. So I suddenly found myself getting more and more involved in the sponsorship side. It was evident at the end of 1978 that we were completely unprepared to go and find another sponsor. Until then, we were one of the best-backed teams in Formula 1, but the departure of Elf changed everything.'

Their loss would be keenly felt. Elf had developed their press relations to a fine degree, thanks to the ever-watchful eye of François Guiter and his front man, Eoin Young. The Elf party at the French Grand Prix had become a not-to-be-missed occasion thanks to the friendly family atmosphere around the pool at a smart hotel on the Mediterranean. On one memorable occasion, though, events appeared to go over the top, prompting Young to think that he would find himself without a job and Tyrrell without a sponsor.

'Life with Elf was great while François Guiter was in charge,' said Young. 'No one was in doubt who was Le Chef when he was around. He was a big man and he had been in the French Resistance as a frogman during World War Two. I remember one of the parties at the Ille Rousse in Bandol when Ken Tyrrell, in schoolboy mode, pushed Guiter fully clothed, in suit and tie, into the pool. There was one of those "Ohmagawd!" hushes when people realized what had happened, and I could see my job going out the window as my boss struggled, half-drowned, to the edge of the pool. I hadn't heard the frogman stories and I was amazed to see there was hardly a ripple. The big man had gone in like a porpoise and there'd been no sign of him, nothing at all, until he gracefully emerged from the water at the other end of the pool.'

Guiter had also been behind the introduction of an end-of-season test session at Paul Ricard when journalists were invited to the South of France to drive the various racing cars that enjoyed Elf sponsorship. In his delightful autobiography, Young recalled a very serious incident that highlighted the caring side of Ken Tyrrell's character.

'I was working in the office at home', Young wrote, 'when François Guiter called to say that an English journalist had been badly injured in a road accident near the circuit after the Elf presentation. He asked if I could bring the journalist's wife to the hospital to be with her husband. In fact it was a New Zealander, Murray Taylor, who wrote for *Motoring News*. Murray had been a passenger in a car driven by another journalist who had been killed instantly when they ran under the back of a mobile crane. Murray's wife Glenys, also a New Zealander, made the trip bravely considering that she didn't know the extent of her husband's injuries. When we were ushered into the intensive care ward, I nearly fainted at the sight of Murray's injuries. But Glenys simply went to his bedside, held his hand and whispered encouragement to him. One brave lady.

'We drove to the hotel where the Tyrrell team happened to be staying for testing at the track. They had heard the news and Ken had set a place for Glenys beside him at the table. I thought this was Uncle Ken being kind and doing his best to cheer up the poor girl after her ordeal. The meal progressed and they chatted, but it soon became apparent that Glenys was beginning to colour and get angry, loudly defending her corner. This didn't seem to be in any script I knew for comforting young ladies in their moment of distress. At one point I thought she was going to hit him! Then Ken gave that bellowing laugh, and that's when Glenys realized he had been winding her up, about New Zealand rugby or some such unlikely subject. He had led her into an argument to take her mind off Murray, and she said she felt so much better for it! It was a typically effective piece of Tyrrell human engineering in action.'

Ken always enjoyed a lively debate over dinner, but discussions around the family table took on a more serious tone at the end of 1978 as the consequences of Elf's and First National's withdrawal began to take hold. 'The loss of Elf took all of us by surprise,' said Bob Tyrrell. 'Nobody had gone out to look for a sponsor before because we didn't have to. So now we were thinking we would go out and find a sponsor the next day – but it didn't work like that. I suddenly found myself as the official sponsorship seeker!'

Bob's first catch actually landed in his lap. The telex machine in the front office at Ockham chattered into life one afternoon and a message in broken English announced that the communication was from Candy, a domestic appliance manufacturer in Italy. They were interested in speaking to someone from Tyrrell about motor racing sponsorship. 'We went to Italy and made a presentation,' said Bob. 'After a period of Italian negotiations, Candy agreed a deal. It was not for anything like the budget Elf had provided, but it was a big help. We didn't have enough money that year, and to be perfectly honest, I don't think we ever quite caught up after that.'

Five rounds of the 1979 championship had already taken place by the time the royal blue cars were entered for the Belgian Grand Prix as Candy Tyrrell-Fords. Pironi cemented the relationship by finishing third, the highest placing the team would achieve that year. Patrick Depailler had moved on to Ligier, and his place had been taken by another Frenchman, Jean-Pierre Jarier. Between them, Pironi and Jarier collected 28 points, just enough to hand Tyrrell the fifth spot in the Constructors' championship, which equalled the team's lowest placing since Tyrrell had begun to build his own cars.

Twenty-eight points might have been considered a disappointment at the time, but never again would the Tyrrell team scale such heights.

19

Tea and Sandwiches

Maurice Phillippe's first ground effect car had been only moderately good, but the next one, Tyrrell 010, was a step forward. The trouble was, the leading teams in the pit lane had taken two steps to Tyrrell's one. Frank Williams had led the way in 1979, his new car moving the ground effect principle on to a level that left Lotus far behind. Phillippe made a good copy of the Williams for the 1980 season, but by then Frank's team had already moved the goal posts even further away.

If the first Grand Prix win for Williams had been a significant landmark in 1979, the first victory for the turbocharged Renault had been an even more important pointer to the future. For the time being, however, the Ford Cosworth DFV continued to hold sway as Alan Jones and Nelson Piquet, representing Williams and Brabham, embarked on an increasingly tense battle for the 1980 World championship. Meanwhile, down in the wood yard, two years for Pironi had proved quite enough and he followed in Depailler's foot-steps to Ligier. 'I learned a great deal with Ken,' Pironi admitted. 'At the time, I felt it was a super team for a young driver to be with because Ken had a very good rapport with newcomers. The team was good on experience too, and I learned an enormous amount. I owe them a great deal. But I have to say that I didn't think either the 008 or 009 were very good designs. They were not competitive cars.

My feeling about Tyrrell was that they had the raw material for success but their cars were simply not good enough or fast enough. If they could have got themselves better organized on that front, they had the back-up and the mechanics to win races.'

Jean-Pierre Jarier hoped that would be the case, and he stayed on for a second season. He was joined by Derek Daly, a young Irish driver who would capture the headlines, usually for the wrong reasons. The Dubliner certainly started off on the right note when he finished fourth at the first race in Argentina in a 009, but his performances went downhill from there. Or dramatically uphill, as things turned out five races later in Monte Carlo.

Jarier and Daly, in Tyrrell-Ford 010s, had qualified in the middle of the grid for this classic procession through the streets. As Tyrrell pointed out before the start, the only hope for his drivers was to stay out of trouble and take advantage of the misfortunes of others. Daly would have done well to heed this advice. As the cars rushed towards the first corner, Ste Devote, the knock-on effect of this well-known bottleneck caused drivers to brake earlier than usual. The mid-field came close to a standstill as a result, but not Daly. Caught out by the dramatic slowing of the car in front, Daly slammed into the back of Bruno Giacomelli's Alfa Romeo, the Tyrrell riding up a rear wheel and launching itself into a crazy journey clean over the top of the Italian car. The Tyrrell twisted and rolled during its brief flight before landing on another car – the Tyrrell driven by Jarier. The good news was that Daly's car had not rolled to the right, into an area peopled by photographers and officials, one of whom was Jean-Marie Balestre, the president of the FIA, the sport's governing body. As Balestre immediately started ranting to all and sundry about the Irishman's heritage, Daly probably wished he *had* actually landed on the president.

Several drivers had been involved in the ensuing mêlée, most of them without the faintest idea as to what had happened. 'There were about four or five cars in various states of disrepair,' Daly recalled. 'The drivers had climbed out and Jean-Pierre was really laying into

Giacomelli, saying it was his fault. Giacomelli said it wasn't, and Alain Prost, who had also been caught in the middle of it all, hadn't a clue what was going on. You see, the thing was, Jean-Pierre hadn't seen me because I had come from above! But the really comical bit was that the fleeting thought went through my mind that I might get away with this!

'I was explaining what happened to Jean-Pierre when Balestre came over, grabbed me by the arm and began telling everyone in the most vindictive manner that I was responsible. I could hardly deny it, but I didn't need that. The drivers accepted the facts reasonably well considering I had just wrecked their race – which, in those days, wasn't stopped despite bits of cars all over the corner.'

The hardest part was still to come. Daly had got through the two days of practice in Monaco with only one brush against a kerb, but on the day before the race he had crashed heavily and spectacularly in a Procar event for BMW sports cars. Now, he had to walk the 500 metres to the pit lane and explain himself to Ken Tyrrell. 'I'll never forget that walk back to the pit,' he said. 'I went up, looked him in the eye and said, "Ken, I'm sorry. It was my fault." He looked at me in disgust and said just one word: "Again." That was it. But he said it slowly and loudly. It was a scalding rebuke of headmasterly quality.

'I lived in Monaco at the time, so I packed up my gear. As I walked back to my apartment, I went by this Ferrari showroom with a yellow Dino 246 in the window. I went down the next day and bought it to make me feel better. It didn't actually make me feel better then, but it does now. I paid $11,000. I still have the car, and it's probably worth $75,000! But I was really pissed off about the accident. Ken never called me during the rest of that week and I don't think we spoke until the next race.'

Tyrrell did not need to labour the point. He had been around long enough to know that these things happen, just as he could never guarantee a driver that his car would be 100 per cent reliable. Even so, as the season wore on, Daly began to wonder just how much misfortune a single driver was meant to endure.

Following an excellent run in the British Grand Prix at Brands Hatch on 13 July, where Daly led home Jarier in fourth and fifth places, the performance of 010 began to fade as rivals stepped up development, something Tyrrell could not afford to do. The drivers began to murmur that the chassis was flexing, but in Austria in mid-August Daly was to suffer something much worse. It was while defending 11th place with his usual vigour that he experienced a driver's worst nightmare: he pushed the brake pedal and nothing happened. Worse still, when he tried to turn into the corner, a quick left-hander, the steering didn't respond. The Tyrrell shot straight off the road and into a cornfield.

'I saw this barbed wire fence coming up and that really frightened me,' Daly recalled. 'I couldn't spin the car. But, by the grace of God, the car went sideways and then backwards, the roll-over hoop behind my head snapping the barbed wire as I went through. I tell you, if I'd still been going forwards . . . well, it didn't bear thinking about. So, the car finally stops and the corn catches fire from the heat of the disc brakes. I was out of there like a shot, believe me.

'They examined the car in great detail and could not find anything wrong. The steering was perfect; the brake pedal was perfect; the car rolled; everything looked okay. It just appeared that I had gone straight off the road. I could tell from Ken's manner that he doubted what I was saying. As they pushed the car onto the transporter, I was standing with my engineer, Brian Lisles. He noticed that the left-front brake disc was not rotating with the wheel. The bolts holding the disc had simply sheared. Everything rotated, but the disc was not connected to the wheel. That was a relief, I can tell you.'

If Daly thought that was bad, he was to have another brake-related problem, this time under even more frightening circumstances, during the Dutch Grand Prix a few weeks later. Holding eighth place with 12 laps to go, Daly reached the end of the 190mph straight and hit the brakes for the hairpin that followed. The left-hand front disc shattered instantly, tearing out the caliper as it did

231

so, the flailing metal then breaking the top link in the suspension. Daly knew he was in for another terrifying ride. 'When I hit the brakes,' he said, 'it was like someone had a hammer under the pedal and they were going bang-bang-bang against my foot. I saw in slow motion the front wheel fold back onto the cockpit. I remember saying to myself, "I hope they see this and realize it's not my fault!"'

Because there was braking of sorts from the right-front wheel, the car veered slightly right, an angle which took it past the catch-fencing designed to arrest any wayward car on the outside of the corner. The Tyrrell skipped across the narrow run-off area and went nose first at unabated speed into a tyre wall stacked against the crash barrier. The impact sent the car high in the air and over the barrier; it came to rest with its nose resting on the top layer of guardrail, pointing at the sky. 'That was the very first time when suddenly my life began to go before me,' Daly continued. 'As I careered towards the barrier, I could hear the ambulance driving from the track to the hospital; I was thinking of my mother at home and how sad she was going to be when she realized how badly hurt I was. This was going to be the big one I'd never had. I knew my legs were going to be smashed, judging by the speed I was going off the road.'

Those of us watching from the inside of the corner were convinced Daly had broken legs, at best. It was with relief that we saw him moving around in the cockpit, and complete amazement that we not only saw him climb out but eventually come running across the track on his way to the pits. Daly had a pale complexion at the best of times; on this occasion, his skin was a ghastly shade of creamy white, but his sense of calm had not deserted him.

'That was lucky!' he remarked at the time, with a grin. 'The tyre barrier did a fantastic job. I knew I was going to hit it very hard, and I just had time to pull back my legs as far as possible. It was a hard impact, but everything seemed to be absorbed and progressive. My legs hurt a bit, but otherwise I'm fine. When the car came to rest, I didn't know where the hell I was. The nose was pointing upwards and all I could see was sky. But I knew I was okay and that was all that mattered. Who's leading, by the way?' Once Daly had reached the pits he was sent to hospital to be checked over, receiving stitches for a cut in his leg. 'The amazing thing was when I came back to the track that night. There was nobody there. My clothes were lying in a corner. I put them on, and I remember thinking that nobody seemed to care. I remember that as being one of the cold sides of F1. In fairness, Ken called the next morning and said, "Derek, I'm truly sorry you had an accident of that magnitude in one of my cars."'

Jarier finished fifth that day, but the remaining three races would produce a single seventh place and another pile of broken parts and damaged bodywork. Daly had mixed feelings when he left at the end of the year. 'It was a great place for a young driver to learn. The first time I drove 010 had been in South Africa. The gear lever was made of a lighter material so I didn't have the mechanical feel I like in a gearbox. During the race, I tore the dogs off one of the gears. When we got back to England, Ken called and said he wanted me to come down to the workshop as soon as I could. He had set up a gear cluster and gear lever and actually had someone go through the working of the gearbox in minute detail so I would see exactly why I had knocked the dogs off it. Instead of simply saying, "Don't do it again!", he had physically showed me what I needed to learn. I don't think I broke a dog ring [a circular, cogged part of the gear selection mechanism] during the rest of my career.

'Ken could be very helpful like that, but you didn't want to be on the receiving end of a froth job. I remember Jean-Pierre and I had qualified quite close together for that race at Zandvoort. We both said the car was actually quite good and we weren't sure what to change to make it better. Ken suddenly exploded! He couldn't understand how two drivers could say the car was good yet they were not at the front of the grid and seemed to have no idea about how to get there. He went mad! We were simply trying to say that the car was good, but it just wasn't quick. He could not buy into that at all.'

When Ken examined his end-of-year accounts, he discovered that the various accidents during 1980 had done much damage to an already thin bottom line. 'When you are in the thick of the European season and racing once a fortnight,' he said, 'it's very difficult to keep your team competitive when you are spending most of the time repairing cars rather than developing them. We had 11 accidents in 1980 and only two of them were the fault of the car. The other nine were driver errors – although I have to say not always our drivers. Money was tight, and we had to make some cost-cutting measures. We used to take one member of the factory to each European race at our expense as a means of getting everyone involved, but we had to stop that because it is quite expensive. We also stopped buying materials far in advance; we simply bought enough to do the next few races. We didn't buy any capital equipment. We didn't take on any more staff, and the number stayed at 43.'

Significantly, despite these difficult, changing circumstances, no one left the team.

'That was really noticeable,' said Steve Leyshon. 'There was an absolute minimum of staff turnover, unlike somewhere like Lotus where there seemed to be different faces at every race, more like a bunch of weekend warriors than a proper race team. It was all to do with the way Ken chose his staff. He didn't pick primadonnas. He chose people he knew would want to make themselves better and work with the team. Ken inspired incredible loyalty. You'd do anything for him. We knew that times in 1980 weren't as good as they had been before and we were under no illusions that it was going to be just as difficult in 1981. But you never thought about leaving.'

The team's problems increased when sponsors Candy withdrew with great regret. The Italian company was simply too small to justify the cost. The first casualty was Karl Kempf and his computerized research, this potentially important avenue of development being cut off in its prime. 'That was a pity,' said Keith Boshier, as he watched from the sidelines while preparing bodywork with his usual meticulous eye for detail. 'Karl was a really clever guy, a nice bloke, always willing to chat with everyone on the workshop. I think, however, that Maurice [Phillippe] sometimes felt Karl was treading on his toes. This was in the days of ground effects, and the cars had to have skirts running along the bottom of the sidepods. When we were being hopelessly outperformed, Karl walked round Brands Hatch and watched the cars. I remember him coming back to the pits and saying he could see what the trouble was: the Williams skirts were on the ground all the time; ours were off and air was getting in. We didn't have the proper springs. But they wouldn't listen. Karl was years ahead of his time, but you can understand others thinking this wasn't what it was all about.'

The Tyrrells were left yet again with nothing more than the maker's name written defiantly in large white letters on the sides of the cars. It made for a sad sight when the team turned up for a non-championship opener for 1981 in South Africa. It rained during practice, and the water highlighted the outline of 'Candy', where the letters had been picked off, on the surface of the team's umbrellas. Ken had even had to go as far as making everyone redundant for a brief period. He was able to keep on only a skeleton staff, virtually closing up shop for a couple of weeks until he found some finance. He didn't owe any money, but there certainly wasn't any coming in. Better to stop than carry on in hope. Still, the mechanics were called back at the last minute and cans of paint were added to the freight to allow the second car to appear in the colours of Deutz (supporting the South African lady driver Desire Wilson at Kyalami) and the black and red of Michelob, in recognition of the paying American driver Kevin Cogan.

Times were not only hard, but confused. Formula 1 had been in danger of tearing itself apart for some time. The collective strength of the teams had grown through the Formula One Constructors' Association (FOCA), and the Ecclestone-led organization had confronted the governing body (FISA) during 1980. The resulting polarization saw manufacturers such as Ferrari, Renault and Alfa Romeo side with FISA, while the likes of Williams, McLaren,

Brabham and, of course, Tyrrell were firmly behind FOCA. Matters had come to a head in South Africa, where the FOCA teams had defiantly run their own race (the last time an entire F1 grid of 19 cars would be powered by the Ford Cosworth DFV). The race at Kyalami did not therefore count towards the 1981 championship, but it did force a compromise and the birth of the Concorde Agreement, the framework of rules by which the sport would be run. At its heart was the recognition that FOCA, not FISA, would look after F1's commercial interests.

'This is a good thing,' said Tyrrell at the time. 'Formula 1 has to be controlled sensibly and FISA hasn't been doing that. To be honest, I didn't see that they were ever going to be capable of doing so. It's far better for FOCA to look after the commercial side of F1. People say that it's wrong that Bernie [Ecclestone] runs a team [Brabham], yet he is effectively running FOCA. I don't think that matters. The fact that he is running a team is neither here nor there. In fact, it gives him a better insight; he knows the current problems. If Bernie wanted to give up being involved in the running of FOCA then we would find somebody else to do it. But he likes doing it, he gets very involved in doing it, and it's a thing he does extremely well. Why not let him do it?'

Why not, indeed. Ecclestone would continue to run FOCA, much to the benefit of the teams, who discovered undreamed-of wealth in the next two decades. But the final extent of Ecclestone's influence would become a matter of deep concern to Ken Tyrrell before the beginning of the new millennium.

For now, though, his worry was keeping the team in racing. Jarier and Daly had moved on, Tyrrell signing the American Eddie Cheever and taking on pay-drivers – Cogan for the US Grand Prix at Long Beach, and Ricardo Zunino in Brazil and Argentina – for the first few races. When it came to the San Marino Grand Prix in May, the first event in Europe, Ken reverted to his preference for bringing on new talent – aided, in part, by a small amount of Italian sponsorship money – by giving a drive to Michele Alboreto, a shy

24-year-old from Milan. A new car, 011, appeared mid-season – not that it made much of a difference; Cheever crashed it during its first outing at Silverstone and was forced to use the 010 for the race. The height of his achievement would be fourth that day in Britain, plus three fifth places elsewhere; the nadir, a failure to qualify in Austria. Alboreto struggled at first, failing to qualify in Spain and Germany, but Ken could see the promise. Latent talent, however, did not pay the bills, and the Tyrrell Racing Organization slumped to eighth equal in the Constructors' championship with a mere 10 points.

The financial struggle intensified to the point where Ken found himself on the horns of a dilemma four races into the 1982 season. The divide between the FOCA teams and the manufacturers aligned with FISA had grown in direct proportion to the increasing power of the turbocharged engines used by the latter. The more financially sound FOCA teams had begun to use large amounts of expensive but strong and lightweight materials in order to produce cars under the 580kg minimum weight limit, and in order to have those cars satisfy the weight limit during post-race scrutineering, someone thought up an urgent need to equip the cars with water-cooled brakes, a requirement that had about as much value as tailoring a driver's seat with velour upholstery.

It worked like this. The water-cooled brakes would require a large water tank. The coolant would be quickly dispersed in the general direction of the brakes – assuming the tank had been filled in the first place – thus giving an immediate weight advantage, the FOCA teams then claiming that the rules permitted the tanks to be refilled completely before post-race scrutineering. When Brabham and Williams did this after finishing first and second in the second round of the championship in Brazil there were immediate protests from Renault and Ferrari. The manufacturers said they merely wanted clarification of an admittedly grey area in the regulations; the FOCA teams scoffed at such feigned innocence.

Matters became much more serious 29 days later when an FIA

appeal tribunal declared that cars should meet the 580kg weight limit at all times during the race. Nelson Piquet and Keke Rosberg were therefore disqualified from their first two places, victory in Brazil handed to the Renault of Alain Prost. There was immediate outrage from FOCA. The first casualty was the San Marino Grand Prix, held during the week following the appeal hearing. Only 14 cars took part at Imola, the majority of FOCA teams having decided to boycott the event. There was a certain amount of unease among the renegades when Tyrrell announced that he felt he had no option but to race. The timing of the dispute could not have been worse for Tyrrell. Having struggled for more than a year without a major sponsor, Ken had negotiated a three-race deal – with the possibility of further involvement – with his old friends from Candy. He could either woo the Italians at their home event and survive, or support FOCA and go out of business. It was with great reluctance that he chose the former.

Ken being Ken, however, he made his presence felt by loudly condemning the water tank ruling and lodging official protests against the Ferraris, Renaults and Toleman-Harts. Not surprisingly, perhaps, his complaints were thrown out. Having tried to hold F1 to ransom, the FOCA teams damaged their image even further by dragging the water tank issue and other matters to the International Chamber of Commerce in Lausanne. It was to be a lost cause; nothing would stop the advance of the turbos. Tyrrell, meanwhile, had lived to fight another day, albeit with much unhappiness over the Imola affair.

At least Ken's faith in Alboreto had been justified as the Italian grew in confidence and began to finish regularly in the points with the 011. Still, Ken was frustrated because the race performances were being compromised by qualifying, when the DFV-powered Tyrrell proved no match for the turbo engines that, significantly for small teams such as Tyrrell, were increasing in numbers elsewhere. Candy's support was most welcome, but the team continued to struggle. Just before round six in Monte Carlo at the end of May,

Ken gave an assessment of his latest position. 'If you had told me that we would have survived this long the way we have, I don't think I would have believed it,' he said. 'We knew that we were working hand-to-mouth and that we were going to have to be very careful. We drew up a very tight budget, which I controlled personally on a week-by-week basis, and we haven't gone over budget at all. I examined every invoice and bill, be it for £10 or £10,000, and cut everything to the bone. We have reduced our staff from 43 to 33 and stopped going testing. We've only done the things we had to do. We've stretched the mileage of our engines. Instead of a rebuild every 500 miles, we extended one particular engine to 900. It's risky, but we haven't broken an engine through over-mileage even though we've just had two expensive failures in Belgium on engines costing £30,000 each.

'That brings other complications. We desperately need to do well in Monte Carlo but we are short of engines. Two arrived back from the test bed just after the truck had left for Monaco. Normally, that would not have been a problem; just fly them down to the South of France. But these aren't normal times! So, we've had to send them by road. That's tied up a man's time when we really need him at the factory. We should have sent the engines in our van, but, quite frankly, we didn't think the van would reach Monte Carlo. We should have replaced it some time ago, but for obvious reasons we can't. Very fortunately, I get a loan car from the Ford Motor Company every year, and have done ever since we started in F1. It's a Granada estate, so we folded down the back seat and away we went. At least that saved the cost of a hire car when we arrived here. It's quite normal for us at the moment. Quite often I will take the Granada and collect engines myself. It saves bringing someone in over the weekend. I feel I may as well do that as sit in the bloody garden!

'But where the cutbacks have hurt most is not being able to do any wind tunnel work. That's been very painful for our engineers, who feel frustrated by not being able to do all the things they want

239

to do. Also, I have always been keen to get the mechanics back from the Grands Prix on the night of the race, which allows them to have a day or two off before the cars arrive back. But now, instead of flying them back, they drive back. We have saved between £400 and £500 that way, but it means they don't get back to Dover until 6 a.m. on the Monday, having not been to bed all night. That's not very good when you've just done three hard days at a race track.

'It's been hard on everybody. The motorhome was one of the first things to go. We have our debriefs in the truck, and instead of hot meals the mechanics have sandwiches. It's not satisfactory, not satisfactory at all. But we can get by without it, even though it's difficult if you have a sponsor come along and you need somewhere to have a chat in private. We just have to make these cutbacks. Candy and our other sponsor, Imola Ceramica, will be stopping after Monaco. That means we will be back to zero again. That's hard when a team needs £1 million to run two cars for a season and hope to score points.'

Nonetheless, Ken continued to be positive as he went on to explain that a test during the winter of 1981–82 at Paul Ricard had produced a minor breakthrough in the understanding of the car. That, coupled with Alboreto becoming number one driver in 1982 on Cheever's departure, had given the team some much-needed encouragement. 'Once Michele started to do a lot of testing, he realized the team was relying on him,' said Tyrrell. 'He responded, and his performance has improved thanks to that and increased confidence in the car.'

Monaco might have been a major disappointment – the Italian lost fifth place with a bent suspension mounting point, the second Tyrrell, driven by Brian Henton, finishing a distant eighth after an early unscheduled pit stop – but Alboreto followed up excellent early-season results by winning points in France, Germany and Italy. His fifth place at Monza on 12 September was particularly timely because Tyrrell had agreed a sponsorship deal with Denim aftershave for this race and the final round in Las Vegas. Tyrrell said he was confident of a good result in the US, but not even his most optimistic forecast would have covered what was about to happen in the heat of Nevada.

20

The Last Hurrah

Ken Tyrrell could barely contain himself. 'Look at this!' he said, stabbing his finger at a blue betting slip. 'Got some money on Michele, have you? He's going to win y'know.' Ken seemed to know more than the bookmakers. This was only the second time the Grand Prix had come to Las Vegas. Judging by the odds being posted across town, the betting offices had not done their homework. The handicappers had concentrated on a three-way fight for the championship. Keke Rosberg, who needed to score only two points, was favourite to take the title while his rivals, John Watson and Niki Lauda, were quoted as outsiders. Watson, though, was favourite to win the race since that was precisely what the Ulsterman needed to do if he was to have any hope of stopping the championship going to Rosberg and Williams. As for the rest, who cared? Ken Tyrrell certainly did. 'Twenty to one for Michele!' he spluttered. 'They must be mad! The mechanics have put their money down. I've got one hundred dollars on him. Get in quick before they realize what's going on.'

It took a while for the message to filter through. From the moment Alboreto set off on his first lap of the circuit at the back of Caesars Palace, the dark green Tyrrell was quick. The Italian revelled in the balance and grip that paid dividends on an unimaginative track zigzagging between concrete walls laid out in the massive parking lot behind the hotel. The car park had been designed to cope with the large crowds attending world title boxing contests. This was also a World championship event – not that you would have known it judging by the sparse numbers braving the heat in the open grandstands. These people understood Ferrari and Mario Andretti; Tyrrell and Alboreto meant nothing. At least not until Thursday evening, by which time the Denim-sponsored car had been fastest in the unofficial practice session in the morning and second quickest in the afternoon. The punters sat up and took notice when Michele was third overall on Friday, the fastest non-turbo on the grid for Saturday's race. The odds were slashed to 3–1. Ken smiled, and double-checked his betting slip.

A win for Alboreto was not necessarily a foregone conclusion. The Renaults of Alain Prost and René Arnoux were on the front row of the grid, almost a second faster than the Tyrrell, but their season thus far had shown that reliability did not match the turbo per-formance, the Frenchmen having scored just two wins apiece. More worrying for Ken was the presence of Eddie Cheever alongside Alboreto, Tyrrell's former driver having had a difficult year with the Talbot-Ligier but very keen to prove a point on home soil. Rosberg, starting from the third row, would not be a problem since he was anxious to stay out of trouble. The McLaren-Fords of Watson and Lauda were even further back.

Tyrrell's worst fears were confirmed when the Renaults shot into the lead and Cheever and Alboreto engaged in a bout of heavy wheel-banging as they fought for position going into the first corner. Alboreto emerged in third place, but with the imprint of a Ligier wheel on his right-hand sidepod and blue paint on a rear wheel. Cheever had come off even worse, his left-front wheel slightly out of alignment. At least it meant the American would not be troubling Alboreto for the remaining 75 laps.

As the Renault drivers squabbled among themselves, it was apparent they were failing to get away from Alboreto as anticipated. Michele knew he merely had to bide his time. The first chink in the

French armour came on lap 20 when Arnoux lost the lead, then trailed into the pits with engine trouble. Freed from the in-house battle with his team-mate, Prost was able to concentrate on winning the race. Bit by bit he stretched his lead to 18 seconds. Then the gap began to shrink as Prost struggled with his brakes and a vibration from the front end of the yellow and white car. On lap 52, Michele Alboreto took the lead of a Grand Prix for the first time. With just 10 laps to go, Ken applied caution and had the pit board order his driver to ease off. Watson had worked his way into second place, but with 30 seconds to make up the Tyrrell seemed safe.

Alboreto, usually silky smooth with the gear lever, fumbled one or two changes at his new leisurely pace, Ken cringing at one stage as the Italian missed fourth when passing in front of the pits. There was no lasting damage. Alboreto cruised home to give Tyrrell their first win since Monaco four long years earlier. Rosberg, by finishing fifth, took the championship. As Rosberg and Alboreto celebrated, Ken cheerfully fingered the betting slip in his top pocket. Everyone was happy.

The people from Denim were particularly delighted, and there seemed no reason why Bob Tyrrell shouldn't be able to secure an even better deal for 1983. 'In those days,' said Bob, 'you could fly to Milan, go down the autostrada and see the people from Imola Ceramica and Giacobazzi, and then pop over to Ragno Tiles and Beta Tools. In the course of a couple of days, you could see the lot. It was an era when there were many Italian companies involved, at a time before Formula 1 effectively outgrew them. They were small companies, but you could pull together maybe a couple of million dollars and build up a package.

'At the end of 1982, we were talking to Benetton in the hope that they would come into F1. As you know, we were also talking to Denim, who had been sponsoring Osella [a small, unsuccessful Italian team], looking for a long-term contract. Denim was owned by Elida Gibbs, which in turn was owned by Unilever. So we had started talking to Denim and we were pretty certain that, with the greatest respect to Osella, Denim wanted to move up a grade. So going into 1983, we had them all ready to be the co-sponsor with Benetton. Denim would have the top half of the car.

'This was before computer graphics. We had everything done up on transparencies with a big picture of the car. We had Denim overlaid on top so you could see how it worked with Benetton on the rest of the car. The whole thing was going to be worth a tidy sum of money for us. We had won the last Grand Prix of 1982. Everything was looking good.

'We had Luciano Benetton come to England with his people. We brought him to the Old Rectory. Mr Benetton sat down. He was looking around, slightly amazed. The first thing he asked was, "Where's the fence around your house to stop the intruders? In Italy everything is guarded." He wanted to know why the windows weren't barred, and where was the guy with the guard dog? That sort of thing!

'We got down to business and showed him our proposal. He took one look at the drawing and immediately lifted off Denim from the top of the car. Then he said quietly, "We go first class at Benetton." As a result of that, I had to phone up a multinational company and say, "I'm sorry, we can't take you." Denim were gutted. So was I. I'd never done it before, and I've never done it since. The final irony, of course, was that Denim went to Williams and stayed with Frank for years and years – a lot longer than Benetton stayed with us!'

In the meantime, Ken had been introduced to David McErlain, a modest but highly successful businessman 20 years Ken's junior. In the years to come, McErlain would quietly help out the team with timely injections of cash to pay for engines and, occasionally, wages if money proved to be tight. The two men would become very close friends, mainly due to Ken's respect for McErlain's integrity and the fact that David was not afraid to gently but firmly point out the error of Ken's ways when the need arose. Ken would never object to such treatment from the right person since it was very much his way.

'Ken's office door was always open to everybody,' said Neil Davis. 'They could go in and he would listen to what they had to say. He would usually give his opinion straight away, and it was always an honest opinion. If you made a silly mistake, you could get a good bollocking from Ken. But, having said that, if you held up your hand and owned up, he would have a go at you and that would be it. Half an hour later, it might be getting near lunchtime and he would come up and say, "Fancy a pub lunch?" Off you'd go, and the subject would not be mentioned. You'd had your bollocking. End of story. Believe me, you could not have worked for a better guy.'

Keith Boshier had a good view of events in Ken's office since the glass fibre workshop was directly opposite. Boshier would use tact when the need arose and pretend not to see important visitors, or to note who was talking to Ken about a possible pay rise or receiving a lecture from the boss. The one unofficial observer Ken did object to was Mutley, a stray retriever cross who had made the wood yard his second home. 'Mutley was a lovely dog, always hanging about the place,' Boshier recalled. 'But, for some reason, he would sit outside Ken's office and stare through the window. Of all the windows to choose, it had to be Ken's. He used to go berserk!'

Boshier might have broken his rule on occasion and had a quiet chuckle if he saw a colleague receive a carpeting in Ken's office, but then he was on the receiving end himself from time to time. 'There was the story of the telephone call,' he said. 'When the girl in the office went home at 5.30 p.m. and a telephone call came through, the bell at the front of the building would ring. If you picked up any of the internal phones, you could answer the outside call. So after 5.30 p.m., it was a case of not using too loud an air tool so that you could hear the bell, get the phone and find out who was ringing. It might be a driver, a sponsor, anyone.

'One night, I answered the phone. It was someone from the press who said they'd heard that such and such a driver was going to sign. Of course, I knew who had been there [in Ken's office] and who hadn't. For some reason, I got a bit carried away and told this journalist that no, we hadn't signed so and so. That was it. I hung up and didn't think any more about it.

'The next morning, Ken came marching over to my workshop and blew my feet off the ground. "What bloody right have you got telling a journalist . . . !" You can imagine the rest. Suddenly, I realized just what I had done. I couldn't believe I had been so stupid, and I apologized profusely. Ken probably went away and laughed about it, but he didn't half frighten me!'

The press were soon on to the story that Benetton had signed a sponsorship deal. The knitwear manufacturer would get good value from its one season with the team, not least from the presentable young American driver who had been drafted in to join Alboreto. For Danny Sullivan, this was a dream come true, thanks, in part, to his friendship with Professor Frank Falkner MD, one of the world's leading paediatricians who had been a long-time fan of F1 and friend of Ken and Norah. Falkner would arrange to have conferences coincide with Grands Prix worldwide so that he could leave the lecture theatre for the pit lane at the first opportunity. He also helped out where he could. In the film *Weekend of a Champion*, for example, it is Falkner who is carrying Jackie Stewart's bag when the world champion goes looking for his flameproof gear before the start of the 1971 Monaco Grand Prix. An urbane and totally charming man, Falkner was a wonderful asset in the Tyrrell pit on the days when he could arrange a handy collision of work and play. It was while lecturing in California that Falkner met Sullivan.

'Looking back on it now, I was so lucky,' said Sullivan. 'Because of his friendship with Frank, Ken was one of the first people I met in motor racing. That was at a non-championship F1 race in California in 1971. I was introduced to Ken and Jackie and Norah, everybody! I was planning to go to England to do a course at the famous Jim Russell Racing Drivers' School, and Ken said I should stay with him for a few days beforehand.

'His son Kenneth picked me up at the airport and took me to Ken and Norah's. The first thing that happened was the BBC were doing a documentary on Jackie and there was a showing at the BBC studio in London. They took me there, and then to an F1 race at Silverstone, where they introduced me to Colin Chapman of Lotus. He flew me in his plane to Norfolk, which happened to be where the Russell school was located. So these are my first few days in motor racing, and I'm thinking, "Hey, this is cool. I could really get into this!"

'After doing the Russell school, I worked the summer of 1971 as a gofer for Ken. The first race I did for him was at Monaco – which, of course, Jackie won. I just helped push tyres around, polish the cars and so on. Sometimes I would pick up people at the airport. Things like that. Then I started racing in Formula Ford, and I leased one of Ken's transit vans to pull around my car. It was £20 for the year! Ken also helped me choose which car to drive by calling Vern Schuppan, a driver who knew about these things. That was the sort of thing Ken would do for you. But with absolutely no fuss. I could see, though, that driving for him would be a different matter!'

Sullivan worked his way through the ranks and achieved enough to have Ken put his name on a list of young drivers to be offered a test for the second seat in 1983. 'Ken wanted me to come over from the States and do this test at Paul Ricard,' said Sullivan. 'There were 10 drivers, and I was the last to get in the car. Why, I don't know. Maybe it was because they thought I wasn't going to be any good. I wanted to be as professional as the other guys, so I watched them as they took their turns at getting into the car. They were changing the pedals and doing this and that and generally fiddling about. So, I'm watching this, and it comes to my turn. I get in the car and start to follow suit. Roger Hill is helping the drivers in and out. I know from my experience with the team that Roger is not the sort to make a lot of comment, so when he speaks you'd better listen, because whatever he has to say could be of some substance. He leans in, grabs my arm and says very quietly but firmly, "Just drive the car." Right! Okay, got that! Everything's fine. The seat's okay.

248

Let's go! I got ten laps – that was it. It was the same for everybody. But I was quickest. Ken never said anything. He didn't say "Good job", nothing like that. We were standing around and he asked if I could be in Brazil in January for another test. He didn't need to ask twice.

'I went to Rio. I got down there early and I sat around for days – the test in those days went on for more than a week. Then, right at the end, I drove the car. I only got a handful of laps and I used a set of Michele's old qualifiers. I was something like two-tenths off Michele's time. Again, Ken didn't say anything. We were getting ready to go to the airport to catch the night flight when I finally said, "Well?" Ken replied, "You selected yourself."

'That was it. I was in the team. There was no big deal, no announcement, no big show of coming over and shaking my hand and saying, "Well done, you've got the drive." It was typical Ken, very understated. But it was a really great moment.'

Sullivan made a big impression on 10 April when he fought with Rosberg's Williams for the lead of the Race of Champions at Brands Hatch. This was due as much to the American's tenacity as to Ken Tyrrell's forethought. The weather, typical for early April, produced a chilly, overcast day for the race. Since tyre warmers had yet to be invented, it was clear to Tyrrell that the tyres would need bringing up to temperature beforehand under controlled conditions. No one seemed to notice the significance of the Tyrrell team sending Sullivan out on several laps during the warm-up period before the start, and then refuelling his car on the grid. By the time the race was a few laps old, Sullivan's tyres were in perfect condition. The rest were relying on the opening laps to bring their tyres up to a decent working temperature, but the fast pace would prove to be too much for the rubber. That was evident when several cars stopped to change tyres; Rosberg's rear Goodyears blistered quite dramatically. Sullivan, meanwhile, was in excellent shape, thanks to Ken Tyrrell's shrewd pre-race assessment.

Sullivan's first championship points came in mid-May with a

fifth place after a steady drive at Monaco that won Tyrrell's approval; for once, here was a youngster who had listened to his instructions after starting from the back row of the grid. 'It wasn't always like that,' said Sullivan. 'The fact that I had known him personally cut no ice. He was really tough, but in a fair way. I remember one race where something was not right with the car and he said, "I don't want you to let people by! You're too nice. Don't let 'em by! If they're faster, they'll find a way through, but don't make it easy!"'

Due to a number of accidents and mechanical problems for Alboreto, the fifth place for Sullivan at Monaco had been the team's best result in five Grands Prix. That changed at the beginning of June when the scene shifted to the streets of Detroit for the United States Grand Prix. The Tyrrell, with its normally aspirated Ford Cosworth, had been suffering badly at the hands of the increasingly powerful turbos, which now accounted for half the field. But the tight turns of Detroit were a different proposition entirely, and it was here that the Ford Cosworth in its latest form had one final shout, appropriately enough on the doorstep of Ford's world headquarters.

In many ways, Ken wanted to pay his last respects. Permission was granted by Benetton for the Tyrrells' noses to carry large Ford ovals. It was a deal that did not involve money, just old fashioned gratitude and diplomacy; it was a means of saying thank you to Ford after a 15-year association that had seen Tyrrell win 32 Grands Prix. Donald Peterson, Ford's executive vice president, was in the pits. So was Edsel Ford II; Michael Kranefuss, the racing boss, worldwide; Stuart Turner, Director of European Motor Sports; Harold Poling, marketing manager; and, of course, the ever-present Jackie Stewart in his role as Ford consultant and television summarizer.

The outcome of the race was not as clear-cut as it had been in Las Vegas eight months before, particularly when Alboreto qualified sixth behind a collection of turbo Ferraris and Brabhams. Neither could anyone tell which type of tyre would stand the punishment of 60 laps on the uneven surfaces of the public roads. And there was the additional element of refuelling, a novelty introduced by

Brabham the previous year, and one the turbo teams had taken up as a matter of necessity. For these reasons, no one could say with any conviction who would win the race, although Tyrrell reckoned he was in with a chance since Alboreto and Sullivan (starting from the middle of the grid) would be running non-stop.

Alboreto had one less rival to worry about when Patrick Tambay stalled his Ferrari at the start, the Tyrrell moving into fourth place a few laps later when Elio de Angelis retired his Lotus. That became third when Andrea de Cesaris began to have trouble with his Alfa Romeo. Then, in no time at all, Alboreto was second, as Arnoux (now driving for Ferrari) and Rosberg made scheduled pit stops at half-distance. Only Piquet remained in front of the Tyrrell, and the thirsty Brabham-BMW turbo too would be stopping soon. Norah sat by the pit wall on a metal packing case, a lap chart spread across her knee, a stopwatch in her right hand (like Ken, Norah wrote with her left hand). Ken stood by her left side, checking positions and lap times. Michele was just four seconds behind. Piquet had to be stopping soon.

With each passing lap, it began to dawn on Ken that the crafty Brabham team had filled Piquet's car to the brim and he was running non-stop. That explained his slow pace early on, when Arnoux had romped into the lead. Now the tactic was paying off handsomely. There didn't seem to be anything Alboreto could do.

Then, with 10 laps remaining and going into a right-hander, Piquet suddenly felt the back end of the Brabham go loose; the left rear tyre had punctured. Alboreto was on to the blue and white car in a flash. By the end of the lap he was in the lead as Piquet made his disconsolate way to the pits. Rosberg was over 10 seconds behind. Ken stood on the pit wall and raised his hands above his head as the pale green car raced across the line for the final time.

Meanwhile, back in Surrey, Keith Boshier was loading a ladder onto the roof of his car and preparing to make the 20-minute drive to the wood yard. There, he and some of his colleagues clambered onto the roof and fixed a Union flag to mark a Tyrrell victory.

'Typical Tyrrell,' said Boshier. 'There wasn't a ladder about the place, so I had to bring my own! The Union Jack was more than 15 years old because it was one we had, shall we say, "liberated" in Albi in France when we were there for an F2 race in 1967. It had become something of an unofficial tradition to raise the flag when we won a race.'

The *Surrey Advertiser* carried a picture of the flag ceremony the following week. It was a timely piece of editorial decision-making, for never again would the Tyrrell Racing Organization savour such a moment. They would not even come close during the rest of the 1983 season, Alboreto scraping just a single point in Holland. Sullivan rounded off the year with a solid seventh place in South Africa, the championship limelight taken by Nelson Piquet as the Brazilian and Brabham humbled Prost and Renault.

'I could not have been with a better team,' Sullivan insisted. 'Ken would just let you go and, if you made a mistake, he would gently pull you back and tell you what to do. My only regret was that I really wanted to stay in Formula 1, but it didn't happen for various reasons. Don't misunderstand me; it worked out great, because I went back to the States and won some races [including the Indianapolis 500]. But I never felt I really got into F1. That was, though, no fault of Ken. He was fantastic to be with. What you got was a lot of little lessons; he didn't pound it into you.

'The classic I remember was at the European Grand Prix, which was the penultimate race of the season. I arrived at Brands Hatch for the warm-up on race morning and the first thing Michele said to me was, "I didn't have anything to do with this." I had no idea what he was talking about. Then Ken told me he was giving my car to Michele – and I had out-qualified him by a second! I got mad because I couldn't understand why he had done that. It wasn't as if Michele was running for the championship or anything like that. I had a big argument with Ken, but all I could do was sort out the car as best I could and go racing. Which is what I did.

'After the race, when everything had calmed down, Ken said,

"You know, I was really proud of you this morning. You fought for what was right. I wasn't going to give you the car, but I was glad you stood up for yourself because that was your right." That was Ken. He wanted you to argue, but not for the sake of the argument. He wanted you to be 100 per cent sure of your position. He wanted you to fight for it. You knew where you stood with Ken because he was always the same.

'I saw how important this was to him in an unexpected way when we were in Austria. Ken and Frank Falkner were coming back from dinner somewhere on one of those little narrow roads and they had an accident. Ken had a few cuts and looked like he had been in a fight; Frank had a broken leg and looked bad to me. Ken said, "For Christ's sake, Frank! Pull yourself together!" I quietly told Ken that I thought Frank looked bad and I didn't think he should speak to him in that way. Ken gave me one of those looks and said, "Don't be silly! I have to talk to him like I always talk to him because if I was anything less he would worry and think there was something wrong." And he was right! Tyrrell psychology at its best.

'Ken did not have the money to do things on the level of the top teams, but you never wanted for anything. You always wanted maybe a faster car, but you never lacked anything. It was the best-organized team that I maybe ever drove for. Ken and Norah created a family ambience and it never changed. Ken never treated anybody differently; there was no hierarchy, not even for the drivers.

'I never realized really how much of an influence he had on my career, right from the early days. It was quiet teaching; "you don't want to be doing that, do it this way". He had a fatherly way of doing it, a scholarly way as well. And I learned so much from the guys who worked for him. Brilliant people. Take Keith [Boshier], who made my seat. It was the best seat, bar none, I ever had in racing. I mean, no one even came close! I used to tell the other people I drove for – you know, big teams with all the facilities – about this guy in a shed down in the wood yard at Tyrrell, and he made me this seat and it was just perfect. He used clay rather than foam [an idea introduced by Jackie Stewart]. We spent about eight hours doing it, but that didn't matter. Keith would say, "Don't worry. Just sit there and I'll get you a cup of tea." That was the Tyrrell team. The most super place to be.'

21

A Load of Balls

The British media received an unexpected invitation to join Ken Tyrrell for dinner at 7.30 p.m. sharp on Wednesday, 22 February 1984. This was unusual on several counts, chief among them the fact that Ken's financial position was such that he could barely afford to buy a round of drinks, never mind a three-course meal for a large group in London's Mayfair Hotel. Benetton had taken their money to Alfa Romeo for 1984 and Tyrrell was known to be the only team planning to run the Ford Cosworth for the full season; the rest of the former Cosworth stalwarts – McLaren, Williams, Brabham, Lotus – had gone down the turbo route. Tyrrell was hardly an attractive proposition for prospective sponsors. He had signed a young German driver by the name of Stefan Bellof, but there was no chance of Ken attracting any of the big names. Not that they were available at this late stage. The start of the season was just over a month away. So what could the story be?

Typically, Tyrrell was revealing nothing as he greeted the press with his usual mix of broad grin and cheeky banter. It was a full turnout of representatives from the specialist magazines, plus the complete array of Fleet Street's finest. That alone said much about the affection inspired by Tyrrell and his team. Dinner would be convivial in such company. But where was the story?

Tyrrell had managed to keep yet another secret. And he kept his guests on tenterhooks. When the final course was complete, and just before coffee, Ken stood up. He thanked his friends from the media for their support over the years and, tongue in cheek, suggested they might be curious to know who his other driver for the coming season was. 'Now you are about to find out,' he announced, barely able to suppress a craggy smile. On that note, the double doors at the end of the room opened and there stood a shy and awkward-looking Martin Brundle. 'I'll never forget that evening,' said Brundle. 'I remember the doors opened, and Murray Walker went "Yeesss!" and started cheering!'

It was indeed good news. Brundle had come to everyone's attention by giving Ayrton Senna a run for his money in the 1983 British Formula 3 championship. Senna had won the title, but Brundle had made him sweat by beating the much-fancied Brazilian on several occasions. Here was someone worth looking at. Brundle's only problem – a familiar one for aspiring British drivers – was lack of money. 'We had no sponsors,' said Bob Tyrrell. 'It would turn out to be completely the wrong thing to do because there were no sponsors about to come out. There were no British companies willing to help. But Dad had a genuine wish. When Martin said he wasn't sure what sponsorship he could bring, Dad told him he didn't have to bring any.' Tyrrell was taking a chance, employing the Englishman on merit and hoping to attract a sponsor along the way. To achieve that, he needed the help of the British press, and they were only too glad to assist. It was a good story after all.

'I'd first met Ken the previous year,' said Brundle. 'I'd just won an F3 race at Oulton Park on a Saturday by beating Senna again and I decided on the spur of the moment to fly to Monza for the next day's Italian Grand Prix. Goodness knows how I managed that because I didn't have a pass or anything. It went okay, and on the way home I introduced myself to Ken and Norah who were on the same flight. I knew I was going to see Ken more formally at some stage because he had already offered a test drive to the top British driver in F3, and it was clear by then that it was going to be me.

When I did the F3 support race at the Austrian Grand Prix, Ken had taken the trouble to come onto the grid and say hello.

'At the end of the year, I got my test. The really good thing was that I had already driven the F1 McLaren about 10 days before as part of a prize they were offering, so I had an idea about what I was letting myself in for because the most powerful thing I'd driven until then had been a 150bhp F3 car.'

Brundle had turned up at Silverstone for the Tyrrell test on a wonderful autumnal morning. The conditions were mild, with a clear sky and no wind, and Brundle had the Grand Prix circuit more or less to himself. He made the most of it. Tyrrell's usual meticulous notes show that Brundle progressed in exactly the manner Ken would have wished to see. Danny Sullivan warmed up the car, then Brundle got in. His first four laps in the Tyrrell 011 were in the high 1m 20s, then he returned to the pits for enough fuel to allow a longer run. The lap times came down with each circuit: 1m 26.22s, 22.40, 21.10, 20.46, 19.55, 19.07, 18.18, 17.59, 17.41, 16.77, 17.52 (Tyrrell noting 'traffic' by this lap), 16.88 and 16.11. After refuelling again, Brundle was into the 1m 15s, going from 15.98 to 15.29, and then clocking his fastest time in the 011 of 1m 14.90s. Interestingly, as John Blunsden had discovered when testing Tyrrell's Formula 2 car in 1966, as soon as the lap times began to rise, Brundle was brought straight in.

Suitably impressed, Ken had a 012 brought from the transporter for Brundle to try in the afternoon. Exactly the same thing happened. After a rear wing adjustment, followed by changes to the front wings, Brundle's lap times fell progressively from 1m 13.90s to 1m 13.22s. After two identical laps at 1m 13.30s, Brundle was brought in. Alboreto had qualified for the British Grand Prix earlier that year with a best lap of 1m 14.65s. The lap record stood at 1m 14.21s. Tyrrell had seen enough.

'I also tested for them in Brazil, which killed me, because I was nowhere near fit enough to handle an F1 car in the heat of Rio,' Brundle recalled. 'But I went quite well and then it was a case of just waiting because Ken didn't have any money. Then he called me down to his office and he said, "I've got some bad news for you: I still don't have any money. But the good news is I'm going to sign you anyway." It was a great feeling.'

Brundle returned to Brazil at the end of March 1984 for the opening race of the season, where he qualified 18th, four places ahead of Bellof. Sixty-one laps of the Jacarepaguá autodrome in Rio de Janeiro would be a tough test for a pair of F1 rookies. Bellof lasted just 11 laps before being sidelined by a broken throttle cable, but Brundle drove steadily and found his name moving up the leaderboard as others ran into trouble. By lap 30 he was 11th; two laps later he was seventh, as both Brabhams and a Ferrari had retired and Nigel Mansell had had an accident in his Lotus. 'Ken's advice had been very much a case of bring it home, just do the best you can,' said Brundle. 'I could hardly believe it when I got into the top six. Then, on the final lap, I was fifth! I remember when I got back to the pits having scored two points, there was an element of disbelief. Ken was wearing that seven-inch-wide grin he had. He was really happy. I think we were all slightly bemused. With all those turbo cars out there, we had been worried about qualifying and just getting in the race. Sure, it would get more and more difficult as time went on, but there we were with two championship points at the end of the first race!'

Bellof opened his score with a sixth place at the end of round three in Belgium, and followed it up with fifth at Imola, a race where Brundle was deeply aggrieved not to have scored points after his car failed to deliver the last few gallons of fuel and caused the blue Tyrrell to roll to a halt. Two races later, Brundle would roll to a halt in a far more spectacular manner.

Qualifying for the Monaco Grand Prix at the beginning of June brought added pressure in the form of an announcement that just 20 of the 27 entries would be allowed to start (the organizers frequently restricted the number of cars on such a tight circuit as theirs). The non-turbo cars would be up against it. Sure enough,

Bellof's was the only normally aspirated car to make the grid when he squeezed into 20th place, but Brundle had come oh so close, a brilliant lap reaching a frightening and premature conclusion. 'I came through the chicane leading to the harbour front faster than I had done before,' said Brundle. 'The lap had been inch perfect. The chicane was bloody near flat out in our car, which meant arriving into the left-hander at Tabac at some staggering speed. The brake pedal went all soggy. I had touched a kerb somewhere and got a bit of knock-off on a pad. The brake balance bar used to run in front of the throttle pedal. As the brake pedal went down it took the balance bar cable with it, across the throttle. As I tried to brake, I actually accelerated, straight into the barrier.'

The Tyrrell hit the metal with the most sickening thump before being flicked on its side and skating down the track. The wheels on the right-hand side were ripped off, and it was only the bulge created by the exhaust pipes that saved Brundle's arm, which had been flung from the cockpit, from being trapped between the car and the road. Brundle's head, meanwhile, had made sharp contact with the track. 'The car was still on its side when they got me out,' Brundle recalled. 'I got on my feet and instinct told me to get back to the pits for the spare car. I remember the crowd cheering, probably as much from relief as anything else because it had been a major accident. Luckily, this was at the back of the pits and I found my way there and got into the spare car. Ken said, "You're okay. You've got eight minutes left and you are 22nd at the moment." I said, "Okay, no problem – which track am I at?" At which point Ken didn't say a word, he simply reached in and switched off the engine. I didn't know where I was. I was trying to remember whether I should turn right or left when I got to the end of the pit lane!'

There was to be drama of a different kind the following day. Cars crashed left, right and centre when the race was run in truly appalling conditions. Alain Prost, starting his McLaren-TAG turbo from pole position, led for the first 10 laps before Nigel Mansell's

Lotus-Renault turbo, going faster than was perhaps wise on the streaming track, moved to the front. Leading a Grand Prix for the first time proved too much for Mansell, and he whacked a barrier. As the field slithered towards self-destruction, the rain intensified, and two drivers, clearly revelling in the conditions, moved into contention. One was Ayrton Senna in a Toleman-Hart turbo; the other was Stefan Bellof in his Tyrrell-Ford. By lap 27, they were second and third, Senna catching the leader hand over fist and Bellof closing in on them both.

Monitoring the track conditions on television screens at race control, the clerk of the course, Jacky Ickx, decided enough was enough. At the end of the 32nd of a planned 78 laps, Ickx gave instructions for the red flag to be shown at the start/finish line – just as Senna roared on to Prost's tail. In theory, the race was not yet over. Time should have been allowed for the organizers to check the weather situation and order a restart if possible, but one Monegasque official took it upon himself to instigate the presentation of the trophy and order the reopening of the track. Prost was the winner, with Senna second and Bellof third. Had the race been allowed to run another lap, Senna would have won; had it been allowed to go even further, the entire Tyrrell team remained convinced that a fourth Monaco Grand Prix victory would have been added to their score. 'Stefan would've walked it,' said Nigel Steer, Bellof's number one mechanic. 'He was catching Senna by a second a lap, but what we didn't know was that Senna would not have lasted much longer. I've since been told by John Walton, Ayrton's number one mechanic at the time, that the Toleman's suspension had broken when Senna jumped the car over the chicane. There was no way he could have lasted more than another couple of laps. That would have been something, Stefan coming from last on the grid to win in a half-distance race!'

Formula 1 was back on the streets three weeks later, this time at Detroit. On the face of it, the team did even better, but in the long term this race would have disastrous consequences and would mark a terrible low for a man whose integrity was beyond dispute.

Ken had continued to fight against the gathering tide of turbo opposition. His only hope for remaining competitive lay with rules that were gradually reducing the capacity of fuel tanks, which would help the more frugal normally aspirated engines and force the turbo brigade to reduce boost, and hence fuel consumption and performance, at a time when refuelling had been banned during the races. However, the weight of turbo opposition had grown to such an overwhelming degree that moves were afoot to retain the existing 220-litre fuel limit rather than reduce it, as planned, to 195 litres. To change the rules in this way would require unanimity among the teams. Tyrrell remained the lone voice against the change.

In the meantime, he was battling on another front to stay competitive. The post-race business of topping up tanks for water-cooled brakes – the cause of the weight-limit furore in 1982 – had been ruled out, but the problem for officials remained in that there was no means of weighing the cars while the race was in progress. Tyrrell had begun to exploit the loophole by adding more water when the car made a late-race stop; in addition to the two gallons being pumped on board, the water brought with it 140lb of lead shot. This was accomplished using a complex device comprising an air canister and two water cylinders with large pistons inside. The mechanics coined the unofficial name 'duck gun' for it, thanks to the use of pellets that ordinarily would have been used to down birds rather than raise the weight of a racing car.

According to Tyrrell, water was being pumped from the car's on-board tank to a spraying mechanism over the engine air intake trumpets. The regulations allowed for the tank's replenishment during the race. Because the water was being pumped in under pressure, it was necessary to have a vent at the top of the tank. The laws of physics dictated that from time to time a certain amount of lead shot would be blown out of the vent, and would inevitably find its way onto the pit lane. 'It was hard to avoid that!' said Steve Leyshon. 'I remember at one race – Imola, I think it was – and we were next door to Arrows. We'd just made a pit stop and Dave Luckett, the

Arrows chief mechanic, appeared with a broom and began sweeping away the lead shot which had landed in their pit!'

'I had no idea what was going on,' said Brundle. 'They didn't tell me anything, and I was incredibly naive then. The first I knew was when someone asked me about this lead shot which was all over the Tyrrell pit after I had made a stop! I hadn't the faintest clue what they were talking about. But I have to say that I did wonder why it was so necessary to take on all that water close to the end of a race and then have the car suddenly feel like it was towing a caravan as I left the pits!'

The duck gun was brought into play, as usual, for the Detroit GP, for which the Tyrrells qualified 11th and 16th, Brundle ahead of Bellof. 'For some reason,' said Brundle, 'Ken convinced himself that Stefan was quicker than me around this circuit. I don't know why. I was always good on street circuits; they were my speciality. We had this system where, if one driver was holding the other up, the guy behind raised his arm. So Stefan was behind me and he had his arm up to say I was holding him up – which was bullshit, because I was tucked up behind some turbos. I got called in to change my tyres, and that released Stefan. On the very next lap, he crashed. It was as if he needed to prove he was faster than me. Anyway, I now had fresh tyres and I just charged. I was absolutely flying.'

Brundle climbed steadily from eighth place, picking off one turbo after another. With 18 laps to go, he was fourth, behind the Lotus of Elio de Angelis. When Alboreto retired his Ferrari with engine trouble, Brundle was third and looking for a way past the Lotus. 'There was a little left-hander near the last chicane, and I nailed him between the two,' Brundle recalled. 'In the remaining seven laps, I caught Nelson Piquet's leading Brabham. As we came out of the chicane for the last time, all the Brabham mechanics were on the race track, so I wouldn't have been able to pass him anyway. One more lap and I know I would have won the race. It was such a nimble car; Nelson's Brabham-BMW was never going to hold me back. The Tyrrell was awesome under braking.

262

'After the race, I was really pleased with myself; you know, I thought I was a bit good that day. I went to dinner still feeling perky – and Ken slapped me down, big time. He said that in Jackie's opinion I shouldn't have overtaken de Angelis where I did, it was too much of a risk. I said that neither he nor Jackie knew that de Angelis had missed a gear out of that corner; he was very slow there and it was easy for me to pass. I had just enjoyed what I thought was the best day of my life so far, but I left that dinner bruised – quite seriously bruised, actually. I can remember that night in the Renaissance Centre very clearly indeed. Ken obviously thought I was too full of myself. In the end, he was right.'

Two weeks later, during practice for the next Grand Prix in Dallas, Brundle wrote himself out of the race and the rest of the season. 'Bellof and I were flying; I think we were third and fourth in the final session before qualifying. It was another street circuit lined by concrete walls. I went out, and it was almost a question of not whether I would be on pole, but by how much. On my first flying lap, I hit the wall and smashed up my feet. I think Ken could see I was going to do that. I had come from winning in F3 to finishing fifth in Brazil to standing on the podium in Detroit. To ending up in hospital. Ken was tremendous. He helped organize the doctors and my trip home. There was none of this, "I told you so", but neither did he sit on the end of the bed and sympathize. He did exactly what he needed to do.'

With Brundle out of action, Ken cast around for a replacement. His eye fell on Stefan Johansson, a lively young Swede worthy of a decent opportunity in F1. 'Being asked to drive for Ken was a lifeline for me,' said Johansson. 'At the time, I had just finished with Spirit-Honda, a small team struggling to survive in F1. I was going to Japan to do Formula 2, which in those days, after having been in F1, was like going to Siberia and being sentenced to work in the coal mines! I got the call from Ken and I was happy to accept. I went straight to the next race, the British Grand Prix at Brands Hatch. I didn't get the chance to test the car beforehand. I went straight there, and out-qualified Bellof!

'Ken was fantastic to deal with, absolutely brilliant. He was such a lovely man. I was a young driver at the time and he was just so good at making you feel comfortable and making you feel good and giving you the confidence. You knew he was pushing you – you were pushing anyway – but he just had that really nice psychological manner that allowed him to get the most out of you. He was very calm, very gentle, not cursing or throwing any wobblies. If you made a mistake, he would put his arm around your shoulder and walk you to the side of the garage – like a dad in a way. It was brilliant. In those few races I probably learned as much as I had in two or three years.

'That Tyrrell was a lovely car to drive – very nice, very nimble. It was a strange car to begin with because it was relatively soft; you always felt the back end was going to go away from you when you turned in. But then it sort of took a set and it really stuck. Once you got over that you could really throw the car around and drive it hard. Of course, it was my bad luck that I joined the team at circuits where the Ford DFV was going to struggle, but I out-qualified Bellof at every race, so I was very satisfied with that.

'Ken paid me a little bit; I can't remember exactly, but it was something like £3,000 a race. But the point was, he paid on the day he said he would, every time. He was 100 per cent in everything he did. It was a great team to work for. The family feeling was incredible. I remember Norah made the lunches. If we happened to be staying in a hotel that did a buffet breakfast, she would clean them out by taking enough food to make lunchtime sandwiches for the boys! And the mechanics were great people, incredibly capable guys. My car never missed a beat. The only pity was, it was for just four races in 1984.'

And there lay the rub. Johansson took part in only four races because the team was not allowed to compete any further. Immediately after the Dutch Grand Prix on 26 August, where Johansson and Bellof finished eighth and ninth respectively, the Tyrrell Racing Organization was banned for the rest of the season and excluded from the 1984 championship as a whole. The entire team was shattered.

The situation had been simmering ever since Detroit. The first six finishers had been inspected in the usual way, officials taking samples of petrol from the fuel tank and water from the 13-litre reservoir on the Tyrrell, in which a quantity of small lead balls was found (surprise! surprise!). Tyrrell claimed this was ballast. But the shock came later when he was told that analysis of the chemical make-up of the water sample had revealed it to be 27.5 per cent aromatics, which was illegal. Tyrrell was accused of breaking the rules on four counts: taking on fuel during the race; using fuel that did not comply with the regulations; equipping the car with fuel lines that were not to the correct specification (namely, the water pipe from the water reservoir, which was now alleged to be carrying fuel!); and using lead ballast that was not fixed to the car in the prescribed manner. Subsequent inquiries revealed that there was, in fact, less than 1 per cent hydrocarbon content in the water, which was well within the rules. Once the scientific technicalities had been waded through, it became apparent that FISA had wrongly interpreted their analysis.

Tyrrell took his case to the FIA Court of Appeal, which sat a few days after the Dutch Grand Prix. The court not only ignored Tyrrell's weighty evidence, it also took the unprecedented step of switching the charges. Suddenly, Tyrrell was guilty on three counts: the presence of hydrocarbons in the water, unsecured mobile ballast and illegal holes in the flat bottom of the car. The 'infinitesimal' (FISA's word) amount of hydrocarbon was put down to the possibility that the water had been transported to the pits in one of the team's fuel churns. On the subject of ballast, Tyrrell proved to the court that there was provision for the scrutineers to place a seal across the opening of the tank, and they had been at liberty to do so before the start of a race. The regulations required the ballast to be secured in such a way that tools were required for its removal; Tyrrell argued that the ballast could not be removed without the aid of tools. FISA then suggested that Tyrrell had been using fuel additives in the first half of the race, flushing them out at the pit stop and adding ballast at the same time – a complete nonsense that did not stand up to scrutiny. The holes in the flat bottom, which had never been mentioned before, were proved to be no more than air vents that had no discernible effect on the car's aerodynamics.

The judges, from Argentina, Austria, Belgium, France, Italy, Portugal and Greece, were completely unmoved by Tyrrell's words, and the severe and outrageous penalty was confirmed. Apart from being branded a cheat, the costs to Tyrrell were enormous. The removal of 13 points also meant the loss of subsidized FOCA travel for the coming year. Tyrrell was being denied its livelihood by what appeared to be nothing more than suspicion. Crucially, of course, Ken would now no longer be in a position to vote in favour of the proposed reduction in fuel capacity. With Tyrrell removed from the scene, there would be unanimity when the votes were cast.

'Ken did talk to me and a couple of others in the office beforehand,' said Roger Hill. 'He said we had a very, very serious problem and we might be banned for the rest of the year. It was over such a very, very small amount of hydrocarbons. If someone took a sample of your blood, you would have more in there than the amount they were pinning on us. It had taken us ages to work out how to get this weight into the car. We weren't breaking the rules. But the stigma was attached to the team, and that upset Ken. He became so disappointed and disillusioned with those involved. I think there were a lot of people behind it, right down to the engine makers for the other teams. But the frustrating thing was, he couldn't do anything about it. He couldn't even get anyone to prove how pathetic the amount in question was; nobody would side with him, yet he knew he was right. There were probably more people cheating than he was, except he wasn't cheating; he was playing by the rules. It was *not* cheating. Ken didn't give in, but that was the only time I ever saw him come close. He was at his wits' end. He knew he was going to be shafted.'

Ken refused to comment at the time. Even in later years, his thoughts, articulated quietly, were brief and to the point. 'Being banned for something we didn't do was ... well, I can normally forgive anybody anything, but I can't in this case,' he stated in 1993. 'Even now, I can't forgive. I never thought about giving up or anything like that because I like motor racing so much. But I felt dreadful, quite dreadful. And so did everybody on the team.'

'Yes, it was a low point,' recalled Steve Leyshon. 'It was a complete joke, because everyone knew exactly what was going on. There was no auxiliary fuel tank, and the hydrocarbon business was a red herring.' 'It wasn't surprising there was stuff like that in the tank,' said another mechanic who wished to remain anonymous. 'Because there were no facilities of any kind in the temporary pits at Detroit, we'd only gone and taken the water from the fucking river! So what d'you expect?'

'We were thrown out for having an auxiliary fuel tank because they had found traces in the water tank,' said Brundle. 'But the joke was, we only had 542bhp available from the engine and we never ever filled our fuel tank up. We could not have used a tankful of fuel even if we had tried! We started Detroit with our fuel tank 80 per cent full; that's all you would use on a street circuit. We could not possibly need an auxiliary fuel tank, but that's what we were thrown out for. I got very upset with Ken, very upset. I was in Harley Street with my legs up in the air for a month – plenty of time to rue my career path having taken a massive dip. A journalist got through to my room at 10 o'clock one night and asked for a comment on Tyrrell's exclusion from the World championship. It was the first I had heard of it. Ken, being the secretive old sod that he was, either didn't take the trouble to, or didn't feel the need to, or didn't even think about letting me know. There I was, lying in hospital, still in an enormous amount of pain, and all my work that year had just been annulled. It still pisses me off to this day. When you look at the number of podiums and points I scored, the 1984 figures are not included. But whenever I quote my points and podiums, I count them in. I've got the trophy at home. That will do for me. Everyone knows what that was really all about, and it had nothing to do with the actual racing.'

22

On the Back Foot

Ken Tyrrell was probably grateful that journalists tend not to be at their best first thing in the morning. As members of the British press waited at Heathrow for a flight to Paris on Monday, 18 February 1985, they were surprised to see Tyrrell preparing to board the same plane. An astute observer would have seen Ken flush slightly when caught off guard and asked what he was doing. His answer – something along the lines of going to talk to a prospective sponsor – seemed to satisfy the writers, who at the time were attaching more importance to looking for a restorative coffee and preparing for a two-day pre-season junket with Renault. Little did they know that Tyrrell was about to visit the very same firm. Even if they were sensitive to his slight stammer when answering, the thought of Ken negotiating for a turbo engine would have seemed as unlikely as the President of Israel ordering a pork chop at a restaurant, even if his life depended on it.

Being a realist, Tyrrell knew he had no choice. Turbocharged engines now ruled the roost, and a customer Renault engine was the most viable option. Finding finance had been made even more difficult thanks to being branded a cheat, a subject Ken was reluctant to discuss. 'In personal terms it's been hurtful in that I felt we weren't banned in 1984 for reasons which were valid,' said Ken. 'I think we were banned because people wanted to change the regulations and we wouldn't agree to do so. So they found another way for our vote to be invalid. How damaging is it to us as a company? It's difficult to say. You could not expect a potential sponsor to understand what really happened, so people probably think that we were cheating. And that probably sticks in the mind of a potential sponsor. Because most of the sponsors are being chased by the same people, I would think that sufficient poison has been put in by our competitors.'

That did not prevent a deal being done in Paris, and the first Renault-powered Tyrrell duly appeared at the French Grand Prix in July. Brundle, who had recovered sufficiently to start the 1985 season in Brazil in March, was to drive the new car. 'This was 014,' said Brundle. 'Unfortunately, it was more or less 012 with a bloody great turbo in the back. It was a monster; not a good car. The team was on the back foot now. They didn't have the money or the infrastructure or the equipment. Then we lost Bellof.'

For months on end, Ken had been trying to persuade his drivers not to take part in sports car racing. Brundle was driving for Jaguar (with whom he would win a world title), but Bellof was more of a worry to Ken because the German had chosen to drive a Porsche 956, a car Tyrrell did not see as being as strong as the Jaguar with its state-of-the-art carbon fibre chassis. 'The 956, with its aluminium chassis, had hurt one or two people,' said Brundle. 'I remember Ken and David McErlain were always trying to talk us out of sports car racing. Ken knew that Stefan could be a bit of a wild boy at times. We were racing at Spa [on 1 September], and I saw the accident. It was a big one. Tom [Walkinshaw, Brundle's entrant] came and told me that Bellof had died and he asked what I wanted to do. I rang Ken straight away. I said simply, "Ken. Stefan's dead." He replied, "I know. Call me Monday." And the line went dead. Ken was a man of very few words on the telephone. Normally, before phoning him, I would make a list. If you ever took a breather at any time, the phone went down. He wasn't being rude; it was just how he was on the telephone. "Okay? Bye." Click. On an occasion such as this, he wouldn't want to talk at all.'

'Ken had really taken a shine to Stefan,' said McErlain. 'I remember we went to a test at Estoril and Stefan said he was thinking of leaving. Ken spent the whole time convincing him to stay. We weren't happy about his sports car racing, so much so that Ken offered to pay the money he was earning from sports cars if he would stop. But Stefan liked the idea of being German and driving for Porsche. His death hit Ken very hard. Ken really thought he had a champion in the making. Everything about Stefan was right: he was slim, wiry, dedicated and had the right temperament. But above all, he was bloody quick.'

The Tyrrell mechanics were distraught. Bellof had not only been fast, he was also hugely popular. 'I was his number one mechanic for two years,' said Nigel Steer. 'That, for me, was almost the best time of my life. Stefan was something else, so much fun to be with. He had this booming laugh and you could hear him in the paddock; you always knew exactly where he was! I remember he came in one day and asked for the shoe sizes of every mechanic. He had a sponsorship deal with Puma and he said he was going to fit us out with trainers. Drivers don't do things like that. Not for their mechanics, anyway. And, even if they say as much, they rarely deliver. But Stefan was as good as his word and he came in some time later with trainers for everyone. There were no airs or graces with him.

'Stefan did pull some moves when he was racing. If this one at Spa had come off [Bellof had been trying to overtake at a risky place] we would have said it was a typical Stefan move. But it didn't come off. Even so, it was a hell of a shock. Everyone was really upset.'

In an interview a few weeks later, Ken talked about losing young drivers and the problems associated with hiring the latest generation of aspiring talent. 'We have been credited with being the talent spotters of motor racing,' he said, 'but in fact it's not as simple as that. A large part of it is because we haven't got the finance to sign the more established drivers. So we have been able to look around and find the people whom we think might make the grade. We have been able to spot the up-and-coming ones.

'People ask me if it's not galling to then lose these drivers to other teams just as they are becoming established. Obviously it's a little frustrating. Having said that, when we sign a driver straight from F3 or F2, we always put them on a three-year contract with an option to renew at the end of each year. So we have the option to get out at the end of a year. Then, once his three-year term is over, it would be unreasonable to sign him for a longer period. So we don't really mind. But we would have loved to keep Alboreto, for example.

'It's obviously terribly, terribly sad when some of our young drivers have fatal accidents. Depailler and Bellof had theirs in cars other than ours. In Patrick's case [killed while testing an Alfa Romeo F1 car at Hockenheim in 1980], he wasn't driving for us anyway in F1. Stefan has been a greater technical loss because he was driving for us when he had his fatal accident in a Porsche. We have lost his services just as he was looking like becoming a future champion. The fact that they were both nice young men and very easy to get on with was perhaps the greatest loss of all.

'In the case of François [Cevert], that was really tragic for us. Apart from anything else, he was a great team member. He liked motor racing and enjoyed driving cars. He was very, very close to Jackie [Stewart], to whom he gave a lot of the credit for his performance. So, at the end of 1973, we'd lost the use of drivers who had finished first and second in so many Grands Prix and all of a sudden we had neither of them for the following year. That was terribly hard to bear.'

Bellof had driven the Tyrrell-Renault just three times before his accident, Ken having continued to run a 012 through the first half of the season. Brundle gave a Ford Cosworth Tyrrell what appeared to be its last race at the new Nürburgring on 4 August. He started from the back of the grid, drove his heart out and finished 10th. And last.

'I was joined by Philippe Streiff for the following year,' Brundle recalled. 'Maurice Phillippe had produced 015, and this was a better car; Streiff and I had some good runs. We finished in the points six times in 1986, and to be perfectly honest that was a sensible target for Tyrrell at the time.'

Tyrrell had secured sponsorship for the new season from Data General and Courtaulds, a move that had brought journalist Stuart Sykes into contact with the team to handle press and PR. Data General might have been providing computer technology, but car-to-pits telemetry – effectively, a spy in the car – was still in its infancy, as Sykes was to discover. 'With Ken's permission, I made a habit of abandoning the pit lane on the Friday morning of each race so that I could go out on patrol around the circuit and watch the cars and drivers at various points. At Spa [at the end of May], I made my way up to the chicane at the very top at Les Combes. At one point, Martin Brundle overcooked it and had a spin, bouncing around a bit over the kerb. It was enough to dislodge the little leather-covered pad attached to the back of the cockpit to cushion his helmeted head. It came spinning out of the car and lobbed over the guardrail where I was standing. In those days my reflexes were still like Mark Waugh's, and I duly took the catch. Rather than keep it as a souvenir, I dutifully returned it to Ken when I got back to the Tyrrell garage. When I explained that it had come off during Martin's spin, Ken grabbed it and yelled, "Spin? What spin? He never told me he had a bloody spin!"'

That indiscretion aside, Brundle was much happier with the 015. 'The car looked better and felt better,' he said. 'I crashed it in Jerez [in April], and at Imola [a fortnight later] I went one better – or worse, I should say – by crashing as I left the pits to go to the grid. I had to run back for the spare car, which was the awful 014. It was a strange season because I was set to get into the points at Monaco when Patrick Tambay tried to overtake me and only succeeded in going right over my head and causing us both to crash.

'But the most disappointing was the final race at Adelaide. I was in third place after Streiff had run out of fuel ahead of me. As I went into the last corner, my fuel reading turned to 000 – and it was right! We had an over-boost button and you could use it three times to overtake. I think I used it four times, and that was just enough to tip the fuel consumption on to the wrong side of zero. I coasted to the line and Johansson [in a Ferrari] beat me to it to take third.

'Qualifying with the turbo engine really was something. I'll never forget Adelaide. They would put in a high altitude turbo and blank off the waste gate for qualifying. That gave you something like 1300bhp! The thing was, you had been trolling round in the morning with 800bhp. Then you would have a two-hour break and get back in the same car with qualifying tyres on it – and 1300bhp! You just can't imagine what that was like. The car was the same weight but with loads more power and grip. But the thing was, you had to be very careful with the qualifying tyres. As soon as you brought them up to temperature, they would start to bite. You didn't want that to happen too early. So you had to coast out of the pits and not use full throttle during the out lap. Then you would come through the last corner, floor the throttle for the first time and . . . wham! The thing would take off like you wouldn't believe on a circuit lined with concrete walls. It was incredible.'

Adelaide in 1986 was Brundle's last race for Tyrrell after three eventful years. The end came just as abruptly as the beginning. 'We were in Mexico City for the penultimate race and I asked Ken what was happening in 1987,' Brundle recalled. 'I wanted to know what was going on because I had some other offers. He said he hadn't got any money together and the Renault deal was coming to an end. He more or less suggested I should seriously consider whatever offers I had. That was it. Nothing more was ever said, and I signed for Zakspeed [a small German F1 outfit] in November. It was the end of a very happy period. Ken gave me my chance with a brilliant team, great people and superb preparation. Ken was such a great source of knowledge and maturity. I absolutely loved being there.'

Brundle's dramatic final lap for Tyrrell in Adelaide had largely gone unnoticed at the end of a hugely theatrical day in terms of the championship. Three drivers – Nigel Mansell, Nelson Piquet and Alain Prost – had gone to Australia with a chance of winning the title. During the course of 82 laps, all three had been in a position to succeed; typically, perhaps, Mansell's departure from the equation had been the most spectacular. A rear tyre burst as the Englishman sped down the back straight at 180mph, and he was lucky to come to rest without harm. Williams, sensing a problem, called in Mansell's team-mate for a precautionary tyre change, the stop for Piquet handing the championship to the effective outsiders, McLaren-TAG. Prost couldn't believe his luck.

Turbocharged engines had dominated the year, but there was a move afoot to have them removed from F1 – a supreme irony when you consider just what Tyrrell had been through in 1984. The first step was to introduce a two-pronged championship for 1987, one division for turbos, the other for normally aspirated engines with the incentive of an increase in capacity from 3 to 3.5 litres. Tyrrell jumped at the chance to compete in the latter for what would be known as the Jim Clark Cup for drivers and the Colin Chapman Trophy for the teams. 'Turbocharged engines are history,' he said, with more than a hint of satisfaction. 'Why should we spend money on engines that will be out of date at the end of the year?' Not surprisingly, the engine chosen by Tyrrell was an uprated version of the Ford Cosworth, known as the DFZ. Streiff was staying with the team for another year, to be joined by Jonathan Palmer. Brian Lisles, who had been with Tyrrell for nearly 10 years, was promoted to chief engineer, while Maurice Phillippe remained as senior design engineer.

Time and technology were marching into Formula 1 from several directions at once. The arrival of Longines timing screens in every garage meant that Norah Tyrrell and her female friends perched along the pit wall had become redundant. A very impressive skill, at which Norah was accepted as being one of the most accomplished, was about to be lost. Gone were the days when the timekeeper could chart the progress of each and every car during practice and the race with the aid of just one stopwatch.

The secret weapon had been a stopwatch with a split facility plus a specially prepared sheet of paper divided into vertical columns – one column per car and each column split vertically in two. During practice, as soon as the first car passed Norah, she would press the start button to set the watch in motion. She would not touch that button again until practice was finished. When the car reappeared at the end of its first flying lap and passed a predetermined focus point – Norah would choose a fence post or advertising hoarding opposite the pits – she would press the split button. The digits would freeze and the number would be written at the bottom of the left-hand column for that particular driver. By pressing the split button again, Norah would see that the watch had not stopped at all but had carried on recording the time. When the car reappeared, she would press the split again, writing the new number above the previous one. Now came the moment for a quick piece of mental arithmetic as the first number was subtracted from the second, the resulting lap time being written alongside, in the right-hand column.

And so the process continued each time the driver blasted past. The tricky bit came when several cars were circulating at once, the split being pressed each time and the lap duly recorded in the column for the driver in question. The 60 minutes of practice would be a controlled frenzy of clicking, writing and calculating, Ken frequently peering over Norah's shoulder and relaying the lap time to a mechanic in readiness for display on the driver's pit board. And as if that were not difficult enough, Norah would chart the entire race, recording lap times (using the same split method on the watch) and race positions for each lap. It had been commonplace in years gone by for Ken to use Norah's handiwork to confront official timekeepers whose lap-scoring competence did not match that of his wife.

'In those days,' said Norah, 'if there was a query, you would get together with the other girls and check the times. If we found we were the same but we differed from the official times, then the team concerned would protest. The girls were excellent at timekeeping, but Michele Dubosc of Ligier was the best ever – quite brilliant.

'I went to more or less every Grand Prix, and I loved it. The thing about doing the lap charts and timing was that all the girlfriends and wives were involved. I can remember in the early days we would go to Dunlop and get a Coke. That was a big deal, because there were no motorhomes or anything like that! But, as a result, it was very matey, very friendly. The girls would clean helmets, give the drivers a drink when they came in, take their visors off. They were very involved, because the drivers didn't have all the people who hang around them now. You could do a lot because you had something to focus on. It's all changed now, of course, but the timing and so on available to the teams is fabulous. It's foolproof, and so fast. You wonder how we got by all those years ago!'

A more foolproof mode of running had returned to the team now that turbos and intercoolers were not part of the package on the latest race car, the 016. Just as significant for Tyrrell was the fact that running costs had been reduced accordingly. 'It's much, much cheaper to have normally aspirated engines rather than a turbo,' Tyrrell explained. 'There is no doubt about that at all. The engine is essentially a 20-year design with which we have enormous experience, and it has run reliably.'

Tyrrell had Brian Hart to thank for that. Hart, a former racing driver of some note, had set up an engine tuning and manufacturing business at Harlow in Essex, his infectious enthusiasm for racing having been transferred to the quality of his workmanship in the engine bay. But not even Hart could make up the difference between the power of the Ford and that of the turbos, Tyrrell becoming the leader of what was clearly a second division. Even so, Palmer scored a fine fifth place at Monaco in May 1987 while on his way to bringing both the Clark and Chapman trophies to Tyrrell.

Tyrrell had made the most of the split championships, but it would be a different story in 1988 when, as part of the programme to remove turbos, their power and fuel capacity were reduced and more teams turned to normally aspirated engines. Added to which the next Tyrrell, designated 017, was a very average car, Palmer and new recruit Julian Bailey struggling to scrape together a pathetic five championship points. This performance was in keeping with the heavily reduced sponsorship, a full package with Courtaulds and Data General in 1987 having given way to stickers for Cavendish Finance (introduced by Bailey) and an even smaller amount of exposure for Camel cigarettes, the tobacco company having been quite prominent on the cars in 1987.

The fact that the tobacco company was there at all had been a surprise to many, since Camel had been fully committed to Lotus and Ayrton Senna. 'We had been having discussions with R J Reynolds [Camel] and a guy called Duncan Lee for quite some time,' Bob Tyrrell explained. 'Finally, I had a phone call from Duncan to say a very small group of teams had been invited to pitch for title sponsorship in 1987, and would I like to come to Winston, Salem, and make a presentation to the board. I said I'd love to.

'Winston is in the heart of tobacco country. I was shown into a huge room with panelled walls and a table which would have stretched from here to the other side of my house. When you do a thing like that, there is a wonderful mix of dread and excitement. I knew I had to sell this normally aspirated formula because we didn't have a turbo. The slogan we had dreamed up was "new sponsor, new formula, right timing". I'd just shown the first slide on a big screen when the chairman, Lester Pullen, stood up and said he couldn't think of worse timing! Why would they want to come into F1 when it was split between turbos and normally aspirated engines? His company wanted stability rather than being associated with something new. My heart sank, because my entire presentation hung on this angle! I thought for a couple of seconds, then took a deep breath. "Mr Pullen," I said, "your company hasn't got to where it is by not taking risks. If you're too frightened to take risks, the last place you should be is Formula 1 because F1 is a risk business – and if you don't like that, you shouldn't be a sponsor." There was silence for what seemed an age. Then he laughed. And the whole board laughed! "Mr Tyrrell, please continue," said Pullen, and he sat down. We were in there for two hours and they were asking all sorts of questions.

'I knew that Lotus were coming the next day with Senna, and eventually we had a letter from Pullen saying really sorry, but they had decided on another team. I rang Duncan and he said Mr Pullen had been very impressed by the Tyrrell presentation but felt he had to go with Senna. I told Duncan to tell Pullen that if he was coming into F1 with Senna and Satoru Nakajima [the Lotus number two in 1987], he wouldn't have a European driver, and we'd got two [Palmer and Streiff]. He agreed to sponsor our drivers in 1987 and then take some space on the cars for 1988. Nobody could quite understand why Camel should be doing that. I think part of the reason was that Lester Pullen happened to like what we had to say. The only problem was that after a good season in 1987, we failed to deliver the following year.'

The 1988 season had barely got into its stride before Ken was painfully aware that he needed to improve his game. The most significant change came in the design department: Maurice Phillippe left, to be replaced in the summer of 1988 by Dr Harvey Postlethwaite, a designer who had been with March, Hesketh, Wolf and Ferrari. The Englishman brought more than just a keen sense of humour and a fine turn of phrase to a team that had fallen behind in the technical stakes. Postlethwaite had been employed by Ferrari in 1981 for his knowledge of the latest techniques. Now he was preparing to do the same for Tyrrell. 'Motor racing has become very sophisticated in recent years,' he said at the time of his appointment. 'The operation at the race track, for example, is much more complex than before. You are not there getting your hands dirty, rolling up your sleeves and banging pop rivets into an aluminium chassis. It's much more about computing and looking at aerodynamic data, much more of an intellectual exercise, and I find that much more interesting. If it's fun and you are enjoying it, then it's worth doing.'

Having been with Ferrari for seven years, Postlethwaite found the move to the former wood yard, like many before him, a major

279

culture shock. 'Actually,' he added, 'shock is not the right word. It's as big a surprise as when I went to Ferrari. Just like then, it's not better, it's not worse, it's different. The thing that's pleasantly surprising is that there are not many people, but those that are here are of a very high standard. Everyone at Tyrrell has to earn his or her keep. The team may have been going through a bad time, but you are instantly reminded that this has been a championship-winning team and a lot of those people are still here. The mechanics here can do anything! They're proper racing mechanics.

'At Ferrari, the problem was finding the right person you needed to get a job done because there was a staff of 250. That's the way they work, and there's nothing wrong with that, but I have to say it's nice to be here, to remind myself what British racing teams are all about. The skill level is very high, and while the resources at Tyrrell may be limited, there is absolutely no problem about getting things done. If you want a washer made up, it happens quickly, thanks to the team's resourcefulness. At Ferrari, you would have to get a drawing done and go through the system. Two days later, you would get your washer. It would be perfectly made. And there would be thousands of them! That's the difference.'

Postlethwaite was well qualified to assess the team's potential, particularly in view of plans to extend the factory and install much-needed equipment. The previous extension had been erected on the understanding that it would be used for servicing the timber lorries, which by this time were non-existent. 'We'd had a prefabricated "Marley" building put up for purposes to do with the timber business,' said Bob Tyrrell. 'When we went to the planners to convert the use to racing, they went berserk. They had no idea there was a racing team there in the first place! We had established use by now, but they were horrified and didn't want it to happen. We went to appeal, and we lost the appeal. In the end, we were allowed to keep the Marley building, and the local residents were quite happy to have us there.' All of which was just as well, otherwise Postlethwaite would have had no basis on which to formulate his plans for the team.

'At this point [in 1988],' Postlethwaite continued, 'we don't have a lot of the things we need to be fully competitive. But it is our intention to put that right. As an indication of our seriousness, we have managed to recruit Jean-Claude Migeot, an aerodynamicist of the highest calibre. We managed to convince him because, among other reasons, the new building we are doing will be up to date, with a composites facility, an autoclave and other things you need to make a state-of-the-art racing car. It won't be lavish, but it will be sufficient. That's always been Tyrrell's way and it will be enough to allow us to get the job done properly. Next year, turbos will be banned and we're back to a level playing field.'

23

Nearly, But Never Again

'Ken did not put me under any pressure. This was my first Grand Prix and he said I should just drive the car and see what happened. We thought it would be good if I just qualified. That would be a start. I qualified – and finished fourth! I'll never forget Ken's big, big grin when I got back to the pits. It was *fantastique*.'

The arrival of Jean Alesi halfway through 1989 brought a mix of emotions. The reason he was there in the first place had become a sore point, since it was because of an unexpected disagreement between Tyrrell and Michele Alboreto. The Italian had rejoined the team after five seasons with Ferrari, a period of varying fortune that had seen Alboreto fight for the championship in 1985 but struggle for much of the time. Alboreto retained personal backing from Marlboro, but the situation became difficult when, five races into the 1989 season, Tyrrell arranged for a renewal of support from Camel. The upshot was a terse exchange that left Tyrrell needing to find a replacement for the French Grand Prix on 9 July. Jean Alesi was driving for Eddie Jordan in Formula 3000, and the Irishman was quick to spot the convenience of having his team also enjoy sponsorship by Camel. A deal was done, and Alesi was entered for the race at Paul Ricard.

Jonathan Palmer was as pleased as anyone else to have a fresh face and more cash come into the team. Palmer's view of F1 had been changed dramatically when he got his hands on the first car designed by Postlethwaite, 018. This had been at Imola at the end of April, where Palmer finished sixth and set the eighth fastest lap. After struggling manfully with the dreadful Tyrrell 017, Palmer knew this was a proper racing car. It might have been painted in Tyrrell's traditional colour of royal blue without a single piece of sponsor identification, but Palmer was cock-a-hoop. His enthusiasm was about to be holed beneath the water line, courtesy of Jean Alesi.

Fourth place at the end of the Frenchman's first race was a sign of things to come, and Palmer struggled to stay on Alesi's prodigious pace. Alesi collected two more points in the Italian Grand Prix in September, but not before he had learned a great deal about Ken's method of dealing with young drivers. 'At Monza, it rained during practice and I had a big, big spin but didn't hit anything,' Alesi recalled. 'I came in and didn't say anything except that I didn't want to go out for a while. Ken came over and asked if something had happened. I told him. He asked me if I had been scared, and I said I had. It was sixth gear! So he said, "Okay, go out again. If you crash, don't worry, there is another car. But it's important that you don't lose confidence." Unbelievable! That was Ken.'

Tyrrell finished fifth in the constructors' series, a reasonable result at first glance, but one which was put into perspective by comparing the team's total of 16 points with the 141 scored by the championship winners, McLaren-Honda. Nonetheless, the promise was there. Postlethwaite and his small team might have been hamstrung by a shortage of funds, but that had not prevented them from producing Tyrrell 018, arguably one of the nicest Tyrrells ever built. 'We knew there was a massive shortage of money all the time, and Ken struggled through it all,' said Roger Hill. 'But we never had to take a pay cut and the cars were always done right. We would just cut back on things which, as far as Ken was concerned, would not make the car go any quicker. If you needed something for the car, you had it. No question about that. But everything else had to wait.'

'That could be really depressing,' said Keith Boshier. 'During the winter, while waiting for sponsorship, you couldn't buy anything, not even a bit of hardboard for a new top on your bench. The finance was locked up, solid. But I don't think we really knew how bad it was half the time. A lot of people would use Tyrrell as a stepping stone to other jobs in F1, particularly on the design side. Being at Tyrrell was a good grounding, almost like an apprenticeship. But the rest of us had become "Tyrrellized", so to speak. Where else would you want to go and work after 10 years here? There was nowhere quite like it, certainly nowhere with that atmosphere. It was easy-going in many ways because everybody was trusted to get on with what they were doing.'

In 1988 and 1989, that work had focused on Tyrrell 017 and Postlethwaite's first car, 018. 'The 017 was a bad car for us,' said Hill. 'It looked good, but it wouldn't go. Even when Harvey took it to a test at Monza for a couple of days and did what he thought was necessary to make the thing work, it still wouldn't go! Harvey was just right for Tyrrell because he made good, straightforward cars that were strong. He understood them, and got people around him who understood what was needed. His first car, 018, was probably one of the best cars we ever made. It was so simple, so light and so easy to work on. Quite brilliant. It seemed we were making a comeback. And we were. For a while.'

Such enthusiasm was fired by an extraordinary performance by Alesi in the United States Grand Prix, the first race of the 1990 season. Starting from the second row of the grid, Alesi mounted an immediate challenge against no less a person than Ayrton Senna. The McLaren-Honda and the Tyrrell-Ford ran wheel to wheel as they fought for the lead. Alesi eventually had to settle for second place, but when new driver Satoru Nakajima brought the team another point for sixth place, Tyrrell's weekend in Phoenix was complete. Alesi was on a high. And that was a worry for Ken.

'He was a fantastic man for a young driver to be with,' said Alesi. 'There was a lot of excitement after Phoenix. We were at Paul Ricard, preparing for Monte Carlo, and I was really excited. I kept saying to Ken, "I'm going to win! I'm going to win!" At the end of the day, he said, "Jean, I need to talk to you." We went into his hire car, he closed the door and said to me, "We already have more points than [at this stage] last year, so I don't want to see you in hospital. Please be careful." I was really surprised. I've never had a team owner or a team manager say that to me before or since because they don't care that much. It really was quite incredible.'

And it worked. Alesi qualified third in Monaco and finished second, splitting the McLarens of Senna and Gerhard Berger. Tyrrell were fourth in the championship with 14 points. The problem was, the blue and white cars would collect just two more points during the remaining 12 races.

By May 1990, Postlethwaite had introduced 019, a responsive and elegant development of the previous car that matched Brian Hart's efforts as he extracted an amazing 625bhp from the Ford Cosworth DFR. Tyrrell had switched to Pirelli, and the package had its competitive moments. Overall, though, the shortage of money and a series of collisions and incidents contributed to the shortfall in points. And there was no escaping the fact that Tyrrell needed a more powerful engine in order to keep pace.

Ken seemed to have found the answer when he arranged to use a Mugen-Honda V10 for 1991, effectively the engine run so successfully by McLaren the previous year. The deal was brokered in part by McLaren and involved a liaison between the two teams as Tyrrell's suspect marketing policy came under McLaren's professional umbrella. 'We had 140 people by now, and Honda wanted a good team with a proper marketing strategy,' said Bob Tyrrell. 'Ron Dennis wanted an exclusive marketing deal that put McLaren in control. That brought us into direct contact with Ekrem Sami, the head of McLaren's marketing and one of the best people in the business. They showed us the importance of how the team should be presented. Ken and I neither knew nor cared before! Ron came to look round the factory. He pointed out, for example, that a wall needed painting. We hadn't noticed!'

For Dennis, the wheel was coming full circle. Some ten years before, he had come to Tyrrell for advice. 'It was at the time I was thinking of entering Formula 1,' he recalled. 'I went to see Ken – I didn't really know him – and asked his opinion. He strongly recommended against it. I can't remember the reasons he gave, but, since I was as stubborn as he was, I was set on coming in anyway, and whatever he said against it was not going to make much difference!

'We had a hand in engineering the supply of Mugen-Honda engines for 1991 and we took over the responsibility of finding and looking after sponsorship for the team. I knew it was a bit of a shock for Ken, but we undertook the task on a clear understanding that a given percentage of the income had to be spent on marketing. I could never get Ken to understand the snowball effect: the better you are, the more money it generates. There was a point where we had improved the show by 90 per cent, and he just wasn't prepared to go that extra little bit. That 10 per cent was a value for money percentage, but he didn't see it. We would constantly argue, but we would always argue as friends.

'I think it's fair to say he had more income in those two years than he ever had. But, in the third year, he still preferred to go back to being independent even though it cost him money. I saw that as being stubborn; he just saw it as a matter of pride, a wish to be his own man.'

The team went into 1991 with a strong package: an evolution of 019, an engine used by the reigning world champions, sponsorship from Braun AG, Pirelli tyres, professional marketing support and two useful drivers, Nakajima and Stefano Modena (Alesi having had the inevitable call to Ferrari), a gifted Italian who appeared to be promising. In theory, the team was in very good shape. The reality was completely different.

At the end of the season, I went to see Ken to find out why his team had just 12 points on the board. He explained that they had started off well with fourth and fifth places in the US Grand Prix at Phoenix, but the engine had turned out to be much heavier than expected. A new gearbox had proved troublesome, but one of the biggest disappointments had been an engine failure just as Modena was challenging Senna for the lead at Monaco. Being typically honest, Ken followed that up by saying that second place at the following race in Canada had been due to the misfortune of others. The season went completely downhill after that.

Then he paused. Leaning across the table and staring me in the eye, he said he did not want to see any of what followed in the piece I was about to write. Having got my agreement, he leaned back in his black leather chair, the same one he'd always had, but now showing a distinct list to starboard. 'Tyres,' he said quietly. 'An absolute bloody disaster. In Mexico, for example, we chose the best tyre they had. For 14 laps, we were right with Senna. Then the tyres blistered and we had to stop and change them. Then that set blistered. Awful. Absolutely awful.' Leaning forward again, Tyrrell then demonstrated why his integrity was beyond reproach. 'I don't want you to say any of that because Pirelli have pulled out and I don't want to bang nails into their coffin. It wouldn't be right. I understand they are having a bad time commercially as well, so this is not the time to rubbish them. You'll have to find a way round that by saying they were a bit disappointing or something. Okay?' His look left no doubt in my mind that this had to be 'okay', otherwise a serious froth job would be on the cards next time we met.

The team had actually taken knocks on several fronts, one of the worst (apart from the tyres) being Postlethwaite's departure mid-season to Sauber, the Swiss team offering him a new challenge as they prepared to enter F1. Nakajima had also announced his intention to retire at the end of the year, and as the going got difficult it seemed to the mechanics that Modena more or less gave up. 'Stefano was a strange guy,' said Roger Hill. 'He could be really quick, but he had some strange – I don't know what they were – superstitions, I suppose. He had to put part of the seat belts on himself. That didn't bother us; if that's what he wanted and it made him go quick, then let him get on with it. But we struggled with the fact that his car had to be on a certain side of the garage. It used to cock up what we were trying to do. We had a system, it was the way we worked, and all of a sudden something which should have been right here was over there. Our job is total repetition, particularly when you are against the clock. So you turn around and something you need is not where you expect it to be, but on the other side. That sounds silly, but it does make a difference.'

There had been a change, too, in the command structure within the team. Ken was chairman, and Bob had been made managing director – he was now effectively running the company. Rupert Manwaring was running the team, and the technical department, having been taken care of by George Ryton in the aftermath of Postlethwaite's departure, was now in the hands of Mike Coughlan. Together, they would enter 1992 with pluses and minus on the balance sheet. Pirelli had been replaced by Goodyear, thus giving Tyrrell the same tyre as everyone else, and the overweight Mugen-Honda had made way for a V10 from Ilmor Engineering, an ambitious young company from Northamptonshire. On the down side, Braun had quit, leaving the Tyrrell 020B looking dangerously bereft of sponsorship once again.

'We had these periods where we used to oscillate between having a great budget and not so much,' said Bob Tyrrell. 'If you had a three-year deal with a sponsor, you could plan and say you were going to invest in the factory or on something else that needed doing. But, for us, it was a case of "thank God we didn't spend the money on that" when the funds suddenly became depleted again. Ultimately, that was the reason we became unsuccessful; we were never quite getting there. We never had everything together at the same time. You would have a sponsor and an engine, but the wrong tyres. Or the right tyres but the engine was no good, or there was no money for development.'

The net result was an even more difficult season, Tyrrell claiming just eight points in 1992 thanks mainly to the professionalism and persistence of Andrea de Cesaris, the F1 veteran having joined the less consistent Olivier Grouillard. The team's reliability record was excellent, but the cars were not quick enough. It was a familiar tale, but hope springs eternal, and when a supply of Yamaha engines was arranged for 1993, Tyrrell didn't have to reach for his chequebook for the first time in 25 years. Bob had unearthed substantial financial support from Japan.

'Following our experience with Honda, we had targeted Japan as an up-and-coming sponsorship market,' he said. 'We had been out there, plodding away for years. We had been talking to people since 1979, but it was like bashing your head against a brick wall. Then we heard Larrousse were in financial difficulty and they had a Japanese driver, Ukyo Katayama. We spoke to Japan Tobacco to see what their plans were and discovered they weren't happy. JT was obviously a very big company and couldn't be associated with a team which might go bust. So, we persuaded JT to come with us for 1993, and we took Ukyo as well.

'After a few months, it became evident that they were planning to do something much bigger than simply centring their Cabin brand around a Japanese driver. The big deal was going to be associated with their Mild Seven brand, and obviously we were hoping to be associated with that. Unfortunately, we did not score a single point [in 1993], Katayama and de Cesaris finishing just a handful of races. The Mild Seven deal went to Benetton. We might not have got the deal anyway, but the difference between success and failure can hinge on things which are sometimes outside your control?'

Meanwhile, Coughlan and Postlethwaite passed each other at the front door as the former left for Ferrari and Harvey returned from the Italian team (which he had joined after a very brief spell at Sauber) for a second stint at Tyrrell. He could hardly complain that he didn't know what he was letting himself in for. 'Oh, I know all about the team,' he said with a grin. 'What's different this time round? That's a leading question! Let's just say I feel perhaps that I am much more a master of my own destiny this time round and generally more comfortable with the situation. [That was

Harvey-speak for the fact that David McErlain had been instrumental in persuading Ken to make Postlethwaite a shareholder in order to tempt him back.] It seems, to put it simply, that the team has sort of stopped, and all we are doing is pressing the right buttons to start it up again. The basic operation is absolutely sound and the same people are here. We've got everything in place, including a good driver pairing, a mix of experience and promise.'

Mark Blundell had joined Katayama for 1994, the Englishman having made a name for himself as a test driver for Williams and McLaren, as well as by racing strongly for Brabham and Ligier. 'I'd just had a particularly good year at Ligier, and Tyrrell was a viable option,' said Blundell. 'They needed someone with experience and the right credentials. I was available, and they had enough money to pay me, which at that time wasn't a bad deal.

'I obviously knew who Ken was, but I'd never had to work with him before and I have to say he was probably the most straightforward man I've ever dealt with in the pit lane. A man of few words in many instances, but he was straight as could be and he paid on the nail. If he said he was going to do something, he'd do it. And if you said you were going to do something, he expected it back.

'When I went to the factory for the first time, I was slightly taken aback when I saw some of the shacks they were still using, and then a fairly modern building alongside. But I soon found it was a very cosy and homely atmosphere. They were a great bunch of guys to be with. It also meant I had the great pleasure of working with Harvey Postlethwaite, a fantastic guy. He had this bright young engineer, Mike Gascoyne, working with him, and together they were really driving the whole project on.

'Unfortunately, the Yamaha engine turned out to be the Achilles heel. But I knew Yamaha from having worked with them at Brabham, where I had scored Yamaha's first World championship point. So I was back in the fold, and in some respects our relationship got even better when I finished third at Barcelona [on 29 May

1994]. That was the first podium Tyrrell had scored since 1991. Unfortunately, we had too many failures, although the problems were rarely related to finger trouble by the mechanics.

'While I was there, Ken's influence was becoming less and less. Bob was having a greater say in the daily running of the team, but Ken was still in the background, still an authority. My biggest memory of Ken Tyrrell is his voice. That will always stick in my mind. It was that and his stature, the office, the chair. He was like a headmaster. There was an aura around him. I wouldn't say we ever had a ruck, but we had some lively discussions, a few raised voices. At the end of it, everyone walked away still speaking; you'd had your say and no one left the room slamming doors. He was strong, as hard as nails. He would say things you didn't want to hear some-times but you couldn't ignore it and there was never any malice attached.

'I was born in 1966, two years before Ken went into F1, so I wasn't really aware of Jackie Stewart and all he and Ken had done together. I started looking at the old photographs and found I could relate to them – the blue cars, Jackie's famous helmet, Ken standing there as the figurehead. I was able to piece it together and could begin to understand why they'd had such a fantastic partnership.

'The thing you learned from Ken was that respect is a worthwhile thing to have. You only have to look round the pit lane to see that there are a lot of shallow people about. But Ken was not one of them. He had true character and depth. Norah was such a lovely lady. To be able to say that I have driven for Tyrrell is great. It was the best experience of my F1 career – by a long way.'

24

Assisting at a Wake

Events at Imola on the afternoon of 1 May 1994 ensured that the date became as significant in motor racing history as 7 April 1968, the day Jim Clark was killed at Hockenheim. Ayrton Senna's fatal accident shook the sport from top to bottom. Initially, the FIA was able to handle the aftermath calmly and avoid a knee-jerk reaction, but the hysterical response worldwide to the death of a top driver – the first fatality in a Grand Prix for 12 years, and, it has to be said, the first to be caught live on television – forced the governing body into visible action.

Changes to slow the cars were introduced with more or less immediate effect, and Harvey Postlethwaite's team at Tyrrell was one of the first to react, thanks to use of the wind tunnel at Southampton University and a new association with Fondmetal Technologies in Italy. One way or another, Tyrrell showed great promise in 1994, so much so that at the beginning of the following year, *Autosport* predicted that the team from Ockham was about to have its 'best season in a long time'. In fact, it would turn out to be one of the worst.

Tyrrell had reluctantly parted with Blundell when there were insufficient funds to pay him. His place for 1995 was taken by Mika Salo, who, apart from having shown promise during two late-season races with Lotus, had the additional benefit of enjoying support from Nokia. Tyrrell had also begun an association with Avenue

Communications, a public relations company. Among their staff was Mark Gallagher, a keen follower of the sport and later to become head of marketing at Jordan. In 1994, however, Gallagher found himself working with Tyrrell.

'We got the job with Tyrrell by being blunt about their situation,' said Gallagher. 'That entailed telling Ken and Bob that a media survey showed that people viewed their team as being like a family shop, one that hadn't moved on. I remember having dinner with Ken and Norah in the Hilton in Brazil. I told Ken, without trying to be sycophantic, that I remembered seeing the British Grand Prix on television with a Tyrrell driven by Jackie Stewart leading the race, and I'd had a Tyrrell poster on my bedroom wall for years. But I didn't say that I thought of him as being in the business for a long time. The sport had moved on in many respects, and the fact was that we had to find a way of raising the team's profile and finding the money to do the job.

'They were having various false starts at that time when it came to rejuvenating the team. There had been a blinding opportunity in 1991, for instance. I thought the Braun sponsorship was brilliant because it was a male-orientated technology product, they were a German company, and the livery on the car was very clean. They had the Mugen-Honda and Stefano Modena, whom I had been following in Formula 3000 and whom I knew, if channelled properly, could be excellent. But that didn't work, and Nokia wasn't turning out to be much better. Nokia had been sold the deal that Tyrrell could go from a low ranking towards the top and that all they needed was money. Nokia gave them quite a big cheque, believing this would be the answer. The difficulty was that the selling of Tyrrell was always being done on rediscovering past glories. "We've won three championships with Jackie Stewart . . . okay, 20 years have gone by, but we still know the magic ingredient." But that was wrong, because they didn't have the infrastructure, the development facilities or the manufacturer behind them. And they occasionally made a wrong choice of personnel – as you do.'

It took a while for Salo to find his feet during his first full season, and his obvious speed had the unfortunate effect of causing Katayama to overdrive while trying to keep pace. One minor disappointment piling on top of another meant the team did not score a single championship point until Monza in September. By the end of the season, a meagre five points was worth ninth in the 1995 Constructors' championship, one of the worst results since Tyrrell had started to build his own cars 25 years before.

Ken handled many interviews on the subject of his anniversary in racing. His answers to dreamy questions about the good old days were typically direct. 'I think a lot of people have nostalgic diarrhoea,' he said, before breaking out in that familiar toothy grin. 'Because of this 25-year thing – and it was the same for the 25th anniversary of our coming into F1 – I've had a lot of questions about the past, and you'd be surprised at the number that finish off by saying, "Ah, those were the days. It's not like it was." Well, that's rubbish. Yes, of course Grand Prix racing has changed, but it's every bit as competitive now as it was in 1968. The cars are different, there's more money and the way we do things is different, but when it comes to going racing – when it comes to *winning* – then it's exactly the same. It's bloody difficult; always has been, always will be.'

Ken's team was about to prove that dictum during the years that followed. Postlethwaite waxed lyrical about the latest Yamaha engine, referring to the V10 as a 'little jewel' when launching Tyrrell 024 on 30 January 1996, but by the end of the year the Japanese gem had become tarnished by technical trouble, a fact which contributed in large part to Katayama and Salo retiring in 16 of the season's 32 starts. Once again, there were a mere five championship points to show for the team's efforts at the end.

It was perhaps no surprise when the four-year partnership with Yamaha was dissolved, Postlethwaite holding out great hope for 1997 with a return to a Ford engine and much-needed reliability. He would get his consistent running, but it would be slow; the Ford V8 was 50bhp down and no match for the V10 engines dominating the front of the field. Even Postlethwaite's enthusiasm was noticeably on the wane when in October he looked forlornly at the 2 next to Tyrrell's name sitting next to last in the 1997 championship table. It was small consolation that the points had been earned as a result of a brilliant non-stop strategy that took Mika Salo to fifth place at Monaco.

'The fact is,' he said, 'we've been punching below our weight. Basically, it's a bloody good team with excellent people and sound organization. We've done everything right – good race strategy, excellent pit stops, Mika and Jos [Verstappen] have driven some cracking races – yet we've been looking at 10th and 11th places at the end of it. We've just been slow in comparison with our rivals. Development in F1 is so fast that when you are 50bhp down, you are nowhere. When you are handicapped like that, the size of the budget doesn't actually matter.'

Irony continued to be unwittingly heaped on the team as new plans were hatched and promises made. An attempt at putting a brave face on the future came in September 1997 when Tyrrell entered a joint venture with European Aviation to build a wind tunnel facility at the airline's base at Bournemouth airport. The catchphrase was 'Tyrrell 2000: Racing towards the Millennium'. Sadly, nothing could have been further from the truth.

Twelve months later, *Autocourse* opened its summary of Tyrrell's 1998 season thus: 'Working for the Tyrrell Racing Organization in 1998 must have been like assisting at a wake. The team was in its death throes, waiting to drift into the hereafter following the buy-out at the beginning of the season by British American Racing. The new team was not due to come on stream until 1999, which left Tyrrell to struggle on as best it could. The technical group, led by Dr Harvey Postlethwaite, and the loyal mechanics down at Ockham ought to get some sort of award for tolerance and fortitude under the most trying circumstances imaginable.'

The new British American Racing team had been announced after a deal had been concluded on 28 November 1997 to purchase Tyrrell. Paul Stoddart, the boss of European Aviation, would eventually buy the cars and equipment and Ken would stay on for a final season, but from 1999 onwards the team would be BAR. Effectively, British American Tobacco had bought the name, had purchased a slot in Formula 1. But they ignored – or failed to see – the most important part of the deal. 'There were a lot of key guys at Tyrrell, a hell of a lot of expertise,' said Mike Gascoyne. 'People like Roger Hill and Dick Gear, guys who knew the business inside out. That's where BAR totally screwed up because they threw that away. They actually showed how inexperienced they were. Ken ran his team for 30 years; some of the people at BAR would last barely three years with ten times the budget Ken had. More than that, they simply dismissed a warmth and atmosphere that had no equal.'

Rumours of the amount paid by BAR ranged from $20 million to $30 million, depending on which publication you read. Either way, it was a tidy sum, one F1 insiders believed had been brokered by Bernie Ecclestone as a form of pension for one of F1's longest-serving members. Others suggested Ecclestone had been behind another bid by the Austro-Canadian Walter Wolf to purchase the team for a price less than that which BAR had finally offered. The story of the buy-out simmered in the columns of the news pages for some weeks; still, its final confirmation surprised some of the personnel at Ockham.

'Ken called in all the managers,' Neil Davis recalled. 'People like myself, the chief mechanic, Harvey and Mike Gascoyne, Rupert Manwaring and George Koopman [the team's financial director, a man with valuable F1 experience who had helped keep the company afloat]. Ken made this announcement that he had decided to sell it up. He was very sad. Obviously he didn't want to. We were dumb-struck. In your heart, you wanted it to keep going, but in your head it couldn't continue the way it was going. We couldn't afford the drivers. We might have had a good car, but we didn't have a good enough engine, so it didn't matter how good the car was; without the driver or the engine, you were snookered. Those things didn't look as if they were going to come. Obviously Bob had his hands tied because it was looking more and more difficult for him to convince people to put money in. There just seemed no alternative, even though it was a hell of a shock, particularly after we had been together all this time.'

'I was surprised. In fact, I was bowled over,' said Keith Boshier. 'I thought Ken would keep going until he dropped. I just couldn't believe it. He was being offered a huge amount of money, and obviously Ken wasn't the only shareholder. What would I have done? I would have done what they did. But it was a shame. The last car, 026, was a good one. We just needed a couple of decent drivers.'

That was a moot point. The worst possible omen for the team came in February 1998 when a press release stated simply that Ken Tyrrell would no longer be part of an organization that was moving into its 30th season of F1 racing. Although Ken would not elaborate, it was certain that he had found it impossible to agree with BAR's plan to hire the Brazilian driver Ricardo Rosset over Ken's preferred choice, Jos Verstappen. The decision was based on the money Rosset could bring to the party – a curious logic given the scandalous amount BAR was due to squander during the seasons that followed. Tyrrell was upset because he felt Verstappen could do a far better job with what looked like being a half-reasonable car. Initial tests with the Tyrrell 026, powered by a Ford V10 rather than the tired V8, had certainly been encouraging, even in the hands of a newcomer, Toranosuke Takagi. 'The issue we have been grappling with for the past month is the significant difference in agendas for Tyrrell and BAR during 1998,' said Ken. 'We at Tyrrell are about to enter our final season, and our priorities are rather more short term than those of BAR, which must plan for its long-term future in F1.' Tyrrell was right. Rosset appeared to act as nothing more than a crash-tester, one who seemed to believe that gravel traps on the outside of corners were there to be used. The team's best result was ninth place for Takagi at Silverstone and Monza.

Tyrrell took little satisfaction from being proved correct. 'Ken had very mixed feelings,' said David McErlain. 'He said it was ironic that all his life he should have motor racing and no money, and now he had money and no motor racing, and he knew which he would rather have. I told him the sale had been the right deal on the day. There are moments in life when you have to make a decision like that, and Ken had made the right one.'

Gascoyne, now highly rated after time spent with Postlethwaite, accepted an offer to join Jordan as technical director and left during the season. 'I took away very fond memories,' said Gascoyne. 'The great thing was that, primarily, the man in charge was an enthusiast. Ken loved the sport. Even in the last few years he used to come to every meeting, and his enthusiasm to get involved was still there. He didn't make decisions any more, but he embraced the whole business of racing – the intrigue, the strategy, what we were going to do, why we were going to do it. He just loved it all. He would sometimes get overexcited and say some classically silly things. He just wanted to be involved, even if it was simply checking the weather. We were in Brazil one year and it was showery and overcast just before the start. Ken came on the radio and said, "I'm out the back and I can tell you that the weather is . . . uncertain." We would just crack up, and we'd have a good laugh about it with him later. In 1994, refuelling came in and Ken absolutely loved the race strategy that came with it. He was a great one for telling you 20 things that covered every possible scenario, and then, when inevitably one of them came to pass, he would say, "I told you so!" You just couldn't help but laugh.'

That may have been so, but Ken's experience and sense of practicality – assets which did not always sit well with bright young engineers – had come into play during the 1997 Monaco Grand Prix. It was Ken who had asked the first question about the possibility of running non-stop in this wet race, a suggestion which was greeted initially with scepticism. In the end, not only was Ken proved right, the two points for fifth place – the only two earned that season – were worth a considerable sum in benefits to the team. In effect, Ken's ability to see the bigger picture had prompted a decision worth $10 million. It proved there was no substitute for experience and old-fashioned excellence.

'We were always behind, but we had an attitude of engineering excellence,' said Gascoyne. 'In some respects we did as much engineering as some of the bigger companies. In the last few years we had a reputation for aerodynamic innovation. But it was frustrating, because we really were unable to keep up thanks to being on the wrong tyres or having the wrong engine. Talking in later years to the guys I had worked with, we all found that the standard of engineering at other teams wasn't that good. You would arrive there thinking, "What can a guy from Tyrrell possibly teach these people?" The other teams had such good facilities and so on. But then you'd look at some of the workmanship and say quietly to yourself, "Well, we'd never have done anything as shoddy as that at Tyrrell!" The problem was, people didn't notice because we were at the back of the grid, but the engineering standards were those of a thoroughly professional team. I don't think people realized how little we had to work with, because the cars looked pretty good and everything was done as it should be. To be honest, you'd walk up the grid and look at something being done by some of the so-called top teams and think, "Well, that's a shower of shit for a start!" It made you appreciate Tyrrell all the more. Everything was done correctly. Tyrrell was always a proper company. It was a real team in that it had a warmth and atmosphere that made it a very special place to work.'

From Postlethwaite's point of view, the departure of Gascoyne was sad but inevitable. 'As the year [1998] went on, we obviously lost a number of key people,' said the man who was effectively in charge of the team. 'But most of them stuck with it and they did an excellent job. The car has been reliable and well turned out; the jobs have been done. It's a huge tribute to the unsung heroes in the background. I think I speak for everyone when I say we had the right to ask, "What the hell did we do to deserve this?" They could quite rightly have been expected to walk away from it, but they didn't. They've done a super, super job. The morale has been fantastic, as good as it's ever been.

'There was this rather grandiose idea that since it was going to be Tyrrell's last year, then "Let's go out on a high note, chaps!" It was never going to be like that. It was always going to be a case of holding our heads up and coming out of this without it being a real disaster. We've managed that. It's not what anyone would have wanted, but, under the circumstances, Tyrrell has finally been put to bed with, I'd like to think, a bit of dignity.'

25

The Legacy

In November 1998 Ken began to complain of stomach pains. Grumbling was not his way, and neither was paying a visit to a doctor. He had kept fit by swimming regularly in the pool at the Old Rectory; as far as the family could recall, his only visit to hospital (apart from when he had crashed at Goodwood) had been to have his varicose veins attended to. That was a hereditary complaint, but this seemed more serious.

A diagnosis of cramp allayed initial fears, but when the problem persisted into the New Year, a visit to a specialist suggested that an exploratory operation was in order. The surgeon discovered a large tumour outside the pancreas, in the ampullary. 'It was very complicated,' said Kenneth Tyrrell. 'In fact, it was so bad that the surgeon did some bypass work to allow the gut to go around the tumour. Basically, he didn't touch the tumour, sewed everything back together again and said what Ken needed was chemotherapy. Ken agreed with Bob and me that he should get a second opinion. The consultant looked at the scans and said that he wouldn't operate. Jackie [Stewart] had said all along that Ken ought to be going to the Mayo Clinic in the United States, but he thought, "Oh no, let's not bother with that."'

Stewart was hardly surprised by Ken's attitude; it was typical of a man who didn't like to make a fuss over personal problems and who

301

could be stubborn, particularly when it came to accepting privileges. 'In many ways, Ken was extraordinarily militant and extremely socialist,' said Stewart. 'He was dead against privilege. I remember most vividly his attitude towards concessions at Monaco. If you had won at Monaco or become world champion, you received a free entry for the Monaco Grand Prix; you were exempt because of what you had done the year before. Then they introduced a rule limiting the number of cars that could start at Monaco. This was quite tricky because you could end up not posting a time if you had broken down or hit a wall. But the previous winner or reigning champion would be allowed to start, no matter what. Ken was vehemently opposed to this. He said this was very bad, that nobody should be privileged in this way. His view was that if we didn't establish a time for whatever reason, then we would set an example and not take up this concession. He thought I should publicly say that nobody should be privileged. I should make it plain that I had a free ticket, but that I would surrender it because everybody ought to be on the same platform. We said as much, and that, for Ken, was important.

'He just could not accept class structure. The Hôtel de Paris, for instance, was a no-go area for him. It was almost anti-social of me to take Ken into the cocktail bar. For years he stayed in a modest hotel outside Monte Carlo. It wasn't until very late on that he was really pushed – probably by Norah! – into staying in the Holiday Inn, or the Beach Plaza as it became known.'

Stewart was all too familiar with cancer and its treatment. Jackie's family had been shaken to the core when his youngest son Paul had contracted the disease. Intensive treatment at the Mayo had saved him. 'Ken phoned me the day before he had the operation,' said Stewart. 'I asked him if he was sure he had the right people. "Don't start!" he said. "I'm totally confident. This is being sorted, so don't even start." Then, once everyone realized it was serious, I got two doctors from the Mayo Clinic to take a look at the scans. I was talking daily with Kenneth and Bob and we arranged for them to come to the apartment belonging to Sid Watkins [the FIA medical delegate] and sit in on a conference call with the Mayo.'

'Dad didn't like to be too up front about his medical condition,' said Kenneth. 'He didn't want to be a part of this, but he wanted Bob and me to hear what the people from the Mayo had to say and to make the decision. We sat in on the conference call and decided instantly what had to be done. We went straight back home and said, "Dad, you'd better pack your bags. We're off!"

'Jackie laid everything on. We also had a lot of help from Dr Ian Hay. It was a bloody great operation and no one but a surgeon in the Mayo, Dr Geoffrey Thompson, would touch it. Ken was desperately weak when he came out, so weak that he couldn't travel. We moved into a hotel, but the problem was he had to have a special diet. Obviously, you can't get what you need from room service, so I went out and bought a stock of food for the room. The first thing I made him – all according to the instructions – was a basic cheddar cheese sandwich. I remember he took one bite and said, "Aw, Jesus Christ, Kenneth. That's the best food I've ever eaten in my life."

'The chances of surviving pancreatic cancer for five years are something like four per cent. We knew this, but Dad had never asked the question. Before going into the Mayo, we went to see an oncologist there. He had done further scans to confirm what had already been said. This man was sitting at his desk when Dad and I walked in. He said to Dad, "Have you got your affairs in order?" Dad was stunned. He'd been brought face to face with the fact that he had cancer in a major way. But now, after the operation, we hoped we had bought more time.'

Even though he no longer owned a team, Ken's interest in racing never waned. Prior to the operation, he had been deeply involved with the British Racing Drivers' Club, assuming the role of president, but not before he had led a stern fight in earlier years against those whom he felt did not have the best interests of the club at heart. 'Ken always had this enormous sense of right and wrong,' Martin Brundle recalled. 'He had a good take on these things. He was as solid as a rock, never afraid to stand up and say what he thought. At times, one or two club members would say some bitter and twisted things, and it really pained me to hear that. But Ken would take the flak. If he believed he was right – and he invariably was – then he would not let go. He was entrenched to the absolute last.'

Tyrrell had demonstrated that most forcibly in 1997, at a time when he was short of money and adopting such a principled stance actually threatened the livelihood of his team. A row had blown up over the Concorde Agreement, the secret covenant between the teams and the governing body by which the sport is run. Most teams had signed a revised version, but Frank Williams, Ron Dennis and Ken Tyrrell had objected to the terms covering intellectual property rights and distribution of the F1 purse. All three refused to sign. The surprise was not that Ken should have strong views, but that he was prepared to risk the loss in income from television money and other sources controlled by Bernie Ecclestone and the administrative arm of the FIA.

'It was something none of us could swallow,' said Dennis. 'This was at a time when Ken was not as economically strong as he would have liked, but Frank and I supported him. That support was always given with the absolute certainty that it would come back somehow, some time. And it did. There was a certain honour – it had always been there – between us, and Ken was a very strong part of that. He would speak his mind, even if it was against his interests, even if it put him in isolation, even when, in a case like this, he had everything to lose.'

Frank Williams, who had received a knighthood for his services to motor sport, was equally impressed but scarcely surprised by Ken's resolve. 'He was good entertainment! When he had what people called a "froth job", it was always a pretty reasoned and powerful argument put in a memorable way. During the dispute over the Concorde Agreement, Ken played a rigid and forceful role, even though he didn't have the funds for the legal battles. Ron and I took care of that, but he was part of the backbone; he had loads of that. He felt passionately about this and he was extraordinarily blunt with Bernie. He was truly as ballistic as the stories you've heard; he had a sort of anger which went almost beyond the limit. But it was reasoned, and he was right.

'He had been taken apart by the FIA in 1984, and that was disgusting. I didn't really know the rights and wrongs of what had happened in his fuel tank – I'm not really interested – but what they did to him was wrong.

'When I got to F1, Ken was friendly and helpful, but a little aloof in some ways because, since he was a top competitor, we would tend to get in his way. He took a tough view on that. I remember once he turned me away from a Silverstone test. I had turned up, not realizing it was exclusive, and begged Ken to let me on the track. He said, "On yer bike, mate!" I respected that. He was up for the championship and he didn't want chaff in the way.

'I will always remember Ken for his immense straightforward-ness; it never diminished in any way, regardless of the situation he might have been in. You always knew what he was thinking. And the other thing I admired was his ability, time and time again, to produce something that was truly newsworthy – like his own car, and then the six-wheeler. No one had a clue. That was really bril-liant. When the team started to decline, his determination never wavered. Having been there myself, I knew what it was like and I just don't know how he paid his way. He was obviously super-frugal. It was an object lesson in how to survive with order rather than with chaos. Ken had great presence and strength of character. He was a pillar. You could anchor yourself to him. That's what happened during the dispute over the Concorde Agreement.'

Ken had the satisfaction of seeing harmony reached before his illness set in. Not surprisingly, given his passion for the sport, he continued to be a keen observer, even though rigorous treatment had to be put in place not long after his return from the Mayo Clinic. 'We came back to England in April 1999,' Kenneth recalled.

'When the cancer started to spread again, the Mayo Clinic recommended Dr Cunningham at the Royal Marsden and Dad began to receive chemotherapy. One of the problems with pancreatic cancer is that, unlike breast cancer, it is uncommon. There are various concoctions of chemo that may best be described as "standard", but there is not much available for pancreatic. When the standard treatment ceases to be effective, they have to start on something else and move into more and more esoteric areas.

'Dad was reacting badly to the chemo, feeling quite ill at times. But he would go back in there and say to the oncologist, "Right, what's next? What are you going to put me on now?" The oncologist said to Bob and me in private that he had never known anyone who kept coming back the way Dad did. He said this stuff makes you feel awful. They did regular scans. It was better for a while. Then it started to get worse.'

Ken refused to give up. He continued to follow the progress of his beloved Tottenham Hotspur even though he was no longer fit enough to travel to the home games at White Hart Lane, but shooting provided his greatest source of enjoyment and relaxation, as it had done for most of his life. As the son of a gamekeeper, it was natural that Ken should have gone rough shooting in the woods close by the yard at Long Reach. Later in life, at an organized shoot in Derbyshire, David McErlain introduced Ken to Paul Tear, a master cutler from Sheffield. 'I first met Ken about 20 years ago,' Tear recalled. 'He took the actual shooting very seriously and, as you might imagine, he was very keen on the etiquette. He was a serious sportsman; to come up to Derbyshire twice a week in the early hours of a winter's morning required a major commitment. But you could tell that he was a country-lover as well. We would stand out on a lovely crisp morning and he would say, "Aren't we lucky to be here?" To be perfectly honest, he made our season for us. He brought a bit of gloss to our lives. He impressed my team because there was no bullshit. He would talk about the races, trusting us not to divulge the gossip we loved to hear. But, really, he was far more interested in us.

'Towards the end, he was not looking well, but he hated talking about himself. The only thing I remember him ever mentioning was this little bum bag he had on his belt. He was so pleased with it because it was carrying the IV needed to pump the chemo into him at regular intervals. "Here, feel this!" he would say with a grin as he invited you to feel the little motor buzzing away at regular intervals. There was a Corinthian spirit about him. He was a lovely, lovely man.'

As word of the seriousness of Ken's illness filtered through the paddocks and motor racing firms of the world, Tyrrell stories were recounted with a chuckle and a shake of the head. The most popular concerned Jackie Stewart during practice for a race at the Nürburgring one year. The Scot had come into the pits and was reeling off a catalogue of trouble; the handling, the tyres, the track, the engine, nothing was right. Tyrrell, clipboard tucked under his arm, listened impassively. When the monologue had finished, he bent down and leaned into the cockpit, his craggy face an inch from Stewart's. 'You think you've got problems?' he roared. 'England are 78 for 6!' The progress, or lack of it, of the England first XI was a matter of concern to Ken, so much so that he kept check at the races by tuning his car radio to the BBC World Service and badgering reporters to obtain the latest score from their sports desks. When time permitted, Ken followed every over of every Test match on television, but he shunned a visit to the ground itself for fear the atmosphere might not be as good as the picture he had built in his mind over the years. If ever there was a game that embodied Ken's feeling for fair play, cricket was it.

His sense of right and wrong never deserted him any more than he would dream of abandoning his true friends. Ken, for instance, stayed in touch with Charles Hewlett, a team-mate from his Ockham soccer-playing days. 'He continued to be very caring and generous,' said Hewlett. 'When my wife and I took on the organization of a [Silver] Jubilee celebration and procession in the village, I had a phone call from Ken. He said, "Charlie, what's all this about the Jubilee?" When I explained what we were trying to do, he said I'd better go and see him, which I did. He said he had vehicles, premises and facilities, and we were to help ourselves. Without further ado, he opened a drawer, pulled out his chequebook and gave me a cheque that was big enough to allow us to go ahead without any more worries. Ken was very much in the background, and of course we made sure he was there at the function, but he was typically low key.

'It was the same with the British Legion Poppy Appeal. I took over the organization of that when my wife died, and Ken was very keen to help. He always made sure there was a box at the factory. That sort of action fitted perfectly with him.

'There were one or two in the village who were worried about Ken's development – the noise and traffic, and so on – but Ken went about it in a very kindly way. It helped to bring Ockham's name to the fore, but he never abused it. It's safe to say there was a great respect for him; he was never at odds with anyone. Personally, I was very proud of what he had achieved.'

Such qualities were typical of a man who had uncomplicated tastes and a straightforward view of life. Hewlett's stories came as no surprise to Jackie Stewart. 'That would have been Ken through and through. He had no sophisticated tastes. He liked his tennis court and his garden, he was very proud of the Old Rectory, but his big treat at night would be getting home and sitting down, with Norah beside him, drinking a gin and tonic. That was heaven for Ken. He would never go and get a suit made or an expensive pair of shoes. That was unnecessary. No matter how much money he had – and he was always spending as much money as he could on his racing team – extravagances were absolutely not on. And yet, after I had helped him with his cancer, two silver gilt vases arrived out of the blue. Just to say thank you. I had never received a present like that in my life from anyone. It was an extravagance. The vases are absolutely beautiful, as if they had been made for my house. It was totally contrary to anything Ken had done before.'

Other Tyrrell drivers were experiencing similar behaviour, even if it was via the telephone rather than through the post. 'I never became close to Ken when I was driving for the team,' said Derek Daly, 'but when I left Britain and came to America and later began television commentary work, Ken would see me doing the IndyCar races. When I came back occasionally to Europe, Ken would hold long conversations and be genuinely interested in what I was doing. He would say how Norah thought my accent had changed a bit, things like that. But the point was, he was almost gushing in his enthusiasm because he wanted to help as much as he could to make me better on television! I was so, so surprised. Then, at the end of 2000, I was inducted into the Motor Sport Hall of Fame in Ireland, and they asked Ken if he would come to the ceremony. He said "Absolutely!", and he was there when I arrived. I couldn't believe it. I thought he looked good and seemed very energetic. Even though he told me the full story about his cancer – only because I had asked – and showed me the IV he had to inject, I didn't realize how ill he was. That was the last time I saw him.'

Martin Brundle had a similar experience as he developed his career as a summarizer on ITV's F1 programmes. 'I actually got a lot closer to Ken through shooting. Towards the end, he opened up a lot more, told me a lot of things. But the boot was on the other foot in a way because he really appreciated my work on TV and went to a lot of trouble to tell me how my commentary made it so much more interesting for him, particularly as he now had to stay at home and watch the races. He would ring up and say, "But how could you know such and such a thing? How could you see that was going to happen?" His interest and his support really meant a lot to me.

'But the strangest thing occurred in late July 2001. I had to ring him about something to do with the BRDC, and as usual I had my list of questions prepared because I had got conditioned to it. When I was done, I said, "Okay, Ken, thanks." He then asked if I had finished all I wanted to say. I said I had, and it then seemed as if he was downloading his mental list. He chit-chatted; he wanted to talk. I remember thinking, "That's so unusual for Ken. I don't like the sound of that.'"

At around the same time in California, Danny Sullivan took a call from Ken. 'I forget the reason for the call, but we talked for about 45 minutes. You didn't have conversations with Ken that lasted that long. I called Frank [Falkner] and said I was worried because that was so unusual. I had this awful feeling that he wanted to be touching base, just to talk for one last time.'

A few weeks later, Jackie Stewart called at the Old Rectory. 'The last few months of his life were very fulfilling, and I am so glad I was able to share a little bit of that time during my visits,' he said. 'I would have missed so much of a side of Ken I hadn't actually got to know. We talked about all sorts of things from the past. It really amused me that he couldn't understand why the Ford Motor Company should have entrusted him to do what he did and supported him to that level. He wanted to know how that had come about. He had no earthly idea that Ford was buying Ken Tyrrell because of who he was, what he was. We had wonderful chats. But on one particular visit in late August, I was quite shocked by how much he had deteriorated.' When Stewart left his dear friend and mentor that day, he knew in his heart of hearts it would be for the last time. Jackie stepped outside the house and broke down.

'It was obvious Ken was dying,' said Kenneth. 'I don't know exactly what happens, but the tumours grow so large that they start to impinge on the organs and they cease to function properly. He was on morphine. Mum would not leave his side for the last couple of days. She just stayed in bed with him.'

Ken passed away early in the morning of Saturday, 25 August 2001.

Stewart was the first to receive the call from the family. Within a matter of hours the news had been flashed around the world thanks to a statement and mark of respect prepared the previous evening by Stewart and Ford. The tributes came from far and wide, some businesslike, some personal, but all filled with a high regard for the man, his team and, in many cases, his family.

'One of the things I fondly remember,' said Ron Dennis, 'is Ken's relationship with Norah, which was just fantastic. Marriage is a difficult contract to have when you are in F1; it's difficult for anyone, but even more so when you had the level of dedication he had. To see their marriage survive throughout, and to see the support and love they gave to each other, was wonderful. It was an example for us all.'

Norah had endured her share of illness too, but, like Ken, she never uttered a word of complaint. Ken's memorial service was a moving mark of respect, but not even the most heartfelt sympathy and support could replace the man she had loved so dearly for nearly six decades.

On 22 May 2002 the *Daily Telegraph* obituary column carried notice of the passing of Norah Tyrrell. It referred to 'the grieving widow of Ken'. Nothing further needed to be said.

During the months following Ken's death, Kenneth and Bob sorted out their father's affairs. It was while rooting around in the cellar of the Old Rectory that they discovered an unexpected legacy. 'Dad had quite a lot of wine,' said Kenneth. 'He wasn't a connoisseur, and he wasn't afraid to say as much, but he used to store his supply in the cellar. I found this wooden case of Château Margaux. There was a note on it, written by Dad. It read: "Half of this case is to be drunk when I die, and half is to be drunk by the family when Norah dies." We knew nothing about it. We stretched his request a little bit by taking four bottles to Derbyshire to say farewell on Ken's behalf to the shooting party, but the Tyrrells – 11 of us, led by Mum – had a dinner party at the Rectory and we drank the wine and toasted Dad. He would have liked that.'

It is a sentiment shared by all who came into contact with Ken Tyrrell, none more so than those who had passed through the wood yard at Ockham. During the research for this book, one theme in particular popped up time after time. It was summed up best by Jo

Ramirez, a man for whom 40 years in motor sport had provided an understanding of what is right and what is wrong – the basic tenet of Ken Tyrrell's life. 'Ken was so helpful and so protective,' said Ramirez. 'Everything he said was right, and it made sense. Those of us who had the pleasure of working for him will treasure those years for ever.'

Tyrrell Racing Organisation
Formula 1 Results

1967

Race & Circuit	*Drivers*	*Car/Engine*	*Result*
German GP, Nürburgring	Jacky Ickx	Matra-Ford MS7	Rtd: Suspension (F2)

1968

Race & Circuit	*Drivers*	*Car/Engine*	*Result*
South African GP, Kyalami	Jackie Stewart	Matra-Ford MS9	Rtd: Engine/Con-rod
	Jean-Pierre Beltoise	Matra-Ford MS7	6th
Spanish GP, Jarama	Jean-Pierre Beltoise	Matra-Ford MS10	5th
Monaco GP, Monte Carlo	Johnny Servoz-Gavin	Matra-Ford MS10	Rtd: Accident/driveshaft
Belgian GP, Spa-Francorchamps	Jackie Stewart	Matra-Ford MS10	4th
Dutch GP, Zandvoort	Jackie Stewart	Matra-Ford MS10	1st
French GP, Rouen	Jackie Stewart	Matra-Ford MS10	3rd
British GP, Brands Hatch	Jackie Stewart	Matra-Ford MS10	6th
German GP, Nürburgring	Jackie Stewart	Matra-Ford MS10	1st
Italian GP, Monza	Jackie Stewart	Matra-Ford MS10	Rtd: Engine
	Johnny Servoz-Gavin	Matra-Ford MS10	2nd
Canadian GP, St. Jovite	Jackie Stewart	Matra-Ford MS10	6th
	Johnny Servoz-Gavin	Matra-Ford MS10	Rtd: Accident
United States GP, Watkins Glen	Jackie Stewart	Matra-Ford MS10	1st
Mexican GP, Mexico City	Jackie Stewart	Matra-Ford MS10	7th
	Johnny Servoz-Gavin	Matra-Ford MS10	Rtd: Ignition

313

Race of Champions, Brands Hatch	Jackie Stewart	Matra-Ford MS10	6th
Gold Cup, Oulton Park	Jackie Stewart	Matra-Ford MS10	1st

1969

Race & Circuit	Drivers	Car/Engine	Result
South African GP, Kyalami	Jackie Stewart Jean-Pierre Beltoise	Matra-Ford MS10 Matra-Ford MS10	1st 6th
Spanish GP, Montjuich Park	Jackie Stewart Jean-Pierre Beltoise	Matra-Ford MS80 Matra-Ford MS80	1st 3rd
Monaco GP, Monte Carlo	Jackie Stewart Jean-Pierre Beltoise	Matra-Ford MS80 Matra-Ford MS80	Rtd: Broken driveshaft Rtd: Broken driveshaft
Dutch GP, Zandvoort	Jackie Stewart Jean-Pierre Beltoise	Matra-Ford MS80 Matra-Ford MS80	1st 8th
French GP, Clermont-Ferrand	Jackie Stewart Jean-Pierre Beltoise	Matra-Ford MS80 Matra-Ford MS80	1st 2nd
British GP, Silverstone	Jackie Stewart Jean-Pierre Beltoise	Matra-Ford MS80 Matra-Ford MS84	1st 9th
German GP, Nürburgring	Jackie Stewart Jean-Pierre Beltoise Johnny Servoz-Gavin	Matra-Ford MS80 Matra-Ford MS80 Matra-Ford MS7 (F2)	2nd Rtd: Damaged upright (6th) Rtd: Engine (F2)
Italian GP, Monza	Jackie Stewart Jean-Pierre Beltoise	Matra-Ford MS80 Matra-Ford MS80	1st 3rd
Canadian GP, Mosport Park	Jackie Stewart Jean-Pierre Beltoise Johnny Servoz-Gavin	Matra-Ford MS80 Matra-Ford MS80 Matra-Ford MS84	Rtd: Collision 4th 6th
United States GP, Watkins Glen	Jackie Stewart Jean-Pierre Beltoise Johnny Servoz-Gavin	Matra-Ford MS80 Matra-Ford MS80 Matra-Ford MS84	Rtd: Engine Rtd: Engine 7th
Mexican GP, Mexico City	Jackie Stewart Jean-Pierre Beltoise Johnny Servoz-Gavin	Matra-Ford MS80 Matra-Ford MS80 Matra-Ford MS84	4th 5th 8th
Race of Champions, Brands Hatch	Jackie Stewart	Matra-Ford MS80	1st
International Trophy, Silverstone	Jackie Stewart	Matra-Ford MS80	3rd

1970

Race & Circuit	Drivers	Car/Engine	Result
South African GP, Kyalami	Jackie Stewart Johnny Servoz-Gavin	March-Ford 701 March-Ford 701	3rd Rtd: Engine
Spanish GP, Jarama	Jackie Stewart Johnny Servoz-Gavin	March-Ford 701 March-Ford 701	1st 5th

Monaco GP, Monte Carlo	Johnny Servoz-Gavin	March-Ford 701	DNS
	Jackie Stewart	March-Ford 701	Rtd: Engine
Belgian GP, Spa Francorchamps	Jackie Stewart	March-Ford 701	Rtd: Engine
Dutch GP, Zandvoort	Jackie Stewart	March-Ford 701	2nd
	François Cevert	March-Ford 701	Rtd: Engine
French GP, Clermont Ferrand	Jackie Stewart	March-Ford 701	9th
	François Cevert	March-Ford 701	11th
British GP, Brands Hatch	Jackie Stewart	March-Ford 701	Rtd: Fire
	François Cevert	March-Ford 701	7th
German GP, Hockenheim	Jackie Stewart	March-Ford 701	Rtd: Engine
	François Cevert	March-Ford 701	7th
Austrian GP, Osterreichring	Jackie Stewart	March-Ford 701	Rtd: Split Fuel line
	François Cevert	March-Ford 701	Rtd: Engine
Italian GP, Monza	Jackie Stewart	March-Ford 701	2nd
	François Cevert	March-Ford 701	6th
Canadian GP, St. Jovite	François Cevert	March-Ford 701	9th
	Jackie Stewart	Tyrrell-Ford 001	Rtd: Broken stub axle
United States GP, Watkins Glen	Jackie Stewart	Tyrrell-Ford 001	Rtd: Engine/oil line
	François Cevert	March-Ford 701	Rtd: Lost rear wheel
Mexican GP, Mexico City	Jackie Stewart	Tyrrell-Ford 001	Rtd: Front Suspension
	François Cevert	March-Ford 701	Rtd: Engine
Race of Champions, Brands Hatch	Jackie Stewart	March-Ford 701	1st
Oulton Park Gold Cup	Jackie Stewart	Tyrrell-Ford 001	7th(heat one)

1971

Race & Circuit	Drivers	Car/Engine	Result
South African GP, Kyalami	Jackie Stewart	Tyrrell-Ford 001	2nd
	François Cevert	Tyrrell-Ford 002	Rtd: Accident
Spanish GP, Montjuich Park	Jackie Stewart	Tyrrell-Ford 003	1st
	François Cevert	Tyrrell-Ford 002	7th
Monaco GP, Monte Carlo	Jackie Stewart	Tyrrell-Ford 003	1st
	François Cevert	Tyrrell-Ford 002	Rtd: Suspension and wheel
Dutch GP, Zandvoort	Jackie Stewart	Tyrrell-Ford 003	11th
	François Cevert	Tyrrell-Ford 002	Rtd: Accident
French GP, Paul Ricard	Jackie Stewart	Tyrrell-Ford 003	1st
	François Cevert	Tyrrell-Ford 002	2nd
British GP, Silverstone	Jackie Stewart	Tyrrell-Ford 003	1st
	François Cevert	Tyrrell-Ford 002	10th
German GP, Nürburgring	Jackie Stewart	Tyrrell-Ford 003	1st
	François Cevert	Tyrrell-Ford 002	2nd

Austrian GP,	Jackie Stewart	Tyrrell-Ford 003	Rtd: Broken driveshaft
Osterreichring	François Cevert	Tyrrell-Ford 002	Rtd: Engine
Italian GP, Monza	François Cevert	Tyrrell-Ford 002	3rd
	Jackie Stewart	Tyrrell-Ford 003	Rtd: Engine
Canadian GP,	Jackie Stewart	Tyrrell-Ford 003	1st
Mosport Park	François Cevert	Tyrrell-Ford 002	6th
United States GP,	Jackie Stewart	Tyrrell-Ford 003	5th
Watkins Glen	François Cevert	Tyrrell-Ford 002	1st
	Peter Revson	Tyrrell-Ford 001	Rtd: Clutch
Race of Champions,	Jackie Stewart	Tyrrell-Ford 001	2nd
Brands Hatch			
Questor GP, Ontario	Jackie Stewart	Tyrrell-Ford 001	2nd
Motor Speedway			
International	Jackie Stewart	Tyrrell-Ford 001	3rd
Trophy, Oulton			
Park			
GKN/Daily Express	Jackie Stewart	Tyrrell-Ford 003	Rtd: Accident
International			
Trophy, Silverstone			
Rothmans World	Jackie Stewart	Tyrrell-Ford 003	3rd
championship	François Cevert	Tyrrell-Ford 002	7th
Victory Race,			
Brands Hatch			

1972

Race & Circuit	Drivers	Car/Engine	Result
Argentine GP,	Jackie Stewart	Tyrrell-Ford 003	1st
Buenos Aires	François Cevert	Tyrrell-Ford 002	Rtd: Gearbox
South African GP,	Jackie Stewart	Tyrrell-Ford 003	Rtd: Gearbox
Kyalami	François Cevert	Tyrrell-Ford 002	9th
Spanish GP, Jarama	Jackie Stewart	Tyrrell-Ford 003	Rtd: Accident
	François Cevert	Tyrrell-Ford 002	Rtd: Engine
Monaco GP,	Jackie Stewart	Tyrrell-Ford 004	4th
Monte Carlo	François Cevert	Tyrrell-Ford 002	Running, not classified
Belgian GP, Nivelles	François Cevert	Tyrrell-Ford 002	2nd
French GP,	Jackie Stewart	Tyrrell-Ford 003	1st
Clermont Ferrand	François Cevert	Tyrrell-Ford 002	4th
	Patrick Depailler	Tyrrell-Ford 004	Running, not classified
European GP,	Jackie Stewart	Tyrrell-Ford 003	2nd
Brands Hatch	François Cevert	Tyrrell-Ford 002	Rtd: Accident
German GP,	Jackie Stewart	Tyrrell-Ford 003	11th (not running, classified)
Nürburgring	François Cevert	Tyrrell-Ford 002	10th
Austrian GP,	Jackie Stewart	Tyrrell-Ford 005	7th
Osterreichring	François Cevert	Tyrrell-Ford 002	9th

Italian GP, Monza	Jackie Stewart	Tyrrell-Ford 005	Rtd: Clutch
	François Cevert	Tyrrell-Ford 002	Rtd: Engine
Canadian GP, Mosport Park	Jackie Stewart	Tyrrell-Ford 005	1st
	François Cevert	Tyrrell-Ford 006	Rtd: Gearbox
United States GP, Watkins Glen	Jackie Stewart	Tyrrell-Ford 005	1st
	François Cevert	Tyrrell-Ford 006	2nd
	Patrick Depailler	Tyrrell-Ford 004	7th

1973

Race & Circuit	Drivers	Car/Engine	Result
Argentine GP, Buenos Aires	Jackie Stewart	Tyrrell-Ford 005	3rd
	François Cevert	Tyrrell-Ford 006	2nd
Brazilian GP, Interlagos	Jackie Stewart	Tyrrell-Ford 005	2nd
	François Cevert	Tyrrell-Ford 006	10th
South African GP, Kyalami	Jackie Stewart	Tyrrell-Ford 006	1st
	François Cevert	Tyrrell-Ford 005	Running, not classified
Spanish GP, Montjuich Park	Jackie Stewart	Tyrrell-Ford 006/2	Rtd: Brakes
	François Cevert	Tyrrell-Ford 006	2nd
Belgian GP, Zolder	Jackie Stewart	Tyrrell-Ford 006/2	1st
	François Cevert	Tyrrell-Ford 006	2nd
Monaco GP, Monte Carlo	Jackie Stewart	Tyrrell-Ford 006/2	1st
	François Cevert	Tyrrell-Ford 006	4th
Swedish GP, Anderstorp	Jackie Stewart	Tyrrell-Ford 006/2	5th
	François Cevert	Tyrrell-Ford 006	3rd
French GP, Paul Ricard	Jackie Stewart	Tyrrell-Ford 006/2	4th
	François Cevert	Tyrrell-Ford 006	2nd
British GP, Silverstone	Jackie Stewart	Tyrrell-Ford 006/2	10th
	François Cevert	Tyrrell-Ford 006	5th
Dutch GP, Zandvoort	Jackie Stewart	Tyrrell-Ford 006/2	1st
	François Cevert	Tyrrell-Ford 006	2nd
German GP, Nürburgring	Jackie Stewart	Tyrrell-Ford 006/2	1st
	François Cevert	Tyrrell-Ford 006	2nd
Austrian GP, Osterreichring	Jackie Stewart	Tyrrell-Ford 006/2	2nd
	François Cevert	Tyrrell-Ford 006	Rtd: Accident
Italian GP, Monza	Jackie Stewart	Tyrrell-Ford 006/2	4th
	François Cevert	Tyrrell-Ford 006	5th
Canadian GP, Mosport Park	Jackie Stewart	Tyrrell-Ford 006/2	5th
	François Cevert	Tyrrell-Ford 006	Rtd: Accident
	Chris Amon	Tyrrell-Ford 005	10th
United States GP, Watkins Glen	Jackie Stewart	Tyrrell-Ford 006/2	Withdrawn
	François Cevert	Tyrrell-Ford 006/3	Practice Accident
	Chris Amon	Tyrrell-Ford 005	Withdrawn

GKN-Daily Express Trophy Race, Silverstone	Jackie Stewart	Tyrrell-Ford 006	1st

1974

Race & Circuit	Drivers	Car/Engine	Result
Argentine GP, Buenos Aires	Jody Scheckter Patrick Depailler	Tyrrell-Ford 006/2 Tyrrell-Ford 005	Rtd: Cylinder head gasket 6th
Brazilian GP, Interlagos	Jody Scheckter Patrick Depailler	Tyrrell-Ford 006/2 Tyrrell-Ford 005	13th 8th
South African GP, Kyalami	Jody Scheckter Patrick Depailler	Tyrrell-Ford 006/2 Tyrrell-Ford 005	8th 4th
Spanish GP, Jarama	Jody Scheckter Patrick Depailler	Tyrrell-Ford 007 Tyrrell-Ford 006/2	5th 8th
Belgian GP, Nivelles	Jody Scheckter Patrick Depailler	Tyrrell-Ford 007 Tyrrell-Ford 007	3rd Rtd: Brake strap
Monaco GP, Monte Carlo	Jody Scheckter Patrick Depailler	Tyrrell-Ford 007 Tyrrell-Ford 006/2	2nd 9th
Swedish GP, Anderstorp	Jody Scheckter Patrick Depailler	Tyrrell-Ford 007 Tyrrell-Ford 007	1st 2nd
Dutch GP, Zandvoort	Jody Scheckter Patrick Depailler	Tyrrell-Ford 007 Tyrrell-Ford 007	5th 6th
French GP, Dijon	Jody Scheckter Patrick Depailler	Tyrrell-Ford 007 Tyrrell-Ford 006/2	4th 8th
British GP, Brands Hatch	Jody Scheckter Patrick Depailler	Tyrrell-Ford 007 Tyrrell-Ford 007	1st Rtd: Engine
German GP, Nürburgring	Jody Scheckter Patrick Depailler	Tyrrell-Ford 007 Tyrrell-Ford 007	2nd Rtd: Accident damage
Austrian GP, Osterreichring	Jody Scheckter Patrick Depailler	Tyrrell-Ford 007 Tyrrell-Ford 007	Rtd: Engine Rtd: Accident
Italian GP, Monza	Jody Scheckter Patrick Depailler	Tyrrell-Ford 007 Tyrrell-Ford 007	3rd 11th
Canadian GP, Mosport Park	Jody Scheckter Patrick Depailler	Tyrrell-Ford 007 Tyrrell-Ford 007	Rtd: Accident/brake failure 5th
United States GP, Watkins Glen	Jody Scheckter Patrick Depailler	Tyrrell-Ford 007 Tyrrell-Ford 007	Rtd: Fuel pipe 6th
Grande Premio Presidenta Medici, Brasilia	Jody Scheckter	Tyrrell-Ford 006/2	2nd

1975

Race & Circuit	Drivers	Car/Engine	Result
Argentine GP, Buenos Aires	Jody Scheckter Patrick Depailler	Tyrrell-Ford 007 Tyrrell-Ford 007	11th 5th

Brazilian GP, Interlagos	Jody Scheckter Patrick Depailler	Tyrrell-Ford 007 Tyrrell-Ford 007	Rtd: Split oil tank Rtd: Accident
South African GP, Kyalami	Jody Scheckter Patrick Depailler	Tyrrell-Ford 007 Tyrrell-Ford 007	1st 3rd
Spanish GP, Montjuich Park	Jody Scheckter Patrick Depailler	Tyrrell-Ford 007 Tyrrell-Ford 007	Rtd: Engine Rtd: Accident
Monaco GP, Monte Carlo	Jody Scheckter Patrick Depailler	Tyrrell-Ford 007 Tyrrell-Ford 007	7th 5th
Belgian GP, Zolder	Jody Scheckter Patrick Depailler	Tyrrell-Ford 007 Tyrrell-Ford 007	2nd 4th
Swedish GP, Anderstorp	Jody Scheckter Patrick Depailler	Tyrrell-Ford 007 Tyrrell-Ford 007	7th 12th
Dutch GP, Zandvoort	Jody Scheckter Patrick Depailler	Tyrrell-Ford 007 Tyrrell-Ford 007	Rtd: Engine (16th) 9th
French GP, Paul Ricard	Jody Scheckter Patrick Depailler Jean-Pierre Jabouille	Tyrrell-Ford 007 Tyrrell-Ford 007 Tyrrell-Ford 007	9th 6th 12th
British GP, Silverstone	Jody Scheckter Patrick Depailler	Tyrrell-Ford 007 Tyrrell-Ford 007	3rd 9th
German GP, Nürburgring	Jody Scheckter Patrick Depailler	Tyrrell-Ford 007 Tyrrell-Ford 007	Rtd: Accident 9th
Austrian GP, Osterreichring	Jody Scheckter Patrick Depailler	Tyrrell-Ford 007 Tyrrell-Ford 007	8th 11th
Italian GP, Monza	Jody Scheckter Patrick Depailler	Tyrrell-Ford 007 Tyrrell-Ford 007	8th 7th
United States GP, Watkins Glen	Jody Scheckter Patrick Depailler Michel Leclere	Tyrrell-Ford 007 Tyrrell-Ford 007 Tyrrell-Ford 007	6th Rtd: Accident Rtd: Engine
British Airways-Daily Mail Race of Champions, Brands Hatch	Jody Scheckter	Tyrrell-Ford 007	Rtd: Engine
Daily Express Trophy, Silverstone	Patrick Depailler	Tyrrell-Ford 007	5th
Swiss GP, Dijon	Patrick Depailler	Tyrrell-Ford 007	2nd

1976

Race & Circuit	*Drivers*	*Car/Engine*	*Result*
Brazilian GP, Interlagos	Jody Scheckter Patrick Depailler	Tyrrell-Ford 007 Tyrrell-Ford 007	5th 2nd
South African GP, Kyalami	Jody Scheckter Patrick Depailler	Tyrrell-Ford 007 Tyrrell-Ford 007	4th 9th
US West GP, Long Beach	Jody Scheckter Patrick Depailler	Tyrrell-Ford 007 Tyrrell-Ford 007	Rtd: Suspension 3rd

Spanish GP, Jarama	Jody Scheckter	Tyrrell-Ford 007	Rtd: Engine
	Patrick Depailler	Tyrrell-Ford P34	Rtd: Accident/brake failure
Belgian GP, Zolder	Jody Scheckter	Tyrrell-Ford P34	4th
	Patrick Depailler	Tyrrell-Ford P34	Rtd: Engine
Monaco GP, Monte Carlo	Jody Scheckter	Tyrrell-Ford P34	2nd
	Patrick Depailler	Tyrrell-Ford P34	3rd
Swedish GP, Anderstorp	Jody Scheckter	Tyrrell-Ford P34	1st
	Patrick Depailler	Tyrrell-Ford P34	2nd
French GP, Paul Ricard	Jody Scheckter	Tyrrell-Ford P34	6th
	Patrick Depailler	Tyrrell-Ford P34	2nd
British GP, Brands Hatch	Jody Scheckter	Tyrrell-Ford P34	2nd
	Patrick Depailler	Tyrrell-Ford P34	Rtd: Engine
German GP, Nürburgring	Jody Scheckter	Tyrrell-Ford P34	2nd
	Patrick Depailler	Tyrrell-Ford P34	Rtd: Accident
Austrian GP, Osterreichring	Jody Scheckter	Tyrrell-Ford P34	Rtd: Accident/Suspension
	Patrick Depailler	Tyrrell-Ford P34	Rtd: Suspension failure
Dutch/European GP, Zandvoort	Jody Scheckter	Tyrrell-Ford P34	5th
	Patrick Depailler	Tyrrell-Ford P34	7th
Italian GP, Monza	Jody Scheckter	Tyrrell-Ford P34	5th
	Patrick Depailler	Tyrrell-Ford P34	6th
Canadian GP, Mosport Park	Jody Scheckter	Tyrrell-Ford P34	4th
	Patrick Depailler	Tyrrell-Ford P34	2nd
United States GP, Watkins Glen	Jody Scheckter	Tyrrell-Ford P34	2nd
	Patrick Depailler	Tyrrell-Ford P34	Rtd: Detached fuel line
Japanese GP, Fuji	Jody Scheckter	Tyrrell-Ford P34	Rtd: Overheating engine
	Patrick Depailler	Tyrrell-Ford P34	2nd
Daily Mail Race of Champions, Brands Hatch	Jody Scheckter	Tyrrell-Ford 007	Rtd: Accident
Graham Hill International Trophy, Silverstone	Jody Scheckter	Tyrrell-Ford 007	3rd

1977

Race & Circuit	Drivers	Car/Engine	Result
Argentine GP, Buenos Aires	Ronnie Peterson	Tyrrell-Ford P34	Rtd: Spun off
	Patrick Depailler	Tyrrell-Ford P34	Rtd: Engine Overheating
Brazilian GP, Interlagos	Ronnie Peterson	Tyrrell-Ford P34	Rtd: Accident
	Patrick Depailler	Tyrrell-Ford P34	Rtd: Accident
South African GP, Kyalami	Ronnie Peterson	Tyrrell-Ford P34	Rtd: Fuel pressure
	Patrick Depailler	Tyrrell-Ford P34	3rd
US West GP, Long Beach	Ronnie Peterson	Tyrrell-Ford P34	Rtd: Fuel line
	Patrick Depailler	Tyrrell-Ford P34	4th

Spanish GP, Jarama	Ronnie Peterson	Tyrrell-Ford P34	8th
	Patrick Depailler	Tyrrell-Ford P34	Rtd: Engine
Monaco GP, Monte Carlo	Ronnie Peterson	Tyrrell-Ford P34	Rtd: Brakes
	Patrick Depailler	Tyrrell-Ford P34	Rtd: Brakes/Gearbox
Belgian GP, Zolder	Ronnie Peterson	Tyrrell-Ford P34	3rd
	Patrick Depailler	Tyrrell-Ford P34	8th
Swedish GP, Anderstorp	Ronnie Peterson	Tyrrell-Ford P34	Rtd: Ignition
	Patrick Depailler	Tyrrell-Ford P34	4th
French GP, Dijon	Ronnie Peterson	Tyrrell-Ford P34	12th
	Patrick Depailler	Tyrrell-Ford P34	Rtd: Accident
British GP, Silverstone	Ronnie Peterson	Tyrrell-Ford P34	Rtd: Engine
	Patrick Depailler	Tyrrell-Ford P34	Rtd: Accident/Brakes
German GP, Hockenheim	Ronnie Peterson	Tyrrell-Ford P34	Rtd: Engine (9th)
	Patrick Depailler	Tyrrell-Ford P34	Rtd: Engine
Austrian GP, Osterreichring	Ronnie Peterson	Tyrrell-Ford P34	5th
	Patrick Depailler	Tyrrell-Ford P34	13th
Dutch GP, Zandvoort	Ronnie Peterson	Tyrrell-Ford P34	Rtd: Ignition
	Patrick Depailler	Tyrrell-Ford P34	Rtd: Engine
Italian GP, Monza	Ronnie Peterson	Tyrrell-Ford P34	6th
	Patrick Depailler	Tyrrell-Ford P34	Rtd: Engine
United States GP, Watkins Glen	Ronnie Peterson	Tyrrell-Ford P34	16th
	Patrick Depailler	Tyrrell-Ford P34	14th
Canadian GP, Mosport Park	Ronnie Peterson	Tyrrell-Ford P34	Rtd: Fuel leak
	Patrick Depailler	Tyrrell-Ford P34	2nd
Japanese GP, Fuji	Ronnie Peterson	Tyrrell-Ford P34	Rtd: Accident
	Patrick Depailler	Tyrrell-Ford P34	3rd
Race of Champions, Brands Hatch	Ronnie Peterson	Tyrrell-Ford P34	Rtd: Engine (10th)

1978

Race & Circuit	Drivers	Car/Engine	Result
Argentine GP, Buenos Aires	Didier Pironi	Tyrrell-Ford 008	14th
	Patrick Depailler	Tyrrell-Ford 008	3rd
Brazilian GP, Rio de Janeiro	Didier Pironi	Tyrrell-Ford 008	6th
	Patrick Depailler	Tyrrell-Ford 008	Rtd: Spun off/brakes
South African GP, Kyalami	Didier Pironi	Tyrrell-Ford 008	6th
	Patrick Depailler	Tyrrell-Ford 008	2nd
US West GP, Long Beach	Didier Pironi	Tyrrell-Ford 008	Rtd: Gearbox
	Patrick Depailler	Tyrrell-Ford 008	3rd
Monaco GP, Monte Carlo	Didier Pironi	Tyrrell-Ford 008	5th
	Patrick Depailler	Tyrrell-Ford 008	1st
Belgian GP, Zolder	Didier Pironi	Tyrrell-Ford 008	6th
	Patrick Depailler	Tyrrell-Ford 008	Rtd: Gearbox

Spanish GP, Jarama	Didier Pironi	Tyrrell-Ford 008	12th
	Patrick Depailler	Tyrrell-Ford 008	Rtd: Engine
Swedish GP, Anderstorp	Didier Pironi	Tyrrell-Ford 008	Rtd: Collision/suspension
	Patrick Depailler	Tyrrell-Ford 008	Rtd: Suspension
French GP, Paul Ricard	Didier Pironi	Tyrrell-Ford 008	10th
	Patrick Depailler	Tyrrell-Ford 008	Rtd: Engine
British GP, Brands Hatch	Didier Pironi	Tyrrell-Ford 008	Rtd: Gearbox mounting bolts
	Patrick Depailler	Tyrrell-Ford 008	4th
German GP, Hockenheim	Didier Pironi	Tyrrell-Ford 008	5th
	Patrick Depailler	Tyrrell-Ford 008	Rtd: Accident
Austrian GP, Osterreichring	Didier Pironi	Tyrrell-Ford 008	Rtd: Accident
	Patrick Depailler	Tyrrell-Ford 008	2nd
Dutch GP, Zandvoort	Didier Pironi	Tyrrell-Ford 008	Rtd: Accident
	Patrick Depailler	Tyrrell-Ford 008	Rtd: Engine
Italian GP, Monza	Didier Pironi	Tyrrell-Ford 008	DNS: Accident at first start
	Patrick Depailler	Tyrrell-Ford 008	DNS: Accident at first start
United States GP, Watkins Glen	Didier Pironi	Tyrrell-Ford 008	10th
	Patrick Depailler	Tyrrell-Ford 008	Rtd: Loose hub assembly
Canadian GP, Montreal	Didier Pironi	Tyrrell-Ford 008	7th
	Patrick Depailler	Tyrrell-Ford 008	5th
Daily Express International Trophy, Silverstone	Patrick Depailler	Tyrrell-Ford 008	Rtd: Accident

1979

Race & Circuit	*Drivers*	*Car/Engine*	*Result*
Argentine GP, Buenos Aires	Didier Pironi	Tyrrell-Ford 009	DNS: Accident at first start
	Jean-Pierre Jarier	Tyrrell-Ford 009	Rtd: Engine
Brazilian GP, Interlagos	Didier Pironi	Tyrrell-Ford 009	4th
	Jean-Pierre Jarier	Tyrrell-Ford 009	DNS: Electrical failure
South African GP, Kyalami	Didier Pironi	Tyrrell-Ford 009	Rtd: Throttle linkage
	Jean-Pierre Jarier	Tyrrell-Ford 009	3rd
US West GP, Long Beach	Didier Pironi	Tyrrell-Ford 009	DNQ
	Jean-Pierre Jarier	Tyrrell-Ford 009	6th
Spanish GP, Jarama	Didier Pironi	Tyrrell-Ford 009	6th
	Jean-Pierre Jarier	Tyrrell-Ford 009	5th
Belgian GP, Zolder	Didier Pironi	Tyrrell-Ford 009	3rd
	Jean-Pierre Jarier	Tyrrell-Ford 009	11th
Monaco GP, Monte Carlo	Didier Pironi	Tyrrell-Ford 009	Rtd: Accident
	Jean-Pierre Jarier	Tyrrell-Ford 009	Rtd: Broken rear upright
French GP, Dijon	Didier Pironi	Tyrrell-Ford 009	Rtd: Suspension
	Jean-Pierre Jarier	Tyrrell-Ford 009	5th

British GP, Silverstone	Didier Pironi	Tyrrell-Ford 009	10th
	Jean-Pierre Jarier	Tyrrell-Ford 009	3rd
German GP, Hockenheim	Didier Pironi	Tyrrell-Ford 009	9th
	Geoff Lees	Tyrrell-Ford 009	7th
Austrian GP, Osterreichring	Didier Pironi	Tyrrell-Ford 009	7th
	Derek Daly	Tyrrell-Ford 009	8th
Dutch GP, Zandvoort	Didier Pironi	Tyrrell-Ford 009	Rtd: Rear suspension
	Jean-Pierre Jarier	Tyrrell-Ford 009	Rtd: Spun off/stuck throttle
Italian GP, Monza	Didier Pironi	Tyrrell-Ford 009	10th
	Jean-Pierre Jarier	Tyrrell-Ford 009	6th
Canadian GP, Montreal	Didier Pironi	Tyrrell-Ford 009	5th
	Jean-Pierre Jarier	Tyrrell-Ford 009	Rtd: Engine
	Derek Daly	Tyrrell-Ford 009	Rtd: Engine
United States GP, Watkins Glen	Didier Pironi	Tyrrell-Ford 009	3rd
	Jean-Pierre Jarier	Tyrrell-Ford 009	Rtd: Collision
	Derek Daly	Tyrrell-Ford 009	Rtd: Accident
Gran Premio Dino Ferrari, Imola	Jean-Pierre Jarier	Tyrrell-Ford 009	5th

1980

Race & Circuit	Drivers	Car/Engine	Result
Argentine GP, Buenos Aires	Jean-Pierre Jarier	Tyrrell-Ford 009	Rtd: Collision damage
	Derek Daly	Tyrrell-Ford 009	4th
Brazilian GP, Interlagos	Jean-Pierre Jarier	Tyrrell-Ford 009	12th
	Derek Daly	Tyrrell-Ford 009	14th
South African GP, Kyalami	Jean-Pierre Jarier	Tyrrell-Ford 010	7th
	Derek Daly	Tyrrell-Ford 010	Rtd: Puncture
US West GP, Long Beach	Jean-Pierre Jarier	Tyrrell-Ford 010	Rtd: Accident
	Derek Daly	Tyrrell-Ford 010	8th
Belgian GP, Zolder	Jean-Pierre Jarier	Tyrrell-Ford 010	5th
	Derek Daly	Tyrrell-Ford 010	9th
Monaco GP, Monte Carlo	Jean-Pierre Jarier	Tyrrell-Ford 010	Rtd: Accident
	Derek Daly	Tyrrell-Ford 010	Rtd: Accident
Spanish GP, Jarama	Jean-Pierre Jarier	Tyrrell-Ford 010	4th
	Derek Daly	Tyrrell-Ford 010	Rtd: Accident
French GP, Paul Ricard	Jean-Pierre Jarier	Tyrrell-Ford 010	14th
	Derek Daly	Tyrrell-Ford 010	11th
British GP, Brands Hatch	Jean-Pierre Jarier	Tyrrell-Ford 010	5th
	Derek Daly	Tyrrell-Ford 010	4th
German GP, Hockenheim	Jean-Pierre Jarier	Tyrrell-Ford 010	15th
	Derek Daly	Tyrrell-Ford 010	10th
Austrian GP, Osterreichring	Jean-Pierre Jarier	Tyrrell-Ford 010	Rtd: Engine
	Derek Daly	Tyrrell-Ford 010	Rtd: Accident/brakes

Dutch GP,	Jean-Pierre Jarier	Tyrrell-Ford 010	5th
Zandvoort	Derek Daly	Tyrrell-Ford 010	Rtd: Accident/brakes
Italian GP, Monza	Jean-Pierre Jarier	Tyrrell-Ford 010	Rtd: Brakes
	Derek Daly	Tyrrell-Ford 010	Rtd: Accident
Canadian GP,	Jean-Pierre Jarier	Tyrrell-Ford 010	7th
Montreal	Derek Daly	Tyrrell-Ford 010	DNS: Accident at first start
	Mike Thackwell	Tyrrell-Ford 010	DNS: car passed to Jarier
United States GP,	Jean-Pierre Jarier	Tyrrell-Ford 010	Running, not classified
Watkins Glen	Derek Daly	Tyrrell-Ford 010	Rtd: Collision/suspension
	Mike Thackwell	Tyrrell-Ford 010	DNQ

1981

Race & Circuit	Drivers	Car/Engine	Result
US West GP,	Eddie Cheever	Tyrrell-Ford 010	5th
Long Beach	Kevin Cogan	Tyrrell-Ford 010	DNQ
Brazilian GP,	Eddie Cheever	Tyrrell-Ford 010	Running, not classified
Rio de Janeiro	Ricardo Zunino	Tyrrell-Ford 010	13th
Argentine GP,	Eddie Cheever	Tyrrell-Ford 010	Rtd: Clutch
Buenos Aires	Ricardo Zunino	Tyrrell-Ford 010	13th
San Marino GP, Imola	Eddie Cheever	Tyrrell-Ford 010	Rtd: Accident
	Michele Alboreto	Tyrrell-Ford 010	Rtd: Accident
Belgian GP, Zolder	Eddie Cheever	Tyrrell-Ford 010	6th
	Michele Alboreto	Tyrrell-Ford 010	12th
Monaco GP,	Eddie Cheever	Tyrrell-Ford 010	5th
Monte Carlo	Michele Alboreto	Tyrrell-Ford 010	Rtd: Accident
Spanish GP, Jarama	Eddie Cheever	Tyrrell-Ford 010	Running, not classified
	Michele Alboreto	Tyrrell-Ford 010	DNQ
French GP, Dijon	Eddie Cheever	Tyrrell-Ford 010	13th
	Michele Alboreto	Tyrrell-Ford 010	16th
British GP, Silverstone	Eddie Cheever	Tyrrell-Ford 010	4th
	Michele Alboreto	Tyrrell-Ford 010	Rtd: Clutch
German GP,	Eddie Cheever	Tyrrell-Ford 011	5th
Hockenheim	Michele Alboreto	Tyrrell-Ford 010	DNQ
Austrian GP,	Eddie Cheever	Tyrrell-Ford 011	DNQ
Osterreichring	Michele Alboreto	Tyrrell-Ford 010	Rtd: Engine
Dutch GP, Zandvoort	Eddie Cheever	Tyrrell-Ford 011	Rtd: Suspension/accident
	Michele Alboreto	Tyrrell-Ford 011	Rtd: Engine (9th)
Italian GP, Monza	Eddie Cheever	Tyrrell-Ford 011	Rtd: Spun off
	Michele Alboreto	Tyrrell-Ford 011	Rtd: Accident
Canadian GP,	Eddie Cheever	Tyrrell-Ford 011	Rtd: Engine (12th)
Montreal	Michele Alboreto	Tyrrell-Ford 011	11th
Caesars Palace GP,	Eddie Cheever	Tyrrell-Ford 011	Rtd: Engine
Las Vegas	Michele Alboreto	Tyrrell-Ford 011	Rtd: Engine (13th)

1982

Race & Circuit	Drivers	Car/Engine	Result
South African GP, Kyalami	Michele Alboreto	Tyrrell-Ford 011	7th
	Slim Borgudd	Tyrrell-Ford 011	16th
Brazilian GP, Rio de Janeiro	Michele Alboreto	Tyrrell-Ford 011	4th
	Slim Borgudd	Tyrrell-Ford 011	7th
US West GP, Long Beach	Michele Alboreto	Tyrrell-Ford 011	4th
	Slim Borgudd	Tyrrell-Ford 011	10th
San Marino GP, Imola	Michele Alboreto	Tyrrell-Ford 011	3rd
	Brian Henton	Tyrrell-Ford 011	Rtd: Clutch
Belgian GP, Zolder	Michele Alboreto	Tyrrell-Ford 011	Rtd: Engine
	Brian Henton	Tyrrell-Ford 011	Rtd: Engine
Monaco GP, Monte Carlo	Michele Alboreto	Tyrrell-Ford 011	Rtd: Front suspension (10th)
	Brian Henton	Tyrrell-Ford 011	8th
United States GP, Detroit	Michele Alboreto	Tyrrell-Ford 011	Rtd: Accident
	Brian Henton	Tyrrell-Ford 011	9th
Canadian GP, Montreal	Michele Alboreto	Tyrrell-Ford 011	Rtd: Gearbox
	Brian Henton	Tyrrell-Ford 011	Running, not classified
Dutch GP, Zandvoort	Michele Alboreto	Tyrrell-Ford 011	7th
	Brian Henton	Tyrrell-Ford 011	Rtd: Throttle linkage
British GP, Brands Hatch	Michele Alboreto	Tyrrell-Ford 011	Running, not classified
	Brian Henton	Tyrrell-Ford 011	8th
French GP, Paul Ricard	Michele Alboreto	Tyrrell-Ford 011	6th
	Brian Henton	Tyrrell-Ford 011	10th
German GP, Hockenheim	Michele Alboreto	Tyrrell-Ford 011	4th
	Brian Henton	Tyrrell-Ford 011	7th
Austrian GP, Osterreichring	Michele Alboreto	Tyrrell-Ford 011	Rtd: Accident
	Brian Henton	Tyrrell-Ford 011	Rtd: Engine/valve spring
Swiss GP, Dijon	Michele Alboreto	Tyrrell-Ford 011	7th
	Brian Henton	Tyrrell-Ford 011	11th
Italian GP, Monza	Michele Alboreto	Tyrrell-Ford 011	5th
	Brian Henton	Tyrrell-Ford 011	Rtd: Accident
Caesars Palace GP, Las Vegas	Michele Alboreto	Tyrrell-Ford 011	1st
	Brian Henton	Tyrrell-Ford 011	8th

1983

Race & Circuit	Drivers	Car/Engine	Result
Brazilian GP, Rio de Janeiro	Michele Alboreto	Tyrrell-Ford 011	Rtd: Collision
	Danny Sullivan	Tyrrell-Ford 011	11th
US West GP, Long Beach	Michele Alboreto	Tyrrell-Ford 011	9th
	Danny Sullivan	Tyrrell-Ford 011	8th
French GP, Paul Ricard	Michele Alboreto	Tyrrell-Ford 011	8th
	Danny Sullivan	Tyrrell-Ford 011	Rtd: Clutch

San Marino GP, Imola	Michele Alboreto	Tyrrell-Ford 011	Rtd: Accident/rear suspension
	Danny Sullivan	Tyrrell-Ford 011	Rtd: Accident
Monaco GP,	Michele Alboreto	Tyrrell-Ford 011	Rtd: Accident
Monte Carlo	Danny Sullivan	Tyrrell-Ford 011	5th
Belgian GP,	Michele Alboreto	Tyrrell-Ford 011	14th
Spa-Francorchamps	Danny Sullivan	Tyrrell-Ford 011	12th
United States GP,	Michele Alboreto	Tyrrell-Ford 011	1st
Detroit	Danny Sullivan	Tyrrell-Ford 011	Rtd: Electrics
Canadian GP,	Michele Alboreto	Tyrrell-Ford 011	8th
Montreal	Danny Sullivan	Tyrrell-Ford 011	DNQ
British GP, Silverstone	Michele Alboreto	Tyrrell-Ford 011	13th
	Danny Sullivan	Tyrrell-Ford 011	14th
German GP,	Michele Alboreto	Tyrrell-Ford 011	Rtd: Fuel pump drive
Hockenheim	Danny Sullivan	Tyrrell-Ford 011	12th
Austrian GP,	Michele Alboreto	Tyrrell-Ford 012	Rtd: Accident
Osterreichring	Danny Sullivan	Tyrrell-Ford 011	Rtd: Accident
Dutch GP, Zandvoort	Michele Alboreto	Tyrrell-Ford 012	6th
	Danny Sullivan	Tyrrell-Ford 011	Rtd: Engine
Italian GP, Monza	Michele Alboreto	Tyrrell-Ford 012	Rtd: Clutch
	Danny Sullivan	Tyrrell-Ford 011	Rtd: Fuel pump drive
European GP,	Michele Alboreto	Tyrrell-Ford 012	Rtd: Engine
Brands Hatch	Danny Sullivan	Tyrrell-Ford 012	Rtd: Fire/broken oil line
South African GP,	Michele Alboreto	Tyrrell-Ford 012	Rtd: Engine
Kyalami	Danny Sullivan	Tyrrell-Ford 012	7th
Race of Champions,	Danny Sullivan	Tyrrell-Ford 011	2nd
Brands Hatch			

1984

Race & Circuit	Drivers	Car/Engine	Result
Brazilian GP,	Martin Brundle	Tyrrell-Ford 012	5th
Rio de Janeiro	Stefan Bellof	Tyrrell-Ford 012	Rtd: Throttle cable
South African GP,	Martin Brundle	Tyrrell-Ford 012	11th
Kyalami	Stefan Bellof	Tyrrell-Ford 012	Rtd: Broken hub
Belgian GP, Zolder	Martin Brundle	Tyrrell-Ford 012	Rtd: Lost wheel
	Stefan Bellof	Tyrrell-Ford 012	6th
San Marino GP, Imola	Martin Brundle	Tyrrell-Ford 012	Rtd: Fuel feed (11th)
	Stefan Bellof	Tyrrell-Ford 012	5th
French GP, Dijon	Martin Brundle	Tyrrell-Ford 012	12th
	Stefan Bellof	Tyrrell-Ford 012	Rtd: Engine
Monaco GP,	Martin Brundle	Tyrrell-Ford 012	DNQ
Monte Carlo	Stefan Bellof	Tyrrell-Ford 012	3rd
Canadian GP,	Martin Brundle	Tyrrell-Ford 012	10th
Montreal	Stefan Bellof	Tyrrell-Ford 012	Rtd: Driveshaft

United States GP, Detroit	Martin Brundle	Tyrrell-Ford 012	2nd
	Stefan Bellof	Tyrrell-Ford 012	Rtd: Accident
United States GP, Dallas	Martin Brundle	Tyrrell-Ford 012	DNQ: practice accident
	Stefan Bellof	Tyrrell-Ford 012	Rtd: Accident
British GP, Brands Hatch	Stefan Johansson	Tyrrell-Ford 012	Rtd: Accident damage
	Stefan Bellof	Tyrrell-Ford 012	11th
German GP, Hockenheim	Stefan Johansson	Tyrrell-Ford 012	9th
	Mike Thackwell	Tyrrell-Ford 012	DNQ
Austrian GP, Osterreichring	Stefan Johansson	Tyrrell-Ford 012	DNQ
	Stefan Bellof	Tyrrell-Ford 012	EXC
Dutch GP, Zandvoort	Stefan Johansson	Tyrrell-Ford 012	8th
	Stefan Bellof	Tyrrell-Ford 012	9th

1985

Race & Circuit	Drivers	Car/Engine	Result
Brazilian GP, Rio de Janeiro	Martin Brundle	Tyrrell-Ford 012	8th
	Stefan Johansson	Tyrrell-Ford 012	7th
Portuguese GP, Estoril	Martin Brundle	Tyrrell-Ford 012	Rtd: Gear linkage
	Stefan Bellof	Tyrrell-Ford 012	6th
San Marino GP, Imola	Martin Brundle	Tyrrell-Ford 012	9th
	Stefan Bellof	Tyrrell-Ford 012	Rtd: Engine
Monaco GP, Monte Carlo	Martin Brundle	Tyrrell-Ford 012	10th
	Stefan Bellof	Tyrrell-Ford 012	DNQ
Canadian GP, Montreal	Martin Brundle	Tyrrell-Ford 012	12th
	Stefan Bellof	Tyrrell-Ford 012	11th
United States GP, Detroit	Martin Brundle	Tyrrell-Ford 012	Rtd: Accident
	Stefan Bellof	Tyrrell-Ford 012	4th
French GP, Paul Ricard	Martin Brundle	Tyrrell-Renault 014	Rtd: Gearbox
	Stefan Bellof	Tyrrell-Ford 012	13th
British GP, Silverstone	Martin Brundle	Tyrrell-Renault 014	7th
	Stefan Bellof	Tyrrell-Ford 012	11th
German GP, Nürburgring	Stefan Bellof	Tyrrell-Renault 014	8th
	Martin Brundle	Tyrrell-Ford 012	10th
Austrian GP, Osterreichring	Stefan Bellof	Tyrrell-Renault 014	Rtd: Out of fuel (7th)
	Martin Brundle	Tyrrell-Ford 012	DNQ
Dutch GP, Zandvoort	Martin Brundle	Tyrrell-Renault 014	7th
	Stefan Bellof	Tyrrell-Renault 014	Rtd: Engine
Italian GP, Monza	Martin Brundle	Tyrrell-Renault 014	8th
Belgian GP, Spa-Francorchamps	Martin Brundle	Tyrrell-Renault 014	13th
European GP, Brands Hatch	Martin Brundle	Tyrrell-Renault 014	Rtd: Water pipe
	Ivan Capelli	Tyrrell-Renault 014	Rtd: Accident

South African GP,	Martin Brundle	Tyrrell-Renault 014	7th
Kyalami	Philippe Streiff	Tyrrell-Renault 014	Rtd: Accident
Australian GP,	Martin Brundle	Tyrrell-Renault 014	Running, not classified
Adelaide	Ivan Capelli	Tyrrell-Renault 014	4th

1986

Race & Circuit	Drivers	Car/Engine	Result
Brazilian GP,	Martin Brundle	Tyrrell-Renault 014	5th
Rio de Janeiro	Philippe Streiff	Tyrrell-Renault 014	7th
Spanish GP, Jerez	Martin Brundle	Tyrrell-Renault 015	Rtd: Engine
	Philippe Streiff	Tyrrell-Renault 014	Rtd: Engine
San Marino GP, Imola	Martin Brundle	Tyrrell-Renault 014	8th
	Philippe Streiff	Tyrrell-Renault 014	Rtd: Transmission
Monaco GP,	Martin Brundle	Tyrrell-Renault 015	Rtd: Accident
Monte Carlo	Philippe Streiff	Tyrrell-Renault 015	11th
Belgian GP,	Martin Brundle	Tyrrell-Renault 015	Rtd: Gearbox
Spa-Francorchamps	Philippe Streiff	Tyrrell-Renault 015	12th
Canadian GP,	Martin Brundle	Tyrrell-Renault 015	9th
Montreal	Philippe Streiff	Tyrrell-Renault 014	11th
United States GP,	Martin Brundle	Tyrrell-Renault 015	Rtd: Electrics
Detroit	Philippe Streiff	Tyrrell-Renault 015	9th
French GP,	Martin Brundle	Tyrrell-Renault 015	10th
Paul Ricard	Philippe Streiff	Tyrrell-Renault 015	Rtd: Fuel leak/fire
British GP,	Martin Brundle	Tyrrell-Renault 015	5th
Brands Hatch	Philippe Streiff	Tyrrell-Renault 015	6th
German GP,	Martin Brundle	Tyrrell-Renault 015	Rtd: Electrics
Hockenheim	Philippe Streiff	Tyrrell-Renault 015	Rtd: Engine
Hungarian GP,	Martin Brundle	Tyrrell-Renault 015	6th
Hungaroring	Philippe Streiff	Tyrrell-Renault 015	8th
Austrian GP,	Martin Brundle	Tyrrell-Renault 015	Rtd: Turbo
Osterreichring	Philippe Streiff	Tyrrell-Renault 015	Rtd: Engine
Italian GP, Monza	Martin Brundle	Tyrrell-Renault 015	10th
	Philippe Streiff	Tyrrell-Renault 015	9th
Portuguese GP, Estoril	Martin Brundle	Tyrrell-Renault 015	Rtd: Engine
	Philippe Streiff	Tyrrell-Renault 015	Rtd: Engine
Mexican GP,	Martin Brundle	Tyrrell-Renault 015	11th
Mexico City	Philippe Streiff	Tyrrell-Renault 015	Rtd: Turbo
Australian GP,	Martin Brundle	Tyrrell-Renault 015	4th
Adelaide	Philippe Streiff	Tyrrell-Renault 015	5th

1987

Race & Circuit	Drivers	Car/Engine	Result
Brazilian GP,	Jonathan Palmer	Tyrrell-Ford DG/016	10th
Rio de Janeiro	Philippe Streiff	Tyrrell-Ford DG/016	11th

San Marino GP, Imola	Jonathan Palmer	Tyrrell-Ford DG/016	Rtd: Clutch
	Philippe Streiff	Tyrrell-Ford DG/016	8th
Belgian GP, Spa-Francorchamps	Jonathan Palmer	Tyrrell-Ford DG/016	DNS: Accident at first start
	Philippe Streiff	Tyrrell-Ford DG/016	9th
Monaco GP, Monte Carlo	Jonathan Palmer	Tyrrell-Ford DG/016	5th
	Philippe Streiff	Tyrrell-Ford DG/016	Rtd: Accident
United States GP, Detroit	Jonathan Palmer	Tyrrell-Ford DG/016	11th
	Philippe Streiff	Tyrrell-Ford DG/016	Rtd: Accident
French GP, Paul Ricard	Jonathan Palmer	Tyrrell-Ford DG/016	7th
	Philippe Streiff	Tyrrell-Ford DG/016	6th
British GP, Silverstone	Jonathan Palmer	Tyrrell-Ford DG/016	8th
	Philippe Streiff	Tyrrell-Ford DG/016	Rtd: Engine
German GP, Hockenheim	Jonathan Palmer	Tyrrell-Ford DG/016	5th
	Philippe Streiff	Tyrrell-Ford DG/016	4th
Hungarian GP, Hungaroring	Jonathan Palmer	Tyrrell-Ford DG/016	7th
	Philippe Streiff	Tyrrell-Ford DG/016	9th
Austrian GP, Osterreichring	Jonathan Palmer	Tyrrell-Ford DG/016	14th
	Philippe Streiff	Tyrrell-Ford DG/016	DNS: Accident at first start
Italian GP, Monza	Jonathan Palmer	Tyrrell-Ford DG/016	14th
	Philippe Streiff	Tyrrell-Ford DG/016	12th
Portuguese GP, Estoril	Jonathan Palmer	Tyrrell-Ford DG/016	10th
	Philippe Streiff	Tyrrell-Ford DG/016	12th
Spanish GP, Jerez	Jonathan Palmer	Tyrrell-Ford DG/016	Rtd: Collision
	Philippe Streiff	Tyrrell-Ford DG/016	7th
Mexican GP, Mexico City	Jonathan Palmer	Tyrrell-Ford DG/016	7th
	Philippe Streiff	Tyrrell-Ford DG/016	8th
Japanese GP, Suzuka	Jonathan Palmer	Tyrrell-Ford DG/016	8th
	Philippe Streiff	Tyrrell-Ford DG/016	12th
Australian GP, Adelaide	Jonathan Palmer	Tyrrell-Ford DG/016	4th
	Philippe Streiff	Tyrrell-Ford DG/016	Rtd: Spun off

1988

Race & Circuit	Drivers	Car/Engine	Result
Brazilian GP, Rio de Janeiro	Jonathan Palmer	Tyrrell-Ford 017	Rtd: Transmission
	Julian Bailey	Tyrrell-Ford 017	DNQ
San Marino GP, Imola	Jonathan Palmer	Tyrrell-Ford 017	14th
	Julian Bailey	Tyrrell-Ford 017	Rtd: Gearbox
Monaco GP, Monte Carlo	Jonathan Palmer	Tyrrell-Ford 017	5th
	Julian Bailey	Tyrrell-Ford 017	DNQ
Mexican GP, Mexico City	Jonathan Palmer	Tyrrell-Ford 017	DNQ
	Julian Bailey	Tyrrell-Ford 017	DNQ
Canadian GP, Montreal	Jonathan Palmer	Tyrrell-Ford 017	6th
	Julian Bailey	Tyrrell-Ford 017	Rtd: Accident

329

United States GP,	Jonathan Palmer	Tyrrell-Ford 017	5th
Detroit	Julian Bailey	Tyrrell-Ford 017	Rtd: Accident (9th)
French GP,	Jonathan Palmer	Tyrrell-Ford 017	Rtd: Engine
Paul Ricard	Julian Bailey	Tyrrell-Ford 017	DNQ
British GP, Silverstone	Jonathan Palmer	Tyrrell-Ford 017	Rtd: Engine
	Julian Bailey	Tyrrell-Ford 017	16th
German GP,	Jonathan Palmer	Tyrrell-Ford 017	11th
Hockenheim	Julian Bailey	Tyrrell-Ford 017	DNQ
Hungarian GP,	Jonathan Palmer	Tyrrell-Ford 017	Rtd: Engine
Hungaroring	Julian Bailey	Tyrrell-Ford 017	DNQ
Belgian GP,	Jonathan Palmer	Tyrrell-Ford 017	Rtd: Throttle cable (14th)
Spa-Francorchamps	Julian Bailey	Tyrrell-Ford 017	DNQ
Italian GP, Monza	Jonathan Palmer	Tyrrell-Ford 017	DNQ
	Julian Bailey	Tyrrell-Ford 017	12th
Portuguese GP, Estoril	Jonathan Palmer	Tyrrell-Ford 017	Rtd: Engine overheating
	Julian Bailey	Tyrrell-Ford 017	DNQ
Spanish GP, Jerez	Jonathan Palmer	Tyrrell-Ford 017	Rtd: Punctured water radiator
	Julian Bailey	Tyrrell-Ford 017	DNQ
Japanese GP, Suzuka	Jonathan Palmer	Tyrrell-Ford 017	12th
	Julian Bailey	Tyrrell-Ford 017	14th
Australian GP,	Jonathan Palmer	Tyrrell-Ford 017	Rtd: Crown wheel and pinion
Adelaide	Julian Bailey	Tyrrell-Ford 017	DNQ

1989

Race & Circuit	Drivers	Car/Engine	Result
Brazilian GP,	Jonathan Palmer	Tyrrell-Ford 017B	7th
Rio de Janeiro	Michele Alboreto	Tyrrell-Ford 017B	10th
San Marino GP, Imola	Jonathan Palmer	Tyrrell-Ford 018	6th
	Michele Alboreto	Tyrrell-Ford 018	DNQ
Monaco GP,	Jonathan Palmer	Tyrrell-Ford 018	9th
Monte Carlo	Michele Alboreto	Tyrrell-Ford 018	5th
Mexican GP,	Jonathan Palmer	Tyrrell-Ford 018	Rtd: Throttle return spring
Mexico City	Michele Alboreto	Tyrrell-Ford 018	3rd
United States GP,	Jonathan Palmer	Tyrrell-Ford 018	Rtd: Electrics (9th)
Phoenix	Michele Alboreto	Tyrrell-Ford 018	Rtd: Gearbox
Canadian GP,	Jonathan Palmer	Tyrrell-Ford 018	Rtd: Accident
Montreal	Michele Alboreto	Tyrrell-Ford 018	Rtd: Electrics
French GP,	Jonathan Palmer	Tyrrell-Ford 018	10th
Paul Ricard	Jean Alesi	Tyrrell-Ford 018	4th
British GP, Silverstone	Jonathan Palmer	Tyrrell-Ford 018	Rtd: Spun off
	Jean Alesi	Tyrrell-Ford 018	Rtd: Spun off
German GP,	Jonathan Palmer	Tyrrell-Ford 018	Rtd: Throttle cable
Hockenheim	Jean Alesi	Tyrrell-Ford 018	10th

Hungarian GP,	Jonathan Palmer	Tyrrell-Ford 018	13th
Hungaroring	Jean Alesi	Tyrrell-Ford 018	9th
Belgian GP,	Jonathan Palmer	Tyrrell-Ford 018	14th
Spa-Francorchamps	Johnny Herbert	Tyrrell-Ford 018	Rtd: Spun off
Italian GP, Monza	Jonathan Palmer	Tyrrell-Ford 018	Rtd: Engine
	Jean Alesi	Tyrrell-Ford 018	5th
Portuguese GP, Estoril	Jonathan Palmer	Tyrrell-Ford 018	6th
	Johnny Herbert	Tyrrell-Ford 018	DNQ
Spanish GP, Jerez	Jonathan Palmer	Tyrrell-Ford 018	10th
	Jean Alesi	Tyrrell-Ford 018	4th
Japanese GP, Suzuka	Jonathan Palmer	Tyrrell-Ford 018	Rtd: Fuel leak
	Jean Alesi	Tyrrell-Ford 018	Rtd: Gearbox
Australian GP,	Jonathan Palmer	Tyrrell-Ford 018	DNQ
Adelaide	Jean Alesi	Tyrrell-Ford 018	Rtd: Electrics

1990

Race & Circuit	Drivers	Car/Engine	Result
United States GP,	Satoru Nakajima	Tyrrell-Ford 018	6th
Phoenix	Jean Alesi	Tyrrell-Ford 018	2nd
Brazilian GP,	Satoru Nakajima	Tyrrell-Ford 018	8th
Interlagos	Jean Alesi	Tyrrell-Ford 018	7th
San Marino GP, Imola	Satoru Nakajima	Tyrrell-Ford 019	Rtd: Accident
	Jean Alesi	Tyrrell-Ford 019	6th
Monaco GP,	Satoru Nakajima	Tyrrell-Ford 019	Rtd: Spun off
Monte Carlo	Jean Alesi	Tyrrell-Ford 019	2nd
Canadian GP,	Satoru Nakajima	Tyrrell-Ford 019	11th
Montreal	Jean Alesi	Tyrrell-Ford 019	Rtd: Accident
Mexican GP,	Satoru Nakajima	Tyrrell-Ford 019	Rtd: Accident
Mexico City	Jean Alesi	Tyrrell-Ford 019	7th
French GP,	Satoru Nakajima	Tyrrell-Ford 019	Rtd: Gear linkage
Paul Ricard	Jean Alesi	Tyrrell-Ford 019	Rtd: Differential
British GP, Silverstone	Satoru Nakajima	Tyrrell-Ford 019	Rtd: Electrics
	Jean Alesi	Tyrrell-Ford 019	8th
German GP,	Satoru Nakajima	Tyrrell-Ford 019	Rtd: Engine
Hockenheim	Jean Alesi	Tyrrell-Ford 019	Rtd: CV joint (11th)
Hungarian GP,	Satoru Nakajima	Tyrrell-Ford 019	Rtd: Spun off
Hungaroring	Jean Alesi	Tyrrell-Ford 019	Rtd: Accident
Belgian GP,	Satoru Nakajima	Tyrrell-Ford 019	Rtd: Engine
Spa-Francorchamps	Jean Alesi	Tyrrell-Ford 019	8th
Italian GP, Monza	Satoru Nakajima	Tyrrell-Ford 019	6th
	Jean Alesi	Tyrrell-Ford 019	Rtd: Spun off
Portuguese GP, Estoril	Satoru Nakajima	Tyrrell-Ford 019	Withdrawn
	Jean Alesi	Tyrrell-Ford 019	8th

Spanish GP, Jerez	Satoru Nakajima	Tyrrell-Ford 019	Rtd: Spun off
	Jean Alesi	Tyrrell-Ford 019	Rtd: Collision/puncture
Japanese GP, Suzuka	Satoru Nakajima	Tyrrell-Ford 019	6th
	Jean Alesi	Tyrrell-Ford 019	Withdrawn
Australian GP, Adelaide	Satoru Nakajima	Tyrrell-Ford 019	Rtd: Spun off
	Jean Alesi	Tyrrell-Ford 019	8th

1991

Race & Circuit	Drivers	Car/Engine	Result
United States GP, Phoenix	Satoru Nakajima	Tyrrell-Honda 020	5th
	Stefano Modena	Tyrrell-Honda 020	4th
Brazilian GP, Interlagos	Satoru Nakajima	Tyrrell-Honda 020	Rtd: Spun off
	Stefano Modena	Tyrrell-Honda 020	Rtd: Gearshift
San Marino GP, Imola	Satoru Nakajima	Tyrrell-Honda 020	Rtd: Transmission
	Stefano Modena	Tyrrell-Honda 020	Rtd: Engine
Monaco GP, Monte Carlo	Satoru Nakajima	Tyrrell-Honda 020	Rtd: Spun off
	Stefano Modena	Tyrrell-Honda 020	Rtd: Engine
Canadian GP, Montreal	Satoru Nakajima	Tyrrell-Honda 020	10th
	Stefano Modena	Tyrrell-Honda 020	2nd
Mexican GP, Mexico City	Satoru Nakajima	Tyrrell-Honda 020	12th
	Stefano Modena	Tyrrell-Honda 020	11th
French GP, Magny-Cours	Satoru Nakajima	Tyrrell-Honda 020	Rtd: Spun off
	Stefano Modena	Tyrrell-Honda 020	Rtd: Gearbox
British GP, Silverstone	Satoru Nakajima	Tyrrell-Honda 020	8th
	Stefano Modena	Tyrrell-Honda 020	7th
German GP, Hockenheim	Satoru Nakajima	Tyrrell-Honda 020	Rtd: Gearbox
	Stefano Modena	Tyrrell-Honda 020	13th
Hungarian GP, Hungaroring	Satoru Nakajima	Tyrrell-Honda 020	15th
	Stefano Modena	Tyrrell-Honda 020	12th
Belgian GP, Spa-Francorchamps	Satoru Nakajima	Tyrrell-Honda 020	Rtd: Slid off
	Stefano Modena	Tyrrell-Honda 020	Rtd: Oil leak/fire
Italian GP, Monza	Satoru Nakajima	Tyrrell-Honda 020	Rtd: Sticking throttle
	Stefano Modena	Tyrrell-Honda 020	Rtd: Engine
Portuguese GP, Estoril	Satoru Nakajima	Tyrrell-Honda 020	13th
	Stefano Modena	Tyrrell-Honda 020	Rtd: Engine
Spanish GP, Barcelona	Satoru Nakajima	Tyrrell-Honda 020	17th
	Stefano Modena	Tyrrell-Honda 020	16th
Japanese GP, Suzuka	Satoru Nakajima	Tyrrell-Honda 020	Rtd: Suspension
	Stefano Modena	Tyrrell-Honda 020	6th
Australian GP, Adelaide	Satoru Nakajima	Tyrrell-Honda 020	Rtd: Collision
	Stefano Modena	Tyrrell-Honda 020	10th

1992

Race & Circuit	Drivers	Car/Engine	Result
South African GP, Kyalami	Olivier Grouillard	Tyrrell-Ilmor 020B	Rtd: Clutch
	Andrea de Cesaris	Tyrrell-Ilmor 020B	Rtd: Engine
Mexican GP, Mexico City	Olivier Grouillard	Tyrrell-Ilmor 020B	Rtd: Engine
	Andrea de Cesaris	Tyrrell-Ilmor 020B	5th
Brazilian GP, Interlagos	Olivier Grouillard	Tyrrell-Ilmor 020B	Rtd: Engine
	Andrea de Cesaris	Tyrrell-Ilmor 020B	Rtd: Electrics
Spanish GP, Barcelona	Olivier Grouillard	Tyrrell-Ilmor 020B	Rtd: Spun off
	Andrea de Cesaris	Tyrrell-Ilmor 020B	Rtd: Oil pressure
San Marino GP, Imola	Olivier Grouillard	Tyrrell-Ilmor 020B	8th
	Andrea de Cesaris	Tyrrell-Ilmor 020B	Rtd: Fuel pressure (14th)
Monaco GP, Monte Carlo	Olivier Grouillard	Tyrrell-Ilmor 020B	Rtd: Gearbox
	Andrea de Cesaris	Tyrrell-Ilmor 020B	Rtd: Gearbox
Canadian GP, Montreal	Olivier Grouillard	Tyrrell-Ilmor 020B	12th
	Andrea de Cesaris	Tyrrell-Ilmor 020B	5th
French GP, Magny-Cours	Olivier Grouillard	Tyrrell-Ilmor 020B	11th
	Andrea de Cesaris	Tyrrell-Ilmor 020B	Rtd: Spun off
British GP, Silverstone	Olivier Grouillard	Tyrrell-Ilmor 020B	11th
	Andrea de Cesaris	Tyrrell-Ilmor 020B	Rtd: Suspension/spun off
German GP, Hockenheim	Olivier Grouillard	Tyrrell-Ilmor 020B	Rtd: Overheating
	Andrea de Cesaris	Tyrrell-Ilmor 020B	Rtd: Engine
Hungarian GP, Hungaroring	Olivier Grouillard	Tyrrell-Ilmor 020B	Rtd: Collision
	Andrea de Cesaris	Tyrrell-Ilmor 020B	8th
Belgian GP, Spa-Francorchamps	Olivier Grouillard	Tyrrell-Ilmor 020B	Rtd: Spun off
	Andrea de Cesaris	Tyrrell-Ilmor 020B	8th
Italian GP, Monza	Olivier Grouillard	Tyrrell-Ilmor 020B	Rtd: Engine
	Andrea de Cesaris	Tyrrell-Ilmor 020B	6th
Portuguese GP, Estoril	Olivier Grouillard	Tyrrell-Ilmor 020B	Rtd: Gearbox
	Andrea de Cesaris	Tyrrell-Ilmor 020B	9th
Japanese GP, Suzuka	Olivier Grouillard	Tyrrell-Ilmor 020B	Rtd: Accident
	Andrea de Cesaris	Tyrrell-Ilmor 020B	4th
Australian GP, Adelaide	Olivier Grouillard	Tyrrell-Ilmor 020B	Rtd: Collision
	Andrea de Cesaris	Tyrrell-Ilmor 020B	Rtd: Fuel pressure/fire

1993

Race & Circuit	Drivers	Car/Engine	Result
South African GP, Kyalami	Ukyo Katayama	Tyrrell-Yamaha 020C	Rtd: Transmission
	Andrea de Cesaris	Tyrrell-Yamaha 020C	Rtd: Transmission
Brazilian GP, Interlagos	Ukyo Katayama	Tyrrell-Yamaha 020C	Rtd: Accident
	Andrea de Cesaris	Tyrrell-Yamaha 020C	Rtd: Electrics
European GP, Donington Park	Ukyo Katayama	Tyrrell-Yamaha 020C	Rtd: Clutch
	Andrea de Cesaris	Tyrrell-Yamaha 020C	Rtd: Gearbox

San Marino GP, Imola	Ukyo Katayama	Tyrrell-Yamaha 020C	Rtd: Engine
	Andrea de Cesaris	Tyrrell-Yamaha 020C	Rtd: Spun off
Spanish GP,	Ukyo Katayama	Tyrrell-Yamaha 020C	Rtd: Spun off
Barcelona	Andrea de Cesaris	Tyrrell-Yamaha 020C	DNQ
Monaco GP,	Ukyo Katayama	Tyrrell-Yamaha 020C	Rtd: Oil leak
Monte Carlo	Andrea de Cesaris	Tyrrell-Yamaha 020C	10th
Canadian GP,	Ukyo Katayama	Tyrrell-Yamaha 020C	17th
Montreal	Andrea de Cesaris	Tyrrell-Yamaha 020C	Rtd: Accident
French GP,	Ukyo Katayama	Tyrrell-Yamaha 020C	Rtd: Damaged sump
Magny-Cours	Andrea de Cesaris	Tyrrell-Yamaha 020C	15th
British GP, Silverstone	Ukyo Katayama	Tyrrell-Yamaha 020C	13th
	Andrea de Cesaris	Tyrrell-Yamaha 021	Running, not classified
German GP,	Ukyo Katayama	Tyrrell-Yamaha 021	Rtd: Transmission
Hockenheim	Andrea de Cesaris	Tyrrell-Yamaha 021	Rtd: Gearbox
Hungarian GP,	Ukyo Katayama	Tyrrell-Yamaha 021	10th
Hungaroring	Andrea de Cesaris	Tyrrell-Yamaha 021	11th
Belgian GP,	Ukyo Katayama	Tyrrell-Yamaha 021	15th
Spa-Francorchamps	Andrea de Cesaris	Tyrrell-Yamaha 021	Rtd: Engine
Italian GP, Monza	Ukyo Katayama	Tyrrell-Yamaha 021	14th
	Andrea de Cesaris	Tyrrell-Yamaha 021	Rtd: Oil pressure (13th)
Portuguese GP, Estoril	Ukyo Katayama	Tyrrell-Yamaha 021	Rtd: Accident
	Andrea de Cesaris	Tyrrell-Yamaha 021	12th
Japanese GP, Suzuka	Ukyo Katayama	Tyrrell-Yamaha 021	Rtd: Engine
	Andrea de Cesaris	Tyrrell-Yamaha 021	Rtd: Accident
Australian GP,	Ukyo Katayama	Tyrrell-Yamaha 021	Rtd: Accident
Adelaide	Andrea de Cesaris	Tyrrell-Yamaha 021	13th

1994

Race & Circuit	Drivers	Car/Engine	Result
Brazilian GP,	Ukyo Katayama	Tyrrell-Yamaha 022	5th
Interlagos	Mark Blundell	Tyrrell-Yamaha 022	Rtd: Accident
Pacific GP, Aida	Ukyo Katayama	Tyrrell-Yamaha 022	Rtd: Engine
	Mark Blundell	Tyrrell-Yamaha 022	Rtd: Accident
San Marino GP, Imola	Ukyo Katayama	Tyrrell-Yamaha 022	5th
	Mark Blundell	Tyrrell-Yamaha 022	9th
Monaco GP,	Ukyo Katayama	Tyrrell-Yamaha 022	Rtd: Gearbox
Monte Carlo	Mark Blundell	Tyrrell-Yamaha 022	Rtd: Engine
Spanish GP,	Ukyo Katayama	Tyrrell-Yamaha 022	Rtd: Engine
Barcelona	Mark Blundell	Tyrrell-Yamaha 022	3rd
Canadian GP,	Ukyo Katayama	Tyrrell-Yamaha 022	Rtd: Spun off
Montreal	Mark Blundell	Tyrrell-Yamaha 022	Rtd: Spun off (10th)
French GP,	Ukyo Katayama	Tyrrell-Yamaha 022	Rtd: Spun off
Magny-Cours	Mark Blundell	Tyrrell-Yamaha 022	10th

British GP, Silverstone	Ukyo Katayama	Tyrrell-Yamaha 022	7th
	Mark Blundell	Tyrrell-Yamaha 022	Rtd: Gearbox
German GP, Hockenheim	Ukyo Katayama	Tyrrell-Yamaha 022	Rtd: Throttle
	Mark Blundell	Tyrrell-Yamaha 022	Rtd: Accident
Hungarian GP, Hungaroring	Ukyo Katayama	Tyrrell-Yamaha 022	Rtd: Accident
	Mark Blundell	Tyrrell-Yamaha 022	5th
Belgian GP, Spa-Francorchamps	Ukyo Katayama	Tyrrell-Yamaha 022	Rtd: Engine
	Mark Blundell	Tyrrell-Yamaha 022	5th
Italian GP, Monza	Ukyo Katayama	Tyrrell-Yamaha 022	Rtd: Accident
	Mark Blundell	Tyrrell-Yamaha 022	Rtd: Accident
Portuguese GP, Estoril	Ukyo Katayama	Tyrrell-Yamaha 022	Rtd: Gearbox
	Mark Blundell	Tyrrell-Yamaha 022	Rtd: Engine
European GP, Jerez	Ukyo Katayama	Tyrrell-Yamaha 022	7th
	Mark Blundell	Tyrrell-Yamaha 022	13th
Japanese GP, Suzuka	Ukyo Katayama	Tyrrell-Yamaha 022	Rtd: Accident
	Mark Blundell	Tyrrell-Yamaha 022	Rtd: Electrics
Australian GP, Adelaide	Ukyo Katayama	Tyrrell-Yamaha 022	Rtd: Spun off
	Mark Blundell	Tyrrell-Yamaha 022	Rtd: Accident

1995

Race & Circuit	Drivers	Car/Engine	Result
Brazilian GP, Interlagos	Ukyo Katayama	Tyrrell-Yamaha 023	Rtd: Spun off
	Mika Salo	Tyrrell-Yamaha 023	7th
Argentine GP, Buenos Aires	Ukyo Katayama	Tyrrell-Yamaha 023	8th
	Mika Salo	Tyrrell-Yamaha 023	Rtd: Collision
San Marino GP, Imola	Ukyo Katayama	Tyrrell-Yamaha 023	Rtd: Spun off
	Mika Salo	Tyrrell-Yamaha 023	Rtd: Engine
Spanish GP, Barcelona	Ukyo Katayama	Tyrrell-Yamaha 023	Rtd: Engine
	Mika Salo	Tyrrell-Yamaha 023	10th
Monaco GP, Monte Carlo	Ukyo Katayama	Tyrrell-Yamaha 023	Rtd: Accident
	Mika Salo	Tyrrell-Yamaha 023	Rtd: Engine
Canadian GP, Montreal	Ukyo Katayama	Tyrrell-Yamaha 023	Rtd: Engine
	Mika Salo	Tyrrell-Yamaha 023	7th
French GP, Magny-Cours	Ukyo Katayama	Tyrrell-Yamaha 023	Rtd: Collision
	Mika Salo	Tyrrell-Yamaha 023	15th
British GP, Silverstone	Ukyo Katayama	Tyrrell-Yamaha 023	Rtd: Fuel pressure
	Mika Salo	Tyrrell-Yamaha 023	8th
German GP, Hockenheim	Ukyo Katayama	Tyrrell-Yamaha 023	7th
	Mika Salo	Tyrrell-Yamaha 023	Rtd: Clutch
Hungarian GP, Hungaroring	Ukyo Katayama	Tyrrell-Yamaha 023	Rtd: Accident
	Mika Salo	Tyrrell-Yamaha 023	Rtd: Throttle
Belgian GP, Spa-Francorchamps	Ukyo Katayama	Tyrrell-Yamaha 023	Rtd: Spun off
	Mika Salo	Tyrrell-Yamaha 023	8th

Italian GP, Monza	Ukyo Katayama	Tyrrell-Yamaha 023	Running, not classified
	Mika Salo	Tyrrell-Yamaha 023	5th
Portuguese GP, Estoril	Ukyo Katayama	Tyrrell-Yamaha 023	DNS: Accident at first start
	Mika Salo	Tyrrell-Yamaha 023	13th
European GP, Nürburgring	Gabriele Tarquini	Tyrrell-Yamaha 023	14th
	Mika Salo	Tyrrell-Yamaha 023	10th
Pacific GP, Aida	Ukyo Katayama	Tyrrell-Yamaha 023	14th
	Mika Salo	Tyrrell-Yamaha 023	12th
Japanese GP, Suzuka	Ukyo Katayama	Tyrrell-Yamaha 023	Rtd: Spun off
	Mika Salo	Tyrrell-Yamaha 023	6th
Australian GP, Adelaide	Ukyo Katayama	Tyrrell-Yamaha 023	Rtd: Engine
	Mika Salo	Tyrrell-Yamaha 023	5th

1996

Race & Circuit	Drivers	Car/Engine	Result
Australian GP, Melbourne	Ukyo Katayama	Tyrrell-Yamaha 024	11th
	Mika Salo	Tyrrell-Yamaha 024	6th
Brazilian GP, Interlagos	Ukyo Katayama	Tyrrell-Yamaha 024	9th
	Mika Salo	Tyrrell-Yamaha 024	5th
Argentine GP, Buenos Aires	Ukyo Katayama	Tyrrell-Yamaha 024	Rtd: Transmission
	Mika Salo	Tyrrell-Yamaha 024	Rtd: Throttle
European GP, Nürburgring	Ukyo Katayama	Tyrrell-Yamaha 024	DNQ
	Mika Salo	Tyrrell-Yamaha 024	DNQ
San Marino GP, Imola	Ukyo Katayama	Tyrrell-Yamaha 024	Rtd: Transmission
	Mika Salo	Tyrrell-Yamaha 024	Rtd: Engine
Monaco GP, Monte Carlo	Ukyo Katayama	Tyrrell-Yamaha 024	Rtd: Throttle/accident
	Mika Salo	Tyrrell-Yamaha 024	5th
Spanish GP, Barcelona	Ukyo Katayama	Tyrrell-Yamaha 024	Rtd: Electrics
	Mika Salo	Tyrrell-Yamaha 024	DNQ
Canadian GP, Montreal	Ukyo Katayama	Tyrrell-Yamaha 024	Rtd: Collision
	Mika Salo	Tyrrell-Yamaha 024	Rtd: Engine
French GP, Magny-Cours	Ukyo Katayama	Tyrrell-Yamaha 024	Rtd: Engine
	Mika Salo	Tyrrell-Yamaha 024	10th
British GP, Silverstone	Ukyo Katayama	Tyrrell-Yamaha 024	Rtd: Engine
	Mika Salo	Tyrrell-Yamaha 024	7th
German GP, Hockenheim	Ukyo Katayama	Tyrrell-Yamaha 024	Rtd: Spun off
	Mika Salo	Tyrrell-Yamaha 024	9th
Hungarian GP, Hungaroring	Ukyo Katayama	Tyrrell-Yamaha 024	7th
	Mika Salo	Tyrrell-Yamaha 024	Rtd: Collision
Belgian GP, Spa-Francorchamps	Ukyo Katayama	Tyrrell-Yamaha 024	8th
	Mika Salo	Tyrrell-Yamaha 024	7th
Italian GP, Monza	Ukyo Katayama	Tyrrell-Yamaha 024	10th
	Mika Salo	Tyrrell-Yamaha 024	Rtd: Engine

Portuguese GP, Estoril	Ukyo Katayama	Tyrrell-Yamaha 024	12th
	Mika Salo	Tyrrell-Yamaha 024	11th
Japanese GP, Suzuka	Ukyo Katayama	Tyrrell-Yamaha 024	Rtd: Engine
	Mika Salo	Tyrrell-Yamaha 024	Rtd: Engine

1997

Race & Circuit	Drivers	Car/Engine	Result
Australian GP, Melbourne	Jos Verstappen	Tyrrell-Ford 025	Rtd: Accident
	Mika Salo	Tyrrell-Ford 025	Rtd: Engine
Brazilian GP, Interlagos	Jos Verstappen	Tyrrell-Ford 025	15th
	Mika Salo	Tyrrell-Ford 025	13th
Argentine GP, Buenos Aires	Jos Verstappen	Tyrrell-Ford 025	Rtd: Fuel pressure
	Mika Salo	Tyrrell-Ford 025	8th
San Marino GP, Imola	Jos Verstappen	Tyrrell-Ford 025	10th
	Mika Salo	Tyrrell-Ford 025	9th
Monaco GP, Monte Carlo	Jos Verstappen	Tyrrell-Ford 025	8th
	Mika Salo	Tyrrell-Ford 025	5th
Spanish GP, Barcelona	Jos Verstappen	Tyrrell-Ford 025	11th
	Mika Salo	Tyrrell-Ford 025	Rtd: Puncture
Canadian GP, Montreal	Jos Verstappen	Tyrrell-Ford 025	Rtd: Air valve
	Mika Salo	Tyrrell-Ford 025	Rtd: Engine
French GP, Magny-Cours	Jos Verstappen	Tyrrell-Ford 025	Rtd: Stuck throttle
	Mika Salo	Tyrrell-Ford 025	Rtd: Engine
British GP, Silverstone	Jos Verstappen	Tyrrell-Ford 025	Rtd: Engine
	Mika Salo	Tyrrell-Ford 025	Rtd: Engine
German GP, Hockenheim	Jos Verstappen	Tyrrell-Ford 025	10th
	Mika Salo	Tyrrell-Ford 025	Rtd: Clutch
Hungarian GP, Hungaroring	Jos Verstappen	Tyrrell-Ford 025	Rtd: Pneumatic leak
	Mika Salo	Tyrrell-Ford 025	13th
Belgian GP, Spa-Francorchamps	Jos Verstappen	Tyrrell-Ford 025	Rtd: Spun off
	Mika Salo	Tyrrell-Ford 025	11th
Italian GP, Monza	Jos Verstappen	Tyrrell-Ford 025	Rtd: Engine
	Mika Salo	Tyrrell-Ford 025	Rtd: Engine
Austrian GP, A1-Ring	Jos Verstappen	Tyrrell-Ford 025	12th
	Mika Salo	Tyrrell-Ford 025	Rtd: Transmission
Luxembourg GP, Nürburgring	Jos Verstappen	Tyrrell-Ford 025	Rtd: Engine
	Mika Salo	Tyrrell-Ford 025	10th
Japanese GP, Suzuka	Jos Verstappen	Tyrrell-Ford 025	13th
	Mika Salo	Tyrrell-Ford 025	Rtd: Engine
European GP, Jerez	Jos Verstappen	Tyrrell-Ford 025	16th
	Mika Salo	Tyrrell-Ford 025	12th

1998

Race & Circuit	Drivers	Car/Engine	Result
Australian GP,	Ricardo Rosset	Tyrrell-Ford 026	Rtd: Gearbox
Melbourne	Toranosuke Takagi	Tyrrell-Ford 026	Rtd: Accident
Brazilian GP,	Ricardo Rosset	Tyrrell-Ford 026	Rtd: Gearbox
Interlagos	Toranosuke Takagi	Tyrrell-Ford 026	Rtd: Engine
Argentine GP,	Ricardo Rosset	Tyrrell-Ford 026	14th
Buenos Aires	Toranosuke Takagi	Tyrrell-Ford 026	12th
San Marino GP, Imola	Ricardo Rosset	Tyrrell-Ford 026	Rtd: Engine
	Toranosuke Takagi	Tyrrell-Ford 026	Rtd: Engine
Spanish GP,	Ricardo Rosset	Tyrrell-Ford 026	DNQ
Barcelona	Toranosuke Takagi	Tyrrell-Ford 026	13th
Monaco GP,	Ricardo Rosset	Tyrrell-Ford 026	DNQ
Monte Carlo	Toranosuke Takagi	Tyrrell-Ford 026	11th
Canadian GP,	Ricardo Rosset	Tyrrell-Ford 026	8th
Montreal	Toranosuke Takagi	Tyrrell-Ford 026	Rtd: Transmission
French GP,	Ricardo Rosset	Tyrrell-Ford 026	Rtd: Engine
Magny-Cours	Toranosuke Takagi	Tyrrell-Ford 026	Rtd: Engine
British GP, Silverstone	Ricardo Rosset	Tyrrell-Ford 026	Rtd: Spun off
	Toranosuke Takagi	Tyrrell-Ford 026	9th
Austrian GP, A1-Ring	Ricardo Rosset	Tyrrell-Ford 026	12th
	Toranosuke Takagi	Tyrrell-Ford 026	Rtd: Accident
German GP,	Ricardo Rosset	Tyrrell-Ford 026	DNQ
Hockenheim	Toranosuke Takagi	Tyrrell-Ford 026	13th
Hungarian GP,	Ricardo Rosset	Tyrrell-Ford 026	DNQ
Hungaroring	Toranosuke Takagi	Tyrrell-Ford 026	14th
Belgian GP,	Ricardo Rosset	Tyrrell-Ford 026	DNS: Accident at first start
Spa-Francorchamps	Toranosuke Takagi	Tyrrell-Ford 026	Rtd: Spun off
Italian GP, Monza	Ricardo Rosset	Tyrrell-Ford 026	12th
	Toranosuke Takagi	Tyrrell-Ford 026	9th
Luxembourg GP,	Ricardo Rosset	Tyrrell-Ford 026	Rtd: Engine
Nürburgring	Toranosuke Takagi	Tyrrell-Ford 026	16th
Japanese GP, Suzuka	Ricardo Rosset	Tyrrell-Ford 026	DNQ
	Toranosuke Takagi	Tyrrell-Ford 026	Rtd: Accident

Index